Object-oriented Software in ANSI C++ Second Edition

Michael A. Smith
School of Computing
University of Brighton

THE McGRAW-HILL COMPANIES

London · Chicago · New York · St Louis · San Francisco · Auckland
Bogotá · Caracas · Lisbon · Madrid · Mexico · Milan
Montreal · New Delhi · Panama · Paris · San Juan · São Paulo
Singapore · Sydney · Tokyo · Toronto

Published by
McGraw-Hill Publishing Company
SHOPPENHANGERS ROAD, MAIDENHEAD, BERKSHIRE, SL6 2QL, ENGLAND
Telephone +44 (0) 1628 502500
Fax: +44 (0) 1628 770224   Web site: http://www.mcgraw-hill.co.uk

---

British Library Cataloguing in Publication Data

A catalogue record for this book is available from the British Library

ISBN 007 709504 9

Library of Congress Cataloguing-in-Publication Data

The LOC data for this book has been applied for and may be obtained from the
Library of Congress, Washington, D.C.

Further information on this and other McGraw-Hill titles is to be found at
http://www.mcgraw-hill.co.uk
Author's Website address: **http://www.mcgraw-hill.co.uk/smithma**

Publishing Director: Alfred Waller
Publisher: David Hatter
Typeset by: the Author
Produced by: Steven Gardiner Ltd
Cover by: Hybert Design

2 3 4 5 C U P 3 2 1 0

Printed in Great Britain

Contents

Preface

This book is aimed at programmers who wish to learn the object-oriented language C++. A knowledge of C, the ancestral language of C++, is not a requirement, as the book assumes no previous knowledge of this language.

The first chapter looks at an object-oriented view of programming. The next two chapters concentrate on the basic data and control structures in the language. The book then moves on to discuss the object-oriented features of the language, using numerous examples to illustrate the ideas of encapsulation, inheritance, and polymorphism. In illustrating these ideas, the discussion is initially restricted to the high level features of the language. By using appropriate constructs, such as the `string` class, the need to use low-level facilities in the language is avoided.

In Chapter 12 a case study in the design and implementation of a board game is used to illustrate the concepts and techniques explored in the earlier chapters of the book. This chapter takes the reader from the initial ideas about the problem, through the design process, to the eventual implementation of a program to play the game between two human players.

After these fundamental issues in program construction have been explored, the book then examines the low level features of the C++ language, in particular those concerned with pointers and address arithmetic. The introduction to the use of pointers and address arithmetic is deliberately deferred until the later chapters of the book, in order to encourage users of the language to employ these features only when building classes which implement higher level constructs.

The Standard Template Library is explored with a chapter on the use and implementation of generic algorithms and a chapter on the use of the standard containers.

The book concludes with chapters on the attributes of a C++ program, and a summary of the important constructs in the language. Self-assessment questions and exercises are suggested for the reader at the end of each chapter.

I would in particular like to thank Corinna, my wife, for putting up with my many long hours in the 'computer room' and her many useful suggestions on the presentation and style used for the material in this book.

Website

Support material for the book can be found on the Authors website:
`http://www.mcgraw-hill.co.uk/smithma`. The material consists of further solutions, source code, artwork and general information about C++.

Further exercises may be obtained by tutors, who may contact the Author, by email.

Changes from the first edition

The general structure of the book has been retained from the first edition. However, a substantial amount of new material has been included to cover additions made to C++ in the ANSI C++ standard. Additionally, most of the original code examples have been re-worked to take advantage of features in ANSI C++.

Michael A. Smith
Brighton, March 1999
m.a.smith@brighton.ac.uk

The example programs shown in this book follow the conventions:

Item in program	Example	Convention used
Actual parameter	value = 2; display(value);	Is in lower case.
Class	**class** Account { };	The first character of the class name is capitalized.
Class attribute / Class member variable: (A global data item that is shared between all instances of the class)	**static float** the_rate;	Is in lower case starting with the_ and is declared in the private part of the class.
Constant	**const** MAX = 10;	Is in upper case.
Enumeration type	**enum** Colour = {RED,BLUE};	Starts with an upper case letter.
Enumeration value	**enum** Colour = {RED,BLUE};	Is in upper case.
Formal parameter	display(int amount)	Is in lower case.
Function	process();	Is in lower case.
Function adapter	bind1st	Is in lower case.
Function object	less<int>()	Is in lower case.
Instance attribute / Class member variable: (Λ data item contained in an object)	**float** the_balance;	Starts with 'the_' and is in lower case.
Instance method / Member function	picture.display()	The function name is in lowercase.
Macro name	NAME	Is in upper case.
typedef	**typedef** char* C_string;	Starts with an upper-case letter.
Variable name / Object	mine p_ch	Is in lower case. A variable holding a pointer starts with 'p_'.

Glossary of terms used

Actual
parameter

The physical item passed to a function. For example, in the following
fragment of code the actual parameter passed to the function print is the
int number.

```
int number = 2;

print( number );
```

ADT

Abstract Data Type. The separation of a data type into two components:
*   the public operations allowed on instances of the type.
*   the private physical implementation of the type.
    (Representation of an instance of the type plus the implementation of
    the operations allowed on an instance of the type.)

Base class

A class from which other classes are derived. Also know in other
languages as a superclass.

C

A language originally designed by Dennis Ritchie, used to rewrite the
Unix operating system. C++ is almost a superset of this language. The
language C was based on the previous languages B and BCPL.

C++ string

A string held as an array of characters in memory terminated by the
character '\0'. This string is of type char *.

Class

The specification of a type and the operations that are performed on an
instance of the type. A class is used to create objects that share a common
structure and behaviour.

The specification of a class Account is as follows:

```
class Account {
public:
  Account();
  float account_balance();
  float withdraw( float );
  void deposit( float );
  void set_min_balance( float );
private:
  float the_balance;
  float the_min_balance;
};
```

Class attribute   A data component that is shared between all objects in the class. In effect it is a global variable which can only be accessed by methods in the class. A class attribute is declared in the private part of the class. For example, the class attribute `the_no_transactions` in the class `Account_R` is declared as follows:

```
class Account_R {
   ...
private:
   float   the_balance;
   float   the_overdraft;
   static int the_no_transactions;
};
```

Class method   A member function in a class that only accesses class attributes. For example, the method `prelude` in the class `Account_R` which sets the class attribute `the_no_transactions` is as follows:

```
void Account_R::prelude()
{
   the_no_transactions = 0;
}
```

Note: As `prelude` is a class method the member function is called without reference to an instance of the class. For example: `Account_R::prelude();`.

Class string   A string held in an instance of class `std::string`. This string may be assigned and compared and the results will be consistent.

Dynamic-binding   The binding between an object and the message that is sent to it is <u>not</u> known at compile-time.

Encapsulation   The provision of a public interface to a hidden (private) collection of data procedures and functions that provide a coherent function.

Formal parameter   In a function body the name of the item that is passed to the function. For example, in the following fragment of code the formal parameter in the function `print` is `value`.

```
void print( int value )
{
   std::cout << value;
}
```

Inheritance

The derivation of a class (derived class) from an existing class (base class). The derived class will have the methods and instance/class attributes in the class plus the methods and instance/class attributes defined in the base class. The class `Account_with_statement` that is derived from the class `Account` is specified as follows:

```
class  Account_with_statement : public Account
{
public:
  Account_with_statement(const std::string="");
  void statement( ostream& );
private:
  std::string the_account_name;
  int         the_statement_no;
};
```

Inspector

A method that does not change the state of the object.

Instance attribute

A data component contained in an object. In C++ these are know as data members of the class. The data members of the class should be declared in the private part of the class specification.

```
class Account {
{

private:
  float the_balance;
}
```

Instance method

A function in a class that accesses the instance attributes (member data items) contained in an object. For example, the method `account_balance` accesses the instance attribute `the_balance`.

```
float Account::account_balance()
{
  return the_balance;
}
```

Instantiation

The creation of an object which deals with a specific type of item for example:

```
    Vector <int> numbers;
```

numbers is an instantiation of the class `Vector <int>`.

Message | The sending of data values to a method that operates on an object. For example, the message 'deposit £30 in account `mike`' is written in C++ as:

```
mike.deposit( 30.00 );
```

Meta-class | An instance of a meta-class is a class. Meta-classes are not supported in C++.

Method | Implements behaviour in an object. A method is implemented as a function in a class. A method may be either a class method or an instance method.

Multiple inheritance | A class derived from more than one base class.

Mutator | A method that changes the state of the object.

Object | An instance of a class. An object has a state that is interrogated / changed by methods in the class. The object mike that is an instance of `Account` is declared as follows:

```
Account mike;
```

Overloading | When an identifier or operator can have several different meanings. For example, the extraction operator << is overloaded with several different definitions to allow a user to write:

```
std::cout << "The sum of 1+2 is " << 1+2 << '\n';
```

Polymorphism | The ability to send a message to an object whose type is not known at compile-time. The method selected depends on the type of the receiving object. For example the message 'display' is sent to different types of picture elements that are held in the heterogeneous collection `picture_elements`.

```
picture_elements[i]->display();
```

Static binding | The binding between a method in an object and the message that it is sent to it is known at compile-time.

Templated class A class which is parameterized with a type or types that are used in the body of the class. For example the following is a declaration of the object `colours` which is an instance of the template class `vector`.

```
std::vector <std:string> colours;
```

To my wife Corinna Lord, daughter Miranda and mother Margaret Smith

and guinea pig Delphi

1 Introduction to programming

A computer programming language is used by a programmer to express the solution to a problem in terms that the computer system can understand. This chapter looks at how to solve a small problem using the computer programming language C++.

1.1 Computer programming

Solving a problem by implementing the solution using a computer programming language is a meticulous process. In essence the problem is expressed in terms of a very stylized language in which every detail must be correct. However, this is a rewarding process both in the sense of achievement when the program is completed, and usually the eventual financial reward obtained for the effort.

Like the planet on which we live where there are many different natural languages, so the computer world also has many different programming languages. The programming language C++ is just one of the many computer programming languages used today.

1.2 Programming languages

In the early days of computing circa 1950's, computer programs had to be written directly in the machine instructions of the computer. Soon assembly languages were introduced that allowed the programmer to write these instructions symbolically. An assembler program would then translate the programmer's symbolic instructions into the real machine code instructions of the computer. For example, to calculate the cost of a quantity of apples using an assembly language the following style of symbolic instructions would be written by a programmer:

```
LDA    AMOUNT_OF_OF_APPLES    ; Load into the accumulator # pounds
MLT    PRICE_PER_POUND        ; Multiply by cost per pound of apples
STA    COST_OF_APPLES         ; Save result
```

Note: Each assembly language instruction corresponds to a machine code instruction.

In the period 1957—1958 the first versions of the high-level languages FORTRAN & COBOL were developed. In these high-level programming languages programmers could express many ideas in terms of the problem rather than in terms of the machine architecture. A compiler for the appropriate language would translate the programmer's high level statements into the specific machine code instructions of the target machine. Advantages of the use of a compiler include:

- Gains in programmer productivity as the solution is expressed in terms of the problem rather than in terms of the machine.

- If written correctly, programs may be compiled into the machine instructions of many different machines. Hence, the program may be moved between machines without having to be re-written.

For example, the same calculation to calculate the cost of apples is expressed in FORTRAN as:

```
COST = PRICE * AMOUNT
```

1.3 Range of programming languages

Since the early days of computer programming languages the number and range of high level languages has multiplied greatly. However, many languages have also effectively died through lack of use. A simplistic classification of the current paradigms in programming languages is shown in the table below:

Type of language	Brief characteristics of the language	Example
Functional	The problem is decomposed into individual functions. To a function is passed read only data values which the function transforms into a new value. A function itself may also be passed as a parameter to a function. As the input data to a function is unchanged individual functions may be executed simultaneously as soon as they have their input data.	ML
Logic	The problem is decomposed into rules specifying constraints about a world view of the problem.	Prolog

Object-oriented	The problem is decomposed into interacting objects. Each object encapsulates and hides methods that manipulate the hidden state of the object. A message sent to an object evokes the encapsulated method that then performs the requested task.	Ada 95 Eiffel Java Smalltalk
Procedural	The problem is decomposed into individual procedures or subroutines. This decomposition is usually done in a top down manner. In a top down approach, once a section of the problem has been identified as being implementable by a procedure, it too is broken down into individual procedures. The data however, is not usually part of this decomposition.	C Pascal

1.3.1   Computer programming languages

A computer programming language is a special language in which a high level description of the solution to a problem is expressed. However, unlike a natural language, there can be no ambiguity or error in the description of the solution to the problem. The computer is unable to work out what was meant from an incorrect description.

For example, in the programming language C++, to print the result of multiplying 10 by 5 the following programming language statement is written:

```
std::cout << ( 10 * 5 );
```

To the non programmer this is not an immediately obvious way of expressing: print the answer to 10 multiplied by 5.

1.3.2   The role of a compiler

The high-level language used to describe the solution to the problem, must first be converted to a form suitable for execution on the computer system. This conversion process is performed by a compiler. A compiler is a program that converts the high-level language statements into a form that a computer can obey. During the conversion process the compiler will tell the programmer about any syntax or semantic mistakes that have been made when expressing the problem in the high-level language. This process is akin to the work of a human translator who converts a document from English into French so that a French speaker can understand the contents of the document.

Once the computer program has been converted to a form that can be executed, it may then be run. It usually comes as a surprise to many new programmers that the results produced from running their program is not what they expected. The computer obeys the programming language statements exactly. However, in their formulation the novice programmer has formulated a solution that does not solve the problem correctly.

1.4 A small problem

A local orchard sells some of its rare variety apples in its local farm shop. However, the farm shop has no electric power and hence uses a set of scales which just give the weight of the purchased product. A customer buying apples, fills a bag full of apples and takes the apples to the shop assistant who weighs the apples to determine their weight in kilograms and then multiples the weight by the price per kilogram.

If the shop assistant is good at mental arithmetic they can perform the calculation in their head, or if mental arithmetic is not their strong point they can use an alternative means of determining the cost of the apples.

1.5 Solving the problem using a calculator

For example, to solve the very simple problem of calculating the cost of 5.2 kilos of apples at £1.20 a kilo using a pocket calculator the following 4 steps are performed:

Pocket calculator	Step	Steps performed
	1	Enter the cost of a kilo of apples: C 1 . 2 0
Display: 6.24 Keys: S M / * 7 8 9 - 4 5 6 + 1 2 3 C 0 . =	2	Enter the operation to be performed: *
	3	Enter the number of kilos to be bought: 5 . 2
	4	Enter calculate =

Note: The keys on the calculator are:

C	*Clear the display and turn on the calculator if off*
S	*Save the contents of the display into memory*
M	*Retrieve the contents of the memory*
*+ - * /*	*Arithmetic operations*
	* * Multiply / Division*
	* + plus - minus*
=	*Calculate*

When entered, these actions cause the calculation 1.20 * 5.2 to be evaluated and displayed. In solving the problem, the problem is broken down into several very simple steps. These steps are in the 'language' that the calculator understands. By obeying these simple instructions the calculator 'solves' the problem of the cost of 5.2 kilos of apples at £1.20 a kilo.

1.5.1 Making the solution more general

The calculation using the pocket calculator can be made more general by storing the price of the apples in the calculator's memory. The price of a specific amount of apples can then be calculated by retrieving the stored price of the apples and multiplying this retrieved amount by the quantity required. For example, to setup the price of apples in the calculator's memory and calculate the cost of 4.1 kilos of apples, the process is as follows:

Pocket calculator	Step	Steps performed
	1	Enter the cost of a kilo of apples: C 1 . 2 0
4.92 S M / * 7 8 9 − 4 5 6 + 1 2 3 C 0 . =	2	Save this value to the calculator's memory: S
	3	Retrieve the value from memory: M
	4	Enter the operation to be performed: *
	5	Enter the number of kilos to be bought: 4 . 1
	6	Enter calculate =

To calculate the price for each customer's order of apples, only steps 3—6 needs to be repeated. In essence, a generalized solution to the problem of finding the price of any quantity of apples has been defined and implemented.

1.6 Solving the problem using the C++ language

To solve the problem of calculating the cost of a quantity of apples using the programming language C++, a similar process to that used previously when using a pocket calculator is followed. This time, however, the individual steps are as follows:

Step	Description
1	Set the memory location `price_per_kilo` to the cost per kilogram of the apples.
2	Set the memory location `kilos_of_apples` to the kilograms of apples required.
3	Set the memory location `cost` to the result of multiplying the contents of memory location `price_per_kilo` by the contents of the memory location `kilos_of_apples`.
4	Print the contents of the memory location `cost`.

Note: Although a shorter sequence of steps can be written to calculate 1.2 multiplied by 5.2 the above solution can easily be extended to allow the price of any number of kilograms of apples to be calculated.

In C++ like most programming languages when a memory location is required to store a value, it must first be declared. This is done for many reasons, some of these reasons are:

- So that the type of items that are to be stored in this memory location can be specified. By specifying the type of the item that can be stored the compiler can allocate the correct amount of memory for the item as well as checking that a programmer does not accidentally try and store an inappropriate item into the memory location.

- The programmer does not accidentally store a value into a memory location `c0st` when they meant `cost`. The programmer accidentally typed zero (0) when they meant the letter (o).

The sequence of steps written in pseudo English is transformed into the following individual C++ statements which, when obeyed by a computer, will display the cost of 5.2 kilograms of apples at £1.20 a kilogram.

Step	Line	C++ statements
	1	`double price_per_kilo;`
	2	`double kilos_of_apples;`
	3	`double cost;`
1	4	`price_per_kilo  = 1.20;`
2	5	`kilos_of_apples = 5.2;`
3	6	`cost = price_per_kilo * kilos_of_apples;`
4	7	`std::cout << cost << "\n";`

Note: *Words in bold type are reserved words in the C++ language and cannot be used*
for the name of a memory location.
The name of the memory location contains the character _ to make the name
more readable. Spaces in the name of a memory location are not allowed.
Each C++ statement is terminated with a ;.
*Multiplication is written as *.*
A newline character is represented by " \n" in C++

The individual lines of code of the C++ program are responsible for the following actions:

Line	Description
1	Allocates a memory location called `price_per_kilo` that is used to store the price per kilogram of apples. This memory location is of type `double` and can hold any number that has decimal places.
2—3	Allocates memory locations: `kilos_of_apples` and `cost`.
4	Sets the contents of the memory location `price_per_kilo` to 1.20. The = can be read as 'is assigned the value'.
5	Assign 5.2 to memory location `kilos_of_apples`.
6	Sets the contents of the memory location `cost` to the contents of the memory location `price_per_kilo` multiplied by the contents of the memory location `kilos_of_apples`.
7	Displays the contents of the memory location `cost` onto the computer screen. The components of this statement are illustrated below: Memory location to be printed Output stream New line `std::cout << cost << "\n";` This is read as 'Into the output stream `std::cout` insert the contents of the memory location `cost` followed by a new line'.

This solution is very similar to the solution using the pocket calculator, except that individually named memory locations are used to hold the stored values, and the calculation is expressed in a more human readable form.

An animation of the above C++ program is shown below. In the animation the contents of the memory locations are shown after each individual C++ statement is executed. When a memory location is declared in C++ inside a function its initial contents are undefined.

C++ statements	price Δ	kilos Δ	cost

`double price_per_kilo;`
`double kilos_of_apples;`
`double cost;`
	U	U	U

`price_per_kilo = 1.20;`	1.20	U	U
`kilos_of_apples = 5.2;`	1.20	5.2	U
`cost = price_per_kilo *` `        kilos_of_apples;`	1.20	5.2	6.24
`std::cout << cost << "\n";`	1.20	5.2	6.24

Note: U indicates that the contents of the memory location are undefined.
Δ Due to lack of room in the title column the variable `price_per_kilo` is represented by `price` and `kilos_of_apples` by `kilos`.

1.6.1   Running the program

The above lines of code, though not a complete C++ program, form the core code for such a program. When this code is augmented with additional peripheral code, compiled and then run, the output produced will be of the form:

```
6.24
```

A person who knows what the program does, will instantly know that this represents the price of 5.2 kilograms of apples at £1.20 a kilogram. However, this will not be obvious to a casual user of the program.

1.7 The role of comments

To make a C++ program easier to read, comments may be placed in the program to aid the human reader of the program. A comment starts with `//` and extends to the end of the line. It is important however, to realize that the comments you write in a program are completely ignored by the computer when it comes to run your program. For example, the previous fragment of code could be annotated with comments as follows:

```
double price_per_kilo;              //Price of apples
double kilos_of_apples;             //Apples required
double cost;                        //Cost of apples

price_per_kilo   = 1.20;            // Set cost to £1.20
kilos_of_apples  = 5.2;             // Kilos required

cost = price_per_kilo * kilos_of_apples; // Evaluate cost
std::cout << cost << "\n";          // print the cost
```

Note: This is an example of comments, the more experienced programmer would probably miss out many of the above comments as the effect of the code is easily understandable.

Comments that do not add to a reader's understanding of the program code should be avoided. In some circumstances the choice of meaning full names for memory locations is all that is required. As a general rule, if the effect of the code is not immediately obvious then a comment should be used to add clarity to the code fragment.

1.8 Summary

The statements in the C++ programming language seen so far are illustrated in the table below:

C++ statement	Description
double cost;	Declare a memory location called cost.
cost = 1.2 * 5.2;	Assign to the memory location cost the result of evaluating 1.2 multiplied by 5.2.
std::cout <<"Hi!";	Print the message Hi!.
std::cout << cost << "\n";	Print the contents of the memory location cost followed by a newline.

Statements of this form allow a programmer to write many different and useful programs.

1.9 A more descriptive program

By adding additional C++ statements, the output from a program can be made clear to all who use the program. For example, the program in Section 1.6 can be modified into the program illustrated below. In this program, a major part of the program's code is concerned with ensuring that the user is made aware of what the results mean.

Line	C++ statements
1	`double price_per_kilo;` `//Price of apples`
2	`double kilos_of_apples;` `//Apples required`
3	`double cost;` `//Cost of apples`
4	`price_per_kilo  = 1.20;`
5	`kilos_of_apples = 5.2;`
6	`cost = price_per_kilo * kilos_of_apples;`
7	`std::cout << "Cost of apples per kilo £ ";`
8	`std::cout << price_per_kilo;`
9	`std::cout << "\n";`
10	`std::cout << "Kilos of apples required K ";`
11	`std::cout << kilos_of_apples;`
12	`std::cout << "\n";`
13	`std::cout << "Cost of apples            £ ";`
14	`std::cout << cost;`
15	`std::cout << "\n";`

Line	Description
1-6	Calculate the cost of 5.2 kilograms of apples at £1.20 per kilogram.
7	Displays the message `Cost of apples per kilo  £` onto the computer screen. The double quotes around the text message are used to signify that this is a text message to be printed rather than the contents of a memory location.
8	Displays the contents of the memory location `cost` onto the computer screen after the above message.
9	Starts a new line of output on the computer screen.
10—12	As for lines 7—9 but this time the message is `Kilos of apples required K` and the memory location printed is `kilos_of_apples`.
13—15	As for lines 7—9 but this time the message is `Cost of apples        £` and the memory location printed is `cost`.

1.9.1   Printing several items in the same statement

The following statements:

```
std::cout << "Cost of apples        £ ";
std::cout << cost;
std::cout << "\n";
```

may be combined into the single statement shown below:

```
std::cout << "Cost of apples        £ " << cost << "\n";
```

1.9.2   Running the new program

With the addition of some extra lines of code, the above program can be compiled and then run on a computer system. Once executed the following results will be displayed:

```
Cost of apples per kilo  £ 1.2
Kilos of apples required K 5.2
Cost of apples           £ 6.24
```

This makes it easy to see what the program has calculated.

1.10   Types of memory location

So far the type of the memory location used has been of type `double`. A memory location of type `double` can hold any number that has a fractional part. However, when such a value is held it is only held to a specific number of decimal places. Sometimes it is appropriate to hold numbers that have an exact whole value, e.g. a memory location `people` that represents the number of people in a room. In such a case the memory location should be declared to be of type `int`.

For example, the following fragment of code uses an `int` memory location to hold the number of people in a room.

```
int room;    // Memory location
room = 7;    // Assigned the number 7
```

The choice of the type of memory location used, will of course depend on the values the memory location is required to hold. As a general rule, when an exact whole number is required, then a memory location of type `int` should be used and when the value may have a fractional part then a memory location of type `double` should be used.

Memory location	Assignment to memory location
int people	people = 2;
double weight	weight = 7.52;

1.11   Repetition

So far, all the C++ programs used in the examples have used straight line code. In straight line code the program consists of statements that are obeyed one after another from top to bottom. There are no statements that affect the flow of control in the program. This technique has allowed us to produce a solution for the specific case of the cost of 5.2 kilograms of apples at £1.20 per kilogram.

Using this strategy, to produce a program to list the cost of apples for a series of different weights would effectively involve writing out the same code many times. An example of this style of coding is illustrated below:

```
double price_per_kilo;              //Price of apples
double kilos_of_apples;             //Apples required
double cost;                        //Cost of apples

price_per_kilo = 1.20;

std::cout << "Cost of apples per kilo  : ";
std::cout << price_per_kilo << "\n";

std::cout <<   "Kilo's  Cost" << "\n";
```

```
kilos_of_apples              = 0.1;
```

```
cost = price_per_kilo * kilos_of_apples;
std::cout <<  kilos_of_apples << "        " << cost << "\n";
```

```
kilos_of_apples              = 0.2;
```

```
cost = price_per_kilo * kilos_of_apples;
std::cout <<  kilos_of_apples << "        " << cost << "\n";
```

etc.

Whilst this is a feasible solution, if we want to calculate the cost of 100 different weights this will involve considerable effort and code. Even using copy and paste operations in an editor to lessen the typing effort, will still involve considerable effort! In addition, the resultant program will be large and consume considerable resources.

1.12   Introduction to the `while` statement

In C++ a `while` statement is used to repeat program statements while a condition holds true. A `while` statement can be likened to a rail track as illustrated in Figure 1.1. While the condition is true the flow of control is along the true track. Each time around the loop the condition is re-evaluated. Then, when the condition is found to be false, the false track is taken.

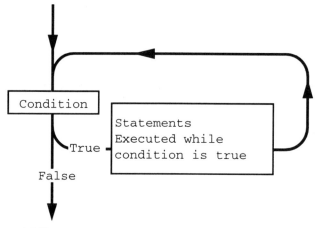

Figure 1.1 The `while` statement as a rail track.

In a `while` loop the condition is always tested first. Due to this requirement if the condition initially evaluates to false then the code associated with the `while` loop will never be executed.

1.12.1　Conditions

In the language C++, a condition is expressed in a very concise format which at first sight may seem strange if you are not used to a mathematical notation. For example, the conditional expression: 'the contents of the memory location `count` is less than or equal to 5' is written as follows:

```
count <= 5
```

Note: The memory location named `count` will need to be declared as:

```
int count;
```

The symbols used in a condition are as follows:

Symbol	Means	Symbol	Means
<	Less than	<=	Less than or equal to
==	Equal to	! =	Not equal to
>	Greater than	>=	Greater than or equal to

If the following memory locations contain the following values:

Memory location	Assigned the value
int temperature;	temperature = 15;
double weight;	weight = 50.0;

then the following table shows the truth or otherwise of several conditional expressions written in C++.

In English	In C++	Condition is
The temperature is less than 20	temperature < 20	true
The temperature is equal to 20	temperature == 20	false
The weight is greater than or equal to 30	weight >= 30.0	true
20 is less than the temperature	20 < temperature	false

Note: As a memory location that holds a `double` value represents a number that is held only to a certain number of digits accuracy, it is not a good idea to compare such a value for equality == or not equality ! =.

1.12.2　A `while` statement in C++

Illustrated below is a fragment of code that uses a `while` statement to write out the text message `Hello` five times:

```
int count;
count = 1;                          //Set count to 1

while ( count <= 5 )                //While count less than or equal 5
{
   std::cout << "Hello" << "\n";// Print Hello
   count = count + 1;              // Add 1 to count
}
```

Note: The statement: count = count + 1; *adds 1 to the contents of* count *and puts the result back into the memory location* count.

In this code fragment, the statements between the { and } brackets are repeatedly executed while the contents of count are less than 5. The flow of control for the above while statement is illustrated in Figure 1.2.

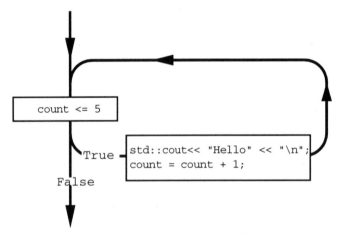

Figure 1.2 Flow of control for a while statement in C++.

1.12.3   Using the **while** statement

The real advantage of using a computer program accrues when the written code is repeated many times, thus saving the implementor considerable time and effort. For example, if we wished to produce a table representing the cost of different weights of apples, then a computer program is constructed that repeats the lines of C++ code that evaluate the cost of a specific weight of apples. However, for each iteration of the calculation the memory location that contains the weight of the apples is changed. A fragment of C++ code to implement this solution is illustrated below:

```
double price_per_kilo;              //Price of apples
double kilos_of_apples;             //Apples required
double cost;                        //Cost of apples
```

```
    price_per_kilo  = 1.20;

    std::cout << "Cost of apples per kilo  : ";
    std::cout << price_per_kilo << "\n";

    std::cout << "Kilo's  Cost" << "\n";
    kilos_of_apples = 0.1;

    while ( kilos_of_apples <= 10.0 )            //While lines to print
    {
      cost = price_per_kilo * kilos_of_apples;   //Calculate cost

      std::cout << kilos_of_apples;              //Print results
      std::cout <<  "        ";
      std::cout << cost << "\n";

      kilos_of_apples = kilos_of_apples + 0.1;   //Next value
    }
```

which when compiled with suitable peripheral code produces output of the form:

```
Cost of apples per kilo  : 1.2
Kilo's  Cost
0.1      0.12
0.2      0.24
0.3      0.36
0.4      0.48
0.5      0.6
0.6      0.72
0.7      0.84
0.8      0.96
0.9      1.08
1.0      1.12
1.1      1.32
1.2      1.44
1.3      1.56
...
 9.9     11.88
10.0     12.0
```

Note: There will need to be additional C++ statements to control the format of the numbers output. See Appendix A on output manipulators for information on controlling the format of the output of numbers.

1.13   Selection

The `if` construct is used to conditionally execute a statement or statements depending on the truth of a condition. This statement can be likened to the rail track illustrated in Figure 1.3 in which the path taken depends on the truth of a condition. However, unlike the `while` statement there is no loop back to re-execute the condition.

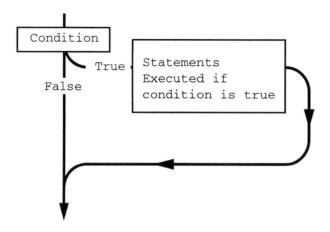

Figure 1.3 The if statement represented as a rail track.

For example, the following fragment of a C++ program only prints out Hot! when the contents of the memory location temperature are greater than 30.

```
int temperature;
temperature = 30;

if ( temperature > 30 )              //If temperature greater than 30
{
    std::cout << "Hot!" << "\n";    // Say its hot
}
```

In this code fragment, the statements between the { and } brackets are only executed if the condition temperature > 30 is true. The flow of control for the above fragment of code is illustrated in Figure 1.4.

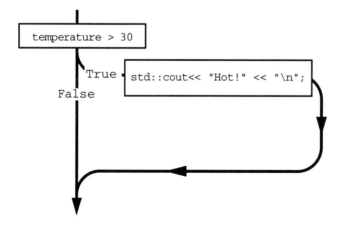

Figure 1.4 The if statement represented as a rail track.

1.13.1   Using the `if` statement

The fragment of program code which was used earlier to tabulate a list of the price of different weights of apples can be made more readable by separating every 5 lines by a blank line. This can be achieved by having a counter `count` to count the number of lines printed and after the 5th line has been printed to insert a blank line. After a blank line has been printed the counter `count` is reset to 0. This modified program is shown below:

```cpp
double price_per_kilo;              //Price of apples
double kilos_of_apples;             //Apples required
double cost;                        //Cost of apples

price_per_kilo  = 1.20;
kilos_of_apples = 0.1;

std::cout <<"Cost of apples per kilo  : ";
std::cout << price_per_kilo << "\n";

std::cout << "Kilo's  Cost";
kilos_of_apples  = 0.0;
int lines_output = 0;

while ( kilos_of_apples <= 10.0 )       //While lines to print
{
  cost = price_per_kilo * kilos_of_apples;  //Calculate cost

  std::cout << kilos_of_apples;         //Print results
  std::cout << "        " ;
  std::cout << cost << "\n";

  kilos_of_apples = kilos_of_apples + 0.1;  //Next value
  lines_output = lines_output + 1;      //Add 1

  if ( lines_output >= 5 )              //If printed group
  {
    std::cout << "\n";                  //  Print line
    lines_output = 0;                   //  Reset count
  }

}
```

which when compiled with additional statements would produce output of the form shown below:

```
Cost of apples per kilo  : 1.2
Kilo's  Cost
0.0      0.0
0.1      0.12
0.2      0.24
0.3      0.36
0.4      0.48

0.5      0.6
0.6      0.72
0.7      0.84
0.8      0.96
0.9      1.08

1.0      1.2
1.1      1.32
1.2      1.44
1.3      1.56
1.4      1.68

etc.
```

1.14   Self-assessment

- What is a computer programming language?

- What do the following fragments of C++ code do?

```cpp
int i;
i = 10;

while ( i > 0 )
{
   std::cout << i ;
   i = i - 1;
}

std::cout << "\n";
```

```cpp
int temperature;
temperature = 10;

if ( temperature > 20 )
{
   std::cout << "It's Hot!";
}

if ( temperature <= 20 )
{
   std::cout << "It's not so Hot!";
}

std::cout << "\n";
```

- What is wrong with the following fragment of C++ code?

```cpp
int value = 3;

if ( value = 2 )
{
    std::cout << "Value is equal to 2";
}
```

- Write a C++ condition expression for the following conditions. In your answer show how any memory location you have used has been declared

  - The temperature is less than 15 degrees centigrade.
  - The distance to college is less than 15 kilometres.
  - The distance to college is greater than or equal to the distance to the football ground.
  - The cost of the bike is less than or equal to the cost of the hi-fi system.

1.15   Paper exercises

Write down on paper C++ statements to implement the following. You do not need to run these solution.

- *Name*
  Write out your name and address.

- *Weight*
  Calculate the total weight of 27 boxes of paper. Each box of paper weighs 2.4 kilograms.

- *Name*
  Write out the text message `"Happy Birthday"` 3 times using a `while` loop.

- *Times table*
  Print the 7 times table. The output should be of the form:
  ```
  7 *  1 =   7
  7 *  2 =  14
  ```
  etc.

  Hint: *Write the C++ code to print the line for the 3rd row, use a variable* row *of type* int *to hold the value 3.*
  ```
  7 *  3 =  21
  ```
  Enclose these statements in a loop that varies the contents of row *from 1 to 12.*

● *Weight table*

Print a table listing the weights of 1 to 20 boxes of paper, when each box weighs 2.4 kilograms.

● *Times table*

Print a multiplication table for all values between 1 and 5. The table to look like:

```
  | 1   2   3   4   5
  -----------------------
1 | 1   2   3   4   5
2 | 2   4   6   8   10
3 | 3   6   9   12  15
4 | 4   8   12  16  20
5 | 5   10  15  20  25
```

Hint: *Write the C++ code to print the line for the 2nd row, use a variable* row *of type* int *to hold the value 2.*

```
  2 | 2   4   6   8   10
```

Enclose these statements in a loop that varies the contents of row *from 1 to 5. Add statements to print the heading:*

```
  | 1   2   3   4   5
  -----------------------
```

2 Software design

This chapter looks at software production in the large. In particular it looks at problems that occur in the development of large and not so large software systems. The notation used by UML (Unified Modelling Language) is introduced as a mechanism for documenting and describing a solution to a problem that is to be implemented on a computer system.

2.1 The software crisis

In the early days of computing, it was the hardware that was very expensive. The programs that ran on these computers were by today's standards incredibly small. In those distant times computers only had a very limited amount of storage; both random access memory and disk storage.

Then it all changed. Advances in technology enabled computers to be built cheaper, with a far greater capacity than previous machines. Software developers thought, "Great! We can build bigger and more comprehensive programs". Software projects were started with an increase in scope and great optimism.

Soon, with projects running over budget and not meeting their client's expectations, the truth dawned: large scale software construction is difficult. The early techniques that had been used in small scale software construction did not scale up successfully for large scale software production.

This can be likened to using a bicycle to travel a short distance. Whilst this is adequate for the purpose, the use of a bicycle is inappropriate if a long distance has to be travelled in a short space of time. You cannot just peddle faster and faster.

2.2 A problem, the model and the solution

In implementing any solution to a problem, we must first understand the problem that is to be solved. Then, when we understand the problem fully, a solution can be formulated.

There are many different ways of achieving an understanding of a problem and its solution. Usually, this involves modelling the problem and its solution using either a standard notation or a notation invented by the programmer. The advantage of using a standard notation is that other people may inspect and modify the description of the problem and its proposed solution. For example, in building a house, an architect will draw up a plan of the various components that are to be built. The client can view the plans and give their approval or qualified approval subject to minor modifications. The builders can then use the plan when they erect the house.

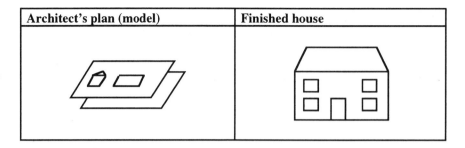

Architect's plan (model)	Finished house

Writing a computer program involves the same overall process. First, we need to understand the task that the computer program will perform. Then we need to implement a solution using the model that we have created.

An easy pitfall at this point is to believe that the model used for the solution of a small problem can be scaled up to solve a large problem. For example, to cross a small stream we can put a log over the stream or if athletic we can even jump over the stream. This approach to crossing a stream however, will not scale up to crossing a large river. Likewise to build a 100-storey tower block, an architect would not simply take the plans for a 2-storey house and instruct the builders to build some extra floors.

In software the same problems of scale exist; the techniques that we use to implement a small program cannot usually be successfully used on a large programming project. The computer literature is full of examples of software disasters that have occurred when a computer system has been started without a full understanding of the problem that is to be solved.

2.2.1   Responsibilities

Since our earliest days we have all been told that we have responsibilities. Initially, these responsibilities are very simple, but as we grow older so they increase. A responsibility is a charge, trust or duty of care to look after something. At an early age this can be as simple as keeping our room neat and tidy. In later life, the range and complexity of items that we have responsibility for, increases dramatically.

A student for example, has the responsibility to follow a course of study. The lecturer has the responsibility of delivering the course to the students in a clear and intelligible manner. The responsibilities of the student and lecturer are summarized in tabular form below:

Responsibilities of a student	Responsibilities of a lecturer
Follow the course of study.	Deliver the course.
Perform to the best of their ability in the exam/assessment for the course.	Set and mark the assessment for the course.
	Attend the exam board for the delivered course.

Software too has responsibilities. For example, a text editor has the responsibility of entering the user's typed text correctly into a document. However, if the text that is entered into the text editor is incorrect or meaningless, then the resultant document will also be incorrect. It is not the role of the text editor to make overall decisions about the validity of the entered text.

In early computing literature, a common saying was "Garbage in, garbage out". Even though the software package implements its responsibilities correctly, the results produced may be at least meaningless, at worse damaging if used.

2.3 Objects

The world we live in is composed of many different objects. For example, a person usually has access to at least some of the following objects:

- A telephone.
- A computer.
- A car.

Each object has its own individual responsibilities. For example, some of the responsibilities associated with the above objects are:

Object	Responsibilities
Telephone	• Establish contact with another phone point. • Convert sound to/from electrical signals.
Computer	• Execute programs. • Provide a tcp/ip connection to the internet.
Car	• Move • Go faster/slower • Turn left/right • Stop.

A responsibility here, is a process that the object performs. For example, a car can move forwards or backwards. However, the car has to be instructed by the driver to perform this task. The object is passive, and only performs an action when instructed to do so.

2.3.1 The car as an object

A car is made up of many components or objects. From a user's perspective some of the major objects that make up a car are:

- The shell or body of the car.
- The engine.
- The gearbox.
- The clutch.
- The battery that provides electric power.

We can think of the body or shell of the car as a container for all the other objects, that when combined, form a working car. These other objects are hidden from the driver of the car. The driver can, however, interact with these objects by using the external interfaces that form part of the car shell. This arrangement of objects is expressed diagrammatically using the UML notation in Figure 2.1.

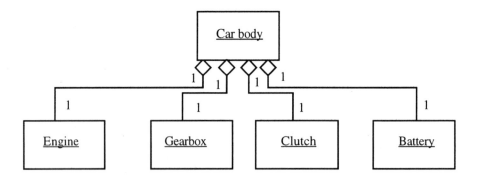

Figure 2.1 Objects that make up a car.

In Figure 2.1 the following style of notation is used:

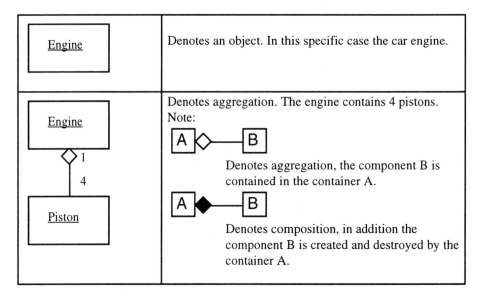

By using this notation, we can express the 'part of' relationship between objects. The engine, gearbox, clutch and battery are 'part of' a car.

2.4 The class

In object-oriented terminology a class is used to describe all objects that share the same responsibilities and internal structure. A class is essentially the collective name for a group of like objects. For example, the following objects all belong to the class car:

Corinna's red car	Mike's silver car	Paul's blue car

Although the objects differ in detail, they all have the same internal structure and responsibilities. Each object is an instance of the class Car. The notation for a class is slightly different from that of an object. The UML notation for a class and an object are illustrated below:

A class	An object (an instance of a class)
Car	<u>Corinna's car</u>

Note: The name of the object is underlined.

It is important to distinguish between a class and an object. A very simple rule is that objects usually have a physical representation, whereas classes are an abstract concept.

2.5 Methods and messages

A method implements a responsibility for a class. For example, some of the responsibilities for the class Car are as follows.

Responsibilities of the class Car
- Start/stop engine
- Go faster/slower
- Turn left/right
- Stop.

An instance of the class Car is an object. By sending a message to the object a hidden method inside the object (a responsibility of the class Car) is invoked to process the message. For example, the driver of the car by pressing down on the accelerator, sends the message 'go faster'. The implementation of this is for the engine control system to feed more petrol to the engine. Normally however, the details of this operation are not of concern to the driver of the car.

2.6 Class objects

We have looked at a car's shell as a container for objects and can look at a laptop computer as a container for several computing devices or objects. A laptop computer is composed of:

- The shell of the laptop, that has external interfaces of a keyboard, touch pad and display screen.
- The local disk drive.
- The network file system.
- The CPU.
- The sound and graphics chipset.

In this analysis, the networked file system is shared between many different laptops, each individual laptop having access to the networked file system. In object-oriented terminology the networked file system is a class object which is shared between all the notebooks.

The concept of a shared object is important as it allows all instances of a class to have access to the same information. Thus, if one instance of a laptop computer creates a file on the network file system, the other notebooks will be able to access the contents of this file.

This arrangement of objects for a laptop computer can be expressed diagrammatically as illustrated using the UML notation in Figure 2.2. Unfortunately in UML there is no way to show diagrammatically that a class item is shared between many classes.

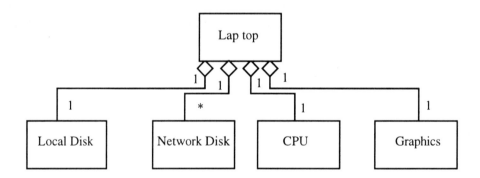

Figure 2.2 Objects that make up a laptop computer from a user's perspective.

Another interesting property of a class object, is that to access it you do not need an instance of the container object. For example, the network file system can be used by devices other than the laptop computers.

2.7 Inheritance

A typical office will usually contain at least the following objects:

- A telephone.
- A fax machine with a telephone hand set.
- A computer.

Each of these objects has their own individual responsibilities. For example, some of the responsibilities of these office objects are:

Object	Responsibilities
Telephone	<ul><li>Establish contact with another phone point.</li><li>Convert sound to/from electrical signals.</li></ul>
Fax machine with a telephone hand set	<ul><li>Establish contact with another phone point.</li><li>Convert sound to/from electrical signals.</li><li>Convert images to/from electrical signals.</li></ul>
Computer	<ul><li>Execute programs.</li><li>Provide a tcp/ip connection to the internet.</li></ul>

Looking at these responsibilities shows that the telephone and fax machine share several responsibilities. The fax machine has two of the responsibilities that the telephone has. We could say that a fax machine is a telephone that can also send and receive images. Another way of thinking about this is that the fax machine can be used as if it were only a telephone. This relationship between classes that represent all telephones and fax machines is shown diagrammatically in Figure 2.3 using the UML notation. In this relationship a fax machine is inherited (or formed from the components) of a telephone.

Inheritance diagram	Responsibilities:
Telephone	Establish contact with another phone point. Convert sound to/from electrical signals.
Fax machine	All the responsibilities of a telephone plus: Convert images to/from electrical signals.

Figure 2.3 Relationship between a telephone and a fax machine.

Note: The superclass (telephone) is the class from which a subclass (fax machine) is inherited.
Inheritance requires you to take all the responsibilities from the superclass; you cannot selectively choose to take only some. However, even though you inherit the responsibilities you do not need to use them.

The inheritance relationship is an important concept in object-oriented programming as it enables new objects to be created by specializing an existing object. In creating the new object, only the addition, responsibilities have to be constructed. The development time for a new software object is reduced as the task of creating the inherited responsibilities has already been done. This process leads to a dramatic reduction in the time and effort required to create new software objects.

2.8 Polymorphism

In a collection of different objects if all the objects are capable of receiving a specific message then this message may be sent to any object in the collection. The method executed when this message is received by an object will depend on the type of the object that receives the message.

For example, in a group of individuals if you ask a person how to take part in their favourite sport, you will probably get many different answers. In effect the message 'How to take part in your favourite sport' is polymorphic in that the answer you get depends on the individual person you select to ask. A tennis player for example, would give a different answer than a golfer.

2.9 Self-assessment

- Explain why the solution to a small problem may not always scale up to solve a much larger and complex problem.

- What is a "Responsibility"?

- What are the responsibilities of:
  - A video camera.
  - An alarm clock.
  - A traffic light.
  - An actress playing the role of Olgar in the *Three sisters* by Chekov.

- What is the relationship between an object, message and a method?

- What classes do the following objects belong to?

apartment	cat	crayon	crystal	dog
guinea pig	igloo	house	ink pen	library
mansion	office block	pencil	rabbit	sheep

  Identify which classes are subclassed from other classes?

- Identify several objects and classes around you at the moment. Can you find responsibilities that any of the objects or classes have in common?

3 Introducing C++ — part 1

This chapter looks at some very simple C++ programs. In introducing these programs the basic control structures of C++ are presented. Apart from the Input and Output statements this part of the C++ language is found in the language C.

3.1 A first C++ program

Like most books on programming, this too starts off with an example program that writes a successful greeting to the user's terminal:

```
#include <iostream>

int main()
{
  std::cout << "Hello world" << "\n";
  return 0;
}
```

which would display the following message on a user's terminal when the program was run:

```
Hello world
```

In the above example program, { and } are used to bracket the body of the function main. This contains the expression std::cout << "Hello world" << "\n"; which writes the string Hello world followed by a newline to the current output stream std::cout. This can be thought of as sending the messages "Hello world" and "\n" to the object std::cout that represents the current output stream. Normally std::cout would be 'attached' to the terminal. The line return 0; returns a result of 0 to the environment that ran the program. By convention a returned value of 0 indicates a successful run of a program. Figure 3.1 shows the structure of a C++ program.

Note: "\n" is simply the C++ way of expressing a string composed of the newline character. The \ character is used to specify that the next character has a special meaning, in this case newline. A full list of escape sequences is given in Appendix G.

The line #include <iostream> is not part of the C++ language. It is a directive to the pre-processor to replace this line by the contents of the file iostream. This file contains definitions about the input output process. It is usually held in one of the system directories of the computer system. This line must always start in column 1.

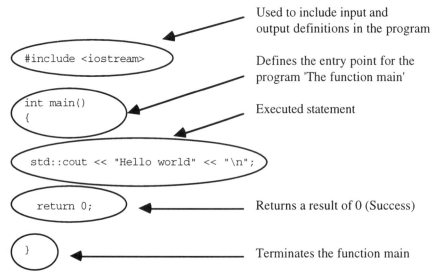

Used to include input and output definitions in the program

#include <iostream>

Defines the entry point for the program 'The function main'

int main()
{

Executed statement

std::cout << "Hello world" << "\n";

return 0;

Returns a result of 0 (Success)

}

Terminates the function main

Figure 3.1 The structure of a C++ program.

The types of the items that are to be output may be mixed as in the case below. The C++ compiler uses the item's type to select the appropriate output form.

```
#include <iostream>

int main()
{
    std::cout << "The Sum of 1+2+3 is " << 1+2+3 << "\n";
    return 0;
}
```

Which would produce the following output when run:

```
The Sum of 1+2+3 is 6
```

3.1.1 Format of a C++ program

A C++ program can be written without regard to format provided that the individual components that make up the program can be recognized. For example, the following is a valid C++ program:

```
#include <iostream>

int main(){std::cout<<"Hello world"<<"\n"; return 0;}
```

Note: The directive #include must be on a line by itself and start in column 1. At least one white space character, for example space is required between any words that are alphabetic such as int and main, so that they can be individually distinguished.

3.1.2   `int main()`

The main unit is prefixed with the keyword int to signify that an integer value is returned as a result of executing the program. By convention a result of 0 indicates the successful running of the program. Remember a program may successfully run yet still produce error messages to a user.

The ANSI standard for C++ requires that all C++ compilers accept a declaration of the form:

```
int main() { }
int main(int argc, char* argv[]) { }
```

Note: The values passed to the function main in the second case are discussed in Appendix K.

for the main program unit. However, other declarations for main may also be accepted by a compiler.

3.1.3   Comments

C++ has two ways of introducing a comment into a program. Firstly:

```
/* An example comment */
```

where the comment is bracketed between /* and */ although it is more usual to write this in the form:

```
/*
 *   This program is a simple test of the C++ compiling system
 *    and writes out the message Hello World to the terminal
 */
```

Note: The / */ comment delimiters may not be nested.*

Secondly:

```
//The rest of the line is a comment
```

Here the comment is introduced by // and is terminated by the newline.

Note: It is good programming practice to comment any code section that is not immediately obvious to a reader of the code.

3.2 A larger C++ program

A complete program to produce a 'count down' is shown below. In this program various constructs that affect the flow of control are introduced.

```
#include <iostream>

int main()
{
  int countdown=10;                    //Start from 10
  while ( countdown > 0 )              //While greater than 10
  {
    std::cout << countdown << "\n";    //Write contents of countdown
    if ( countdown == 3 )             //If equal to 3
    {
      std::cout << "Ignition" << "\n"; // Write Ignition
    }
    countdown--;                       //Decrement countdown by 1
  }
  std::cout << "Blast Off" << "\n";    //Write Blast off
}
```

Note: That `countdown--;` *is the C++ idiom for decrementing the contents of a variable by 1. This could also have been written as:*
`countdown = countdown - 1;`

When run this would produce:

```
10
9
8
7
6
5
4
3
Ignition
2
1
Blast Off
```

3.3 Repetition: `while`

```
while ( countdown > 0 )
{
  // Body of loop
}
```

The above statement repeatedly executes the code between { and } until the condition `countdown > 0` is no longer true.

Note: The ( )s around the condition are mandatory.
The { and } brackets are only required if there is more than one statement to execute repeatedly. Many people, however, would always put in the {} to show the bounds of the loop.

3.4 Selection: `if`

```
if ( countdown == 3 )
{
  // Body of if statement
}
```

This executes the code between { and } if the condition `countdown == 3` is true.

Note: Equality is written ==
This can lead to many mistakes, as it is easily confused with assignment, which is written as =

Not equality is written as ! =. For example, to test if `countdown` is not yet zero the following code is written:

```
if ( countdown != 0 )
  std::cout << "Not yet zero" << "\n";
```

Note: As only one statement was selected to be executed when the condition was true the enclosing { and } were not required.

3.4.1   `if else`

An `else` part may be added to an `if` statement as follows:

```
if ( countdown != 0 )
  std::cout << "Not yet zero" << "\n" ;
else
  std::cout << "Now zero" << "\n" ;
```

Note:

Must be included

```
if ( countdown != 0 )
    std::cout << "Not yet zero" << "\n" ;
else
    std::cout << "Now zero" << "\n" ;
```

The ; before the else must be present as it terminates the previous statement.

3.5 Other repetition constructs

3.5.1 **for**

The for statement in C++ is written as:

```
for ( int countdown = 10; countdown  > 0; countdown-- )
{
  // Body of for statement
}
```

Note: The variable controlling the for loop countdown may be declared inside the ()s. When the control variable for the loop is declared within the for statement its scope is the body of the loop. See also Section 26.4 on legacy compilers.

which in this example steps countdown through the values 10 to 1. This is equivalent to the following while statement:

```
{
  int countdown = 10;
  while ( countdown  > 0 )
  {
    // Body of loop
    countdown--;
  }
}
```

*Note: countdown--; is the C++ idiom for: countdown = countdown - 1;
In the for statement any of the components between the ;s may be omitted.*

3.5.2 **do while**

In some cases it is a requirement that the loop is executed at least once, in which case the do while statement may be used. For example, the above for statement could in this case have been written as:

```
int countdown = 10;
do
{
  // Body of loop
  countdown--;
} while ( countdown > 0 );
```

3.6 Other selection constructs

3.6.1 `switch`

The following rather inelegant series of `if` statements may be combined:

```
if ( number == 1 )
  std::cout << "One";
else if ( number == 2 )
  std::cout << "Two";
else if ( number == 3 )
  std::cout << "Three";
else
  std::cout << "Not One,Two or Three";
std::cout << "\n";
```

into the `switch` statement shown below.

```
switch( number )
{
  case 1 :
    std::cout << "One";
    break;
  case 2 :
    std::cout << "Two";
    break;
  case 3 :
    std::cout << "Three";
    break;
  default :
    std::cout << "Not One,Two or Three";
}
std::cout << "\n";
```

In the switch statement however, an explicit 'break' out must be specified, otherwise control will drop to the next case label. This break out of the `switch` statement is performed by the `break` statement.

Note: A case label must be both a value which can be contained in an integer machine word and a compile time constant.
If break is omitted execution will continue through the case label to the next statement.

3.6.2   Conditional expression statement

The expression:

```
( number == 0 ? "zero" : "not zero" )
```

delivers the string `"zero"` or `"not zero"` depending on the value of `number`. This could be used in a longer expression to print the 'form' of number as in:

```
std::cout <<"number is "<< (number==0 ? "zero" : "not zero") << "\n";
```

3.6.3   The `break` statement

As shown above, the break statement may be used to cause control to be passed to the exit of a switch statement. The break statement may also be used to terminate the execution of the looping constructs `while`, `do while` and `for`.

Note: Be careful — A break statement in the wrong place may be disastrous!

The code below will print out the numbers 9 to 0:

```
counter = 10;
while ( counter > 0 )
{
    counter--;
    std::cout << counter << " ";
}
cout << "\n";
```

```
9 8 7 6 5 4 3 2 1 0
```

However, by use of a break statement the loop may be terminated early, in this case when the value of counter is equal to 3:

```
counter = 10;
while ( counter > 0 )
{
    counter--;
    if ( counter == 3 )
        break;
    std::cout << counter << " ";
}
cout << "\n";
```

The effect is that only the numbers 9 to 4 are printed:

```
9 8 7 6 5 4
```

3.6.4 The `continue` statement

The `continue` statement is rather unusual in that its effect is to abandon the current execution path through the code, and proceed to the next iteration.

```
counter = 10;
while ( counter > 0 )
{
  counter--;
  if ( counter == 3 )
    continue;
  std::cout << counter << " ";
}
cout << "\n";
```

The result of the above code is simply that the number 3 is not printed.

```
9 8 7 6 5 4 2 1 0
```

Continue may also be used in do while and for statements, to abandon the current execution path through the loop and resume execution on the next iteration.

Note: In producing guidelines for writing C++ code, some people would only allow break to be used to exit from a case statement and would not allow continue to be used at all.

3.7 Input and output

In C++ input and output (I/O) are performed using the << (insertion) and >> (extraction) operators. Input and output functions are not part of the C++ language but are provided by library objects and methods, in fact any person could write their own I/O system. However, it is usual to use the standard set of objects and methods provided by the standard I/O library.

The operators << and >> are not dedicated to the I/O process but are simply existing C++ operators overloaded with a new definition. Overloading is the process of giving another meaning to an existing operator or function.

3.7.1 Output

The insertion operator << is used to send a value to the current output stream as follows:

```
std::cout << 42;
```

Which would write 42 to the stream associated with `std::cout` (Current output). In C++ `std::cout` is usually automatically connected to a user's terminal so no other functions need to be called.

The style of the resulting output may be specified by using output manipulators as follows:

```
std::cout << std::setprecision(2);
```

which would cause output of all floating point numbers to be displayed to two decimal places.

Note: For this output statement no physical output is performed. The style for the output of all subsequent floating point numbers is simply set to be 'display as a decimal number with two places of decimals'.

The manipulator `std::setprecision` is usually used in conjunction with:

```
std::cout << std::setiosflags(std::ios::fixed);  //Display in x.y format
std::cout << std::setiosflags(std::ios::showpoint);//Show all places
```

Output may also be sent to other output streams, for example:

```
std::cerr << "Error in data" << "\n";
```

would send the message to the error stream. Normal writing to `std::cerr` guarantees that the message will be displayed on the user's terminal.

3.7.2   Input

The extraction operator `>>` allows a user to input data values into their program. For example:

```
int height;
std::cin >> height;
```

will read an integer value into the variable height.

One problem with input is that all white space characters (space, tab and newline) are by default ignored. The consequence of this is that if you write a C++ program to copy the text:

```
In C++ the operator:
   <<    is used for output
   >>    is used for input
```

character by character from the input stream `std::cin` to the output stream `cout` then the output would look like:

```
InC++theoperator:<<isusedforoutput>>isusedforinput
```

The solution is to use the manipulator:

```
std::cin >> std::resetiosflags( std::ios::skipws );
```

to unset the option which requests white space to be ignored.

Note: In using input and output manipulators the header file:

```
#include <iomanip>
```

should be included in your program.
Appendix A contains a fuller description of the major I/O functions.

3.7.3   The namespace `std`

In a large program written by many people, there is always the danger of two programmers choosing the same name for an item. To prevent this and to avoid clashes with names in the standard libraries a namespace is used to provide an encapsulation for named items.

The standard library objects, functions etc. are all contained within the namespace `std`. To access an item from the namespace `std` the name of the library item is prefixed with `std::`. Hence the objects `cout` and `cin` are always accessed using `std::cout` and `std::cin` respectively. The concept of namespace is more fully discussed in Chapter 13.

Library item	Explanation
`std::cout`	The current output stream object in the namespace `std`.
`std::ios::skipws`	An item `skipws` that is in the namespace `ios` that itself is contained in the namespace `std`. (This is not strictly true but will do for now.)

3.8 The , operator

The following program acts as a simple software tool to copy its input, character by character, to its output. In C++ `cout` is the standard output stream and `std::cin` is the standard input stream.

The , operator delivers the result of its second argument. In this program the , operator is used to deliver the result of the second argument in the expression:

```
std::cin >> ch , !std::cin.eof()
```

This avoids having to repeat the statement std::cin >> ch;.

Note: The types of the two operands to the , operator may be different as in this case.

```
#include <iostream>
#include <iomanip>

int main()
{
  char ch;                                   //Declare ch
  std::cin >> std::resetiosflags( std::ios::skipws );
  while ( std::cin >> ch , !std::cin.eof() )  //not end of file
  {
    std::cout << ch;                          //Output the ch read
  }
  return 0;
}
```

Note: The line:
```
std::cin >> std::resetiosflags( std::ios::skipws );
```
requests that the input stream delivers all characters including the white space characters. The white space characters are; space tab and newline.

This program can be used on a Unix system as a simple software tool to print the contents of a file. If the compiled program simple_cat were run, then it could be used to print the contents of a file Text as follows:

```
% simple_cat < Text
C++ was initially designed by Bjarne Stroustrup between
1980-1983 and was initially invented to help write event
driven simulations.
As the name implies it is the next increment from C
combining the concept of classes from Simula67 together
with features from BCPL the original inspiration for C.
In many ways C++ is a superset of C.
```

3.9 Self-assessment

- What are the major differences so far between C++ and any other computer programming languages known to you?

- Can a mixture of a simple if with no else part and a while construct represent everything that can be expressed with an if else or do while construct?

- What is the result of the expression 1 == 2? Why is it different from the invalid expression 1 = 2?

- What is output when the following line is executed?

```
std::cout << "C++ was designed by Bjarne Stroustrup" << "\n";
```

- Can any switch statement be replaced by an equivalent statement made up of nested if else statements? Is the converse true? In each case explain your answer.

- Are break and continue statements necessary in C++?

- Why does C++ have two looping constructs while and do while?

- When should comments be introduced into a program?

- What does the following program do and is it good programming practice?

```
#include <iostream>
int main()
{
  int sum = 0;

  for( int count = 1; count < 100; count++ )
  {
    sum = sum + count;
    if ( sum > 1000 )
    {
      std::cout << count << "\n";
      count = 100;
    }
  }
}
```

- What is the difference between = and ==?

3.10   Exercises

Construct the following programs:

● *Numbers*
  A program to write out the numbers 32 to 126 using a while loop.

● *Times Table*
  A program to print out the 5 times table so that the output is in the following form:

```
5 *  1 =   5
5 *  2 =  10
5 *  3 =  15

.  .  .

5 * 12 =  60
```

● *Times Table the general case*
  A program to print out any times table. You will need to ask the user which times table is required.

```
int num; std::cin >> num;
```

would read a decimal number into num.

● *Series*
  A program to print out items in the series 1 1 2 3 5 8 13 . . . until the last term is greater than 10000.

● *Order*
  A program to read in three numbers and print them out in ascending order.

4 Introducing C++ — part 2

This chapter looks at some of the simple data items that can be described in C++.

4.1 Introduction

```
int countdown;
```

In the examples presented so far, the only type of objects declared have been of type `int` or `char`. The exact representation or 'range of values' that an object of type `int` can take, may well differ between implementations of C++. It all depends on the size in bytes of a machine word, on the computer used.

Note: The standard header file `<limits>` and `<float.h>` will contain minimum and maximum values for the data types implemented on a particular system.

C++ allows a variable to be initialized at the same time that it is declared, as in the example below.

```
int countdown = 10;
```

4.2 Declarations of data items

Data items can be declared at different points in a program. One such location is the point at which executable statements occur. It is, however, more usual for the declaration to be located at the start of a function or after an opening {.

```
#include <iostream>
int main()
{
  int   green_cars = 23;      // When a data item is declared
  int   red_cars   = 20;      //  it can also be given an initial value.
  std::cout << "Number of green cars  = " << green_cars << "\n";
  std::cout << "Number of red cars    = " << red_cars << "\n";

  int total = green_cars + red_cars;
  std::cout << "Total number of cars  = " << total << "\n";
  return 0;
}
```

4.2.1　Identifiers

A C++ identifier (such as a variable name or function name) is composed of upper and lower-case characters, numeric digits and the underscore character '_'. The maximum length of an identifier is unlimited, but it must start with a letter.

4.3　Fundamental types of C++

The inbuilt data types or fundamental types are as follows:

Type	May also be specified as	Commentary
char		Holds a character
unsigned char		Unsigned version of char
signed char		Signed version of char
bool		A Boolean value
wchar_t		Wide char
int	signed int signed	A machine word that holds an integer number
unsigned int	unsigned	Unsigned version of int
short	signed short int signed short short int	May have less precision than an int
unsigned short	unsigned short int	Unsigned version of short
long	long int	May have more precision than an int
unsigned long	unsigned long int	Unsigned version of long
float		A number held in floating point form
double		May have more precision than a float
long double		May have more precision than a double

Note:　A float, double and long double are stored as a floating point number. The rest of the fundamental types are stored as an exact quantity.

The unsigned types will be able to store a larger positive number than their signed types.

The precision of items declared with these data types may vary, depending on the compiler or machine used.

The representation of char may be either signed or unsigned. This is to allow implementors the choice of the architectural representation of a char.

4.4　Typedef

One problem in writing a program in C++, is that the precision of a number cannot be specified. To make matters worse, the precision of the fundamental types may change between implementations of the language. For a programmer this can cause many problems. Consider the following code fragment:

```
int big_number = 100000;
```

On some computers this will fail, as an `int` will have been defined to be only two bytes wide. Two bytes will only allow an `int` to be in the range -32768 to 32767. The solution to this problem is to allow a user to define a new data type which would represent the large number in terms of an existing data type. This is achieved with the typedef statement as follows:

```
typedef int Integer;

Integer big_number;
```

which would equate `int` with the new type `Integer`. On a machine where an `int` is two bytes wide and a `long int` is four bytes wide, the `typedef` statement could be changed to:

```
typedef long Integer;
```

Normally, `typedef` statements would be contained in a single header file, so that only a small number of changes would have to be made to a program to allow it to run on another machine.

Note: Typedef does not introduce a new type, rather it is an alias for an existing type specification.

4.5　The types `float`, `double`, `long double`

An instance of the type `int` holds numbers to an exact value. In the solving certain problems the numbers that are manipulated will not be an exact value. For example, a person's weight is 80.45 kilograms. An instance of the type `float` is a variable which can hold a number which has decimal places. Thus in a program a person's weight can be held in the variable `weight` which is declared as follows:

```
float weight = 80.45;
```

An instance of the type `float` is implemented as a floating point number. A floating point number holds a value to a specific number of decimal digits. This will in many cases be an approximation to the exact value which the programmer wishes to store. For example, a 1/3 will be held as 0.333 ... 33. The following table shows how various numbers are effectively stored in floating point form to 6 decimal places:

Number	Scientific notation	Floating point form
80.45	$0.8045 * 10^2$	+804500 +02
0.008045	$0.8045 * 10^{-2}$	+804500 −02
0.333333	$0.333333 * 10^0$	+333333 +00

Note: In reality the floating point number will be held in binary.

The main consequence of using a floating point number is that numbers are held to an approximation of their true value. Calculations using floating point numbers will usually only give an approximation to the true answer. However, in many cases this approximation will not cause any problems. An area where this approximation will cause problems is when the value represents a monetary amount.

In the definition of C++ `double` is defined to have the same or greater precision than a `float` and a `long double` to have the same or greater precision than a `double`.

4.6   Const declarations

To make a program more readable, constants can be given symbolic names. The declaration of a constant is very similar to that of a normal variable, the only difference is, of course, that no value can subsequently be assigned to it.

```
const int       MAX = 10;
const long double PI  = 3.14159265358979323846264338327 9L;
```

Note: It is good programming practice to use a const declaration for any value other than 0 or 1.

To differentiate easily between const items and variable items, const items are shown in UPPER case.

The use of L after the number to indicate a `long double` constant. Appendix I lists the different type of literals that may be declared in a C++ program.

4.7   Enumerations

Variables may be restricted to have specific values. In the example below a new type is created named `Colour` which may only have the values `red`, `blue` or `green`. A compile time error would be generated if any other value were assigned to a variable of type `Colour`.

```
enum Colour   {RED,BLUE,GREEN};     //Enumeration

Colour car;
car = RED;
switch ( car )
{
  case RED :
    std::cout << "Car is red";
    break;
  case BLUE :
    std::cout << "Car is blue";
    break;
  case GREEN :
    std::cout << "Car is green";
    break;
}
```

Note: The compiler represents RED as 0, BLUE as 1 etc. However, these values can be changed with enum Colour { RED= 2, BLUE = 4, GREEN}. GREEN would take the next value which in this case is 5. In most cases, it would be considered poor programming practice to explicitly ask the compiler to represent an enumeration with a specific value.

The use of a break statement at the end of each case label, which causes a break out of the switch statement to the following statement.

4.8 Arithmetic operators

The arithmetic operators in C++ are:

+	Addition
–	Subtraction
*	Multiplication
/	Division
%	Modulus or Remainder

Note: Division: If both operands are of type integer then the result will be an integer division of the operands. However, if one of the operands is a floating point number then the result will be floating point division of the operands.

Modulus: Both operands must be integer.

For example, the following program:

```
#include <iostream>

int main()
{
  std::cout << 5/2 << "\n";    //Integer division
  std::cout << 5/2.0 << "\n"; //Floating point division (5.0/2.0)
  std::cout << 5%2 << "\n";    //Modulus
  return 0;
}
```

when compiled and run will produce:

```
2
2.5
1
```

4.8.1   Monadic arithmetic operators

–	negation
+	positive form

4.9 Relational operators in C++

==	equal
!=	not equal
<	less than
>	greater than
<=	less than or equal
>=	greater than or equal

Note: Yet another warning that equality is written as == and not as =, which is the operator for assignment.

Only the fundamental data types may be compared with these relational operators. In particular comparing two string literals to determine, equality or the collating sequence, will not give the expected result. The reason a string literal comparison will not give the expected result, is explained in Section 8.12.3.

For example:

```
std::cout << (  temperature > -10 ? "Maybe warm" : "Very cold" );
```

4.10   Logical operators

&&	logical and
||	logical or

These may be used to construct complex conditional expressions as in:

```
if ( year == 2004 && month == 2 )
{
  //29 days
}
```

Appendix F contains a list of the priority of all the operators. C++ sensibly has && and || as a lower priority than the relational operators.

Note: In evaluating a conditional expression, the left to right evaluation will stop as soon as a definite result is established. This lazy evaluation may cause problems if it is required to execute all parts of the condition. Section 3.12.1 illustrates how to prevent lazy evaluation of an expression.

4.10.1   Monadic logical operator

!	not

This delivers the inverse of the boolean expression or boolean value. For example:

```
std::cout << ( !my_birthday ? "normal day" : "My birthday" );
```

4.11   The type `bool`

The type `bool` declares a variable to hold a truth value. For example, the Boolean variable `Christmas` is used in the following fragment of code.

```
bool christmas = day == 25 && month == 12;

if ( christmas )
{
  std::cout << "Happy christmas" << "\n";
}
```

4.11.1   Alternative to `bool`

Originally C++ did not contain a `bool` data type. To facilitate the manipulation of boolean values the following `int` values where used instead:

Truth value	Represented by `int` value
true	Any value other than 0
false	0

Whilst the use of an `int` value to represent truth values is not recommended its use can result in compact source code. For example, a code sequence to write a line of 40 minus characters is written as:

```
int count = 40;
while( count )
{
  count--; std::cout << "-";
}
```

To retain compatibility with this original way of processing truth values, an instance of a `bool` is promoted to the following `int` values:

Declaration	`std::cout << (int) res;`
bool res = true;	1
bool res = false;	0

4.12   Bitwise operators

These are used for operating on integer quantities. Most programs will require the use of these operators only occasionally.

&	bitwise and
|	bitwise or
^	bitwise xor
<<	pattern << n ; left shift pattern by n binary places
>>	pattern >> n ; right shift pattern by n binary places

Note: The operators << and >> in the examples presented have only been used, so far,
for input and output. This is because C++ allows operators to be overloaded
with a new meaning. This concept is discussed more fully in Chapter 15.

For example, the following program:

```
#include <iostream>

int main()
{
  for ( int i=1; i<=4; i++ )
  {
    std::cout << ( 32>>i ) << "\t" << ( 32<<i ) << "\n";
  }
  return 0;
}
```

when compiled and run will produce:

```
16        64
8         128
4         256
2         512
```

Note: " \ t " is the C++ way of expressing a tab character. Appendix G gives a full
listing of the escape sequences that can be included in a string or literal constant.
The different uses of << as an output insertion operator and as a left shift
operator.

4.12.1   Warning using | and & as logical operators

Though | and & can be used as logical operators, it is not recommended as lazy
evaluation will not be performed. For example:

Expression	what is evaluated

`if ( temperature > 20  & sunny() )`
`{`
`  work_outside();`
`}`
	Both the expression `temperature>20` and the function `sunny()` are evaluated even if the temperature is <= 20 degrees.

4.12.2   Monadic bitwise operators in C++

~	bitwise not

This operator changes all 0s to 1s and all 1s to 0s in a word.

4.13   The `sizeof` operator

The `sizeof` operator may be used to deliver the size of a C++ data type. In the example code below, it is used to print the size in bytes of some of the inbuilt data types.

```
#include <iostream>

int main()
{
  std::cout << "Sizes of types" << "\n";
  std::cout << "char        " << sizeof(char) << "\n";
  std::cout << "short       " << sizeof(short) << "\n";
  std::cout << "int         " << sizeof(int) << "\n";
  std::cout << "bool        " << sizeof(bool) << "\n";
  std::cout << "long        " << sizeof(long) << "\n";
  std::cout << "float       " << sizeof(float) << "\n";
  std::cout << "double      " << sizeof(double) << "\n";
  std::cout << "long double " << sizeof(long double) << "\n";
  return 0;
}
```

When run on two different computers the following results were obtained:

Sun sparc based	PC 80x86 DOS based

`Sizes of types`
`char        1`
`short       2`
`int         4`
`bool        1`
`long        4`
`float       4`
`double      8`
`long double 8`
	`Sizes of types`
	`char        1`
	`short       2`
	`int         2`
	`bool        1`
	`long        4`
	`float       4`
	`double      8`
	`long double 10`

Note: If your program is to be run on more than one machine this information may be vital.

4.14   Promotion of variables

Like many languages, C++ has strict rules about type conversion when arithmetic operations are performed. However, C++ will perform type conversions (promotions) in many places to allow an operation to take place. For the unwary this can lead to errors. Fortunately these promotions are mostly intuitive.

In any arithmetic operation using the inbuilt arithmetic operations, the contents of variables are promoted if necessary to a form in which the operation can be performed. This process is composed of several stages.

In an expression involving `Operand1 operator Operand2`

● If either `Operand1` or `Operand2` is a:

long double	then the other operand is converted to a	long double
double	then the other operand is converted to a	double
float	then the other operand is converted to a	float

● Otherwise the integer promotions take place on both operands. These are:

    ● If all values of the types (`char`, `signed char`, `unsigned char`, `short  int`, or `Unsigned  short  int`) can be represented as an `int` then the instance of the type is converted to an `int`. Otherwise, the instance of the type is converted to an `unsigned int`.

    ● For instances of the types (`wchar_t`, or enumeration type) the value is converted to the first of the following types that can represent all the values: `int`, `unsigned  int`, `long`, or `unsigned long`.

    ● An instance of type `bool` is converted to an instance of the type `int` with `false` as 0, and `true` as 1.

For example, an instance of a `char` will be promoted to an instance of an `int`.

● If either `Operand1` or `Operand2` is a:

unsigned long	then the other operand is converted to a	unsigned long

● When one of the operands is a `long  int` and the other is an `unsigned int`:

If `long  int` can be made to represent the `unsigned  int` then the `unsigned int` will be converted to a `long  int`.

If `long  int` cannot be made to represent the value of the `unsigned int` both the operands will be converted to `unsigned long  int`.

● If either `Operand1` or `Operand2` is:

long	then the other operand is converted to a	long
unsigned	then the other operand is converted to a	unsigned

The promotion of variables can be illustrated by the following three-stage process for an expression involving two operands:

First Stage If any of the operands are of the following type:	Second Stage Then the operand will be promoted to the lower ranking of the two types below, which can hold the quantity.	Third Stage Then if both operands are of different ranking then the lowest ranking operand will be promoted to the same rank as the higher.	
`char`			Low ranking
`signed char`			
`unsigned char`			
`short int`			
`unsigned short int`			
`wchar_t` (See note)			
`bool`			
	`int`		
	`unsigned int`		
		`long int`	
		`unsigned long int`	
		`float`	
		`double`	
		`long double`	High ranking

Note: *The promotion model used does not require an intermediate promotion. For an expression, involving a* `short int` *and a* `double`*, the* `short int` *will be promoted to a* `double`*.*

An instance of a `wchar_t` *is converted to an instance of the first of the following types (* `int, unsigned int, long,` *or* `unsigned long` *) that can hold all values of the type* `wchar_t`*.*

The special case noted above when the operands are `long int` *or* `unsigned int`*.*

For example in the following fragment of code:

```
short int units = 5;
float price     = 123.45;

std::cout << units * price;
```

In the expression `unit * price`, the integer promotions take place firstly to promote the `short int` to an `int`. Then both operands are brought up to the same rank, in this case `float`.

4.15   Casts

In C++, one data type may be converted to another type by use of a cast. For example, a number may be converted to a character as follows:

```
std::cout << (char) 65;
```

which would print out a capital A. This assumes, of course, that the computer is working with the ASCII character set.

Note: C++ will do some conversions automatically for a programmer. However, in the above example, the output routines determine how to output a quantity from its type, so the cast was necessary.

An alternative functional notation is also available:

```
std::cout << char(65);
```

Note: There will be cases when the functional notation cannot be used, as the notation is also used to describe another construct (constructor to a class item). For this reason it is best to use the first notation where the type is enclosed in brackets so that the 'functional notation' can be used to indicate the call of a constructor.

4.16   Shortcuts increment and decrement

In C++ there are several shortcuts for adding or subtracting an amount from a variable. The most widely used are probably the increment and decrement operators ++ and --. These, however, have different effects depending on their placement.

Operator	Before a value e.g. ++cost	After a value e.g. cost++
++	Increments the value by 1 unit then delivers the result	Delivers the value then increments the value by 1 unit
--	Decrements the value by 1 unit then delivers the result	Delivers the value then decrements the value by 1 unit

For example, if cost has an initial value of 10 in each case, then:

C++ expression	Delivered as the result of the expression	Value of cost after the evaluation of the expression
++cost	11	11
cost++	10	11
--cost	9	9
cost--	10	9

Note: These operators can be applied to any of the arithmetic and pointer types. Pointers are fully discussed in Chapter 17.

4.16.1   Other shortcuts

Another common construct that can be simplified is the expression:

```
item = item operator expression;
```

where operator is one of the C++ operators such as + - * / etc. This can be rewritten in a shorter form, as:

```
item operator= expression;
```

For example:

Long form	Shortened form
`money = money + 100;`	`money += 100;`
`reduce_price = reduce_price/2;`	`reduce_price /= 2;`

4.17   Expressions

C++ does not have assignment statements but does have expression statements. The difference is that what looks like an assignment statement is in fact an expression, which delivers a result. Thus a C++ programmer can write:

```
int a,b,c;
a = b = c = 0;
```

to set the values of a, b and c to 0. This occurs because = (assignment) delivers the value of the quantity assigned.

However, the following is also a valid expression:

```
i;
```

It delivers the contents of i, which is immediately discarded.

Note: This may well disguise an error of omission on behalf of the implementor of the code.

4.18   Summary of operators

In C++ the operations allowed on the data types are indicated below. In this table `int` also represents its `short`, `long`, `signed` and `unsigned` versions, whilst `float` also represents its `double` and `long` forms.

operator	description	Allowed on		
		char	int	float
+	Addition	✓ ?	✓	✓
−	Subtraction	✓ ?	✓	✓
/	Division	✓ ??	✓	✓
*	Multiplication	✓ ??	✓	✓
%	Modulus (or remainder)	✓ ??	✓	

operator	description	Allowed on		
		char	**int**	**float**
<<	Left shift	✓	✓	
>>	Right shift	✓	✓	
&	bitwise and	✓	✓	
|	bitwise or	✓	✓	
^	bitwise xor	✓	✓	
&&	logical and	✓	✓	
||	logical or	✓	✓	

✓	Allowed
✓ ?	Allowed but be careful; this may not be what you want!
✓ ??	Allowed but do you really want to do this!!

Note: In the table int and float denote any type of int or float for example, `unsigned int` and `long double`.

4.19   Self-assessment

● How are variables declared in C++, and where may a declaration appear?

● What is the precision of an integer in C++?

● How may an instance of one of the standard data types be converted into another of the standard data types? Are there any restrictions/prohibitions?

● List the inbuilt data types of C++. Can you give a relationship between all the inbuilt data types using `sizeof`?

● What is the difference between:

```
    int i = 10; std::cout << i++;
and
    int i = 10; std::cout << ++i;
```

● With the following declarations:

```
    char c;      int i;      double d;    unsigned int u;
```

what is the type of the result of the following expressions:

```
c + i;           d + u;              i + d;
c + c;           i + i;              u + u;
(char) i + c;    (double) i + i;     c + u;
```

- When does the division operator deliver an integer, and when does it deliver a floating point number?

- When executed what will the following print?

```
int main()
{
  int number = 512;
  number <<= 4;
  std::cout << number;
  std::cout << "\t" << (1&3) << "\t" << (5%(4>>1)));
  return 0;
}
```

4.20   Exercises

Construct the following programs:

- *Character Codes*
  A program to write out the characters that are internally represented by the numbers 32 to 126.

  The output should look like this:

  ASCII char A is represented internally by internal code 65
  ASCII char B is represented internally by internal code 66

- *Character Count*
  A program to count the number of characters taken from the standard input. This can then be used as a software tool to count the number of characters in a text file.

- *Upper Case*
  A program to capitalize the first character of a sentence.

- *Primes*
  A program to print all prime numbers between 1 and 1000.

- *Perfect numbers*
  A program to print all perfect numbers between 1 and 1000. A perfect number is a number with factors which, when added together, add up to the number. For example 6 is a perfect number (factors 1,2,3) and 28 is also a perfect number (factors 1,2,4,7,14).

- *Number of 1 bits in a number*
  A program which will input an integer number and print out how many binary 1 bits there are. For example, if the number 5 was input the answer would be 2, and if 8 was input the answer would be 1.

●   *Encrypt*

A simple encryption algorithm is to exclusively or (xor C++ operator ^) each character of a text message with a bit pattern. Then the same process can be repeated on the encrypted text to reveal the original message. Write a program to carry out this encryption/decryption.

For example:

```
'A'          01000001          Encrypted    00110001
key          01110000          key          01110000
    xor      --------              xor      --------
Encrypted    00110001          decrypted    01000001
```

Hint: *Use a 7 bit key to avoid binary data.*

5 Classes

This chapter introduces the concept of the class. A class is an elegant way of encapsulating code and data which interact together into a single unit. This single unit can then be used to create instances of the class termed objects.

5.1 Introduction

The world in which we live is populated by many devices and machines that make everyday living easier and more enjoyable. The TV, for instance, is viewed by almost every person in the country, yet few understand exactly what happens inside 'the box'. Likewise, there are many millions of motorists who drive regularly and do not need a detailed knowledge of the workings of a car to make effective use of it.

To many people, their knowledge of a car is as shown in Figure 5.1

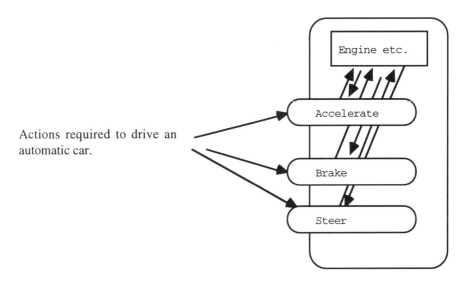

Figure 5.1 Basic understanding of working of an automatic car.

The details of what happens inside the car are not important for most day-to-day driving.

In essence the world is populated with many objects which have an interface that allows the humblest of persons to make effective use of the item. We sometimes criticize the interfaces as being ineffective and difficult to use, yet in most cases we would prefer to use the objects as they stand, rather than having to perform the task by other means.

Likewise in the software world, there are objects that a user or programmer can make effective use of without having to know how the object has been implemented. On a very simple level a C++ program may declare variables to hold floating point numbers, which can then be used for arithmetic operations to sum, multiply, etc. these values. Most programmers however, do not know the exact details of how these operations are performed; they accept the interface provided by the programming language.

At one point it was fashionable for programming languages to provide a rich set of data types. The designers of these languages hoped the data types provided would be adequate for all occasions. The problem was, and still is, that no one language could ever hope to provide all the different types of item that a programmer may need or wish to use.

C++ gives a programmer the ability to declare new data objects, together with a range of operations that may be performed on an instance of the object. Naturally, a programmer may also use objects that have been defined by other programmers.

5.2   Objects, messages and methods

A car can be thought of as an object. The car contains complex details and processes that are hidden from the driver. For example, to make the car go faster the driver presses the accelerator pedal. The car receives the message 'go faster' and evokes an internal method to speed up the engine.

In the above description of driving a car many object-oriented ideas have been used. These ideas are as follows:

object	An item that has a hidden internal structure. The hidden structure is manipulated or accessed by internal methods invoked by a user sending a message to the object.
message	A request sent to an object to invoke a method.
method	A set of actions that manipulates or accesses the internal state of the object. The implementation of these actions is hidden from a user of the object.

5.3   The class

In C++ an object is an instance of a class. An object combines variables and the code which manipulates these variables into a single named item.

The important concept is that the class is a specification of an object, it is in effect a description of storage combined with a description of the operations or methods that may be performed on this storage. An instance of the class must be created before any physical operations can be performed. Each physical representation will contain a copy of the data items that may be manipulated with the operations provided. An object can be represented diagrammatically as shown in Figure 5.2.

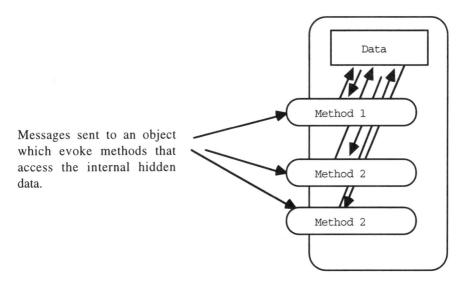

Figure 5.2 Outline of operations on an object.

In this example, the operations on the data are referred to as methods. The use of software objects leads to a much clearer form of program design and can allow the re-use of the class in other programs.

Note: *The concept of binding code and data together to form a class, is often referred to as encapsulation.*

5.3.1 An object for a bank account

Before looking in detail at the implementation of an object that represents a bank account, it is appropriate to consider the messages that might be sent to such an object. For a very simple type of bank account these messages would be:

- Deliver the account balance.
- Deposit money into the account.
- Set the minimum balance for the account (overdraft limit).
- Set-up the account.
- Withdraw money from the account.

Each message invokes a method which has the following responsibilities:

Method/Constructor	Responsibility
`Account`	Set up the initial state of the account (constructor).
`account_balance`	Return the balance of the account.
`deposit`	Deposit money into the account.

`set_min_balance`	Set the overdraft limit:
	    0.00 no overdraft.
	    -10.00 overdraft of £10.00 pounds allowed.

`withdraw`	Withdraw money from the account, but only if there is sufficient funds or an overdraft is allowed.

The state of the object is represented by two float variables:

Instance variable	Represents
the_balance	The current balance.
the_min_balance	The overdraft limit. A value of -200.00 would allow an overdraft of £200.00 for the account.

Note: The instance variables are hidden from a user of the object.
The instance variables are prefixed with the_ to emphasize their role.

For example, to deposit £100.00 into the Account object mike the following notation is used:

```
mike.deposit(100.00);
```

This is read as: send the message deposit to the object mike with a parameter of £100.00. Another way of thinking about this is to imagine the object mike as a person to whom messages can be sent. In this case we tell the object mike to deposit £100.00 into their account.

To withdraw money from the account a programmer sends the message withdraw to the object mike with a parameter representing the amount of money to be withdrawn. The implementation of the method will check that the person has sufficient funds in their account to allow the transaction to take place. If they have insufficient funds or are not allowed an overdraft facility then an amount of £0.00 is returned. For example, to withdraw £20.00 from mike's bank account the following notation is used.

```
float obtained = mike.withdraw(20.00);
```

The variable obtained will contain the actual amount withdrawn from the bank account.

This can be thought of as asking mike to see if £20.00 can be withdrawn from their account. The object mike then replies with the amount of money that has been withdrawn.

5.3.2   Putting it all together

The following program demonstrates the sending of these messages to instances of Account objects mike and cori.

```
#include <iostream>
#include <iomanip>

//Specification and implementation of class Account
```

```
int main()
{
  Account mike, cori;
  float obtained;

  std::cout << std::setiosflags( std::ios::fixed );       //Format x.y
  std::cout << std::setiosflags( std::ios::showpoint ); //0.10
  std::cout << std::setprecision(2);                      //2 dec places

  mike.deposit( 100.00 );
  cori.deposit( 120.00 );

  std::cout<< "Mike's    account = " << mike.account_balance() << "\n";
  std::cout<< "Corinna's account = " << cori.account_balance() << "\n";

  mike.set_min_balance( -100.00 );
  std::cout<< "Mike    withdraws : " << mike.withdraw(120.00) << "\n";
  std::cout<< "Corinna withdraws : " << cori.withdraw(20.00)  << "\n";

  std::cout<< "Mike's    account = " << mike.account_balance() << "\n";
  std::cout<< "Corinna's account = " << cori.account_balance() << "\n";
  return 0;
}
```

Note: This program will require the inclusion of the definition of the class Account
before it can be compiled successfully.

Which when compiled and run delivers the following results:

```
Mike's    account = 100.00
Corinna's account = 120.00
Mike    withdraws : 120.00
Corinna withdraws : 20.00
Mike's    account = -20.00
Corinna's account = 100.00
```

5.3.3   Implementation issues

The class Account uses a float to hold the balance of the account. This is not the best strategy as a floating point number is only held to a specific number of places. Thus, there is the danger of rounding errors when a large balance is held in the account.

5.4 Functions

The methods in the class are implemented as C++ functions. A function is simply a grouping of code that can be executed to perform an action. In executing the function access to data items declared in the class and information passed as parameters to the function will be made. The state of the object is defined by the current contents of variables defined in each object.

In the bank account example above, there are:

Methods (Implemented as functions)	Hidden data items (Representing the state of the object)

`Account`
`account_balance`
`withdraw`
`deposit`
`set_min_balance`
	`the_balance`
	`the_min_balance`

`Account` is a special case. Note that it has the same name as the class and is called a constructor. This function is called automatically when an instance of the class is created. The constructor in the class `Account` has the responsibility of setting the initial amount in a person's bank account to £0.00 and the minimum balance that must be kept in the account to £0.00.

With the declaration:

```
Account mike;
```

the compiler inserts code to call the constructor `Account`, which is implemented as the constructor function `Account` shown below:

```
Account::Account()
{
   the_balance = the_min_balance = 0.00;
}
```

Note: A constructor does not return a value.
The use of the scope resolution operator :: to say that the constructor function
Account is a member of the class Account.

The function `account_balance` is a more typical C++ function and is used to deliver the amount of money in a person's bank account.

```
float Account::account_balance()
{
   return the_balance;
}
```

The type of the result returned from a function is specified before the name, in this case a `float`:

The type of the result

```
float Account::account_balance()
{
     return the_balance;
}
```

The actual value delivered

When the message `account_balance` is sent to an object the C++ function `account_balance` is executed. For example, the following expression will cause the balance in the object `mike` to be printed. Remember the result of sending the message `account_balance` to the object `mike` is a `float` value representing the current balance of the account.

```
std::cout << mike.account_balance();
```

Note: `the_balance` *referred to in the function will be the* `the_balance` *in the object* `mike`. *Each different object that is an instance of the class* `Account` *will have their own copy of* `the_balance`.

5.4.1   Parameters to a function

Any number of values (actual parameters) may be passed to a function, so that the data items that the function operates on may be varied. In the case below, a single value is used to pass the amount of money to be withdrawn from the account. Figure 5.3 shows an overview of the layout of the function `withdraw`.

Type of returned result   Value passed to function

```
float Account::withdraw( float money )
{
   if ( the_balance-money >= the_min_balance )
   {
     the_balance = the_balance - money;
     return money;
   } else {
     return 0.00;
   }
}
```

Value returned

Figure 5.3 Overview of the method `withdraw` implemented as a function.

In C++ there can be any number of parameters to a function (including 0) but only a single item can be delivered as a result of the function. There are ways of returning multiple items, but this involves the use of the parameter mechanism, to export values back to the calling environment. The `return` statement causes an immediate exit from the function.

To withdraw £20.00 from `mike`'s account the following code is written:

```
obtained = mike.withdraw(20.00);
```

Note: In producing guidelines for writing C++ code, some people would only allow a single return statement in a function, which would be the last statement in the function.

5.4.2   Void functions

A function does not need to return a value, as demonstrated by the function `deposit` shown below, where an amount of money is deposited into a person's bank account.

```
void Account::deposit( float money )
{
  the_balance = the_balance + money;
}
```

Note: A void function can use the statement `return;` to cause an immediate exit from the function.

For example, the fragment of code:

```
mike.deposit(250.00);
```

would deposit £250 into `mike`'s bank account.

5.5   Specification and implementation of the class `Account`

The C++ class that represents an `Account` is split into two specific components:

●   The specification of the class:

The specification of the class describes what the class does, but not how it is done. This view whilst human readable, is mainly used by the compiler to check that a programmer has used an instance of the class correctly. Extra documentation would be required to tell a programmer what the class does.

● The implementation of the class:

The implementation of the class describes the implementation of the methods that are called when a message is sent to an instance of the class. This would not normally be visible to a programmer using the class as it can be compiled independently and then linked to a user program.

5.5.1   The specification of the class `Account`

The C++ specification of the class `Account` is:

```
class Account {
public:
  Account();
  float account_balance();          //Return the balance
  float withdraw( float );          //Withdraw from account
  void deposit( float );            //Deposit into account
  void set_min_balance( float );    //Set minimum balance
private:
  float the_balance;                //The outstanding balance
  float the_min_balance;            //The minimum balance
};
```

In effect this describes the signature of the messages that can be sent to an instance of the class `Account`. These are C++ prototypes of the functions that will be used to implement the methods in the class.

The specification for the class `Account` is itself split into two distinct sections a `public` part which is visible to a programmer and a `private` part which contains components that are not visible to a programmer.

Unfortunately, the storage that the object uses has to be declared in the specification part of the class. This is declared in the `private` part of the class and hence will not be accessible to a programmer. This is so that the compiler will know how much memory to allocate for each object of the class `Account` that it creates. Later on in Section 17.13 a method for hiding this storage will be discussed.

The access rights to members of a class is controlled by the visibility modifiers `public` and `private`. The visibility of items in a class is shown in Figure 5.4

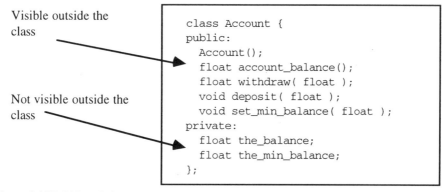

Figure 5.4 Visibility of class members in the specification.

By default all members in a class are private until a label `public` is met. From then on members are visible outside of the class.

Note: It is good programming practice to make data members private to the class and to make public only those member functions of the class which a client will use.

5.5.2   The implementation of the class `Account`

The implementation of the class `Account` contains the body of the functions whose prototypes where contained in the specification part of the class. The function body is shown to belong to the class `Account` using the scope resolution operator ::.

```
Account::Account()
{
   the_balance = the_min_balance = 0.00;
}

float Account::account_balance()
{
  return the_balance;
}

float Account::withdraw( const float money )
{
  if ( the_balance-money >= the_min_balance )
  {
    the_balance = the_balance - money;
    return money;
  } else {
    return 0.00;
  }
}

void Account::deposit( float money )
{
  the_balance = the_balance + money;
}

void Account::set_min_balance( float money )
{
  the_min_balance = money;
}
```

5.5.3   The whole class `Account`

The following table shows the specification and the implementation of the class Account side by side.

Specification	Implementation

`class Account {`
`public:`
` Account();`
` float account_balance();`
` float withdraw( float );`
` void deposit( float );`
` void set_min_balance(float);`
`private:`
` float the_balance;`
` float the_min_balance;`
`};`
	`Account::Account()`
	`{`
	` the_balance = the_min_balance = 0.00;`
	`}`
	
	`float Account::account_balance()`
	`{`
	` return the_balance;`
	`}`
	
	`float Account::withdraw(float money)`
	`{`
	` if(the_balance-money>=the_min_balance)`
	` {`
	`  the_balance = the_balance - money;`
	`  return money;`
	` } else {`
	`  return 0.00;`
	` }`
	`}`
	
	`void Account::deposit( float money )`
	`{`
	` the_balance = the_balance + money;`
	`}`
	
	`void Account::`
	`     set_min_balance( float money )`
	`{`
	` the_min_balance = money;`
	`}`

To the compiler and the user the role of these two parts is as follows:

Class	Role
Specification	Details what the class does.
Implementation	Details how the class performs these operations.

5.5.4   Hierarchy of components in a class

The visibility hierarchy for the Class `Account` is shown in Figure 5.5 below.

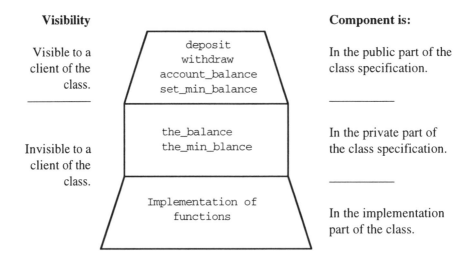

Visibility   **Component is:**

Visible to a   deposit   In the public part of the
client of the   withdraw   class specification.
class.   account_balance
                      set_min_balance

_____   _____

                      the_balance   In the private part of
Invisible to a   the_min_blance   the class specification.
client of the
class.
                                             _____

                      Implementation of   In the implementation
                      functions   part of the class.

Figure 5.5 Visibility of methods and instance attributes of the Class `Account`.

5.5.5   Terminology

The following terminology is used to describe the components of a class.

Terminology	Example: in class Account	Explanation
Data member (Instance attribute Δ)	the_balance	Represents the state of an object. The declaration for the data member is in the private part of the specification. In this book the name of a data member is prefixed with the_.
Member function (Instance method Δ method Δ)	deposit	A function used to access the data members in an object.

Note: The terminology Δ'ed is taken from the language Smalltalk

5.6 A personal account manager

The specification for a personal account manager, implemented on a small electronic notebook with an LCD display, presents the user with a menu on the first few lines of the display, in the form:

```
B - Balance

W - Withdraw

D - Deposit

E - Exit

Input selection:
```

The bottom lines of the display would enable the user to provide any input values required and give room to display any results.

In the example screens below, the user input is shown in **bold** type. For example, if option D were selected, then after the user had input £100, the bottom of the display would look like:

```
Amount to deposit = 100
Balance = 100
```

If using option W, the user specified that £80 had been withdrawn, then the display at the bottom of the screen would look like this:

```
Amount to withdraw = 80
Balance = 20
```

Finally, a user could request their current balance by selecting option B. In this case the display area at the bottom would show:

```
Balance = 20
```

5.6.1 The program

The complete program apart from the specification and implementation of the class Account is shown below. Normally the program will never terminate, as this would lose the amount stored in the simulated bank account.

```
#include <iostream>
#include <iomanip>

//Declaration and implementation of class Account
```

```
int main()
{
  std::cout << std::setiosflags( std::ios::fixed );      //Format x.y
  std::cout << std::setiosflags( std::ios::showpoint ); //0.10
  std::cout << std::setprecision(2);                     //2 dec places

  Account mine;
```

The program loops repeatedly displaying a menu of the transactions that may be performed.

```
while ( true )
{
  char action;
  float obtain,process;

  std::cout << "\n";
  std::cout << "B - Balance"  << "\n" << "\n";
  std::cout << "W - Withdraw" << "\n" << "\n";
  std::cout << "D - Deposit"  << "\n" << "\n";
  std::cout << "E - Exit"     << "\n" << "\n";

  std::cout << "Input selection: ";
  std::cin >> action;
```

A switch statement is used to select between the different transactions that a user may request.

```
  switch ( action )
  {
    case 'B' : case 'b' :
      std::cout << "Balance = " << mine.account_balance() << "\n";
      break;

    case 'W' : case 'w' :
      std::cout << "Amount to withdraw : ";
      std::cin >> process;
      obtain = mine.withdraw( process );
      if ( obtain > 0.00 )
        std::cout << "Withdrawn " << obtain << "\n";
      else
        std::cout << "Not enough funds" << "\n";
      break;

    case 'D' : case 'd' :
      std::cout << "Amount to deposit : ";
      std::cin >> process;
      mine.deposit( process );
      break;
```

```
      case 'E' : case 'e' :
        return 0;

      default  :
        std::cout << "Invalid selection" << "\n";
    }
  }
  return 0;
}
```

Note: *The input data is not checked for either being a valid number or that it is sensible. For example, it is possible to withdraw a negative amount of money from the account.*

5.7 Mutators and inspectors

The methods in a class can either be inspectors or mutators. The role of each of these methods is illustrated in the table below:

Method is a	Role of method	Example from class **Account**
Inspector	Does not change the state of the object.	`account_balance`
Mutator	Changes the state of the object.	`withdraw` `deposit`

5.7.1 Enforcing a member function to be an inspector

The property of a member function to be an inspector can be guaranteed by post fixing the member function with the reserved word `const`. For example, to guarantee that the member function `account_balance` is an inspector its specification is written as:

```
float account_balance() const;          //return the balance
```

and its implementation as:

```
float Account::account_balance() const
{
  return the_balance;
}
```

The compiler will now check that the member function does not change any data member of the class. A compile time error message is generated if in the `const` member function an attempt is made to change a data member.

5.8   Keeping specification and implementation together

Though not recommended the specification and implementation of a class can be combined. In essence the body of the method is included in the specification part of the class. For example, the class Account could have been written as:

```cpp
class Account {
public:
  Account()
  {
     the_balance = the_min_balance = 0.00;
  }

  float account_balance() const
  {
     return the_balance;
  }

  float withdraw( const float money )
  {
     if ( the_balance - money >= the_min_balance )
     {
       the_balance = the_balance - money;
       return money;
     } else {
       return 0.00;
     }
  }

  void deposit( const float money )
  {
     the_balance = the_balance + money;
  }

  void set_min_balance( const float money )
  {
     the_min_balance = money;
  }
private:
  float the_balance;        //Balance of account
  float the_min_balance;    //Minimum balance (Overdraft limit)
};
```

This however, will result in less elegant solution as a user of the class can now see the implementation code.

5.9 Self-assessment

● How do you declare an instance of the class Account?

● When an instance of a class is declared is any code executed?

● How does a programmer code the sending of a message to an instance of a class?

● What is contained in a class?

● What are the advantages of keeping the specification and implementation of a class separate?

● Why might a member function in a class have the same name as the class?

● What are the advantages of holding data and the code that operates on the data together?

● Should a member function in a class be private? Explain your answer.

● Should a data member in a class be public? Explain your answer.

● How can you arrange for private data members in a class to be accessed?

● Would you ever want to declare a class within a class?

5.10 Exercises

Construct the following classes:

● *Safer_Account*
The class to represent a bank account shown earlier had little or no error checking on the values of parameters passed to it. Rewrite this class with strict error checking so that, for example, a negative amount of money cannot be deposited into a bank account.

● *Performance*
A class to describe the state of seats for an individual performance at a cinema. This class has the following methods:

Method	Responsibility
available	Return true if there are n seats available for the performance otherwise return false.
book	Book n seats. The number of seats booked is returned, hence a result of 0 indicates failure.
cancel	Cancel the booking for seats already booked.
remaining	Return the number of seats not booked for this performance.

Construct the following programs:

● *Test programs*
A program to test the class `Safer_Account`.
A program to test the class `Performance`.

● *Cinema*
A program to deal with the day-to-day administration of bookings for a cinema for a single day. Each day there are three separate performances. An early afternoon performance at 1pm, an early evening performance at 5pm, and the main performance at 8.30pm.

The program should be able to handle the booking of cinema seats for any of these three performances and supply details about the remaining seats for a particular performance.

6 Functions

This chapter discusses the role of functions in a C++ program. Functions will normally be members of a class. However, there will be times when they can be usefully used outside of this encapsulating mechanism.

6.1 Introduction

As shown earlier, a function is simply a grouping together of several C++ expressions, which can be called from any appropriate part of a program. Functions allow a programmer a degree of abstraction in solving a problem. However, they can be used more powerfully in combination with data items to form a class.

Functions, however, cannot be nested. This means that a function cannot be declared within another function. The reason for this is to allow very efficient access to data items as well as simplifying the run-time realization of the program.

The function shown in Figure 6.1 sums the two float values passed as parameters.

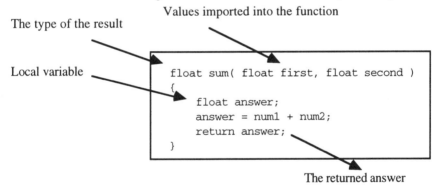

Figure 6.1 A function to return the sum of its two parameters.

6.1.1 Using a function

The following program displays the combined weight of some apples and oranges.

```
#include <iostream>
float sum( float first, float second)
{
  float answer;
  answer = first + second;
  return answer;
}
```

```
int main()
{
  float apples_weight  = 1.21;      //In Kilograms
  float oranges_weight = 1.51;

  std::cout << "Total weight of fruit in kilograms is "
            <<  sum( apples_weight, oranges_weight ) << "\n";
  return 0;
}
```

Note: The value passed may also be a literal value, for example:
```
     std::cout << sum( 10.2, 3.4 ) << "\n";.
```

Which when compiled and run will produce the following results:

```
Total weight of fruit in kilograms is 2.72
```

6.1.2   Terminology

The following terminology is used when describing the process of calling a function:

Terminology	Explanation	Example
Actual parameter	The variable or literal value passed to the function.	`apples_weight`
Formal parameter	The name of the parameter when accessed inside the function.	`first`

When the function `sum` is called it is passed two actual parameters `apples_weight` and `oranges_weight`. In the implementation of the function the formal parameters `first` and `second` are used when access to the parameters are required.

6.1.3   Local variables to a function

When a variable is declared inside a function its lifetime is that of the function. When the function is entered, space for the variables is created automatically on a run-time stack. At the exit point from the function, the storage space for the variable is returned back to the system.

Note: It is good programming practice to only allow a function to access:

- *Parameters to the function.*
- *Local variables.*
- *Data items contained in the class of which this function is a member*

6.1.4   Function prototype

In C++ all functions have to be specified before use. If the function has not already been defined then a function prototype is used to tell the compiler the specification or signature of the function. For the function sum the prototype would be as follows:

```
float sum( float, float );
```

Note: *If a function is a member of a class then its specification (signature) is contained in the class specification.*
If a function is defined before its first use then a function prototype does not need to be specified.
The name of the formal parameter can be omitted in the function prototype.

6.1.5   Void functions

If a function does not return a result then it is declared as a void function. For example the function display_name could be written with its prototype as:

```
void display_name();
int main()
{
  display_name();
  return 0;
}
void display_name()
{
  cout << "A N Other";
}
```

Note: *The empty brackets in a function with no parameters may be replaced by (void) to indicate more visibly that there are no parameters. However, the compiler will always check that the correct number of parameters have been used in the call. See Section 21.13 for how to call a function with a variable number of parameters.*

6.2   Call by value/call by reference

In C++ actual parameters are passed to a function using two separate processes, these process are:

●   Call by value
      A copy is made of the actual parameter and this copy is used as the formal parameter inside the function. Using this mechanism information can only be imported into the function.

● Call by reference

A reference to the actual parameter is used as the formal parameter inside the function. Any changes to the formal parameter will consequently change the actual parameter passed to the function. Using this mechanism information can be imported and exported from the function. This mechanism is implemented by passing the memory address of the actual parameter to the function.

For example, writing a function `swap` to interchange the contents of two variables requires data to be both imported and exported from the function. In the examples, below only the function `swap` will interchange the contents of the two actual parameters `pcs_room_1` and `pcs_room_2`.

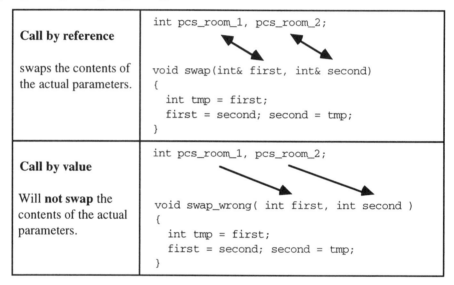

Call by reference
 	
swaps the contents of the actual parameters.
	```int pcs_room_1, pcs_room_2;```
	
	```void swap(int& first, int& second)```
	```{```
	`    int tmp = first;`
	`    first = second; second = tmp;`
	```}```

Call by value
 	
Will **not swap** the contents of the actual parameters.
	```int pcs_room_1, pcs_room_2;```
	
	```void swap_wrong(int first, int second)```
	```{```
	`    int tmp = first;`
	`    first = second; second = tmp;`
	```}```

Note: Call by reference is specified by postfixing the type of the formal parameter with an &.

Only in the case of the function `swap` *will the values contained in the variables* `pcs_room_1` *and* `pcs_room_2` *be changed.*

6.2.1   Putting it all together

Using the function `swap_wrong` will not achieve the desired effect of swapping the contents of the actual parameters. This is because a copy of the actual parameter is used as the formal parameter inside the function. Any changes made to these formal parameters are lost when the function is exited.

```
#include <iostream>

void swap_wrong( int first, int second )
{
  int tmp = first;
  first = second; second = tmp;
}
```

```
int main()
{
  int pcs_room_1 = 4;
  int pcs_room_2 = 8;

  swap_wrong( pcs_room_1, pcs_room_2 );

  std::cout << "PC's room 1 = " << pcs_room_1 << "\n";
  std::cout << "PC's room 2 = " << pcs_room_2 << "\n";
  return 0;
}
```

When run this would produce:

```
PC's room 1 = 4
PC's room 2 = 8
```

Note: In this program the number of PC's in each room has not be swapped, as the
actual parameter is passed by value.

However, using the function `swap` will achieve the desired effect of swapping the
contents of the actual parameters.

```
#include <iostream>

void swap( int& first, int& second )
{
  int tmp = first;
  first = second; second = tmp;
}
int main()
{
  int pcs_room_1 = 4;
  int pcs_room_2 = 8;

  swap( pcs_room_1, pcs_room_2 );

  std::cout << "PC's room 1 = " << pcs_room_1 << "\n";
  std::cout << "PC's room 2 = " << pcs_room_2 << "\n";
  return 0;
}
```

When run this would produce:

```
PC's room 1 = 8
PC's room 2 = 4
```

Note: The C++ way of specifying that a parameter is passed by reference, is to append
& to the parameter type (e.g. `int&`). The full implications of & will be explained
later in Chapter 17.

If an actual parameter is passed by reference to a function it must be a non constant value. The consequence of this is that a literal value may not be passed by reference to a function.

6.3   `const` parameters to a function

To add extra security to functions the `const` specifier may be added to a parameter description to indicate that this parameter is read only inside the body of the function. If a write to this formal parameter is accidentally coded by a programmer then a compile time error message is generated.

```
void wrong( const int item, const char& ch )
{
  item = 123;     //Will fail at compile time
  ch = 'A';       //Will also fail at compile time
}
```

Note: A call by reference does not copy the item, instead a reference to the item (contained in a machine word) is passed.

By using the `const` prefix the code for a function can be made more secure. In particular if a large item is to be passed by reference to a function for efficiency reasons, then the `const` qualifier will prevent an accidental change to the actual parameter.

6.3.1   Summary parameter passing

Parameter specified as: (Using as an example an `int` formal parameter)	Item passed by	Allowed to change formal parameter	Changes exported
`int` item	value	Yes	No
`const int` item	value	No	No
`int&` item	reference	Yes	Yes
`const int&` item	reference	No	No

Note: This can be used to give a similar effect to IN and OUT parameters in Ada.

The effect of using `const` with an array parameter is discussed later in the section parameter access rights for pointers and arrays in Section 17.4.1.

6.4 Recursion

In a very old computer dictionary, recursion might be mischievously defined as:

'If you do not understand recursion see the entry for recursion.'

Note: Recursion is simply solving part of a problem and then recalling the solution mechanism again to evaluate the remainder. This 'recursion' goes on until all parts of the problem are solved.

6.4.1   Recursive functions

Recursion is the ability of a procedure or function to make a call on itself from within its own code body. Whilst this initially may seem a strange idea, it can lead to very elegant code sequences that otherwise would require many more lines of code. In certain exceptional cases recursion is the only way to implement a problem.

An example of a recursive function to write a number using only character based output is sketched in outline below:

Write a number: (`write_number`)

- Split the number into two components
  - (a)   The first digit (remainder when number divided by 10).
  - (b)   The other digits (number divided by 10).

  For example:
  123 would be split into:
  3   (first digit)
  12   (other digits).

- If the other digits are greater than or equal to 10 then write the other digits by recursively calling the code to write a number.

- Output the first digit as a character.

The sequence of calls made is

Call	Implemented as
`write_number( 123 )`	`write_number(12);` output first digit 3
`write_number( 12 )`	`write_number(1);` output first digit 2
`write_number( 1 )`	output first digit 1

This process is diagrammatically expressed in Figure 6.2.

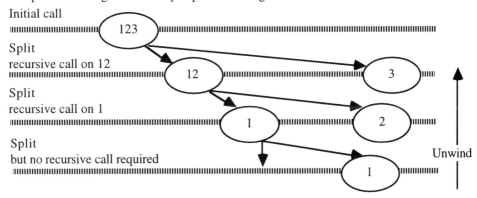

Figure 6.2 Illustration of recursive calls to print the number 123.

The process works by solving a small part of the problem, in this case how to output a single digit, then re-executing the code to solve the remainder of the problem, that is, to output the other digits. In this particular example, the recursive call is made before the solution of the remainder of the problem. This still works as the problem to be solved 'the number to be output' is reduced in size in each recursive call.

However, for recursion to work, the code must reduce the problem to be solved before recalling itself recursively. If this does not take place then endless recursive calls will ensue, which will cause eventual program failure when the system cannot allocate any more memory to support the recursion. Stack space is used on each recursive call to store any parameters or local variables plus the function support information.

```cpp
void write_number( const int number )
{
  int number_to_print = number;
  if ( number < 0 )                        //Make +ve
  {
    number_to_print= -number; cout << "-";
  }
  int first_digit  = number_to_print%10;   //Split
  int other_digits = number_to_print/10;   //
  if ( number_to_print >= 10 )             //More than 1 digit
  {
    write_number( other_digits );          //Other digits
  }
  std::cout << (char) (first_digit + (int) '0'); //First digit
}
```

6.4.2   Putting it all together

The function `write_number` could be used in a program as follows:

```cpp
int main()
{
  write_number( 12345 );
  cout << "  ";
  write_number( -123 );
  cout << "\n";
  return 0;
}
```

which when run would produce:

```
12345  -123
```

6.5 Inline vs. out of line code

When the compiler builds the executable code for a C++ program, there are two distinct approaches in generating the code for functions. These approaches are inline and out of line. The philosophies behind these two approaches are explained below by illustrating the different effect when generating code for calls to the function `swap`.

● Inline

A copy of the code body for the function `swap` is generated each time a call to the function is encountered. This is illustrated in Figure 6.3.

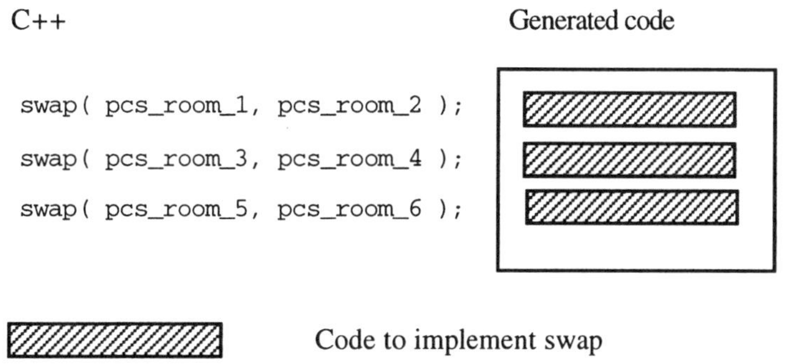

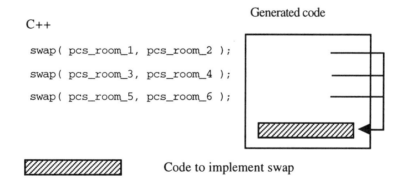

Figure 6.3 Code generated for an inline function.

● Out of line

A single copy of the code body for the function `swap` is generated and calls to this single copy are placed at the points where the function is called. This is illustrated in Figure 6.4.

Figure 6.4 Code generated for an out of line function

6.5.1   When code is inline or out of line

The choice of implementation technique for a function depends in part on where and how the function has been declared. The programmer can also direct the compiler to compile a function inline. However, the compiler is allowed to reject this advice.

In normal circumstances the following will cause a function to be declared inline or out of line.

Inline code	●	A function declaration is prefixed by the keyword inline. The declaration of the body occurs before its first use.
	●	The body of the member function is declared within the class specification. See Section 5.8 for an example of this style of declaration.
Out of line code	●	The body of the member function is declared outside the class specification.
	●	A normal function declaration.

However, if the function is very large, contains looping constructs or is recursive the compiler will normally reject the inline directive.

6.5.2   Advantages/disadvantages

The following table summarizes the advantages and disadvantages of placing a function's code inline or out of line.

	Advantages	Disadvantages
Inline code	Fast to execute	Potentially large code size
Out of line code	Small code size	Slower to execute

6.5.3   Example of an inline function

In the program shown below, each call to the function swap will be replaced by the body of the function.

```
#include <iostream>

inline void swap( int &first, int &second )
{
  int tmp = first;
  first = second; second = tmp;
}

int main()
{
  //Calls to swap
}
```

Note: The body of the function must be defined before the first call to the function.

6.6 Overloading of functions

Overloading is a process which allows the same name to represent several processes in a program. The compiler chooses the appropriate process to use from the context or other additional information provided.

This is best illustrated by an example where the overloaded name is a function:

```
#include <iostream>
#include <string>
```

```
void what_is_this( const char );
void what_is_this( const int );
void what_is_this( const std::string );
void what_is_this( const float );
void what_is_this();
```

Note: The use of `std::string` *to describe an instance of the class* `string`, *this standard class provides sophisticated string handling capabilities, in particular string comparison and assignment. Appendix D lists the members of this class.*

```
void what_is_this( const char c)
{
  cout << "Is a character value " << c << "\n";
}

void what_is_this( const int i)
{
  cout << "Is an integer value " << i << "\n";
}

void what_is_this( const float f)
{
  cout << "Is a float value " << f << "\n";
}

void what_is_this( const std::string str )
{
  cout << "Is a string value " << str << "\n";
}

void what_is_this()
{
  cout << "A function with no parameters" << "\n";
}
```

```
int main()
{
  what_is_this( 1 );
  what_is_this( (float) 1.1 );   //Remember 1.1 is a double const

  what_is_this( 'A' );
  what_is_this( "Hello" );
  cout << "\n";
  return 0;
}
```

which, when run, would print the type and value of the argument passed to `what_is_this`.

```
Is an integer value 1
Is a float value 1.1
Is a character value A
Is a string value Hello
```

Of course, for this to happen, the actual function called must be different in each case. The name `what_is_this` is overloaded by five different functions. The actual binding to the function to be called, is worked out by the compiler at compile time from the actual parameter passed.

6.7 Different number of parameters to a function

As the compiler can distinguish between overloaded names, a function `larger` can be written to deliver the larger of its parameters as follows:

```
#include <iostream>

int larger( const int, const int );
int larger( const int, const int, const int );

int larger( const int a, const int b)
{
  return a>b ? a: b;
}

int larger( const int a, const int b, const int c)
{
  return larger(a,b)>c ? larger(a,b) : c;
}
```

Note: The function `larger` *with three parameters is defined in terms of the function* larger *with two parameters. The compiler resolves which version of* `larger` *to call by virtue of the number of* int *actual parameters.*

6.7.1   Putting it all together

Then the following code can be written:

```
int main()
{
  int num1 = 5, num2 = 4, num3 = 6;

  cout << "Of " << num1 << ", " << num2 ;
  cout << " the larger is " <<  larger(num1,num2) << "\n";
  cout << "Of " << num1 << ", " << num2 << ", " << num3;
  cout << " the larger is " <<  larger(num1,num2,num3) << "\n";
  cout << "\n";
  return 0;
}
```

When run this would produce:

```
Of 5, 4 the  larger is 5
Of 5, 4, 6 the  larger is 6
```

6.8   Default values to parameters

If a default value is given to a formal parameter, then the actual parameter may be omitted when the function is called. The only restriction is that if a formal parameter has a default value, then all formal parameters to the right must also have a default value.

Thus, the following function sum, can be written to return the sum of its parameters:

```
int sum( const int, const int=0, const int=0);   // Specification

int sum( const int a, const int b, const int c)  // Implementation
{
  return a+b+c;
}
```

Note: The way that default values are given for the second and third parameters to the function sum.
It would be an error to repeat the default values on the implementation of the function sum.

6.8.1   Putting it all together

```
int main()
{
  int num1 = 5, num2 = 4, num3 = 6;

  cout << "Of " << num1 ;
  cout << " the sum is " << sum(num1) << "\n";
  cout << "Of " << num1 << ", " << num2 ;
  cout << " the sum is " << sum(num1,num2) << "\n";
  cout << "Of " << num1 << ", " << num2 << ", " << num3;
  cout << " the sum is " << sum(num1,num2,num3) << "\n";
  cout << "\n";
  return 0;
}
```

When run this would produce:

```
Of 5 the sum is 5
Of 5, 4 the sum is 9
Of 5, 4, 6 the sum is 15
```

Remember the actual code generated by the compiler for the function `sum` will involve the passing of three actual parameters. For example:

Programmer writes	Compiler generates
sum(num1)	sum(num1,0,0)
sum(num1,num2)	sum(num1,num2,0)

6.9 Matching a function call to a function declaration

The promotion model described in Section 4.14 is used to promote actual parameters to the type that the called function has been declared with.

The declarations of the two functions:

```
void print_this_as_int( const int );
void print_this_as_double( const double );

void print_this_as_int( const int i)
{
  std::cout << "Is an integer value " << i << "\n";
}

void print_this_as_double( const double i )
{
  std::cout << "Is an double value " << i << "\n";
}
```

if called with the following different types:

```
int main()
{
  print_this_as_int( 1 );
  print_this_as_int( (short) 2 );
  print_this_as_int( (unsigned short) 3 );
  print_this_as_int( 'A' );

  std::cout << "\n";
  print_this_as_double( (short) 1 );
  print_this_as_double( 2 );
  print_this_as_double( (float) 2.2 );
  print_this_as_double( (double) 3.3 );
  return 0;
}
```

would produce these results:

```
Is an integer value 1
Is an integer value 2
Is an integer value 3
Is an integer value 65

Is an double value 1
Is an double value 2
Is an double value 2.2
Is an double value 3.3
```

Note: The character constant `'A'` *is promoted to an int.*

Warning

Unfortunately C++ will also allow:

```
int main()
{
  print_this_as_int( (float) 1.1 );
  print_this_as_int( (double) 2.2 );
  return 0;
}
```

which will compile and give the following results:

```
Is an integer value 1
Is an integer value 2
```

Note: Most compilers will give a warning to indicate the loss of precision in the above cases.

6.9.1   Ambiguity

With overloaded function names there can be an ambiguity which the compiler cannot resolve. Consider the case of the two functions whose prototypes are:

```
void print_this( const int );
void print_this( const double );
```

The compiler will not know which overloaded function to call for the code sequence:

```
print_this( (short) 2 );          //Ambiguity
print_this( (long double) 3.3 );  //Ambiguity
```

The compiler will produce an error message for both statements indicating that it does not know whether to call the function:

```
            print_this( const int )
or          print_this( const double )
```

Member functions

This matching process also takes place for member functions of a class.

6.9.2   Undesirable conversions

As seen in the examples above, the matching of parameters to function declarations may involve a conversion between types. This is not always what is wanted as in the case of a function which is required to return the larger of two numbers. The mechanism described above would convert the values used in the function call, to the type declared in the function specification.

For example, with the following definition of a function `larger`:

```
double larger(const double, const double);

double larger(const double first, const double second)
{
  return first > second ? first : second;
}
```

the following code sequence:

```
larger( 1, 4 )
```

would return 4 as type double. The actual parameters 1 and 4 will be promoted to double literals so that the above function `larger` may be called.

6.10 Function templates

A function template is a specification for a whole family of functions. The function template specification defines a generic function that the compiler will use as a template for generating specific functions depending on the actual parameters used in a call to the function.

Figure 6.5 illustrates the components of a template function for a function `larger`.

```
template <class Type>
```
Specifies that 'Type' is to take the type of the actual parameters used in the function call

```
Type larger( const Type first, const Type second )
{
    return first > second ? first : second;
}
```

Figure 6.5 Components of a template function.

This declaration is similar to a normal function declaration except that: the types of the actual parameters used in the function are given symbolic names that are declared in the template specifier. The specifier **template** **<class** Type> indicates that Type is to take the type of the actual parameter passed to the function.

6.10.1 Example of use

The following example program uses the function template `larger` as follows:

```
int main()
{
    std::cout <<  larger(5, 4)        << "\n";
    std::cout <<  larger(9.99, 4.64 ) << "\n";
    return 0;
}
```

which when compiled with the code for the function template `larger` and run will produce the following output:

```
5
9.99
```

6.10.2   Overloading a function template name

Two function templates to implement the return of the maximum of two and three numbers are shown below:

```
template <class Type>
Type larger(const Type first, const Type second)
{
  return first > second ? first : second;
}

template <class Type>
Type larger(const Type first, const Type second, const Type third)
{
  return larger(larger(first, second), third);
}
```

Note: Parameters to the overloaded template function larger *must be of the same type.*
The operator > must be defined between the two parameters.
A function template does not need a prototype.

Using the above template functions the following code could be written:

```
int main()
{
  std::cout <<  larger(5, 4)              << "\n";
  std::cout <<  larger(10, 30, 20)        << "\n";
  std::cout <<  larger(9.99, 4.64, 3.14) << "\n";
  std::cout <<  larger('M', 'A', 'S')     << "\n";
  return 0;
}
```

which would produce these results:

```
5
30
9.99
S
```

Warning

The code below if compiled:

```
  std::cout <<  larger(4, 5.9)         << "\n";
  std::cout <<  larger('A', 66)        << "\n";
```

would produce two compile time errors, as in both cases the parameters are of a different type.

A possible solution would be to define a new function as follows:

```
template <class Type1, class Type2>
Type1 larger_2g(const Type1 first, const Type2 second)
{
  return first > (Type1) second ? first : (Type1) second;
}
```

When compiled with the following test program:

```
int main()
{
  std::cout <<  larger_2g(4, 5.9)        << "\n";
  std::cout <<  larger_2g('A', 66)       << "\n";
  return 0;
}
```

the output will be:

```
5
B
```

this however, may not always be what is required.

Note: If this templated function is used in conjunction with the previous template function   larger then it must have a different name as the compiler would not be able to resolve which version of the templated function to use.
The result of the function is of the type of the first actual parameter.

6.11   Order of function matching (overloaded functions)

The protocol C++ uses to match a function call with its definition involves three distinct matching strategies:

- If an exact match between the function and its parameters can be found use this definition.

  else

- See if a match can be made between the function and its parameters by using a function template.

  else

- See if a match can be made between the function and its parameters by using overloading resolution.

An ambiguity will occur if more than one match can be made in the stage which first delivers a match.

6.11.1   Overload resolution

Overloading resolution involves the following process:

- For each parameter of the function, find all the overloaded function definitions which can match this parameter.

- There should be only one function definition which has a match for all the parameters. If there is, then this is the function definition to use, otherwise an ambiguity error is deemed to have occurred.

6.12   Self-assessment

- From a programming safety point of view, what are the advantages of passing actual parameters by value?

- Why is call by reference required for actual parameters, when a function can return a value as the result of executing a function?

- What is a function prototype and why is it needed?

- When might overloading of function names be used?

- What are the advantages/disadvantages of overloading names in a program?

- Why does C++ need a scope resolution operator?

- Why can a recursive function not be inline?

- What is the purpose of void in a function declaration?

- Is it meaningful/sensible for a function with prototype `void interesting()` to be used in a program?

- What are the advantages/disadvantages of writing a templated function rather than just a normal function?

- When would you implement a function as a templated function, rather than a normal function?

- What is overload resolution?

6.13 Exercises

Construct the following functions:

- *arithmetic*

  Write a function `arithmetic`, whose specification is:

  ```
  int arithmetic(int operand1, char op, int operand2);
  ```

  Which delivers the result of performing the dyadic operator op between the two formal parameters `operand1` and `operand2`. For example:

  ```
  std::cout<<"the sum     of 1 and 2 is "<< arithmetic(1, '+', 2);
  std::cout<<"the product of 2 and 3 is "<< arithmetic(2, '*', 3);
  ```

- *arithmetic templated*

  Re-write the function `arithmetic` as a templated function.

Construct the following program:

- *Simple desk calculator*

  Write a program to implement a desk calculator that has no operator precedence. For example, if the formula 2+3*4 where input the result would be 20.

- *Desk calculator*

  Write a program to implement a desk calculator. For example, if the formula 2+3*4 where input the result would be 22.

7 Separate compilation

This chapter shows how a C++ program can be split into several units which may be compiled independently. This process greatly enhances the ability to reuse components from existing programs.

7.1 Introduction

To help manage the source code for a large or moderately large program, the sources for the classes used in the program are split into separate files. Naturally for each class there are two distinct files:

- A file containing the class specification.
- A file containing the class implementation.

The specification of the class is included, using the #include directive, in each file which uses the class. The usual convention is to name this file with the class name and an extension of .h. For example, the file which contains the specification of the class Account would be named Account.h and contain:

```
#ifndef CLASS_ACCOUNT_SPEC
#define CLASS_ACCOUNT_SPEC

class Account {
public:
  Account();
  float account_balance() const;      //Return the balance
  float withdraw( const float );      //Withdraw from account
  void deposit( const float );        //Deposit into account
  void set_min_balance( const float ); //Set minimum balance
private:
  float the_balance;                  //The outstanding balance
  float the_min_balance;              //The minimum balance
};

#endif
```

Note: To prevent this specification code being included accidentally twice in a file, the code is surrounded by the following pre-processor directives.

`#ifndef ACCOUNT_SPEC`	*If the pre-processor symbol ACCOUNT_SPEC does not exist then the following text is to be compiled.*
`#define ACCOUNT_SPEC`	*Define the pre-processor symbol ACCOUNT_SPEC.*
`#endif`	*Terminate the conditional inclusion of code.*

These act in a very similar way to a normal if statement. The only difference is that they are executed at compile-time.

The method `account_balance` *is an inspector which is enforced by post fixing the method with the reserved word* `const`.

The use of `const` *to make formal parameters read only.*

Likewise the implementation of the class `Account` is placed in a separate file. By convention this is named with the class name and has an extension `.cpp`. This also may be surrounded by the conditional compilation directives. For example, the file which contains the implementation of the class `Account` would be named `Account.cpp` and contain:

```
#ifndef CLASS_ACCOUNT_IMP
#define CLASS_ACCOUNT_IMP

#include "Account.h"

Account::Account()
{
  the_balance = the_min_balance = 0.00;
}

float Account::account_balance() const
{
  return the_balance;
}

float Account::withdraw( const float money )
{
  if ( the_balance-money >= the_min_balance )
  {
    the_balance = the_balance - money;
    return money;
  } else {
    return 0.00;
  }
}

void Account::deposit( const float money )
{
  the_balance = the_balance + money;
}
```

```
void Account::set_min_balance( const float money )
{
    the_min_balance = money;
}

#endif
```

Note: *The inclusion of the specification of the class* Account *using the pre-processor*
directive #include "Account.h"

A program to test the class Account is shown below:

```
#include <iostream>
#include <iomanip>

#include "Account.h"

int main()
{
    std::cout << std::setiosflags( std::ios::fixed );     //Format x.y
    std::cout << std::setiosflags( std::ios::showpoint ); //0.10
    std::cout << std::setprecision(2);                    //2 dec places

    Account mike;
    float obtained;

    std::cout << "Account balance = " << mike.account_balance() << "\n";

    mike.set_min_balance( -100.00 );
    std::cout << "Overdraft       = " << 100.00 << "\n";
    obtained = mike.withdraw(20.00);
    std::cout << "Money withdrawn = " << obtained << "\n";
    std::cout << "Account balance = " << mike.account_balance() << "\n";

    mike.deposit(100.00);
    std::cout << "Money deposited = " << 100.00 << "\n";
    std::cout << "Account balance = " << mike.account_balance() << "\n";

    obtained = mike.withdraw(20.00);
    std::cout << "Money withdrawn = " << obtained << "\n";
    std::cout << "Account balance = " << mike.account_balance() << "\n";
    return 0;
}
```

Note: *The inclusion of the specification of the class* Account *using the pre-processor*
directive #include "Account.h". *However, the implementation code will*
not be included as this is compiled separately.

7.2 Actual compilation

The exact details of the compilation process, will differ between machines, however using g++ (The Free Software Foundations C++ compiler) it would be:

Command	Commentary
g++ -c Account.cpp	Compile the implementation code into the object code file Account.o.
g++ -c test.cpp	Compile the test program into the object code file test.o.
g++ test.o Account.o	Link together the object code for the test program and the implementation code for the class Account into an executable image.

Integrated project development systems allow the user to tell the system all the C++ source program files that make up a project and then let the system re-build the project using minimum recompilation.

7.3 Separate compilation and the `inline` directive

If separate compilation is used and inline functions are required then these functions must be included in the specification part of the class. This is so that the compiler knows which code to inline.

If the inlined functions where defined in a separately compiled implementation part, the overall compilation would fail at link time. The reason is that as the functions are specified as `inline` in the separately compiled implementation, no code would be generated for these functions. The compiler when compiling the main program which uses these member functions, simply puts in a reference to the member function which will be resolved at link time. As there is no such body to the member function the overall compilation process will fail at link time.

The solution is to place the `inline` implementation of the function in the specification part of the class. For example, if the member function `account_balance` and the constructor of the class are to be inlined then the new specification for the class will be:

```
#ifndef CLASS_ACCOUNT_SPEC
#define CLASS_ACCOUNT_SPEC

class Account {
public:
  Account();
  float account_balance() const;        //Return the balance
  float withdraw( const float );        //Withdraw from account
  void deposit( const float );          //Deposit into account
  void set_min_balance( const float );  //Set minimum balance
private:
  float the_balance;                    //The outstanding balance
  float the_min_balance;                //The minimum balance
};
```

```
//Inline components
//These have to be here

inline Account::Account()
{
  the_balance = 0.00;
}

inline float Account::account_balance() const
{
  return the_balance;
}

#endif
```

The implementation of the class would be the same except of course for the omission of the code for the constructor and the member function `account_balance`.

7.4 A personal account manager revisited

The personal account manager implemented in Section 5.6 performed all input and output as part of the main program. By creating a class `TUI` to perform the input and output this allows the separation of the I/O process from the main logic of the program. This will allow a greater flexibility

The responsibilities of the class `TUI` are:

Method	Responsibility
menu	Set up the menu that will be displayed to the user. Each menu item is described by a string.
event	Return the menu item selected by a user of the TUI.
message	Display a message to the user.
dialog	Solicit a response from the user.

The C++ specification is:

```
#ifndef CLASS_TUI_SPEC
#define CLASS_TUI_SPEC
#include <string>

class TUI
{
public:
  enum Menu_item { M_NONE, M_1, M_2, M_3, M_4, M_5, M_6 };
  TUI();
  void menu(std::string="", std::string="", std::string="",
            std::string="", std::string="", std::string="");
  Menu_item event();
  void message( std::string );
  void dialogue( std::string, float& );
  void dialogue( std::string, int& );
```

```
protected:
  void display_menu_item( std::string, std::string );
private:
  std::string the_men_1, the_men_2, the_men_3;
  std::string the_men_4, the_men_5, the_men_6;
};

#endif
```

Note: The access protected *is discussed fully in Section 11.5 The protected areas in
the specification of a class contains methods that are used by other methods in
the class, but are not required to be visible outside of the class.*

The use of std::string *to describe an instance of the class* string, *this
standard class provides sophisticated string handling capabilities, in particular
string comparison and assignment. Appendix D lists the members of this class.*

For example, if an instance of the TUI had been declared with:

```
TUI screen;
```

then, to set-up the menu system:

```
[a]   Print
[b]   Calculate

Input selection:
```

the following code sequence would be used:

```
screen.menu( "Print", "Calculate" );
```

The user's response to this menu is elicited with the function event. The function
event returns an enumeration representing the menu item selected. For example, if the
user selected option [b] then the code:

```
    switch ( screen.event() )
    {
      case TUI::M_1 :              // Print

      case TUI::M_2 :              // Calculate
    }
```

associated with label M_2 would be obeyed.

*Note: The selected menu item is indicated by an enumeration M_1 for menu item 1,
M_2 for menu item 2, etc.*

The scope resolution operator :: *is used to indicate that M_1 and M_2 are
members of the class TUI.*

7.4.1 A string stream

The C++ I/O classes allow data to be written into memory as well as written to an output device. An instance of the class `ostrstream` is an object which is used in the same way as the object `cout` For example, the following code writes the earth's diameter to the object `memory`:

```
std::ostrstream memory;              //string stream
long earth_diameter = 12756;         //In Kilometres

memory << earth_diameter << '\0';    //Write into memory
```

The character `'\0'` is sent to the object `memory` to signify the end of the characters stored in memory. The method `str()` delivers a C++ string representing the data written into memory. For example, to convert the long number in the object `earth_diameter` into the string `number`, the following code is used:

```
#include <iostream>     // Basic IO stream
#include <strstream>    // string stream class

int main()
{
  std::ostrstream memory;              //String stream
  long earth_diameter = 12756;         //In Kilometres

  memory << earth_diameter << '\0';    //Write into memory

  std::string number = memory.str();   //Assign to a string

  std::cout << "Earth's diameter is " <<
               number << " kilometres" << "\n";
  return 0;
}
```

Which when compiled and run will produce the following output:

```
Earth's diameter is 12756 kilometres
```

Warning

Memory used to store the C++ string delivered by the method `str` is not returned to the system. The consequence of this is that the code will leak memory every time it is executed.

7.4.2 Putting it all together

A programmer can display a message using the method `message` which has as its parameter the text to be output. Likewise, a programmer can initiate a dialogue with the user by using the overloaded version of the method `dialog` that returns a floating point number. The `TUI` currently only supports dialogues that solicit a floating point number or integer number.

The program below uses the class `TUI` to manage the input and output in a program that converts miles to kilometres.

```cpp
#include <iostream>     // Basic IO stream
#include <iomanip>      // IO manipulators
#include <strstream>    // string stream class
#include "TUI.h"

int main()
{
  TUI    screen;                                 //Interaction screen
  float miles;                                   //Miles input
  const double M_TO_K = 1.609344;                //Conversion

  screen.dialogue("Miles   ", miles);            //Dialogue

  std::ostrstream text;                          //String stream
  text << std::setiosflags( std::ios::fixed );   //Float style
  text << std::setiosflags( std::ios::showpoint );
  text << std::setprecision(2);
  text << "Equals   : " << miles * M_TO_K
       << " kilometres" << '\0';
  screen.message( text.str() );                  //Result
  return 0;
}
```

Note: The use of the string stream to facilitate the conversion of the number of kilometres into a string.

Which when compiled with the class `TUI` would result in the following interaction:

```
Miles    : 50.0
Equals   : 80.47 kilometres
```

7.4.3 Implementing the personal account manager

An example interaction with the personnel account manager is as follows:

```
[a]   Deposit

[b]   Withdraw

[c]   Balance

[d]   Quit

Input selection: c
Balance = 4.55
```

Note: The Quit option allows an orderly exit from the program.

A program to implement a personnel account manager using the classes `Account` and `TUI` is as follows:

```
#include <iostream>        // Basic IO stream
#include <iomanip>         // IO manipulators
#include <strstream>       // string stream class
#include "Account.h"       // Account class specification
#include "TUI.h"           // TUI class specification

int main()
{
  Account mine;            //My Account
  TUI screen;             //Interaction screen
  float amount;           //money

  screen.menu("Deposit", "Withdraw", "Balance", "Quit" );
```

The individual requests are processed using a switch statement.

```
while ( true )
{
  switch ( screen.event() )
  {
```

When the deposit menu option is selected the following code processes the request.

```
    case TUI::M_1 :
      screen.dialogue("Amount to deposit", amount);
      if ( amount >= 0.0 )
      {
        mine.deposit( amount );
      } else {
        screen.message("Amount must be positive");
      }
      break;
```

The code to process a withdrawal is as follows:

```
case TUI::M_2 :
  screen.dialogue("Amount to withdraw", amount);
  if ( amount >= 0.0 )
  {
    float get = mine.withdraw( amount );
    if ( get <= 0.0 )
      screen.message("Sorry not enough funds");
  } else {
    screen.message("Amount must be positive");
  }
  break;
```

The code to process a balance enquiry uses a string stream to capture the text to be displayed.

```
case TUI::M_3 :
  {
    std::ostrstream text;                       //Str stream
    text << std::setiosflags( std::ios::fixed );    //Float style
    text << std::setiosflags( std::ios::showpoint );
    text << std::setprecision(2);
    text << "Balance = " << mine.account_balance()
         << '\0';
    screen.message( text.str() );               //"Bal ... "
  }
  break;
```

```
    case TUI::M_4 :
      return 0;
    }
  }
  return 0;
}
```

7.4.4   Implementation of the class TUI

In the implementation of the class TUI the constructor sets the menu items to be the empty string. This is performed so that if a user programmer forgets to call the method menu the code will still function consistently.

```
#ifndef CLASS_TUI_IMP
#define CLASS_TUI_IMP

#include "TUI.h"

TUI::TUI()
{
  the_men_1 = the_men_2 = the_men_3 =
  the_men_4 = the_men_5 = the_men_6 = "";
}
```

The method `menu` records the menu items for later display.

```cpp
void TUI::menu( std::string m1, std::string m2, std::string m3,
                std::string m4, std::string m5, std::string m6 )
{
  the_men_1 = m1; the_men_2 = m2; the_men_3 = m3;
  the_men_4 = m4; the_men_5 = m5; the_men_6 = m6;     //Store names
}
```

The member function `event` after displaying the menu items solicits from the user a selection of one of the menu items. The code prevents a user from selecting a non existent (Empty string) menu item.

```cpp
TUI::Menu_item TUI::event()
{
  Menu_item choice = M_NONE;
  while ( choice == M_NONE )
  {
    display_menu_item( "[a]  ", the_men_1 );  //First menu item
    display_menu_item( "[b]  ", the_men_2 );  //Second ..
    display_menu_item( "[c]  ", the_men_3 );
    display_menu_item( "[d]  ", the_men_4 );
    display_menu_item( "[e]  ", the_men_5 );
    display_menu_item( "[f]  ", the_men_6 );
    char  selection;
    cout << "Input selection: "; std::cin >> selection;
    switch ( selection )
    {
      case 'a' : case 'A' :
        if ( the_men_1 != "" ) choice = M_1;
        break;
      case 'b' : case 'B' :
        if ( the_men_2 != "" ) choice = M_2;
        break;
      case 'c' : case 'C' :
        if ( the_men_3 != "" ) choice = M_3;
        break;
      case 'd' : case 'D' :
        if ( the_men_4 != "" ) choice = M_4;
        break;
      case 'e' : case 'E' :
        if ( the_men_5 != "" ) choice = M_5;
        break;
      case 'f' : case 'F' :
        if ( the_men_6 != "" ) choice = M_6;
        break;
      default  :
        break;
    }
    if ( choice == M_NONE )
      message( "Invalid response" );
  }
  return choice;                          //User selection
}
```

The protected member function `display_menu` will only displays none null menu items. Remember, a programmer using this class may only require a few menu items to be displayed.

```
void TUI::display_menu_item( std::string prompt, std::string name )
{
  if ( name != "" )                          //Not null std::string
  {
    std::cout << prompt << name << "\n" << "\n";
  }
}
```

The member function `message` displays a text message onto the output device.

```
void TUI::message( std::string mes )
{
  std::cout << mes << "\n" << "\n";   //Message to user
}
```

The member function `dialogue` has two implementations to allow a response of either a floating point number or an integer number.

```
void TUI::dialogue( std::string mes, float& answer )
{
  std::cout << mes << " : ";        //User prompt
  std::cin >> answer;               //Read user response
  std::cout << "\n";
}
void TUI::dialogue( std::string mes, int& answer )
{
  std::cout << mes << " : ";        //User prompt
  std::cin >> answer;               //Read user response
  std::cout << "\n";
}
#endif
```

7.4.5　Putting it all together

Using the (command line compiler g++ the above program could be compiled using the following invocations:

Command	Commentary
g++ -c Account.cpp	Compile the implementation code into the object code file `Account.o`.
g++ -c TUI.cpp	Compile the implementation code into the object code file `TUI.o`.
g++ -c main.cpp	Compile the main program.
g++ main.o Account.o TUI.o	Link the main program with the implementation code for the classes `Account` and `TUI` to form an executable image.

The following is an example of the interactions that may be made when the two classes Account and TUI are compiled with the main program and run.

```
[a]  Deposit

[b]  Withdraw

[c]  Balance

[d]  Quit

Input selection: a
Amount to deposit : 10.00

[a]  Deposit

[b]  Withdraw

[c]  Balance

[d]  Quit

Input selection: b
Amount to withdraw : 5.45

[a]  Deposit

[b]  Withdraw

[c]  Balance

[d]  Quit

Input selection: c
Balance = 4.55
```

7.5 Self-assessment

- When working as a member of a team what are the advantages of separately compiling the class implementation and only allowing other members of the team read access to the specification?

- How does splitting a large program into individual files that are separately compiled help a team of programmers develop a program?

- When working as a member of a team it is important to control who has access to individual files. Why is this?

- Why must a programmer deal with inline functions specially when separately compiling a class?

7.6 Exercises

- Using the personal account manager program as an example, split an existing program of yours into separate specification and implementation components. Compile this program using separate compilation.

8 Arrays

This chapter describes the array construct which implements a low level collection for like objects. Unfortunately the use of C++ arrays can lead an unwary programmer into many pitfalls. Higher level constructs are however available in the Standard Template Library, which remove many of these deficiencies.

8.1 Arrays

Like most languages C++ allows a programmer to hold and manipulate many instances of a like item using arrays. However, arrays are not all they seem to be at first sight, and for the unwary programmer this can lead to disastrous situations.

The declaration for an array of 5 integer objects is as follows:

```
const int NUMBER = 5;
int room[NUMBER];
```

Arrays always start at element 0, so a 5 element array room has elements 0 to 4. Individual elements are accessed by using a subscript to select the n'th element of the array. For example, to set element 2 of the array room to the value 15 the following assignment statement is used:

```
room[2] = 15;
```

The following statements store values representing the size of rooms in square metres into individual elements of the array room.

```
room[0]=20; room[1]=30; room[2]=15; room[3]=40; room[4]=10;
```

After the above statements have been executed, the contents of the array room will be as follows:

Contents of the array room	Subscripts of individual elements of room				
	0	1	2	3	4
20 30 15 40 10	20	30	15	40	10

When an array is declared several elements may be initialized to a specific value. For example, to set the array elements in room to have initial values of 20, 30, 15, 40 and 10 the following declaration is used:

```
int room[NUMBER] = { 20, 30, 15, 40, 10 };
```

This sets element 0 to 20, element 1 to 30, element 2 to 15 etc.

Note: *It is an error to have too many initializers.*
If there are too few initializers, the remaining elements are set to int () who's value is zero.

8.2 Using arrays

The following example program calculates the total size in square meters of 5 rooms. The size in square meters of the individual rooms is held in the array room.

```cpp
#include <iostream>

int main()
{
  const int NUMBER = 5;
  int room[NUMBER] = { 20, 30, 15, 40, 10 };

  std::cout << "Total area of all " << NUMBER << " rooms = ";

  int total = 0;
  for ( int i=0; i<NUMBER; i++ )
  {
    total = total + room[i];
  }

  std::cout << total << " Square metres" << "\n";
  return 0;
}
```

When the above program is compiled and then run the output produced is:

```
Total area of all 5 rooms = 115 Square metres
```

8.3 No subscript checking with C++ arrays

Many programming languages check the validity of an array subscript to make sure that it is valid. If the subscript is outside the valid index values for the array, then a run-time error message is usually generated and the program terminated. In C++ there is no run-time check to make sure that the array bound used to access an element of an array is valid. This stems from the original requirement to make the compiled code of a C program fast and lean. If the previous program had been incorrectly written as:

```
int main()
{
  const int NUMBER = 5;
  int room[NUMBER] = { 20, 30, 15, 40, 10 };

  std::cout << "Total area of all " << NUMBER << " rooms = ";

  int total = 0;
  for ( int i=0; i<=NUMBER; i++ )        // <-- WRONG --- i can be 5
  {
    total = total + room[i];
  }

  std::cout << total << " Square metres" << "\n";
  return 0;
}
```

then an access to element `room[5]` is attempted, the result of which is undefined. The probable result will be that the contents of the memory location after the end of the array `room` are added to `total`.

Note: The mistake is that the for loop index goes from 0 to 5 instead of from 0 to 4.

This type of error usually leads to errors in a program that are very difficult to detect. The moral of this section is to be very careful when constructing code that accesses an array in C++. Fortunately, there is a solution to this problem. Sections 20.2 and 25.4 describe solutions to this problem.

In making accesses to an array fast and lean, C /C++ arrays are not self-describing, and hence an array holds no information about the number of elements contained within it.

8.4 Multidimensional arrays

The following table illustrates a declaration, and how individual members of a multidimensional array are accessed.

Declaration	Conceptual	Access to shaded element	Physical representation in memory
int vector[4];		vector[2]	
int table[3][4];		table[1][2]	

Declaration	Conceptual	Access to shaded element	Physical representation in memory
int cube[2][3][4];		cube[0][1][2]	

Note: In accessing consecutive elements in memory the rightmost subscript will change the most rapidly.
To make efficient access to a large array on a paged machine, the innermost loop should change the rightmost subscript. Otherwise, the inner loop will access elements scattered widely throughout the array.

8.5   A single dimension array as a parameter to a function

Actual parameters when arrays are always passed to the called function by reference; the implication of this is that rather than passing the whole array, a reference to the array is passed. This mechanism saves time as well as space as only a reference to the array (a single machine word) is passed rather than having to copy the whole array. However, it also means that writing to the arrays formal parameter (if not declared const) will change the array that has been passed as an actual parameter.

The following function sum returns the sum of the elements in an integer array. As arrays in C++ are not self describing, the size of the array must be passed to the function to convey the number of elements in the array to the function sum. The implementation of the function sum is:

```
int sum( int vec[], int size )
{
  int total = 0;
  for ( int i=0; i<size; i++ )
  {
    total = total + vec[i];
  }
  return total;
}
```

Note: In the declaration of the formal parameter vec, no size is specified. This is a consequence of C++ arrays not being self describing. An array declared in this fashion is termed an open array.

The function sum developed above is used in the following program which calculates the number of people occupying several rooms in a building:

```
int main()
{
  const int ROOMS = 4;
  int people[ROOMS] = { 2, 3, 1, 3 };

  std::cout << "Total number of people in the rooms is "
            << sum( people, ROOMS ) << "\n";
  return 0;
}
```

When compiled and run this will produce the following output:

```
Total number of people in the rooms is 9
```

8.6 Multidimensional arrays as parameters to a function

As arrays in C++ are not self-describing, when an array of n dimensions is passed as an actual parameter to a function, only its last n-1 bounds are specified. This size information is used by the compiler to calculate how to access individual elements of the array in the body of the function. As the description of the bounds must be a compile-time constant, this limits the generality of the function.

For example, it would prove difficult, to write a general function that could operate on an arbitrarily sized matrix (two-dimensional array). One way round this problem is to use the low level primitive pointer. (Pointers are fully explained in Chapter 17.)

As the bounds of an array are not checked at run-time, the bound of the first subscript is omitted. The compiler is able to work out the position of the elements of the array from the bounds of the other subscripts.

For example, a program which prints the contents of a 2D array and flips the elements left to right first defines the size of the array using a const declaration:

```
#include <iostream>

const int ROW    = 3;
const int COLUMN = 4;
```

Then the prototypes for the two functions that print and flip the array elements from left to right are defined. In C++ the size of the first dimension is not defined as there is no array bound checking. However, the sizes for subsequent dimensions need to be defined so that the compiler can work out the position of the selected element of the array.

```
void print( const int table [][COLUMN] );
void flip_left_right( int table [][COLUMN] );
```

The program first populates the array and then prints the 2D array twice, the second time after the array elements are flipped from left to right.

```cpp
int main()
{
  int numbers[ROW][COLUMN];

  for( int i=0; i<ROW; i++ )              //Populate elements
    for( int j=0; j<COLUMN; j++ )
      numbers[i][j] = i*10+j;             // with ROW,COLUMN co-ordinates

  std::cout << "Original array" << "\n";
  print( numbers );                       //Print 2D array numbers
  flip_left_right( numbers );             //Flip left right
  std::cout << "Flipped  array" << "\n";
  print( numbers );                       //Print 2D array numbers
  return 0;
}
```

The print functions implementation is shown below:

```cpp
void print( const int table[][COLUMN] )
{
  for( int i=0; i<ROW; i++ )              //For each row
  {
    for( int j=0; j<COLUMN; j++ )         // For each column in row
    {
      std::cout << table[i][j] << "\t";   //  Print element
    }                                     // End for
    cout << "\n";                         // new line
  }                                       //End for
}
```

and the function `flip_left_right` implementation is:

```cpp
void flip_left_right( int table[][COLUMN] )
{
  for( int i=0; i<ROW; i++ )              //For each Row
  {
    for( int j=0; j<COLUMN/2; j++ )       // For each element
    {                                     //   in column
      int temp = table[i][j];             //
      table[i][j] = table[i][COLUMN-j-1]; //   mirror
      table[i][COLUMN-j-1] = temp;
    }                                     // End for
  }                                       //End for
}
```

Note: *The first dimension of the 2D array is not required; it is left as an open subscript. When an array is passed as a parameter, it is passed by reference. By specifying that the formal array parameter is* const, *writes to the formal array from the body of the function are prevented .*

When run, the lines of code above will produce the following output:

```
Original array
0          1          2          3
10         11         12         13
20         21         22         23
Flipped    array
3          2          1          0
13         12         11         10
23         22         21         20
```

Note: It is very easy to make mistakes in C++ by exceeding the bounds of an individual dimension or the bounds of the total array.
Mechanisms are available in C++ to prevent this from happening. Solution are described in Sections 20.2 and 25.4.

8.6.1 Initializing of arrays

Arrays may be initialized at the time of declaration as follows:

```
int vec[10]        = { 0,1,2,3,4,5,6,7,8,9 };
```

Note: If all values are not supplied, then the remaining elements are initialized to Type() where type *is the type of the array. For the inbuilt types this will deliver 0.*

The subscript may be omitted in which case the size of the array will be large enough to contain all the elements.

A shorthand for initializing an array of characters is allowed; instead of providing the values as individual character constants a C++ string may be used:

```
char name[] = "Brighton";
```

However, the end string terminator is also stored so the above shorthand declaration is equivalent to:

```
char name[] = { 'B', 'r', 'i', 'g', 't', 'o', 'n', '\0' };
```

Note: Trying to initialize an array with too many values will generate an error.

Initializing arrays of higher dimensions

This is done in a similar way, except that {}s can be used to group the items for each dimension as in:

```
int table[2][3]    = { {1,2,3}, {4,5,6} };
int cube[2][3][4] = { { {1,2,3,4}, {5,6,7,8}, {9,10,11,12} },
                      { {1,2,3,4}, {5,6,7,8}, {9,10,11,12} } };
```

Note: It is allowable to omit the inner {}s.

8.7 Initializing arrays of objects

Where the object has a constructor it may be initialized in a similar way to an array of a fundamental type such as int. See Section 8.6 and Section 15.9.

8.8 Case study: the game of noughts and crosses

The children's game of noughts and crosses is played on a three-by-three grid of squares. Players either play X or O. Each player takes it in turn to add their mark to an unoccupied square. The game is won when a player has three of their marks in a row either diagonally, horizontally or vertically. If no unoccupied square remains, the game is a draw (Figure 8.1).

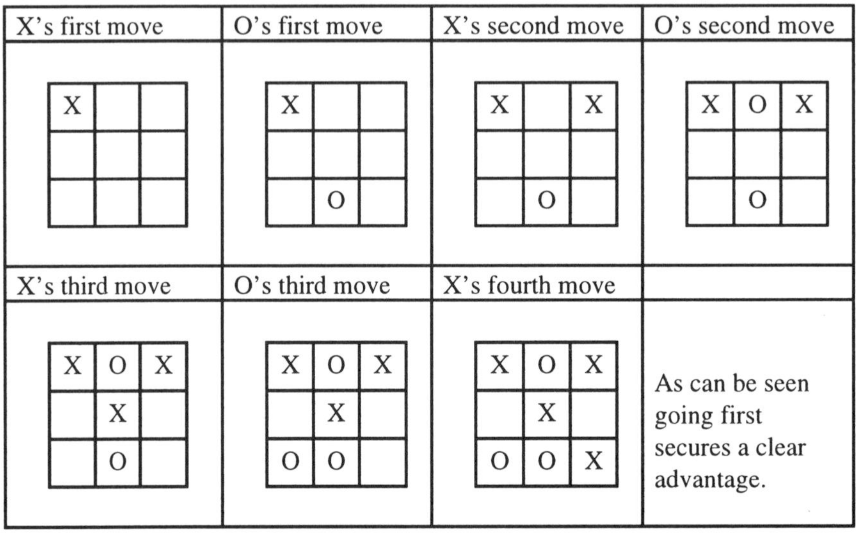

Figure 8.1 A game of noughts and crosses

The game consists of the board and the two players who take it in turns to place an X or O on the board. This conceptual model of the game is shown in Figure 8.2.

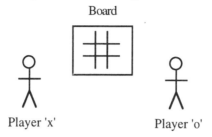

Figure 8.2 Conceptual model of the game of noughts and crosses.

A program to display the current state of a game of noughts and crosses between two human contestants is developed with the aid of a class `Board`. The responsibilities of the class `Board` are as follows:

Method	Responsibility
add	Add the player's mark to the board. The player's move is specified by a number in the range 1 to 9 and their mark by a character.
valid	Return true if the presented move is valid. The method checks that the move is in the range 1 to 9 and that the specified cell is not occupied.
view	Return a string representing the pieces on the board. For example, the final state of the board seen earlier in the example game is represented by the string `"XOX X OOX"`
situation	Return the current state of the noughts and crosses board.

The C++ specification for the class is:

```
#ifndef CLASS_BOARD_SPEC
#define CLASS_BOARD_SPEC
#include <string>

class Board
{
public:
  enum Game_result { WON, DRAWN, PLAYABLE };
  Board();
  bool valid( const int pos ) const;           //Move valid ?
  void add( const int pos, const char piece );  //Add to Board
  std::string view() const;                      //Return view
  Game_result situation() const;                 //State of game
private:
  static const int SIZE_TTT=9;                   //Must be 9
  char the_sqrs[SIZE_TTT];                        //Playing grid
  int  the_moves;                                 //Moves made
};

#endif
```

8.8.1   Using subscripts with a string

A string may be subscripted to allow access to individual characters. The string in effect may be treated as an array with bounds from 0 to `length()-1`. For example a function to convert a string to lower case is implemented as:

```
void to_lower_case( std::string& str )
{
  for ( int i=0; i<str.length(); i++ )
  {
    str[i] = tolower( str[i] );
  }
}
```

Note: This code uses the library function `tolower` *the prototype of which is defined in the header file* `<ctype>`*. Appendix C details the components in the header file* `<ctype>`*.*

8.8.2   An instance of a string stream with no memory leaks

Previously when using a string stream it was noted that memory is claimed but not released. By allocating the memory for the instance of the string stream, this memory leak is avoided. For example, to create an instance of a string stream `text` that can hold a maximum of 100 characters the following declarations are used:

```
const int MAX_BUF = 100;            //Max size of text area
char buf[MAX_BUF];                  //Holds written text
ostrstream text(buf, MAX_BUF);      //text is a string stream
```

Information is written into memory using the normal I/O extraction operator as follows:

```
long earth_diameter = 12756;        //In kilometres

text << "Earth's diameter is " <<
        earth_diameter << " kilometres" << '\0';

std::string message = text.str();
std::cout << message << "\n";
```

Note: The character `'\0'` *must be added to the end of the characters in memory. The method* `str()` *delivers a C++ string that is used to initialize* `message`*.*

When compiled with suitable declarations it would produce:

```
Earth's diameter is 12756 kilometres
```

8.8.3   Driver program for noughts and crosses game

The main program code is responsible for eliciting the moves from the two human players of the game. The game continues until either a player has won or no more moves can be made on the board. The interaction is performed using an instance of the class TUI to isolate I/O from the driver program. Using the class Board shown above and the class TUI, the C++ code for the driver program is:

```cpp
#include <iostream>
#include <string>

//The class Board and class TUI

std::string as_text_pic( std::string );            // Text pic of board

int main()
{
  char player;                                     //Either 'X' or 'O'
  Board oxo;                                        //Instance of Board
  Board::Game_result game_is = Board::PLAYABLE;     //State of Board
  TUI screen;

  player = 'X';                                    //First player
  while ( game_is == Board::PLAYABLE )              //While playable
  {
    int move;
    std::string who=std::string("Player ")+player; //Player X/O
    screen.dialogue(who + " enter move", move);    //Request move
    if ( oxo.valid( move ) )                        // Valid
    {
      oxo.add( move, player );                      //Add to board
      screen.message( as_text_pic(oxo.view()) );    //Display board
      game_is = oxo.situation();                    //Game is
      switch ( game_is )
      {
        case Board::WON  :                          // Won
          screen.message( who + " wins" );
          break;
        case Board::DRAWN :                         // Drawn
          screen.message( "It's a draw" );
          break;
        case Board::PLAYABLE :
          switch ( player )                         // Playable
          {
            case 'X' : player='O'; break;           //   'X' -> 'O'
            case 'O' : player='X'; break;           //   'O' -> 'X'
          }
          break;
      }
    } else {
      screen.message( "Move invalid" );             //Invalid move
    }
  }
  screen.message( "" ); screen.message( "" );
  return 0;
}
```

Note: The use of the scope resolution operator : : to access the named constants of the enumeration Board_state *defined in the class* Board.
A string may also be subscripted to allow access to individual characters of the string.

The function as_text_pic returns a string representing the board that is suitable for display on a text based output device. The input to the function is the string returned from the method view that gives the contents of each square on the noughts and crosses board. A new string is created that contains each character on the board followed by appropriate characters to form a character representation of the board.

Image of the board showing the position of each character contained in the string returned from view.	Positions (in the string returned from the method view).	Text to be appended to form a pictorial representation of the board.
1 | 2 | 3 --------- 4 | 5 | 6 --------- 7 | 8 | 9	1,2,4,5, 7 and 8 3 and 6 9	`"	";`  `"\n---------\n";`  `"\n";`

This results in the creation of a string which represents a two-dimensional character view of the noughts and crosses board. The function as_text_pic is defined as follows:

```
std::string as_text_pic( std::string rep )
{
  std::string res = "";
  for( size_t i=1; i<=rep.length(); i++ )
  {
    res += rep[i-1];                    //Add counter;
    switch ( i )                        // after adding counter
    {
      case 3 :
      case 6 :                          // Add row separator
        res += "\n---------\n";
        break;
      case 9 :                          // Add new line
        res += "\n";
        break;
      case 1 : case 2 : case 4 :
      case 5 : case 7 : case 8 :        // Add Col separator
        res += " | ";
        break;
    }
  }
  return res;                           //Textual picture of board
}
```

Note: size_t *is defined in the header file* <stddef.h>

The output from a typical interaction between two human players is shown below:

X's first move	O's first move	X's second move	O's second move

`X | |`
`---------`
`| | |`
`---------`
`| | |`
	`X | |`
	`---------`
	`| | |`
	`---------`
	`| O |`
		`X | | X`
		`---------`
		`| | |`
		`---------`
		`| O |`
			`X | O | X`
			`---------`
			`| | |`
			`---------`
			`| O |`

X's third move	O's third move	X's forth move	

`X | O | X`
`---------`
`| X |`
`---------`
`| O |`
	`X | O | X`
	`---------`
	`| X |`
	`---------`
	`O | O |`
		`X | O | X`
		`---------`
		`| X |`
		`---------`
		`O | O | X`
			As can be seen going first secures a clear advantage.

8.8.4   Board implementation

In the implementation of the class `Board` the constructor sets the board to a defined state of all spaces.

```cpp
#ifndef CLASS_BOARD_IMP
#define CLASS_BOARD_IMP
#include "Board.h"

Board::Board()
{
  for ( int i=0; i<SIZE_TTT; i++ )
  {
    the_sqrs[i] = ' ';
  }
  the_moves = 0;
}
```

The functions `valid` returns `true` if the square selected is not occupied by a previously played counter.

```cpp
bool Board::valid( const int pos ) const
{
  return (pos >= 1 && pos <= SIZE_TTT) && the_sqrs[pos-1] == ' ';
}
```

Note: *As C++ uses lazy evaluation the RHS of the && operator will only be evaluated if the LHS is true.*
If, however, the & operator had been used, then both sides would have been evaluated.

The functions `add` adds a player's mark to the board. A pre-condition of using this method is that the move must have been validated by the method `valid`.

```
void Board::add( const int pos, const char piece )
{
  the_sqrs[ pos-1 ] = piece;
  the_moves++;
}
```

The method `view` returns a view of the current state of the board.

```
std::string Board::view() const
{
  std::string res = "";
  for( int i=1; i<=SIZE_TTT; i++ )
  {
      res += the_sqrs[i-1];
  }
  return res;
}
```

To determine the current situation each possible win line is checked. This is achieved by storing in the two-dimensional array `win_lines` all the possible co-ordinates for each win line. In the two-dimensional array, the first index selects the win line whilst the second index selects the three co-ordinates for the win line.

A check is made for each win line to see if all the marks are either `'X'` or `'O'`. If no win line is discovered then a check for a draw is made.

```
Board::Game_result Board::situation() const
{
  const int WL = 8;                    //Number of win lines
  const int LL = 3;                    //Length of a line
  int win_lines[WL][LL] = { {0,1,2}, {3,4,5}, {6,7,8},
                            {0,3,6}, {1,4,7}, {2,5,8},
                            {0,4,8}, {2,4,6} };
  for ( int i=0; i<WL; i++ )                            //For each
  {                                                     // win line
    char first_cell = the_sqrs[ win_lines[i][0] ];
    if ( first_cell != ' ' &&                          //Not space
         first_cell == the_sqrs[ win_lines[i][1] ] &&
         first_cell == the_sqrs[ win_lines[i][2] ] )
      return WON;                                       //3 in line
  }
  if ( the_moves >= SIZE_TTT ) return DRAWN;            //

  return PLAYABLE;                                      //Still playable
}

#endif
```

8.9 A stack built using an array

A stack is a structure used to store and retrieve data items. Data items are pushed onto the structure and retrieved in the reverse order in which they were added. This is commonly referred to as 'first in last out'. This process is illustrated in Figure 8.3.

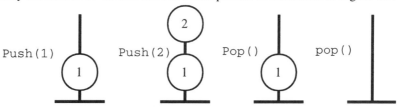

Figure 8.3 Example of operations on a stack.

Note: Every time a C++ function is called, its return address is pushed onto a stack. Then, when an exit is made from the function, the return address is retrieved from the stack. This is how nested calls to functions are made.

Every time a function is called the address of the instruction following the function call is pushed onto a stack. When an exit is made from the function this address is removed from the stack and control transferred to it.

The responsibilities for a stack object are:

Method	Responsibility
empty	Return true if the stack is empty.
pop	Remove the top item on the stack, no result is returned.
push	Push a new item onto the stack.
size	Return the number of elements in the stack.
top	Return the top item on the stack, the stack is unchanged.

The definition of a class to represent a stack is as follows:

```
#ifndef CLASS_STACK_SPEC
#define CLASS_STACK_SPEC

#include <ctype.h>

class Stack {
public:
  Stack();
  bool empty() const;                //Stack empty
  size_t size() const;               //Size of collection
  int top() const;                   //Return top item
  void push( const int );            //Push item onto stack
  void pop();                        //Pop top item from stack
private:
  static const int MAX_ELEMENTS=5;
  int   the_elements[MAX_ELEMENTS];  //Items in Stack
  int   the_tos;                     //Top of Stack pointer
};

#endif
```

Note: The type `size_t` is defined in the header file `<ctype.h>`, and is used to define the size of the collection contained in the stack.

The stack is implemented as an array of integers with `tos` holding the index of the last item added.

The constructor for the class sets the stack to a defined state with `the_tos` representing the index of the top item; -1 is used to signify an empty stack.

```
#ifndef CLASS_STACK_IMP
#define CLASS_STACK_IMP
#include <stdexcep>

Stack::Stack()
{
   the_tos = -1;                         //Empty
}
```

The member functions `empty` and `size` are used to interrogate the state of the stack. The function `empty` is used to determine if the stack is empty.

```
bool Stack::empty() const
{
   return the_tos < 0;                   //Is empty
}
```

The member function `size` returns the number of elements in the stack.

```
size_t Stack::size() const
{
   return the_tos+1;                     //Elements in stack
}
```

The member function `top` returns the top item on the stack. The stack is not changed. It is a requirement in implementing this function that there is at least one element in the stack. If there are no elements in the stack, an exception is raised. Chapter 14 describes in more detail the exception mechanism that devolves the responsibility for handling failure to the user of the class.

Exceptions are a clean way of handling failure, however, they should only be used in exceptional circumstances. When an exception is raised, control is transferred to a handler for the exception. This is usually provided by the programmer who sends the messages to an instance of the stack. If no such provision is made, then the program is aborted with a fatal error. The exception classes are defined in the header file `<stdexcep>`.

```
int Stack::top() const
{
  if ( the_tos < 0 ) {                    //Stack empty
    throw std::range_error("Stack: underflow");
  }
  return the_elements[ the_tos ];         //Top item
}
```

The member function `push` is responsible for adding a new item onto the stack. If this is not possible an exception is `thrown`.

```
void Stack::push( const int item )
{
  if ( the_tos >= MAX_ELEMENTS-1 ) {      //Free space
    throw std::range_error("Stack: overflow");
  }
  the_elements[ ++the_tos ] = item;       //Add item
}
```

The member function `pop` removes the top item from the stack. Again, there is a consistency check on the feasibility of the operation.

```
void Stack::pop()
{
  if ( the_tos < 0 ) {                    //Stack empty
    throw std::range_error("Stack: underflow");
  }
  the_tos--;                              //Remove
}
```

The class is safe, in that there is no way incorrect use could cause it to fail by accessing outside the bounds of the array `elements`. However, an exception is raised if:

- An attempt is made to remove an item from an empty stack.
- An attempt is made to add an item when the stack is full.
- An attempt is made to access a non-existent top item.

8.9.1   Introduction to the exception mechanism

Exceptions are thrown by means of the `throw` construct, and caught using the `catch` construct. The `try` block, forms the container for these constructs. For example, in the fragment of code below, an exception `range_error("Too many items")` is thrown and is caught.

```
int main()
{
  try {

    if ( data_values > MAX_DATA_VALUES )
      throw std::runtime_error("Too many items");
  }
  catch ( std::runtime_error& err )
  {
    cout << "Fail: " << err.what() << "\n";
  }
  return 0;
}
```

Note: *The method what delivers the string "Too many items" that was used in*
       the creation of the class constant range_error("Too many items").
       The exception mechanism is discussed in Chapter 14 and namespace in Chapter
       13.

8.9.2   Putting it all together

Using the above class Stack the following code 'tests' the class with some simple data.

```
#include <iostream>
int main()
{
  Stack numbers;
  char ch;
  while ( std::cin >> ch, !std::cin.eof() )
  {
    try
    {
      switch ( ch )
      {
        case '+' :                              //push item onto stack
        {
          int num; std::cin >> num; numbers.push(num);
          break;
        }
        case '-' :                              //pop item from stack
        {
          int num = numbers.top();
          std::cout << "Num = " << num << "\n";
          numbers.pop();
          break;
        }
      }
    }
    catch ( std::range_error&  err )
    {
      cerr << "\n" << "Fail: " << err.what() << "\n";
    }
  }
  return 0;
}
```

When an attempt is made at performing an invalid operation on the stack, the exception `range_error` is thrown, and is caught by the exception handler. The exception handler prints an error message to the error stream and exits the program.

Note: *That 'white space' is ignored on input.*
When an exception is thrown, the normal mechanism for destroying objects that are now out of scope is invoked.

When run with the data:

```
+1 +2 +3 +4 - - - - -
```

the following results will be produced:

```
Num = 4
Num = 3
Num = 2
Num = 1

Fail: Stack underflow
```

8.10   A computerized bank system

Arrays in C++ can hold objects as well as variables. For example, to build a program to implement the computer system for a very simple bank would require an array of bank accounts. To implement this a class `Bank` is defined which has the following responsibilities:

Method	Responsibility
account_balance	Return the balance for a particular customer's account.
deposit	Deposit money into a specified customer's account.
last_account_no	Return the last account number.
set_min_balance	Set the overdraft limit for a customer.
statement_summary	Print a summary statement of the account.
valid	Check if an account number is valid.
withdraw	Withdraw if possible money from a customer's account.

The C++ specification for the class `Bank` is:

```
#ifndef CLASS_BANK_SPEC
#define CLASS_BANK_SPEC
```

```
class Bank {
public:
  Bank();
  ~Bank();
  float account_balance(const int) const;        //Balance
  float withdraw( const int, const float );       //Withdraw
  void deposit( const int, const float );         //Deposit
  void set_min_balance(const int, const float);//Set minimum balance
  int last_account_no() const;                    //Last account no.
  void statement_summary( ostream&, const int ) const;
private:
  static const int MAX_CUSTOMERS=100;
  Account customer[MAX_CUSTOMERS];                //Customers accounts
};

#endif
```

Note: As the specification contains an array, if the number of the items in the array were changed by changing MAX_CUSTOMERS, then the implementation code would have to be recompiled. In this case there would only be source re-use. ~Bank() is a function which is called whenever an instance of the class Bank is finished with. This will happen, for example, when the function or block it was declared in is exited. This function is called a destructor. Destructors are more fully discussed in Section 11.6.

When declaring an array of classes, the class must have a constructor which takes no parameters if a declaration of the form:

```
Account  customer[MAX_CUSTOMERS]; //Customers accounts
```

is to be used.

Note: In the declaration above, the constructor for Account will be called MAX_CUSTOMER times.

To initialize an array of instances of a class with specific values, see Section 15.9. The implementation of the class Bank is as follows:

```
#ifndef CLASS_BANK_IMP
#define CLASS_BANK_IMP
#include "Bank.h"
```

The constructor and destructor for the class Bank are responsible for restoring and saving the information held in customers' bank accounts, between invocations of the program. The constructor is called after the storage for an instance of bank is created and the destructor is called just before the storage is returned back to the system. By adding appropriate code here the contents of the bank can be held beyond the lifetime of the executing program.

```
Bank::Bank()
{
   //Code to set up the bank accounts
}

Bank::~Bank()
{
   //Code to save the money on deposit
}
```

Note: Constructors and destructor are fully discussed in Section 11.6.

The member functions `account_balance, withdraw, deposit` and `set_min_balance` call the relevant member function in the class `Account`:

```
float Bank::account_balance(const int client) const
{
   return customer[client].account_balance();
}

float Bank::withdraw( const int client, const float money )
{
   return customer[client].withdraw( money );
}

void Bank::deposit(const int client, const float money)
{
   customer[client].deposit( money );
}

void Bank::set_min_balance(const int client, const float money)
{
   customer[client].set_min_balance( money );
}
```

The member function `last_account_no` returns the number of the last account. Valid account numbers in `piggy` an instance of the class Bank run from:

```
   0 .. piggy.last_account_no().
```

```
int Bank::last_account_no() const
{
   return MAX_CUSTOMERS-1;
}
```

The member function `statement_summary` prints a summary of the balance of the account.

```
void Bank::statement_summary( std::ostream& s, const int client ) const
{
  s << "Bank statement summary -";
  s << " account number " << client << "\n";
  s << "£" << customer[client].account_balance();
  s << " on deposit" << "\n";
}

#endif
```

The components to access the member function in an array of classes are as shown in Figure 8.4.

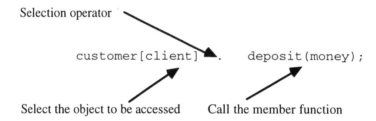

Figure 8.4 Components in accessing a bank account.

8.10.1   Putting it all together

Using the above class Bank the following program can be written:

```
//Code for class Bank

int main()
{
  Bank  piggy;                        //A very small bank
  float obtained;
  int customer = piggy.last_account_no();

  piggy.statement_summary(std::cout,customer);

  std::cout << "\n" << "Transaction Deposit £100.00" << "\n";
  piggy.deposit(customer, 100.00);
  piggy.statement_summary(std::cout, customer);

  std::cout << "\n" << "Transaction withdraw £20.00" << "\n";
  obtained = piggy.withdraw(customer, 20.00);
  std::cout << "piggy Bank gives £" << obtained << "\n";
  piggy.statement_summary(std::cout, customer);

  std::cout << "\n" << "Transaction Deposit £50.00" << "\n";
  piggy.deposit(customer, 50.00);
  piggy.statement_summary(std::cout, customer);
}
```

which when run will produce the following results:

```
Bank statement summary - account number 99
£0 on deposit

Transaction Deposit £100.00
Bank statement summary - account number 99
£100 on deposit

Transaction withdraw £20.00
piggy Bank gives £20
Bank statement summary - account number 99
£80 on deposit

Transaction Deposit £50.00
Bank statement summary - account number 99
£130 on deposit
```

Note: The constructor for Account *will be called for each element of the array customer in the class* Bank.
Likewise any destructor will be called for each element of the array customer, when the storage for an instance of the class Bank *goes out of scope.*

8.11 The part_of relation

In the example above, an Account is part_of a Bank. An instance of the class Bank contains instances of the class Account.

8.12 Arrays and strings

In C and C++ low level strings are represented by an array of characters terminated by the special marker character '\0'. The marker character '\0' is represented by the bit pattern for zero (a byte whose bits are all zeros). This marker character is required so that the end of the string can be determined. For example:

```
char message[] = { 'H', 'e', 'l', 'l', 'o', '\0' };
```

would declare an object message which represents a C++ string. This may be printed using the normal I/O mechanism as shown in the program below:

```
int main()
{
  char message[] = { 'H', 'e', 'l', 'l', 'o', '\0' };
  std::cout << message << "\n"
  return 0;
}
```

which when compiled and run would produce:

```
hello
```

Note: The declaration for message may have been written as:
        `char message[] = "Hello";`
        In this style the marker character '\0' is automatically added at the end of the
        characters in the string.

8.12.1   C++ string constants

A string constant is represented by an array of characters terminated by the special
marker character '\0'. For example, in the program:

```
#include <iostream>

int main()
{
  std::cout << "Hello world" << "\n";
  return 0;
}
```

the string "Hello world" is in fact an array of characters terminated by the special
marker character '\0'.

By using a special marker character as the last character of the array, software that
processes the array can determine how many characters are contained in the string. This
is achieved by searching forward from the zero'th element of the array for the element
containing the marker character.

This representation is completely different from that used by the class
std::string seen earlier in Section 6.6. However, a string constant, for example
"Hello world" is always represented by this method. The class string when
using string constants, converts the array representation to its own internal
representation.

8.12.2   Example of using a C++ string

The following function write prints its single parameter a C++ string to cout.

```
void write( const char vec[] )
{
  int i = 0;
  while ( vec[i] != '\0' )
  {
    std::cout << vec[i];
    i++;
  }
}
```

The function `write` can be used as follows:

```
int main()
{
  write( "Hello world" );
  write( "\n" );
  return 0;
}
```

Note: "Hello world" is an initialized array of characters which is passed by reference to the function `write`.

When executed it would produce:

```
Hello world
```

8.12.3   Advantages and disadvantages of using C++ strings

Whilst using a character array to represent a string will result in code that is efficient, there is always the danger of misuse. Though in some cases less efficient, the use of instances of the class `string` to represent strings provides the programmer with a mechanism that is safer and easier to use. The following table summarizes the major differences between a string declared using:

* The class `string`.
* An array of characters or pointer to character's.
  (The concept of pointers is discussed fully in Chapter 17.)

	Declaration of a		
Object a may be	**std::string a**	**char a[10]**	**Commentary**
assigned	✓	✗	Arrays may not be assigned.
passed by reference to a function	✓	✓	Arrays may only be passed by reference.
passed by value to a function	✓	✗	Arrays may only be passed by reference to a function.
compared	✓	✗	Comparing arrays does not deliver a comparison of the elements. [1]
assigned or compared with a C++ string literal	✓	✗	Arrays may not be assigned or compared. [2]

Notes:
[1]   In the code fragment

```
char name1[] = "Mike"; char name2 = "Mike";
if ( name1 = name2 ) cout << "names are equal" << "\n";
```

the contents of the arrays are not compared, instead the physical address of the start of the arrays is compared. In the above example, the comparison will always deliver false. Chapter 17 explains the use of pointers in more detail.

[2]   *By overloading definitions of comparison operators and providing appropriate constructors the class* string *implements comparison and assignment between C++ strings and instances of the class* string. *Chapter 15 shows how to overload the standard operators.*
A declaration of an array may be assigned an initial value.

8.13   A class to manipulate a person's name and address

Individual people are represented by an instance of the class Person. The responsibilities of this class are:

Method	Responsibility
Person	Sets the person's name and address.
address_line	Return the n'th line of a person's address as a string.
lines_in_address	Return the number of lines in the person address.
name	Returns the person's name as a string.
set_address	Change the details about a person's name and address.

The parameter to the constructor and the method set_address is a string literal of the form "Mike Smith/Brighton", where the start of each new line in the address is indicated by a '/' character.
The C++ specification for this class is as follows:

```
#ifndef CLASS_PERSON_SPEC
#define CLASS_PERSON_SPEC
#include <string>

class Person {
public:
  Person( const std::string name = "Unknown" );
  void set_address( const std::string );           //Set new address
  std::string name() const;                         //Return name
  int lines_in_address() const;                     //Lines in address
  std::string address_line( const int) const;       //line #n of address
private:
  std::string the_details;                          //Persons details
};

#endif
```

Note: The details about a person are stored as an instance of the class string. *The string may be accessed using an array index operation. However, the validity of the subscript is not checked for.*

The constructor for the class `Person` and the method `set_address` stores a person's name and address details for later retrieval.

```
#ifndef CLASS_PERSON_IMP
#define CLASS_PERSON_IMP
#include "Person.h"

Person::Person( const std::string details )
{
  set_address( details );
}

void Person::set_address( const std::string details )
{
  the_details = details;
}
```

The member function `name` returns the person's name, which is retrieved using the member function `address_line`. It is a requirement that the first line of the address is a person's name.

```
std::string Person::name() const
{
  return address_line(1);
}
```

Note: The use of `const` *after the specification of the function* `name`. *This indicates that the member function will not modify any item in the instance of the class. A* `const` *member function is the only function that can be called on a* `const` *instance of a class.*

The member function `lines_in_address` returns the total number of lines in the person's address.

```
int Person::lines_in_address() const
{
  int lines = 1;
  for ( size_t i=0; i<the_details.length()-1; i++ )
  {
    if ( the_details[i] == '/' ) lines++;
  }
  return lines;
}
#endif
```

The member function `address_line` delivers the n'th line of the person's address. This function uses the method `substr` to deliver a slice of an existing string. The parameters to the method `substr` are:

Method	Parameter no	Type	Description
substr	1	const size_t	Start position of slice.
	2	const size_t	No. of characters in slice.

Appendix D lists other methods of the standard C++ class `string`.

```
std::string Person::address_line( const int line ) const
{
  const int last_char = the_details.length()-1;
  int line_on = 1;
  for ( int i=0; i<last_char; i++ )
  {
    if ( line_on == line )
    {
      for ( int j=i; j<last_char; j++ )
      {
        if ( the_details[j] == '/' )
        {
          return the_details.substr( i, j-i );
        }
      }
      return the_details.substr( i, last_char-i+1 );
    }
    if ( the_details[i] == '/' ) line_on++;
  }
  return "";
}
```

8.13.1 Putting it all together

```
//code for class Person

int main()
{
  Person me( "Mike Smith/University of Brighton/"
             "School of Computing/Brighton" );
  for ( int i=1; i<=me.lines_in_address(); i++ )
  {
    std::cout << me.address_line(i) << "\n";
  }
  std::cout << "\n\n";
  return 0;
}
```

Note: Two or more consecutive strings are assembled by the compiler into a single string. In this way a long string may be written in an elegant and easily readable way.

When run, the program produces the following output:

```
Mike Smith
University of Brighton
School of Computing
Brighton
```

8.14   Self-assessment

● Why is the use of arrays in C++ likely to lead to programming errors which may not be detected?

● Is there any restriction to what type of items an array can be made-up of?

● In accessing an array, which subscript changes most rapidly when accessing locations in consecutive memory? Why is this knowledge important?

● Are there any limitations on the number of dimensions that an array might have?

● How is an array of objects declared?

● When an array of objects is declared, how many times is the object's constructor called?

8.15   Exercises

Construct the following program:

● *Noughts and crosses with computer player.*
Add an extra method to the class `Board`, that returns a suggested move for a player.

● *Library*
A program which maintains the state of books in a small school library. Each book in the library has a class mark which is a number in the range 1—999. Two or more identical books will have a different class mark. A person may:

  ● Check a book out of the library.
  ● Reserve a book which is out on loan.
  ● Inquire as to the current status of a book.

The program should be able to handle the above day-to-day transactions. In addition, a facility should be included which will provide a summary about the current status of the books in the library. For example:

```
Books in library 100
Books on loan    = 5
Books reserved   = 2
Books on shelves = 93
```

Hint: *Create a class for a book. The responsibilities of the book class are:*

Method	Responsibility
`loan`	Marks the book as being on-loan.
`missing`	Marks the book as missing.
`reserved`	Marks the book as being reserved.
`returned`	Returns a book to the library.
`state`	Returns the state of the book: `on_shelf`, `on_loan`, etc.

9 Templates

The template mechanism allows classes to be made generic. A templated class is in effect a parameterized type. A programmer can choose which specific type to use for the templated class when they instantiate an instance of the class. By creating templated classes the scope for code re-use is considerably increased. However, usually more effort is required when creating a templated class.

9.1 Introduction to templated classes

The code for the class `Stack`, introduced in Section 8.9, can only be used when a stack of integers is required. By creating a templated class a programmer can create a specific instance of the class to work for a specific type. A templated class is also referred to as a parameterized type. For example, a templated class `Stack` is specified as follows:

```
#ifndef CLASS_STACK_SPEC
#define CLASS_STACK_SPEC

#include <ctype.h>

template <class Type>
class Stack {
public:
  Stack();
  bool empty() const;                      //Stack empty
  size_t size() const;                     //Size of collection
  const Type& top() const;                 //Return top item
  Type& top();                             //Return top item
  void push( const Type );                 //Push item onto stack
  void pop();                              //Pop top item from stack
private:
  static const int MAX_ELEMENTS=5;
  Type   the_elements[MAX_ELEMENTS]; //Items in Stack
  int    the_tos;                          //Top of Stack pointer
};
```

Note: The `Type` used in the stack is specified as a parameter with the template header.

The method top returns a reference to the item in the collection to avoid unnecessary copying of objects. However, there now has to be two versions of the method:

Method signature	Called when:
`Type& top();`	a reference to a mutable object is required.
`const Type& top() const;`	a reference to a const object is required.

This is so that the correct version of the method `top` will be called for the following code:

Declaration	Call of top	Method used
const Stack <**int**> c	c.top()	**const** Type& top() **const**;
Stack <**int**> m	m.top()	Type& top() **const**;

The components in the templated class are illustrated in Figure 9.1. In this figure some of the components in the specification are omitted.

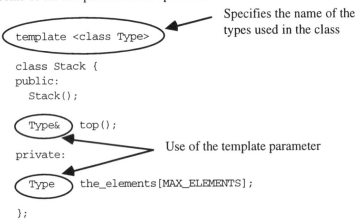

```
template <class Type>

class Stack {
public:
    Stack();

    Type&   top();
private:

    Type    the_elements[MAX_ELEMENTS];

};
```

Specifies the name of the types used in the class

Use of the template parameter

Figure 9.1 Components of a templated class.

An instance of a specific stack is instantiated with:

```
Stack <int>  int_stack;      //Integer Stack
Stack <char> char_stack;     //Character Stack
```

Note: *However, using a parameterized type will not allow a stack to be composed of items of different types. Later on in Chapter 16, it will be shown how polymorphic objects can be used to achieve the effect of having different types of objects processed in the same way. This, however, may not always be what is required.*

Some early implementations of the C++ language do not support templates. In this case a work round using macros may be made. A mechanism for achieving the effect of a template using the macro processor is described in Section 26.9.

The implementation part of the stack is specified in a similar way using the template construct. This is used to specify the names acting as type parameters before specifying the body of each member function.

```
#include <stdexcept>

template <class Type>
Stack<Type>::Stack()
{
    the_tos = -1;                        //Empty
}
```

Figure 9.2 illustrates the implementation of a method in a templated class.

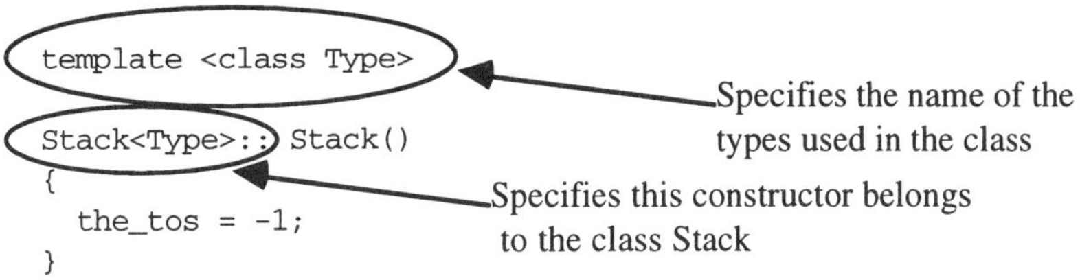

Figure 9.2 Implementation of a method in a templated class.

The member functions `empty` and size are now:

```
template <class Type>
bool Stack<Type>::empty() const
{
  return the_tos < 0;                //Is empty
}

template <class Type>
size_t Stack<Type>::size() const
{
  return the_tos+1;                  //Elements in stack
}
```

Whilst the member functions `top push` and `pop` are:

```
template <class Type>
const Type& Stack<Type>::top() const
{
  if ( the_tos < 0 ) {              //Stack empty
    throw std::range_error("Stack: underflow");
  }
  return the_elements[ the_tos ];    //Top item
}

template <class Type>
Type& Stack<Type>::top()
{
  if ( the_tos < 0 ) {              //Stack empty
    throw std::range_error("Stack: underflow");
  }
  return the_elements[ the_tos ];    //Top item
}
```

Note: The two versions of the method top *a version that is used on a const stack and a version that is used on a non const stack. These are required so that when dealing with:*

> *A const stack*
>> *A reference to a const (read only) object is returned.*
> *A non const stack*
>> *A reference to a mutable (read/write) object is returned.*

```
template <class Type>
void Stack<Type>::push( const Type item )
{
  if ( the_tos >= MAX_ELEMENTS-1 ) {      //Free space
    throw std::range_error("Stack: overflow");
  }
  the_elements[ ++the_tos ] = item;      //Add item
}
```

```
template <class Type>
void Stack<Type>::pop()
{
  if ( the_tos < 0 ) {                    //Stack empty
    throw std::range_error("Stack: underflow");
  }
  the_tos--;                              //Remove
}
#endif
```

Note: A parameterized class may have many types as parameters. For example, the
class Stack could have two parameterized types by using:

```
template <class Type1, class Type2>
class Stack {

      ....

}
```

9.2 Multiple parameters to a template class

As with a template function a templated class may have multiple parameterized types. In addition a parameterized type can be used to specify a specific value of a type. For example, with the class stack, the size of the array used to hold the stack elements can be specified as one of the parameters to the template. The specification for this class is:

```
#ifndef CLASS_STACK_SPEC
#define CLASS_STACK_SPEC
#include <ctype.h>

template <class Type, const int MAX_ELEMENTS=5>
class Stack {
public:
  Stack();
  bool empty() const;                 //Stack empty
  size_t size() const;                //Size of collection
  const Type& top() const;            //Return top item
  Type& top();                        //Return top item
  void push( const Type );            //Push item onto stack
  void pop();                         //Pop top item from stack
private:
  Type  the_elements[MAX_ELEMENTS];   //Items in Stack
  int   the_tos;                      //Top of Stack pointer
};
#endif
```

The implementation of the member function push is now:

```
#include <stdexcep>

template <class Type, const int MAX_ELEMENTS>
void Stack<Type,MAX_ELEMENTS>::push( const Type item )
{
  if ( the_tos >= MAX_ELEMENTS-1 ) {     //Free space
    throw std::range_error("Stack: overflow");
  }
  the_elements[ ++the_tos ] = item;      //Add item
}
```

Note: The implementation of the other member functions follows the same pattern.

An instance of this class Stack is declared as:

```
Stack <int,10> int_stack;      //Integer Stack with 10 elements
Stack <char> char_stack;       //Character Stack with default number
                               // of elements
```

9.3 Problems with templated classes

When a template class is used there is no binding contract between the user of the class and the implementor of the class on how the templated class is to be used. In many cases there will be no problems as any type can be used as the parameter to the templated class. However, if for example arithmetic is performed on an instance of the templated classes actual parameter then the parameter must be an arithmetic type or a type that supports the arithmetic operators used. Consider, a templated version of the class Account seen in Section 5.3.1 whose specification is:

```
#ifndef CLASS_ACCOUNT_SPEC
#define CLASS_ACCOUNT_SPEC

template <class Type>
class Account {
public:
  Account();
  Type account_balance() const;        //return the balance
  Type withdraw( const Type );         //withdraw from account
  void deposit( const Type );          //deposit into account
  void set_min_balance( const Type );  //Set minimum balance
private:
  Type the_balance;                    //The outstanding balance
  Type the_min_balance;                //The minimum balance
};

#endif
```

The implementation of the class is as follows:

```
#ifndef CLASS_ACCOUNT_IMP
#define CLASS_ACCOUNT_IMP

template <class Type>
Account<Type>::Account()
{
  the_balance     = Type();               //Zero
  the_min_balance = Type();               //Zero
}
```

Note: The use of a constructor to return the zero for the type. In the case of the inbuilt arithmetic types this returns their zero value. Hence int () *return zero.*

```
template <class Type>
Type Account<Type>::account_balance() const
{
  return the_balance;
}

template <class Type>
Type Account<Type>::withdraw( const Type money )
{
  if ( the_balance - money >= the_min_balance )
  {
    the_balance = the_balance - money;
    return money;
  } else {
    return Type();                        //Zero
  }
}

template <class Type>
void Account<Type>::deposit( const Type money )
{
  the_balance = the_balance + money;
}

template <class Type>
void Account<Type>::set_min_balance( const Type money )
{
  the_min_balance = money;
}

#endif
```

9.3.1   Putting it all together

Using the above templated class Account the following code can be written:

```
int main()
{
  Account <double> mike;
  double obtained;

  std::cout << std::setiosflags( std::ios::fixed );     //Format x.y
  std::cout << std::setiosflags( std::ios::showpoint ); //0.10
  std::cout << std::setprecision(2);                    //2 dec places

  std::cout << "Account balance = " << mike.account_balance() << "\n";

  mike.deposit(100.00);
  std::cout << "Account balance = " << mike.account_balance() << "\n";

  obtained = mike.withdraw(20.00);
  std::cout << "Money withdrawn = " << obtained << "\n";
  std::cout << "Account balance = " << mike.account_balance() << "\n";

  mike.deposit(50.00);
  std::cout << "Account balance = " << mike.account_balance() << "\n";
  return 0;
}
```

Which when compiled with suitable header files and run will produce:

```
Account balance = 0.00
Account balance = 100.00
Money withdrawn = 20.00
Account balance = 80.00
Account balance = 130.00
```

Alternatively the class could have been parameterized with the type `long` to give an account where the amount is held as an exact quantity. This could be used for countries where there is only a single unit used for their currency.

```
int main()
{
  Account <long> mike;
  long obtained;

  std::cout << "Account balance = " << mike.account_balance() << "\n";

  mike.deposit(10000);
  std::cout << "Account balance = " << mike.account_balance() << "\n";

  obtained = mike.withdraw(2000);
  std::cout << "Money withdrawn = " << obtained << "\n";
  std::cout << "Account balance = " << mike.account_balance() << "\n";

  mike.deposit(5000);
  std::cout << "Account balance = " << mike.account_balance() << "\n";
  return 0;
}
```

When compiled with suitable header files and run will produce:

```
Account balance = 0
Account balance = 10000
Money withdrawn = 2000
Account balance = 8000
Account balance = 13000
```

9.3.2   The problem

However, an implementor cannot specify restrictions to the type that is parameterized with the class. Thus a programmer could foolishly write:

```
int main()
{
  Account <char> strange;              //Compiles

  strange.deposit(97);
  std::cout << "mike Balance = " << strange.account_balance() << "\n";
  return 0;
}
```

which when compiled and run would produce:

```
mike Balance = a
```

But worse, a programmer could have used the following instantiation of the class
Account:

```
  Account < Account<int> > wrong;
```

Note: The space between > > so that this is not confused with the >> operator.

Thought this does not compile, the error message is far from helpful, indicating an error in the code of the templated class where + is used between instances of the actual parameter type Account<int>. Hence the documentation for a templated class needs to carefully define what actual parameters to the templated class are allowed. The users of a templated class should be aware of any limitations in the types that can be used as actual parameters to the instantiation.

9.4 Separate compilation and template classes

When templated classes are used, there must be a unique implementation for each different instantiation of the class. The easiest way to guarantee this is to use a single file that contains both the specification and implementation of the templated class.

Some compilers have a compile time switch to specify that the code for the templated function be generated when a particular file is compiled.

9.5 Self-assessment

- To what extent do templated classes increase the possibility of code-reuse?

- Should all classes be templated? Explain your answer?

- What problems can occur for a user of a templated class?

- What documentation should be provided with a templated class?

- Why are there two versions of the method `top` in the class `Stack`?

9.6 Exercises

Construct the following classes:

- *Store*
  A store for data items which has as its template parameters:
    - The type of the index used.
    - The type of the data item used.

  and the following methods:

Method	Responsibility
`put`	Adds a `[key,data]` pair to the store.
`get`	Using the supplied `key` retrieves the data item associated with the `key` from the data store.
`contains`	Returns true if the `key` is present in the data store.

A possible specification for this class is:

```
#ifndef CLASS_STORE_SPEC
#define CLASS_STORE_SPEC

template <class Index_type, class Item_type>
class Store {
public:
  Store();
  void put( const Index_type key, const Item_type data);
  Item_type& get( const Index_type key );
  const Item_type& get( const Index_type key );
  bool contains( const Index_type key);
private:
  static const int MAX = 5;
  class Cell
  {
  public:
    Index_type index;            //Index into store
    Item_type  item;             //Value stored
  };
  Cell the_data[ MAX ];          //Store
  int  the_next;                 //Next index
};

#endif
```

Which when completed would allow the following fragment of code to be written:

```
Store <std::string, int> parts;

parts.put( "doors" , 4 );
parts.put( "sides" , 2 );

std::cout << "Number of doors = "
          << parts.get( "doors" ) << "\n";
```

● *Better store*
Modify the above class to allow the size of the array to be specified when an instance of the class Store is instantiated.

10 Static variables and functions

This chapter looks at the storage class static. This storage class is used to specify that the lifetime of the object is that of the program.

10.1 Static variables

When a variable is declared, its lifetime is either:

- For the lifetime of the program.
  In which case the variable is declared outside of a function.

- For the lifetime of the executing function.
  In which case the variable is declared (as `auto`) inside a function.
  See Section 27.2 for a fuller description of the storage class `auto`.

Note: The case of an item declared in a class is examined later.

However, there are times when a function needs to remember state information which will be used the next time it is called. This, of course, could be achieved with a declaration of a global variable outside the function, but any other function would also be able to see and modify this variable. The variable can be more usefully declared inside the function, and given the storage class static. This, in effect, produces a global declaration with visibility only within the function.

For example, the function:

```
int unique_number()
{
  static int number = 0;
  return number++;
}
```

would return a new unique number every time it was called.

Note: The declaration is only processed once.

10.1.1   Static variables in a class

Whenever a new instance of a class is declared, a new copy of all the class's data members are created. In most cases this is exactly what is required. However, there will be times when instances of a class need to share data. This could be accomplished with a global variable, but the danger here is that other parts of the program will also be able to see and even change the global variable.

A member variable declared as static in a class, is shared between all instances of that class. This static form of a member variable is also termed a class attribute, as it is an attribute of the whole class and not individual objects.

This process is illustrated below for two classes Ex that contains only data members and Ex2 that contains both normal data members and static data members:

● The class Ex that contains only data members, is used in a program to declare two objects. The program and resultant memory layout are shown below:

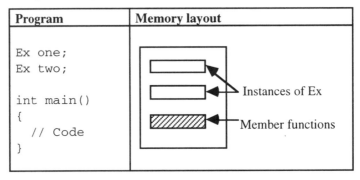

If a member function is declared inline then there will be a copy of its code for each call to the member function.

● The class Ex2 that contains data members and static data members, is used in a program to declare two objects. The program and resultant memory layout are shown below:

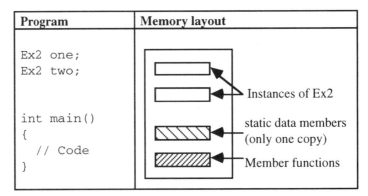

Remember, if a member data item in a class is declared static then regardless of how many instances of the class are created, there will only be a single instance of the static data member.

10.2   Account with an audit trail

A class `Account` that records the total number of transactions processed, uses a static member data item to record the number of transactions made across all instances of `Account`.

The responsibilities for this new class `Account` are:

Method	Responsibility
prelude	Reset the audit trail.
audit_trail	Print the audit trail.
account_balance	Return the balance of the account, record the transaction.
deposit	Deposit money into the account, record the transaction.
set_min_balance	Set the overdraft limit, record the transaction.
withdraw	Withdraw money from the account, but only if there is sufficient funds or an overdraft is allowed, record the transaction.

The C++ specification for the new class `Account` is as follows:

```
#ifndef ACCOUNT_SPEC
#define ACCOUNT_SPEC

class Account {
public:
  Account();
  static void prelude();               //Initialize no_transactions
  float account_balance() const;       //Return the balance
  float withdraw( const float );       //Withdraw from account
  void deposit( const float );         //Deposit into account
  void set_min_balance( const float ); //Set minimum balance
  static void audit_trail(ostream&);   //Simple audit trail
private:
  float the_balance;                   //The outstanding balance
  float the_min_balance;               //The minimum balance
  static int the_no_transactions;      //For audit trail
};

#endif
```

In this class two new member functions have been added, `prelude` which initializes the static variable `the_no_transactions` to 0 and `audit_trail` that prints out the total number of transactions made on all accounts.

These functions have both been declared as static which allows them to be called without reference to an instance of Account.

Note: *A static member function can only access static members of the class. However, it may access non-static members, when it has access to an instance of the class passed as a parameter.*

A static member function is called by prefixing the method name with the class in which it is implemented.

```
Account::prelude();   //Class Name :: Static member function
```

The implementation of the new class Account would begin as follows:

```
#ifndef ACCOUNT_IMP
#define ACCOUNT_IMP
#include "Account.h"

int Account::the_no_transactions;

Account::Account()
{
  the_balance     = 0.00;              //Opening balance
  the_min_balance = 0.00;              //No overdraft
}

void Account::prelude()
{
  the_no_transactions = 0;
}
```

The specification of the static variable the_no_transactions does not allocate any storage; this must be allocated explicitly. A convenient place for this allocation is with the implementation code of the class. The reason for this explicit declaration of storage is that the specification may be included many times in a program, if it is compiled as separate units.

The method audit_trail that writes out the number of transactions performed so far on all account, is implemented as follows:

```
void Account::audit_trail(ostream& ostr)
{
  ostr << "The total number of transactions was ";
  ostr << the_no_transactions;
  ostr << "\n";
}
```

The rest of the implementation for this class follows the previous implementation except of course that the no_of_transactions is incremented for each valid transaction. For example, the transaction deposit now becomes:

```
float Account::withdraw( const float money )
{
  the_no_transactions++;
  if ( money <= the_balance+the_min_balance && money > 0.00 )
  {
    the_balance = the_balance - money;
    return money;
  } else {
    return 0.00;
  }
}

#endif
```

This may be used as follows:

```
int main()
{
  std::cout << std::setiosflags( std::ios::fixed );       //Format x.y
  std::cout << std::setiosflags( std::ios::showpoint ); //0.10
  std::cout << std::setprecision(2);                      //2 dec places

  Account mike, corinna;
  float obtained;

  Account::prelude();

  mike.deposit(100.00);
  std::cout<< "Mike's    account = "<<mike.account_balance()<< "\n";

  obtained = mike.withdraw(20.00);
  std::cout<< "Mike's    account = "<<mike.account_balance()<< "\n";

  mike.deposit(50.00);
  std::cout<< "Mike's    account = "<<mike.account_balance()<< "\n";

  corinna.deposit( 200.00 );
  std::cout<< "Corinna's account = "<<corinna.account_balance()<< "\n";

  Account::audit_trail(std::cout);
  return 0;
}
```

which when compiled and run will produce the following results:

```
mike Balance    = 100.00
mike Balance    = 80.00
mike Balance    = 130.00
corinna Balance= 200.00
The total number of transactions was 8
```

Note: The way a new class was created from an existing class. This can be performed in a cleaner way which promotes code re-use using the concept of inheritance. This is explained in detail in the Chapter 11.

10.3   Self-assessment

- What is the difference between a static data member and normal data member in a class?

- What restrictions are placed on a static member function?

- If you declare a data member in a class as static what else do you have to do?

- When can a member function in a class be called without referring to an instance of the class? Explain why this is so?

10.4   Exercises

Construct the following function:

- *Random number*
  That returns a new random number each time it is called. A very simple strategy to use to give a pseudo random number is to square the middle bits of a static unsigned long and divide the result by 100. This will give a pseudo random number in the range 0 .. 99.

11 Inheritance

This chapter introduces a way of re-using existing classes. This is done via a mechanism that allows a new class to be created out of an existing class or classes. This new class is termed a derived class. In the new class additional member functions and member data items are added to extend the functionality of the original class.

11.1 Account with statement

The class `Account` described earlier in Section 5.3 had no facility to print a mini-statement of the balance of the account. A new class `Account_with_statement` can be created by editing the original `Account` class. However, this has several disadvantages.

- The implementor of the new class `Account_with_statement` has to work with the implementation of the original account. Inevitably the implementor will become involved in the detail of the original class. They may accidentally change data members of the original class, which will result in inconsistencies when the original member functions are called.

- If the implementation code for the class `Account` where amended, then the class `Account_with_statement` would have to be recreated to accommodate these changes.

- In testing the new class, all the methods of the original class `Account` must also be re-tested.

The responsibilities of the class `Account_with_statement` are:

Method	Responsibility
Account Δ	Set up the initial state of the account.
account_balance Δ	Return the balance of the account.
deposit Δ	Deposit money into the account.
set_min_balance Δ	Set the overdraft limit 0.00 no overdraft.
withdraw Δ	Withdraw money from the account.
statement	Return a string representing a mini-statement of the balance of the account.
Account_with_statement	Set up the initial state of an instance of Account_with_statement.

Note: Methods marked Δ have already been written as they are in the class `Account`.

The class `Account_with_statement` has:

Methods	All the methods of the class `Account` plus the additional method: `statement`.

Data members	All the data members of the class `Account` plus the additional data members:
	`the_account_name`
	     holds the name of the account
	`the_statement_no`
	     holds the number of the next statement.

Inheritance allows the creator of a class to inherit all the components of an existing class and add new features that specialise the original class. This process is illustrated in Figure 11.1.

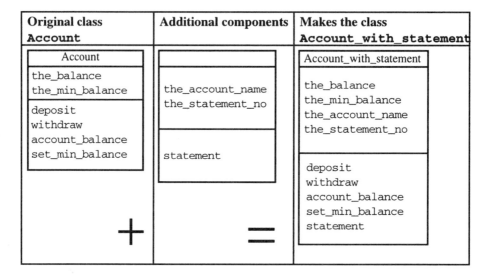

Figure 11.1 The members of the class `Account_with_statement`.

Note: This is not UML syntax, rather a visual representation of the effect of adding additional components to an existing class.

11.1.1 A class diagram showing the inheritance relationship

The above relationship of inheritance is shown in the UML class diagram illustrated in figure 11.2 below.

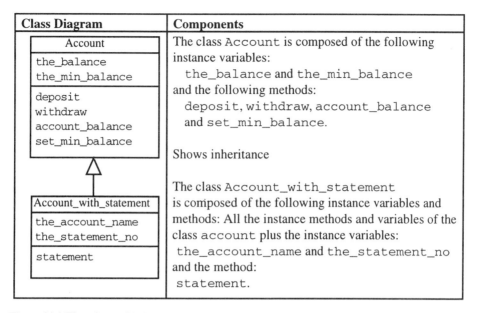

Class Diagram	Components

Account
the_balance
the_min_balance
 	
deposit
withdraw
account_balance
set_min_balance
 	
△
 	
Account_with_statement
the_account_name
the_statement_no
 	
statement
	The class `Account` is composed of the following instance variables:
	    `the_balance` and `the_min_balance`
	and the following methods:
	    `deposit`, `withdraw`, `account_balance`
	    and `set_min_balance`.
	
	Shows inheritance
	
	The class `Account_with_statement` is composed of the following instance variables and methods: All the instance methods and variables of the class `account` plus the instance variables:
	    `the_account_name` and `the_statement_no`
	and the method:
	    `statement`.

Figure 11.2 The relationship between the classes `Account` and `Account_with_statement`.

11.1.2   Terminology

In describing inheritance the following terminology is used:

Terminology	Description	Example
Base class	A class from which other classes are inherited from.	`Account`
Derived class	A class that is inherited from a base class.	`Account_with_statement`

11.1.3   C++ Specification of the class `Account_with_statement`

The C++ specification of the class `Account_with_statement` that inherits the methods and data members from the class `Account` is:

```
#ifndef CLASS_ACCOUNT_WITH_STATEMENT_SPEC
#define CLASS_ACCOUNT_WITH_STATEMENT_SPEC
#include <string>
#include <iostream>
#include "Account.h"
class Account_with_statement : public Account
{
public:
  Account_with_statement(const std::string=""); //Constructor
  std::string statement();                       //Return statement
private:
  std::string the_account_name;                  //Name of account
  int         the_statement_no;                  //Number of statement
};
#endif
```

Note: The header file for the specification includes the specification for the class
Account.

Figure 11.3 illustrates the syntax for deriving a new class from an existing class.

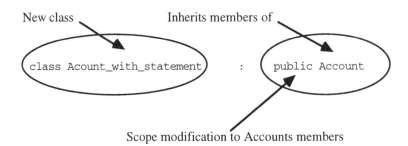

Figure 11.3 Account_with_statement inheriting from the class Account.

Note: The scope modification public to the members of the base class will be
discussed in detail in Section 11.5. In this case it makes all the non-private
members of Account visible to an implementor and user of the class
Account_with_statement.

When the base class Account is used to form the derived class
Account_with_statement the visibility that the derived class has of components
in the base class is the same as any other client of the class. In particular this means that
the derived class cannot access the private components of the base class.

11.1.4 C++ Implementation of the class **Account_with_statement**

The implementation of the derived class account_with_statement is:

```
#ifndef CLASS_ACCOUNT_WITH_STATEMENT_IMP
#define CLASS_ACCOUNT_WITH_STATEMENT_IMP
#include "Account_with_statement.h"

Account_with_statement::Account_with_statement(const std::string name)
{
  the_account_name = name;
  the_statement_no = 1;
}
```

Note: Before the constructor Account_with_statement is called the constructor
Account in the base class will be called.
The constructor has a formal parameter, which has a default value of the empty
string. This default value is defined in the specification of the class.

The member function `statement` returns as a string a mini-statement of the balance of the account. As the derived class cannot see the private data member `the_balance` in the base class, it uses the public member function `account_balance` to deliver the balance of the account. As the message `account_balance` is sent to the same object that the method `statement` is acting on the object name can be omitted. Section 17.14 describes how to access directly the object that the current method is acting on.

```
std::string Account_with_statement::statement()
{
  const int MAX_BUF = 100;                   //Max size of text area
  char buf[MAX_BUF];                         //Holds written text
  std::ostrstream text(buf, MAX_BUF);        //text is a string stream
  text << std::setiosflags( std::ios::fixed );      //Fixed point x.y
  text << std::setiosflags( std::ios::showpoint ); //Show all places
  text << std::setprecision(2);                     //2 dec places
  text << "Mini-statement #" <<
          the_statement_no++ << "  for " <<
          the_account_name   << "\n" << "\n" <<
          "Balance of account is #" <<
          account_balance() << "\n" << '\0';
  return std::string( text.str() );
}

#endif
```

11.1.5 Putting it all together

Inheritance has saved considerable time and effort in the production of the class `Account_with_statement`. A simple test program for this class is shown below:

```
#include <iostream>

//Specification of the class Account_with_statement

int main()
{
  Account_with_statement mike("Mike"), corinna("Corinna");
  float obtained;

  mike.deposit(100.00);
  corinna.deposit(250.00);
  mike.deposit(20.00);
  std::cout << mike.statement()    << "\n";     //Statement for Mike

  obtained = mike.withdraw(30.00);
  std::cout << mike.statement()    << "\n";     //Statement for mike
  std::cout << corinna.statement() << "\n";     //Statement for Corinna
  return 0;
}
```

Note: *The syntax for passing a value to a constructor* `mike("Mike")`.
If the object mike had been declared as:
  `Account_with_statement mike;`
then the constructors formal parameter would take the default value. Naturally if a default value had not been specified the above declaration would have resulted in a compile time error.

which when compiled and run produces the following output:

```
Mini-statement #1  for Mike

Balance of account is £120.00

Mini-statement #2  for Mike

Balance of account is £90.00

Mini-statement #1  for Corinna

Balance of account is £250.00
```

11.2 The is_a relation

The class `Account_with_statement` has the relationship is_a to the class `Account`. A programmer can substitute an instance of the class `Account_with_statement` for an instance of the class `Account` in a program and the effect of the program will stay the same. However, the relationship is not symmetrical as an instance of the class `Account` cannot always be substituted for an instance of the class `Account_with_statement` in a program.

11.3 A savings account

Having already created the class `Account` to deal with a bank account, it is appropriate to think about how an interest-bearing account may be defined. This new account will pay interest on the current balance held in the account at the end of each day.
 An interest-bearing account is the same as an ordinary account but includes ways of specifying the daily interest rate and the actions of accumulating the daily interest and adding this to the outstanding balance at the end of the accounting period.
 In the example below, the default annual interest rate on the account is 10%, which on a daily basis represents 0.026116%.

The responsibilities for the class in addition to all those of an Account are:

Method	Responsibility
`interest_accumulate`	Accumulate the interest gained so far.
`interest_credit`	Add the accumulated interest to the account, resetting the accumulated interest to 0.00.
`end_of_day`	Calculate the interest on the daily balance. This method uses the member function `interest_accumulate` to record the accumulated interest.
`prelude`	Set the daily interest rate.
`set_min_balance`	No action, hence prevents an overdraft being set.

The C++ specification for this class is:

```
#ifndef CLASS_INTEREST_ACCOUNT_SPEC
#define CLASS_INTEREST_ACCOUNT_SPEC
#include "Account.h"

class  Interest_Account : public Account
{
public:
  Interest_Account();
  static void prelude( const float );  //Set up interest rate
  void end_of_day();                   //calculate the interest
  void interest_credit();              //Add the interest to account
  void set_min_balance( const float ); //Override (Null action)
protected:
  void interest_accumulate(const float);  //total
private:
  float the_accumulated_interest;      //Interest gained
  static float the_interest_rate;      //interest rate
};

#endif
```

Note: The inclusion of the specification for `Account` in the class specification for `Interest_Account`.

The role of a `protected` member of a class will be discussed fully later in this chapter in Section 11.5. Essentially protected restricts access of the member function to only other member functions of the class and member functions in a derived class.

The class Interest_Account has the following methods:

In the class Interest_Account	Inherited from Account
`Interest_Account`	`Account`
`interest_accumulate`	`account_balance`
`interest_credit`	`deposit`
`end_of_day`	`set_min_balance`
`prelude`	`withdraw`
`set_min_balance (See Note)`	

Note: The member function set_min_balance *in the class* Interest_account *overrides the method* set_min_balance *in the base class* Account.

and data items:

In the class Interest_Account	Inherited from Account
the_accumulated_interest	the_balance
the_interest_rate	float the_min_balance

As can be seen from the above new class Interest_Account this mechanism saves considerable time and effort, as code from a previously defined class can be re-used to make a new class.

However, this re-use is conditional on existing classes performing suitable operations.

The implementation part of this new class is as follows:

```
#ifndef CLASS_INTEREST_ACCOUNT_IMP
#define CLASS_INTEREST_ACCOUNT_IMP
#include "Interest_Account.h"

const float RATE = 0.00026116;                    //Default 10% interest

float Interest_Account::the_interest_rate=RATE;   //Declare storage

Interest_Account::Interest_Account()
{
  the_accumulated_interest = 0.0;
}
```

The member function prelude is responsible for initializing the static member of the class. Remember, if a data member of a class is declared as static, then only one copy of this data item exists which is shared by all the instances of the class.

```
void Interest_Account::prelude(const float ir)
{
  the_interest_rate = ir;
}
```

The member function set_min_balance overrides the member function in the base class. The implementation of this overridden function is null, preventing a user changing the minimum balance in an instance of Interest_Account. Unfortunately this can be circumvented by the use of the scope resolution operator, the process is detailed in Section 11.3.3.

```
void Interest_Account::set_min_balance( const float )
{
  return;
}
```

The member functions `end_of_day`, `interest_accumulate` and `interest_credit` are responsible for processing the interest on the account.

At the end of each working day the method `end_of_day` will be called and will accumulate the interest in the member variable `the_accumulated_interest` using the method `interest_accumulate`. This accumulated interest will be deposited into the customer's account at the end of the accounting period using the member function `interest_credit`.

```
void Interest_Account::end_of_day()
{
  interest_accumulate(
    account_balance() * the_interest_rate );
}
```

```
void Interest_Account::interest_accumulate(const float ai )
{
  the_accumulated_interest += ai;
}
```

```
void Interest_Account::interest_credit()
{
  deposit( the_accumulated_interest );
  the_accumulated_interest = 0.0;
}

#endif
```

Note: Each instance of `Interest_Account` will contain the member variables `the_balance`, `the_min_balance` and `the_accumulated_interest`.

11.3.1 Call of a constructor in the base class

The constructor for an object of type `Interest_Account` will use the constructor for `Account` to set up the initial balance in the account. This does not have to be explicitly called as the constructor for the base class has no parameters.

```
Interest_Account::Interest_Account()
{
  the_accumulated_interest = 0.0;
}
```

Note: If the constructor for `Account` had a parameter, then the constructor for `Interest_Account` would have been specified in a slightly different way to allow a parameter to be passed to the constructor of `Account`. This is fully explained in Section 11.8.

10.4.1.1   Order of calling constructors and destructors

The constructor in the base class is called first, followed by the constructor in the
derived class. When the object's storage is released the destructor in the derived class
will be called first, followed by the destructor in the base class.

11.3.2   Putting it all together

The following code uses the class Interest_Account:

```
//Class Account
//Class Interest_Account

void process();

int main()
{
  const float DAILY_RATE = 0.00026116;   //10% Annual rate
  Interest_Account::prelude(DAILY_RATE);

  std::cout << std::setiosflags( std::ios::fixed );       //Format x.y
  std::cout << std::setiosflags( std::ios::showpoint ); //0.10
  std::cout << std::setprecision(2);                      //2 dec places
  process();
  return 0;
}
```

The function process then tests the class Interest_Account:

```
void process()
{
  Interest_Account mike;
  float obtained;

  mike.deposit(1000.00);
  std::cout << "Account balance = " << mike.account_balance() << "\n";

  obtained = mike.withdraw(200.00);
  std::cout << "Money withdrawn = " << obtained << "\n";
  std::cout << "Account balance = " << mike.account_balance() << "\n";

  mike.deposit(50.00);
  std::cout << "Account balance = " << mike.account_balance() << "\n";

  mike.end_of_day();
  mike.interest_credit();
  std::cout << "Account balance = " << mike.account_balance() << "\n";
}
```

and produces the following output:

```
Account balance = 1000.00
Money withdrawn = 200.00
Account balance = 800.00
Account balance = 850.00
Account balance = 850.22
```

Note: As the bank account is held as a floating point number, the actual amount held when large may not be exact to two decimal places.

11.3.3   Calling an overridden member function

The member function `set_min_balance` in the base class that was overridden in the derived class may be called by use of the scope resolution operator as follows:

```cpp
int main()
{
  Interest_Account mike;
  float obtained;

  mike.Account::set_min_balance( -250.00 );
  obtained = mike.withdraw(250.00);

  mike.end_of_day();
  mike.interest_credit();
  std::cout << "Account balance = " << mike.account_balance() << "\n";
  return 0;
}
```

which when compiled with suitable declarations and run will produce:

```
Account balance = -250.07
```

Note: This works because the method deposit *that is called by* interest_credit *does not check whether its parameter is negative.*
The only way of preventing a method in the base class being called is to inherit the base class protectively or privately. Section 11.5 describes this process.
The interest rate charged by the bank is the same as given to customers, this is a very generous gesture.

11.4   A saving account with tiered interest rates

A class which has been derived from a base class may itself be used as a base class to derive other classes. For example, the bank may wish to introduce a savings account with a tiered rate of interest. With this type of account the more money that is saved, the higher the interest paid on the account. The base interest rate offered, however, is the same as an Interest_Account.

Amount in account	Annual interest rate	Daily interest rate (365 day year)
less than £10000	10%	0.026116%
£10000 - £24999.99	11%	0.028596%
£25000+	12%	0.031054%

The responsibilities for the class in addition to all those of an Interest_Account are:

Method	Responsibility
prelude	Set the daily interest rates.
end_of_day	Calculate the interest on the daily balance, adding this to an accumulating total for the interest gained so far on the account.

The specification for the class would be:

```
#ifndef CLASS_SPECIAL_INTEREST_ACCOUNT_SPEC
#define CLASS_SPECIAL_INTEREST_ACCOUNT_SPEC
#include "Interest_Account.h"

class  Special_Interest_Account : public Interest_Account
{
public:
  void static prelude( const float, const float, const float );
  void end_of_day();
private:
  static float the_interest_rate1;
  static float the_interest_rate2;
  static float the_interest_rate3;
};

#endif
```

Note: There is no explicit constructor. If a constructor is not provided a default constructor is created. This default constructor will call the constructor in the base class. In this case the constructor in Interest_Account.

while the implementation of the member functions would be:

```
#ifndef CLASS_SPECIAL_INTEREST_ACCOUNT_IMP
#define CLASS_SPECIAL_INTEREST_ACCOUNT_IMP
#include "Special_Interest.h"

const float R1 = 0.00026116;    //10%
const float R2 = 0.00028596;    //11%
const float R3 = 0.00031054;    //12%

float Special_Interest_Account::the_interest_rate1 = R1;
float Special_Interest_Account::the_interest_rate2 = R2;
float Special_Interest_Account::the_interest_rate3 = R3;
```

```
void Special_Interest_Account::prelude
    (const float ir1, const float ir2, const float ir3)
{
  the_interest_rate1 = ir1;
  the_interest_rate2 = ir2;
  the_interest_rate3 = ir3;
}

void Special_Interest_Account::end_of_day()
{
  float money =  account_balance();
  if ( money < 10000 )
    interest_accumulate( account_balance()*the_interest_rate1 );
  else if ( money < 25000 )
    interest_accumulate( account_balance()*the_interest_rate2 );
  else
    interest_accumulate( account_balance()*the_interest_rate3 );
}

#endif
```

The member function `end_of_day` overrides the function `end_of_day` in the class `Interest_Account` to provide the extra functionality. The effect of this is that an instance of the class `Special_Interest_Account` cannot be used where an object of type `Interest_Account` is required. Though the inheritance mechanism is used to produce a specialization of `Interest_Account` it does not have the relationship 'is a' to `Interest_Account`.

If the member function `end_of_day` had to call the member function `end_of_day` in the class `Interest_Account` then the scope resolution operator `::` would be used as follows:

`Interest_Account::end_of_day()` to distinguish between the two functions `end_of_day`.

11.4.1 Putting it all together

The following code uses the class `Special_Interest_Account`:

```
//Class Special_interest_account

#include <iostream>

void process();

int main()
{
  const float DAILY_RATE_R1 = 0.00026116;   //10% Annual rate
  const float DAILY_RATE_R2 = 0.00028596;   //11% Annual rate
  const float DAILY_RATE_R3 = 0.00031054;   //12% Annual rate

  Special_Interest_Account::prelude(
      DAILY_RATE_R1, DAILY_RATE_R2, DAILY_RATE_R3 );
```

```
std::cout << std::setiosflags( std::ios::fixed );        //Format x.y
std::cout << std::setiosflags( std::ios::showpoint );   //0.10
std::cout << std::setprecision(2);                       //2 dec places

process();
return 0;
}
```

```
void process()
{
    Special_Interest_Account mike;
    float obtained;

    std::cout << "Account balance = " << mike.account_balance() << "\n";

    mike.deposit(20000.00);
    std::cout << "Account balance = " << mike.account_balance() << "\n";

    obtained = mike.withdraw(2000.00);
    std::cout << "Money withdrawn = " << obtained << "\n";
    std::cout << "Account balance = " << mike.account_balance() << "\n";

    mike.deposit(50.00);
    std::cout << "Account balance = " << mike.account_balance() << "\n";

    mike.end_of_day();
    mike.interest_credit();
    std::cout << "Account balance = " << mike.account_balance() << "\n";
}
```

and produces the following output:

```
Account balance = 0.00
Account balance = 20000.00
Money withdrawn = 2000.00
Account balance = 18000.00
Account balance = 18050.00
Account balance = 18055.16
```

Inheritance can cut down considerably the amount of code that has to be written for an application but, to use inheritance effectively, careful planning is required!

11.5   Visibility of class members

The visibility of a member of a class to the outside world, and to other classes which may inherit the class, depends on how it has been declared in the class. In essence there is a hierarchy of visibility.

```
class Account
{
public:
   // Visible to client of the class
protected:
   // visible to an inheriting class, but not
   //  visible to client of the class
private:
   // Not visible to client or inheriting class
}
```

The following table summarizes the visibility of class members. For each case, possible items that may be described in this way are suggested.

Member of the class declared as	Visibility of the class member to a user of the class	Examples of items which might be declared in this way
Public	To all items within scope of this class.	Functions visible to a user of the class.
Protected	To another class member and any class member of a class which inherits this class publicly.	Functions which are used to build the functions visible to a user of the class and would be useful to a derived class.
Private	Only to another class member.	Variables, and any functions which should not be used even by a derived class.

Note: Items are by default considered private until a visibility label is met.

11.5.1   Visibility modifiers

This visibility of base class members to a client of the derived class can be changed when the derived class is declared. This is effected by the use of one of the following scope modifications: private, protected, or public. Shown below is the effect of scope modification on the visibility of base class members in class Base to a client of the derived class Derived.

Scope of item in the class Base	Scope to a user of the derived class when the declaration is: class Derived : Δ Base { };		
	Δ = public	Δ = protected	Δ = private
public	public	protected	private
protected	protected	protected	private
private	private	private	private

This is illustrated graphically for public and private inheritance in Figure 11.4. In this diagram, the visibility of base class members in the derived class are shown.

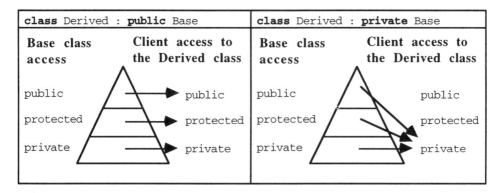

Figure 11.4 Effect of public and private inheritance of a base class.

For example, with the declaration of the classes Base and Derived shown below:

```
class Derived : protected Base          class Base
{                                       {
public:                                 public:
   //Members of Derived class              int inspect();
                                           void mutate();
};                                      protected:
                                           void build();
                                        private:
                                           int the_data;
                                        };
```

The visibility of the inherited members from the class Base in the class Derived is:

Members of the class Base	Visibility of the members of the base class to a client of the class Derived
inspect, mutate	protected
build	protected
the_data	No access

To prevent a user of a derived class seeing public members in the base class the base class must be inherited either privately or protectively. To selectively allow access to member functions in the base class requires the derived class to contain a public overridden version of each of these member functions. The implementation of the overriding method in the derived class calls the base class member. For example, to allow access to the member function inspect but not to allow access to the member function mutate would require the following code for the class Derived:

```
class Derived : protected Base
{
public:
  int inspect();
  //Members of Derived class
};

int Derived::inspect()
{
  return Base::inspect();
}
```

Note: As protected inheritance is used, the member functions inspect *and* mutate *are visible to a class that inherits from the class* Derived.

11.6   Constructors and destructors

As seen previously a constructor for a class will be called, if one has been specified when an instance of that class is created.

A destructor may also be specified which will be called just before the instance of the class variable goes out of scope and any storage is released back to the system. An instance of a class will usually go out of scope when the block in which it has been declared is exited.

For example, the responsibilities of a Room are as follows:

Method	Responsibility
size	Return the size in square metres
Room	Construct an instance of a Room.
~Room	Destruct an instance of a Room

An instance of the class Room is used in a program as follows which describes room 422 in the Watts building. This room has the name w422.

```
watts_building()
{
  Room w422(50);              //declare an instance of Room


}
```

The constructor for the class Room is called when the object w422 is declared; the constructor in this case takes a mandatory parameter that describes the number of square metres of office space.

The destructor ~Room is called when the block containing an instance of the class Room is exited.

11.7   A class to describe a room

This demonstration class describes a room in a building. An instance of the class holds the size of the room in square metres. A member function `size` returns the size of the room.

The constructor initializes an instance of room with its size. The destructor ~Room simply records the fact that the instance of room has gone out of scope and has hence been destroyed.

The specification of the class is:

```
#ifndef CLASS_ROOM_SPEC
#define CLASS_ROOM_SPEC

class Room {
public:
  Room(const int);              //Constructor
  ~Room();                      //Destructor
  void size() const;            //Display size of room
private:
  int the_size_sq_metres;       //Size in square metres
};

#endif
```

The implementation would be:

```
#ifndef CLASS_ROOM_IMP
#define CLASS_ROOM_IMP

Room::Room(const int sq_metres)
{
  the_size_sq_metres = sq_metres;
  std::cout << "Constructor Room       :" <<
             " size in square metres = " << sq_metres << "\n";
}

Room::~Room()
{
  std::cout << "Destructor Room" << "\n";
}

void Room::size() const
{
  std::cout << "Method Room::size()    :" <<
             " size in square metres = " << the_size_sq_metres << "\n";
}

#endif
```

11.7.1   Putting it all together

The above class Room is used in a program which contains the following function.

```
void proc_room()
{
  Room w422(50); w422.size();
}
```

The output from the program when it is compiled with suitable declarations and run is:

```
Constructor Room        : size in square metres = 50
Method Room::size()     : size in square metres = 50
Destructor Room
```

11.8   A class to describe an office

This demonstration class is derived from the class Room and describes an office in a building. The class Office is initialized with the size of the office and the number of staff members who can be accommodated.

The specification for the class is:

```
#ifndef CLASS_OFFICE_SPEC
#define CLASS_OFFICE_SPEC
#include "Room.h"

class Office : public Room {
public:
  Office( const int, const int );   //Constructor
  ~Office();                        //Destructor
  void staff() const;               //Display number of staff
private:
  int the_no_staff;                 //The number of staff
};

#endif
```

The implementation for the class is:

```
#ifndef CLASS_OFFICE_IMP
#define CLASS_OFFICE_IMP

Office::Office( const int size, const int no_staff) : Room(size)
{
  the_no_staff = no_staff;
  std::cout << "Constructor Office    :" <<
              " number of staff = " << the_no_staff << "\n";
}
```

```
Office::~Office()
{
  std::cout << "Destructor Office" << "\n";
}

void Office::staff() const
{
  std::cout << "Method Office::staff() :" <<
              " number of staff = " << the_no_staff << "\n";
}

#endif
```

The constructor for `Office` cannot in this case implicitly call the constructor for `Room`, as the size of the room has to be specified as a parameter to the constructor. This is called explicitly as illustrated in Figure 11.5.

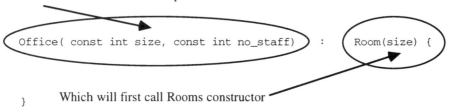

Figure 11.5 Call of a constructor explicitly in the base class.

11.8.1 Putting it all together

The above class `Office` could be used in a program which contains the following function.

```
void proc_office()
{
  Office w418(24,2); w418.staff(); w418.size();
}
```

The output from the program when this function was called would be as follows:

```
Constructor Room       : size in square metres = 24
Constructor Office     : number of staff = 2
Method Office::staff() : number of staff = 2
Method Room::size()    : size in square metres = 24
Destructor Office
Destructor Room
```

Note: The order in which the constructors and destructors are called for an instance of a class which is derived from a base class.

11.9   Initializing data members of a class

The constructor mechanism can be used to initiate individual data members of an object when the object is created. This allows a const data member to be initialized when the object is created. For example, the specification of the class Room could have been defined as:

```
#ifndef CLASS_ROOM_SPEC
#define CLASS_ROOM_SPEC

class Room {
public:
   Room(const int);                //Constructor
  ~Room();                         //Destructor
   void size() const;              //Display size of room
private:
   const int the_size_sq_metres;   //Size in square metres
};


#endif
```

and the implementation of its constructor as:

```
Room::Room(const int sq_metres) : the_size_sq_metres(sq_metres)
{
   std::cout << "Constructor Room        :" <<
             " size in square metres = " << sq_metres << "\n";
}
```

This allows the data member the_size_sq_metres to be declared as a const and hence be immutable. Likewise the specification of the class Office could be changed to:

```
class Office : public Room {
public:
   Office( const int, const int );  //Constructor
  ~Office();                        //Destructor
   void staff() const;              //Display number of staff
private:
   const int the_no_staff;          //The number of staff
};
```

Then the implementation of the constructor for the class Office would be as follows:

```
Office::Office( const int size, const int no_staff)
   : Room(size), the_no_staff(no_staff)
{
  std::cout << "Constructor Office     :" <<
               " number of staff = " << the_no_staff << "\n";
}
```

Note: The explicit call to the constructor of Room *as well as the initialization of the data member* the_no_staff.

11.10 Multiple inheritance

So far a new class has been created for a single existing class, which itself may have been created from another class. In some situations, what is required is to create a new class based on two or more existing classes. This concept is often referred to as multiple inheritance.

As an example, consider the class Interest_Account which provides a class for representing an interest-bearing account. The name of the account holder is not specified as part of the account. A new class Named_Account can be created from the existing classes Interest_Account and Person which will allow the following operations on an instance of the class.

- All the operations in the class Account.
- All the operations in the class Person.
- The ability to return a mini-statement for the account holder.

The responsibilities of this new class would be all the responsibilities of the classes Account and Person plus the additional responsibilities of:

Method/Constructor	Responsibility
Named_Account	Construct the initial values in the account.
mini_statement	Return as a string a summary of the account in the form of a mini-statement.

The C++ specification for this class is:

```
#ifndef CLASS_NAMED_ACCOUNT_SPEC
#define CLASS_NAMED_ACCOUNT_SPEC
#include "Interest_account.h"
#include "Person.h"

#include <string>

class Named_Account : public Interest_Account, public Person
{
public:
  Named_Account( const std::string = "", const float = 0.0f);
  std::string mini_statement() const;
};

#endif
```

The member functions of the class `Named_Account` are shown in the table below:

From the class `Interest_Account`	From the class `Person`	In the class `Named_Account`
account_balance interest_accumulate interest_credit end_of_day deposit Interest_Account prelude set_min_balance withdraw	address_line lines_in_address name set_address	mini_statement

whilst the data members are shown in the following table:

From the class `Interest_Account`	From the class `Person`	In the class `Named_Account`
the_interest_rate the_accumulated_interest the_balance the_min_balance	the_details	

The implementation of the class `Named_Account` is:

```
#ifndef CLASS_NAMED_ACCOUNT_IMP
#define CLASS_NAMED_ACCOUNT_IMP

#include <strstream>
Named_Account::Named_Account( const std::string details,
                              const float amount) :
  Person(details), Interest_Account()
{
  deposit( amount );
}
```

The only member function `mini_statement` returns as a string the name of the account holder followed by the current balance of their account. The implementation of this methods calls the member function `name` in the class `Person` and the member function `account_balance` in the class `Account`.

```
std::string Named_Account::mini_statement() const
{
  const int MAX_BUF = 200;                 //Max size of text area
  char buf[MAX_BUF];                       //Holds written text
  std::ostrstream text(buf, MAX_BUF);      // as a string stream
  text << "Mini Statement for   : " << name() << "\n";
  text << "Balance of account is : £" << account_balance();
  text << "\n" << '\0';
  return std::string( text.str() );
}
#endif
```

The relationship between the classes Account, Interest_Account, Named_Account and Person is illustrated in Figure 11.6.

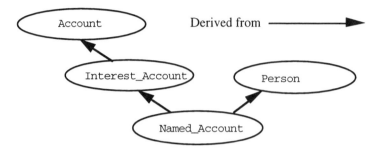

Figure 11.6 Class hierarchy for Named_Account.

For an object of type Named_Account the order of calling the base class's constructors is shown in Figure 11.7.

Named_Account::Named_Account(const string details, const float amount) :

Figure 11.7 Order of calling constructors.

The code body of the constructor in Named_Account deposits amount into the account, by calling the member function deposit implemented in the class Account.

Note: *The constructors are called from left to right.*
If the constructors are not explicitly stated, then the order used for calling the constructors for the base classes, is the order in which the compiler processes the base class definitions.

If classes are constructed carefully, then the possibility for re-use is considerably enhanced. However, there will be cases when the class does not do exactly what is required, in which case a re-working of the base class may be the only answer.

11.10.1 Putting it all together

The class Named_Account can now be used in a program as follows:

```
#include <iostream>
void process();                        // prototype
int main()
{
  const double DAILY_RATE = 0.00026116;   //10% Annual rate
  Named_Account::prelude(DAILY_RATE);

  process();
  return 0;
}
```

The function `process` illustrates the processing of transactions on an instance of the class `Named_Account`.

```
void process()
{
  Named_Account a_n_other( "A N Other/Brighton" );

  std::cout << a_n_other.mini_statement();
  a_n_other.deposit(500);
  std::cout << "Deposit £500" << "\n";
  std::cout << a_n_other.mini_statement();

  a_n_other.end_of_day();
  a_n_other.interest_credit();
  std::cout << "Add interest at end of day" << "\n";
  std::cout << a_n_other.mini_statement();
}
```

Note: The use of the prelude to initialize the variable containing the interest rate payable on the account.

When run, the program would produce the following results:

```
Mini Statement for     : A N Other
Balance of account is : £0.00
Deposit £500
Mini Statement for     : A N Other
Balance of account is : £500.00
Add interest at end of day
Mini Statement for     : A N Other
Balance of account is : £500.13
```

11.11 Accessing base class objects

When using a derived object the base object or objects may be accessed as objects in their own right. This access of a base object can be accomplished in two distinct ways.

- Assignment of a derived object to an object of the same type as one of its base classes, causes the base object only to be assigned.

- Passing a derived object to a function who's formal parameter type is that of one of its base classes.

11.11.1 Assigning the base class object (assignment)

Using the above example of the derived class `Named_Account`, the following code may be written:

```
Named_Account savings( "M Smith/Brighton/UK" );

Person          mike = savings;   //Person object
Interest_Account ia  = savings;   //Interest_account object
Account         na   = savings;   //Account object
```

The compiler truncates the object `savings` to just the components required for the base objects. However, it is not allowed to perform the following:

```
Named_Account    corinna = na    //NO
```

as the compiler does not know how to convert an instance of an `Account` into an instance of a `Named_Account`. However, this could be performed if there was a constructor of `Named_Account` whose formal parameter was of type `Account`.

11.11.2 Assigning the base class object (implied assignment)

An instance of the class `Named_Account` can be used as if it were an instance of its base classes. For example, the function `print_label` prints out an address label for an instance of person.

```
void print_label( std::ostream& ostr, Person& details )
{
  ostr << details.name() << "\n";
  for ( int i=1; i<=details.lines_in_address(); i++ )
  {
    ostr << details.address_line(i) << "\n";
  }
}
```

whilst the function `print_balance` prints out the current balance in an account:

```
void print_balance( std::ostream& ostr, Account& acc )
{
  ostr << "Balance of account is : £" <<
          acc.account_balance() << "\n";
}
```

11.11.3 Putting it all together

These two functions may be called with an actual parameter of type `Named_Account` as illustrated in the following code fragment:

```cpp
int main()
{
  Named_Account a_n_other( "A N Other/Brighton/England/BN2 4GJ" );

  a_n_other.deposit(100.00);

  print_label(   std::cout, a_n_other ); //Process as Person
  print_balance( std::cout, a_n_other ); //Process as Account
  return 0;
}
```

Which when compiled and run will produce:

```
A N Other
Brighton
England
BN2 4GJ
Balance of account is : 100.00
```

11.12 Static binding

In the examples shown so far, the binding between the call of a member function in an object and the code that is eventually executed, is evaluated at compile time. This is commonly referred to as static binding. The implication of this is that the programmer knows in advance what object the member function is called on.

For example, it would not be possible to deal with an array of bank accounts which are composed of different types of account.

Later in Chapter 16, a mechanism for dealing with an array of objects of different types will be shown.

11.13 Inherited functions

The table below summarizes which functions are inherited and which are not.

Type of function	Inherited	Must be a	Created by default
The constructor(s)	No	Member function	Yes
The destructor	No	Member function	Yes
Member function(s)	Yes		No
Friend function(s)	No		No

Note: Friend functions are described in Section 15.4.2.

11.14 Inheritance of the same base class

Using multiple inheritance can sometimes produce a class made from multiple copies of the same base class. To prevent this from happening, the keyword `virtual`, can be prefixed to the name of the base class.

In the examples below, two base classes C1 and C2 have the specification and implementation.

Class C1:	Class C2:
```cpp\nclass C1\n{\npublic:\n C1();\n\n //C1's interface\n};\nC1::C1() { cout << "C1 "; }\n```	```cpp\nclass C2\n{\npublic:\n C2();\n\n //C2's interface\n};\nC2::C2() { cout << "C2 "; }\n```

These base classes are used in the construction of two derived classes D1 and D2.

Class D1:	Class D2:
```cpp\nclass D1: virtual public C1,\n virtual public C2\n{\npublic:\n D1();\n\n //D1's interface\n};\nD1::D1() { cout << "D1 "; }\n```	```cpp\nclass D2: virtual public C1\n{\npublic:\n D2();\n\n //D2's interface\n};\nD2::D2() { cout << "D2 "; }\n```

Note: The keyword virtual *is used as a prefix when the class C1 or the class C2 are used in the derivation of the new classes.*

At a later stage the classes D1, D2 and C2 are used to derive a new class E1 which will only contain a single copy of the classes C1 and C2.

```cpp
class E1 : public D1, public D2, virtual public C2
{
public:
  E1();
  //Public interface of E1
};

E1::E1() { cout << "E1 "; }
```

The class hierarchy for the above classes is:

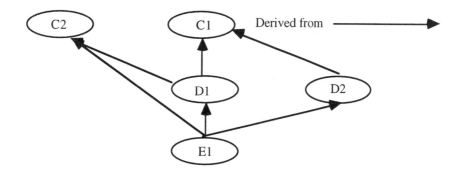

If the class E1 were used in the program:

```
int main()
{
  E1 object;
}
```

the output would be:

```
C1 C2 D1 D2 E1
```

Note: *The order of calling the constructors is a simple left to right evaluation as specified in the derived class.*

$$E1 \; \rightarrow \; D1 \quad D2 \quad C2^{\Delta} \qquad \textit{then E1 constructor}$$
$$D1 \; \rightarrow \; C1 \quad C2 \qquad \textit{then D1 constructor}$$
$$D2 \; \rightarrow \; C1^{\Delta} \qquad \textit{then D2 constructor}$$

Δ *Class not included.*

Had the virtual keyword not been used, then multiple copies of the classes C1 and C2 would have been included. The results from running the program modified to exclude the keyword `virtual` would be:

```
C1 D1 C1 C2 D2 C2 E1
```

Note: *The omission of virtual before the class C2 in the derivation of E1 would have resulted in an extra copy of the class C2 being included.*

11.15 Self-assessment

- How can the concept of inheritance save time in the production of software?

- Can a method in a derived class have the same name as a method in the base class?

- How can the member function in a base class, which has been overridden by a member function in the derived class, be called from a member function of the derived class?

- What is static binding?

- What is the purpose of public, protected and private in a class definition?

- What is a destructor?

- If a base class has a constructor and a new class is derived from it, what constructor has the new class?

- What do you need to do when inheriting from a base class whose constructor takes a parameter?

- Under what circumstances would you declare a member variable static?

- Under what circumstances would you declare a member function static?

- If the language C++ did not have multiple inheritance, how could you implement the class Named_Account?

11.16 Exercises

Construct the following class using inheritance:

- *Account_with_close*
  A class which has all the methods of Account plus the additional method of can_close and close. The responsibilities of these methods are:

Method	Responsibility
can_close	Determines if the account can be closed. An account can only be closed if there is no overdraft.
close	Withdraws the outstanding balance of the account.

This however is only allowed to happen if the account is not overdrawn.

Construct the following program:

- *Test*
  A program to test the class Account_with_close.

Construct the following classes:

- *Employee_pay*
  A class Employee_pay which represents a person's salary has the following methods:

Method	Responsibility
set_hourly_rate	Set the hourly rate.
add_hours_worked	Accumulate the number of hours worked so far.
pay	Deliver the pay for this week.
reset	Reset the hours worked back to zero.
hours_worked	Deliver the number of hours worked so far this week.
pay_rate	Deliver the hourly pay rate.

Tax is to be deducted at 20% of total pay.

- *Better_employee_pay*
A class Better_employee_pay which represents a person's salary. This extends the class *Employee_pay* to add the additional methods of:

Method	Responsibility
set_overtime_pay	Set the overtime pay rate.
normal_pay_hours	Set the number of hours in a week that have to be worked before the overtime pay rate is applied.
pay	Deliver the pay for this week. This will consist of the hours worked at the normal pay rate plus the hours worked at the overtime rate.

Construct the following program:

- *test*
A program to test the classes Better_employee_pay and Employee_pay.

Construct the following class:

- *Employee_pay_with_repayment.*
A class Employee_pay_with_repayment which represents a person's salary after the deduction of the weekly repayment of part of a loan for travel expenses. This extends the class Better_employee_pay to add the additional methods of:

Method	Responsibility
set_deduction	Set the weekly deduction
pay	Deliver the pay for this week. This will include the deduction of the money for the employee loan if possible.

Remember to include the possibility of an employee not being able to repay the weekly repayment of their loan as they have not worked enough hours.

- test
A program to test the class Employee_pay_with_repayment.

- *Company*
A class Company that has the following methods:

Method	Responsibility
`add_hours_worked`	Accumulate the number of hours worked so far for a particular employee.
`normal_pay_hours`	Set the number of hours in a week that have to be worked before the overtime pay rate is applied for a particular employee.
`pay`	Deliver the pay for this week for a particular employee. This will consist of the hours worked at the normal pay rate plus the hours worked at the overtime rate.
`reset`	Reset the hours worked back to zero for a particular employee.
`set_hourly_rate`	Set the hourly rate for a particular employee.
`set_overtime_pay`	Set the overtime pay rate for a particular employee.

Note: The class is a container class for an array of 100 instances of the class `Better_employee_pay`. The messages sent to an instance of this class are delegated to the object for the specific employee.

● *Payroll*

A program that implements the payroll for a small company of upto 100 employees. An individual transaction with the program consists of a single line of the form:

<Action> <Employee Number> [<Parameters>]

Where:

<Action> is

S Sets the hourly rate for this employee.
O Sets the overtime hourly rate for this employee.
N Sets the number of hours normally worked in a week for this employee. If an employee works over this number of hours then they will be paid at an overtime rate.
A Enters hours worked by this employee so far this week.
P Prints the pay earned by the employee for this week. This includes the deduction of 20% tax on total pay.
R Reset the number of hours worked back to zero so that data for the next week can be entered.

<Employee Number> is:
A number in the range 1 to 100.

<Parameters> are:
Any additional values associated with the transaction.

Typical transactions

S 1 5.00	Set the hourly rate for employee 1 as £5.00 per hour
O 2 7.50	Set the overtime rate for employee 2 to be £7.50 per hour.
P 2	Print the total pay earned by employee 2 for this week. [Remember tax is deducted as 20% of total pay.]
A 3 5	Employee 3 has worked 5 hours today.

12 The game of four counters

This chapter goes through the construction of a simple board game using an object-oriented approach.

12.1 Four counters

This simple children's board game is played on a vertical board of cells, six rows by seven columns. Each player takes it in turn to drop a coloured counter into one of the columns of cells on the board. The dropped counters pile up on top of each other to form a vertical column of counters in the cells. A player announces a win when they have four of their counters next to each other in the board either vertically, horizontally, or diagonally.

For example, in a game between two people using black and white counters the board might be as follows, after:

7 moves with white to play next

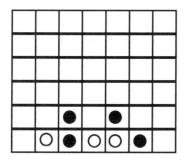

9 moves with white to play next

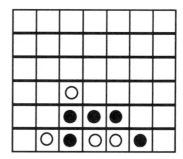

11 moves and a win for black

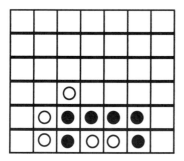

Commentary:

After move 7, white has made a tactical error by not dropping a counter into column 4.

After move 9, black is in an unassailable position and wins easily on move 11.

12.1.1   A program to play four counters

A controller of the game (game's master) asks each player in turn for a move. When a move is received from a player, the board is asked to validate the move. If this is a valid move the counter of the current player is dropped into the board. The board is displayed and the new state of the board is evaluated. This process is repeated until either a player wins or the board is filled. The player making the last move is asked to announce the result of the game.

The interactions by the controller with the system are shown in Figure 12.1

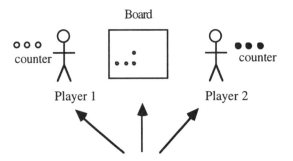

Figure 12.1 Interactions by the controller with the objects in the system.

In the English description of the problem, nouns indicate potential objects and verbs indicate potential messages sent to these objects.

With the major **nouns** indicated in bold and the major *verbs* indicated in bold italics, the specification for the game can now be read as:

This simple children's board **game** is *played* on a vertical **board** of **cells** six rows by seven columns. Each **player** takes it in turn to *drop* a coloured **counter** into one of the columns of **cells** on the **board**. The dropped **counters** pile up on top of each other to form a vertical column of **counters** in the **cells**. A **player** *announces* a win when they have four of their **counters** next to each other in the **board** either vertically, horizontally, or diagonally.

A controller of the **game** (game's master) *asks* each player in turn for a move. When a move is received from a **player**, the **board** is asked to *validate* the move. If this is a valid move the **counter** of the current **player** is *dropped* into the **board**. The **board** is *displayed* and the new state of the board is *evaluated*. This process is repeated until either a **player** wins or the **board** is filled. The **player** making the last move is asked to *announce* the result of the **game**.

The major objects and verbs identified are:

Objects (nouns)	Messages (verbs)
board	announce
cell	ask
counter	display
player	drop
game	evaluated
	play
	validate

The following messages are sent to individual objects:

```
board
```
> Display a representation of the board.
> Drop a counter into a column.
> Evaluate the current state of the board.
> Validate a proposed move.

```
player
```
> Announce the result of the game.
> Ask for the next move.

```
cell
```
> Drop a counter into a cell on the board.

```
counter
```
> Display a representation of the counter.

```
game
```
> Play the game.

It is more appropriate to deal with classes than to deal with objects. For example, `Board` is the class to which the object `board` belongs. Using this approach the messages sent to these classes can be refined into the following list:

Class	Message	Responsibility of method
Board	display	Display a representation of the board.
	drop_in_column	Drop a counter into a column.
	evaluate	Evaluate the current state of the game: win, draw or still playable.
	move_ok_for_column	Check if a player can drop a counter into a column.
	reset	Reset the board to empty.
Player	announce	Announcing that the player has either won or drawn the game.
	counter_is	Return the counter used by the player.
	get_move	Get the next move from the player.

Cell	clear	Clear a cell.
	colour	Return the colour of the counter in the cell.
	contents	Return the counter contained in the cell.
	drop	Drop a counter into the cell.
Counter	colour	Return the colour of the stored counter.
	view	Return a printable representation of the counter.
Game	play	Play the game.

Note: Some of the original messages (verbs) have been renamed to a more specific name when producing this list.

In looking at the methods that belong to the above list of classes, methods that belong to the classes `Counter`, `Player`, and `Board` are split into two distinct categories:

- Methods that perform I/O, or will have an interaction with objects that perform I/O.
- Methods that deal with changing the state or examining the state of the object but involve no direct or indirect I/O.

Inheritance is used to split each of the classes `Counter`, `Player`, and `Board` into two classes:

- A base class whose methods involve no I/O.
- A derived class that inherits from the base class and adds methods that perform I/O or have an I/O interaction.

The classes used in building an implementation of the game C4 will now be:

Class	An instance of which is:
Board	The board for the C4 game, that communicates with the outside world using the TUI class for I/O.
Basic_board	The board for the C4 game.
Player	A player of the game C4, that communicates with the outside world using the TUI class for I/O.
Basic_player	A player of the game C4.
Cell	One of the 42 cells held in the C4 board.
Counter	A counter used in playing the C4 game, that returns a representation that the TUI class can print.
Basic_counter	A counter used in playing the C4 game.
TUI	Used to communicate with the outside world. The class is shown in Section 7.4.
Game	Used to play the game C4.

This decomposition allows many of the classes to be re-used when building a graphical version of four counters.

12.2   Class diagram

A class diagram for the game of four counters is shown below in Figure 12.2

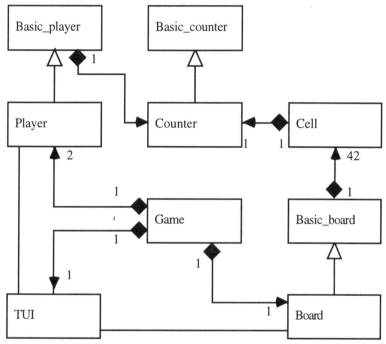

Figure 12.2 Relationship between the classes in the game of four counters.

Note: A line between classes shows a relationship.

12.3   Specification of the C++ classes

The C++ class specifications for the above classes are implemented as follows:

Class	C++ specification

Game	```class Game {```
	```public:```
	``` void play();```
	```};```

Basic_Counter	```class Basic_counter {```
	```public:```
	``` enum Counter_rep { NONE=' ', WHITE='o', BLACK='x' };```
	``` Basic_counter(const Counter_rep=NONE);```
	``` Counter_rep colour() const; //Returns counters colour```
	```};```

Class	C++ specification

Counter	```class Counter : public Basic_counter {```
	```public:```
	  ```Counter(const Counter_rep=NONE);```
	  ```char view() const; //As a character```
	```};```

Basic_player	```class Basic_player {```
	```public:```
	  ```Basic_player(Counter); //Player plays counter ...```
	  ```Counter counter_is() const; //Return players counter```
	```};```

Player	```class Player : public Basic_player {```
	```public:```
	  ```Player(Counter);```
	  ```int get_move(TUI&, const bool=false) const; //Get Move```
	  ```void announce(TUI&, const Board::Game_result) const; //Result```
	```};```

Cell	```class Cell {```
	```public:```
	  ```Cell();```
	  ```void clear(); //Clear the cell```
	  ```void drop(const Counter c); //Drop into cell```
	  ```Basic_counter::Counter_rep colour() const; //Counter colour```
	  ```const Counter& contents() const; //Counter```
	```};```

Basic_board	```class Basic_board {```
	```public:```
	  ```enum Game_result { DRAW, WIN, PLAYABLE };```
	  ```Basic_board(const int rows=DEF_ROWS,```
	    ```const int columns=DEF_COLUMNS);```
	  ```void reset(const int rows=DEF_ROWS,```
	    ```const int columns=DEF_COLUMNS);```
	  ```void drop_in_column(const int, const Counter);```
	  ```bool move_ok_for_column(const int) const;```
	  ```Game_result evaluate() const;```
	```};```

Board	```class Board : public Basic_board {```
	```public:```
	  ```Board(const int rows=DEF_ROWS, const int columns=DEF_COLUMNS);```
	  ```void Board::display(TUI&) const;```
	```};```

Note: In the C++ class specifications only the public members are shown.

The messages sent to instances of the major class Game are show below in the sequence diagram illustrated in Figure 12.3

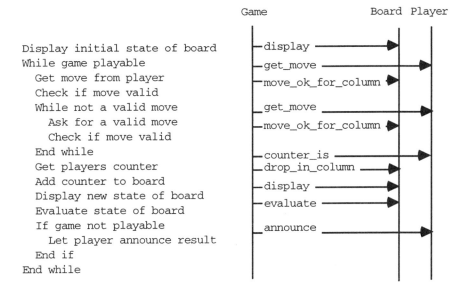

Figure 12.3 Sequence diagram for the game C4.

Note: A sequence diagram, shows the messages sent to objects in the program.

12.4   The implementation

Once the above work has been done, the task of generating the actual code for the program is quite straightforward. The C++ class specifications have been agreed allowing individual software engineers to implement the individual classes. The only exception will be for inherited classes which need to use protected member functions in a base class when implementing methods in the derived class.

12.4.1   The class Game

The class Game contains a single method that plays the game of C4 between two human players. The complete specification for this class is:

```
#ifndef CLASS_GAME_SPEC
#define CLASS_GAME_SPEC

class Game
{
public:
  void play();
private:
  TUI    the_screen;              //Vdu/keyboard
  Board  the_brd;                 //The playing board
  Player the_ply[2];              //The players
};

#endif
```

The code for the method `play` uses instances of the classes TUI, Board, Player to facilitate playing the game of C4 between two human players. This is based on the interaction diagram developed in Figure 12.3.

```cpp
#ifndef CLASS_GAME_IMP
#define CLASS_GAME_IMP

#include "Counter.h"                          //Counter
#include "Player.h"                           //Player
#include "Board.h"                            //Board
#include "Game.h"                             // Game

void Game::play()
{
  the_ply[0] = Player( Counter(Counter::BLACK) ); // Black counter
  the_ply[1] = Player( Counter(Counter::WHITE) ); // White counter

  Board::Game_result game_is = Board::PLAYABLE;
  int current = 0;                            //Current player

  the_brd.display(the_screen);                //Display the board
  while ( game_is == Board::PLAYABLE )        //While playable
  {
    int move = the_ply[current].get_move(the_screen);  //Get move
    while ( !the_brd.move_ok_for_column(move) )         //Is valid
    {
      move = the_ply[current].get_move(the_screen, true);
    }
    Counter plays = the_ply[current].counter_is(); //Plays with
    the_brd.drop_in_column(move, plays);           //Add to board

    the_brd.display(the_screen);                   //Display new board
    game_is = the_brd.evaluate();
    if ( game_is == Board::PLAYABLE )
      current = ( current == 0 ? 1 : 0 );          //Next player
    else
      the_ply[current].announce(the_screen,game_is); //Result
  }
}

#endif
```

12.4.2   The class Basic_counter

The colour of the counter is represented internally by `Counter_rep`. The constructor for `Basic_counter` has a default value of NONE, the default value is used when a cell on the board is populated with no counter. This pretence is required because without using pointers there is no way of selectively having a counter as a member or not a member of a cell on the board. The other member function of the class is responsible for returning the colour of the counter.

The specification of the class `Basic_counter` is as follows:

```
#ifndef CLASS_BASIC_COUNTER_SPEC
#define CLASS_BASIC_COUNTER_SPEC

class Basic_counter {
public:
  enum Counter_rep { NONE=' ', WHITE='o', BLACK='x' };
  Basic_counter(const Counter_rep=NONE);
  Counter_rep colour() const;              //Returns counters colour
private:
  Counter_rep the_colour;                  //The counters colour
};
```

The member functions of the class are implemented in-line for efficiency:

```
inline Basic_counter::Basic_counter(const Counter_rep colour)
{
  the_colour = colour;
}

inline Basic_counter::Counter_rep Basic_counter::colour() const
{
  return the_colour;
}

#endif
```

The implementation of the class `Basic_counter` is:

```
#ifndef CLASS_BASIC_COUNTER_IMP
#define CLASS_BASIC_COUNTER_IMP
#include "Basic_counter.h"

#endif
```

Note: As all the member functions of the class have been implemented in-line, this file is in effect null. It is provided purely for compatibility purposes.

12.4.3 The class `Counter`

The class `Basic_counter` is specialized into the class `Counter`. The method `view` returns a textual representation of a counter suitable for printing using the class `TUI` (see Section 7.4.4).

```
#ifndef CLASS_COUNTER_SPEC
#define CLASS_COUNTER_SPEC
#include "Basic_counter"
#include <stdexcept>
```

```
class Counter : public Basic_counter {
public:
  Counter(const Counter_rep=NONE);
  char view() const;                        //As a character
private:
};
```

Note:　*As constructors are not inherited, any constructors in the base class which need*
　　　to be accessible need to called explicitly from a derived class constructor.

Again the member functions of the class are implemented in-line for efficiency:

```
inline Counter::Counter(const Counter_rep colour)
            : Basic_counter( colour )
{
}

inline char Counter::view() const
{
  switch ( colour() )
  {
    case WHITE : return 'o';
    case BLACK : return 'x';
    case NONE  : return ' ';
    default    : throw std::runtime_error("Counter::view");
                 return '?';   // Keep compiler happy
  }
}

#endif
```

Note:　*The construct* throw *is used to signal an internal consistency failure. This*
　　　construct throw is fully discussed in Chapter 14.

The implementation of the class Counter is:

```
#ifndef CLASS_COUNTER_IMP
#define CLASS_COUNTER_IMP
#include "Counter.h"

#endif
```

Note:　*As all the member functions of the class have been implemented in-line the*
　　　implementation file contains no code.

12.4.4   The class Basic_player

The specification for the class `Basic_player` is as follows:

```
#ifndef CLASS_BASIC_PLAYER_SPEC
#define CLASS_BASIC_PLAYER_SPEC

#include "Counter.h"

class Basic_player {
public:
  Basic_player( Counter );          //Player plays counter ...
  Counter counter_is() const;       //Return players counter
private:
  Counter the_players_counter;      //Plays with counter ...
};
```

The method `counter_is` is implemented in-line for efficiency:

```
inline Counter Basic_player::counter_is() const
{
  return the_players_counter;
}

#endif
```

The implementation of the class `Basic_player` is:

```
#ifndef CLASS_BASIC_PLAYER_IMP
#define CLASS_BASIC_PLAYER_IMP

#include "Basic_player.h"

Basic_player::Basic_player( Counter plays_with )
{
  the_players_counter = plays_with;
}

#endif
```

12.4.5   The class `Player`

The class `Basic_player` is specialized into the class `Player` which allows the player to input a move and display information about the game using the class `TUI`.

```
#ifndef CLASS_PLAYER_SPEC
#define CLASS_PLAYER_SPEC

#include "Basic_board.h"
#include "basic_player.h"
#include "TUI.h"

class Player : public Basic_player
{
public:
  Player( Counter );
  int  get_move(TUI&, const bool=false) const;        //Get Move
  void announce(TUI&, const Board::Game_result) const; //Result
private:
};
#endif
```

In the implementation of the class `Player` all I/O is performed via the class `TUI`.

```
#ifndef CLASS_PLAYER_IMP
#define CLASS_PLAYER_IMP

#include <string>
#include <stdexcept>
#include "Player.h"

Player::Player( Counter plays_with ) : Basic_player( plays_with )
{
}
```

Note: As constructors are not inherited, the constructor in the base class that has a parameter is called explicitly from the derived class constructor.

The method `get_move` uses the class `TUI` to perform the interaction with the real player in the outside world.

```
int Player::get_move(TUI& vdu, const bool repeat) const
{
  int move;
  if ( repeat )                               // Repeated request
    vdu.message("Invalid last choice");       //  Castigate
  std::string input = "Move for player ? is ";
  input[16] = counter_is().view();            // Set player
  vdu.dialogue( input, move );                // Ask for move
  return move-1;
}
```

Note: The expression `counter_is().view()` sends the message view to the object delivered by the method `counter_is`. The method `counter_is` is implemented in the class `Basic_player`.

The method `announce` announces the result of the game using the class `TUI`.

```
void Player::announce(TUI &vdu, const Board::Game_result what) const
{
  switch ( what )
  {
    case Board::WIN :
      {
      std::string result = "Player ? wins";
      result[7] = counter_is().view();
      vdu.message( result );
      }
      break;
    case Board::DRAW :
      vdu.message( "The game is a draw" );
      break;
    case Board::PLAYABLE :
      vdu.message( "The game is still playable" );
      break;
    default :
      throw std::runtime_error("Player::announce");
  }
}
#endif
```

*Note: The case PLAYABLE is never used, but is included in the code for completeness
and to facilitate any changes that may be made to how the game is played.*

12.4.6   The class `Cell`

The specification for an individual cell in the board is as follows:

```
#ifndef CLASS_CELL_SPEC
#define CLASS_CELL_SPEC

#include "Counter.h"

class Cell {
public:
  Cell();
  void clear();                              //Clear the cell
  void drop(const Counter c);                //Drop into cell
  Basic_counter::Counter_rep colour() const; //Counter colour
  const Counter& contents() const;           //Counter
private:
  Counter the_counter;                       //The counter
};
```

The constructor for `Cell` and the method `clear` use an instance of a counter initialized to NONE to indicate that the current cell does not contain a white or black counter.

The colour of this counter is examined by appropriate member functions. To make the implementation efficient, all of the member functions of `Cell` are made in-line.

```
inline Cell::Cell()
{
    the_counter = Counter(Basic_counter::NONE);
}
inline void Cell::clear()
{
    the_counter = Counter(Basic_counter::NONE);
}
```

The method `drop` adds a black or white counter to the cell.

```
inline void Cell::drop(const Counter c)
{
    the_counter = c;
}
```

The method `colour` returns the colour of the counter contained in the cell. A colour of NONE indicates that there is no counter in the cell.

```
inline Basic_counter::Counter_rep Cell::colour() const
{
    return the_counter.colour();
}
```

The method `contents` delivers a reference to the counter contained in the cell, to preserve encapsulation a `const` reference is delivered so that the counter cannot be modified.

```
inline const Counter& Cell::contents() const
{
    return the_counter;
}
#endif
```

The file which contains the implementation of the class `Cell` is defined as:

```
#ifndef CLASS_CELL_IMP
#define CLASS_CELL_IMP
#endif
```

Note: All the member functions of the class have been implemented in-line. Hence the implementation file contains no code.

12.4.7   The class `Basic_board`

The class `Basic_board` is by far the most complex class in the program. The complexity is derived from the need to ask an instance of `Board` about the current state of the game. In the implementation of `Basic_board` several protected member functions are added to facilitate:

- The implementation of the member function `display` in the derived class.

- The implementation of the member function `evaluate`.

```
#ifndef CLASS_BASIC_BOARD_SPEC
#define CLASS_BASIC_BOARD_SPEC

#include "Counter.h"
#include "Cell.h"

const int MAXROW       = 9;   //Maximum Rows
const int MAXCOLUMN    = 9;   //Maximum Columns

const int DEF_ROWS     = 6;   //Default number of rows
const int DEF_COLUMNS = 7;   //Default number of columns

const int STONES_IN_A_WIN_LINE = 4;

class Basic_board {
public:
  enum Game_result { DRAW, WIN, PLAYABLE };
  Basic_board(const int rows=DEF_ROWS,
              const int columns=DEF_COLUMNS);
  void reset(const int rows=DEF_ROWS,
              const int columns=DEF_COLUMNS);
  void drop_in_column( const int, const Counter);
  bool move_ok_for_column( const int ) const;
  Game_result evaluate() const;
protected:
  //Functional decomposition & inheritance
  int max_counters_in_line() const;
  int counters_in_dir( const int, const int, const int,
                       const Basic_counter::Counter_rep ) const;
  //For inheritance
  const Counter& contents( const int, const int ) const;
  int row_size() const;
  int column_size() const;
private:
  Cell the_grid[MAXROW][MAXCOLUMN]; //Basic_board played on
  int the_height[MAXCOLUMN];        //Height of counters col
  int the_row_size;
  int the_column_size;              //Size of playing area
  int the_last_col;
  int the_last_row;                 //Last counter placed
  int the_no_empty_cells;           //No. of cells still empty
};
```

Note: The use of protected member functions which are used internally by the class and are also available to an inheriting class.

Again for efficiency reasons, the member functions below have been implemented in-line. These member functions will be used in the implementation of `display` in the derived class `Board`.

```
inline const Counter& Basic_board::contents( const int r,
                                             const int c) const
{
  return the_grid[r][c].contents();
}

inline int Basic_board::row_size() const
{
  return the_row_size;
}

inline int Basic_board::column_size() const
{
  return the_column_size;
}
#endif
```

Note: The method `contents` *returns a* `const` *reference to a cell contained in the board.*

The implementation of `Board` is as follows:

```
#ifndef CLASS_BASIC_BOARD_IMP
#define CLASS_BASIC_BOARD_IMP

#include "Basic_board.h"
#include <stdexcept>

Basic_board::Basic_board(const int rows, const int columns)
{
  reset(rows,columns);
}
```

The method `reset` returns the board to a defined state in which all cells contain an invisible `Counter`.

```
void Basic_board::reset(const int rows, const int columns)
{
  the_row_size = rows; the_column_size=columns;
  for (int c=0; c<the_column_size; c++ )
  {
    for (int r=0; r<the_row_size; r++ )
    {
      the_grid[r][c].clear();
    }
    the_height[c] = 0;
  }
  the_last_row       = the_last_col   = 0;
  the_no_empty_cells = rows*columns;
}
```

The proposed move is validated by the member function `move_ok_for_column`.

```cpp
bool Basic_board::move_ok_for_column(const int column) const
{
  if ( column>=0 && column<the_column_size  )
  {
    if ( the_height[column] < the_row_size )
    {
      return true;
    }
  }
  return false;
}
```

The method `drop_in_column` records the new height of the selected column and then adds the counter c to this column. A pre-condition of using this member function is that the move has been validated by the member function `move_ok_for_column`.

```cpp
void Basic_board::drop_in_column(const int column, const Counter c)
{
  the_last_col = column; the_last_row = the_height[column];
  the_grid[ the_height[column] ][column].drop(c);
  the_height[column]++;
  the_no_empty_cells--;
}
```

The current state of the board is determined by the member function `evaluate`.

```cpp
Basic_board::Game_result Basic_board::evaluate() const
{
  return max_counters_in_line() >= STONES_IN_A_WIN_LINE ? WIN :
         (the_no_empty_cells == 0 ? DRAW : PLAYABLE );
}
```

The strategy for `max_counters_in_line` is to find the longest line of counters all of the same colour, starting from the position into which the last counter was dropped. This involves the recursive function `counters_in_dir` which counts the number of counters in the colour of the last move, made in a particular compass direction.

For any position on the board there are potentially eight directions to check. As a winning line will go through the current position, this will only involve checking four lines. Figure 12.4 illustrates the possible directions to check.

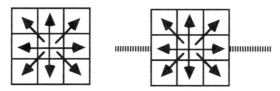

Figure 12.4 Directions to check when a move has been made.

Note: Each line is composed of two line segments which travel in opposite directions.

The member function `max_counters_in_line` adds together the number of counters in the two opposite directions, to form the number of counters in the longest continuous line.

```
int Basic_board::max_counters_in_line() const
{
    int max_counters = 0;
    Basic_counter::Counter_rep counter =
        the_grid[the_last_row][the_last_col].colour();
    if (counter==Basic_counter::NONE) return false;
    for( int dir=1; dir<=4; dir++)
    {
        int counters_in_a_line =
            counters_in_dir(dir,the_last_row,the_last_col,counter)+
            counters_in_dir(dir+4,the_last_row,the_last_col,counter)-1;
        if ( counters_in_a_line > max_counters )
            max_counters = counters_in_a_line;
    }
    return max_counters;
}
```

The code for `counters_in_dir` is recursive, returning either 0 if there are no more counters in the current direction, or 1 + the number of counters in the current direction starting from the next cell. Each time the function is entered a check is made to see if the position to be looked at is off the edge of the board.

```
int Basic_board::counters_in_dir( const int dir,
                const int r_cord, const int c_cord,
                const Basic_counter::Counter_rep counter) const
{
    int r = r_cord; int c= c_cord;
    if ( ( r >= 0 && r < the_row_size )     &&
        ( c >= 0 && c < the_column_size ) &&      //On the board
        ( the_grid[r][c].colour() == counter ) )  // players counter
    {
        switch ( dir )
        {
            case 1 :        c++; break;    //
            case 2 : r++; c++; break;    //    8   1   2
            case 3 : r++;      break;    //
            case 4 : r++; c--; break;    //    7   .   3
            case 5 :        c--; break;    //
            case 6 : r--; c--; break;    //    6   5   4
            case 7 : r--;      break;    //
            case 8 : r--; c++; break;
            default: throw std::runtime_error("Board::counters_in_dir");
        }
        return 1 + counters_in_dir( dir, r, c, counter );
    } else {
        return 0;
    }
}
#endif
```

Note: *The check used for the boundary of the board at the entry to the function.*
The default case in the case statement to capture internal errors. In testing the code this condition occurred.
The construct throw *is fully explained in chapter 14.*

12.4.8   The class Board

The class Board extends a Basic_board to allow the printing of the current state of the board to a text-based terminal.

```
#ifndef CLASS_BOARD
#define CLASS_BOARD

#include "Basic_board.h"

class Board : public Basic_board {
public:
  Board(const int rows=DEF_ROWS, const int columns=DEF_COLUMNS);
  void Board::display(TUI&) const;
private:
};

#endif
```

The implementation of the class Board is as follows:

```
#ifndef CLASS_BOARD_IMP
#define CLASS_BOARD_IMP

#include <iostream>
#include <strstream>
#include "Board.h"

Board::Board(const int rows, const int columns) :
            Basic_board( rows, columns )
{
}

void Board::display(TUI& vdu) const
{
  const int MAX_BUF = 500;              //Max size of text area
  char buf[MAX_BUF];                    //Holds written text
  ostrstream text(buf, MAX_BUF);        // as a string stream

  text << "  ";
  for (int c=1; c<=column_size(); c++)  //Board column number
    text << c << "   ";
  text << "\n";
```

After the headings to each column have been written out, the individual contents of each cell are displayed.

```
  for (int r=row_size()-1; r>=0; r-- )    //For each row in Board
  {
    text << "| ";
    for (int c=0; c<column_size(); c++ ) // For each column
    {
      text << contents(r,c).view();       //  write cell contents
      text << " | ";
    }
    text << "\n";                         //End of row
  }
  for (int c=1; c<=column_size(); c++)    //Bottom of board
    text << "----";
  text << "-" << "\n" << "\n" << '\0';    //

  vdu.message( text.str() );              //Write to TUI
}

#endif
```

Note: *Protected member functions in the class* `Basic_board` *are used to access the physical state of the board.*

12.4.9   Putting it all together

The main program sends the message `play` to an instance of the class Game.

```
#include "Game.h"

int main()
{
  Game().play();                          //Play
  return 0;
}
```

Note: `Game()` *delivers an instance of the class Game to which the message* `play` *is sent.*

A typical interaction is shown below:

Commentary and move	Board after move(s) has been made
After 5 moves player o drops their counter into column 2. `Move for player o is  :  `**`2`**	```1 2 3 4 5 6 7` `| | | | | | | |` `| | | | | | | |` `| | | | | | | |` `| | | | | | | |` `| | | | | x | | |` `| | o | x | o | o | x | |` `----------------------------`
Player x to go next and plays: `Move for player x is  :  `**`3`**	```1 2 3 4 5 6 7` `| | | | | | | |` `| | | | | | | |` `| | | | | | | |` `| | | x | | x | | |` `| | o | x | o | o | x | |` `----------------------------`
Player o plays a poor move: `Move for player o is  :  `**`3`** allowing x to play: `Move for player x is  :  `**`4`** This results in an unbeatable position for x.	```1 2 3 4 5 6 7` `| | | | | | | |` `| | | | | | | |` `| | | o | | | | |` `| | | x | x | x | | |` `| | o | x | o | o | x | |` `----------------------------`
Player o can only block one end of the row of three x's. `Move for player o is  :  `**`2`** Player x responds with the winning move: `Move for player x is  :  `**`6`**	```1 2 3 4 5 6 7` `| | | | | | | |` `| | | | | | | |` `| | | | | | | |` `| | | o | | | | |` `| | o | x | x | x | x | |` `| | o | x | o | o | x | |` `----------------------------` `Player x wins`

12.5   Self-assessment

- The method `get_move` in the class `Player` is an inspector method. Is this a good idea?

- Should the `player` class be able to see an instance of the board? Explain your answer.

- How easy would it be to modify the code for the game of four counters so that the game is played using a graphical interface? For example, to produce HTML output so that the results can be displayed by a web browser, or any other graphical interface known to you.

12.6   Exercises

● *Go back to previous move*
Modify the method `play` in the class `game` to allow a user to request the game to be restarted from a previous move.

Hint: Use an array of instances of `Board` that represent each previous move.

Construct the following class using inheritance:

● *Board_with_suggested_move*
A class which has all the methods of `Board` plus the additional method of `computers_move`. The additional responsibility of this class is:

Method	Responsibility
`computers_move`	Return a column number representing a good move for the computer to make.

Construct the following programs:

● *Computer game*
A program which plays the game of four counters between a human player and the computer.

● *Graphical C4*
A program which plays the game of four counters between a human player and the computer using a graphical interface on a web page.

● *Draughts*
A program which facilitates the playing of the game of draughts between two human players.

● *Reversi*
A program which facilitates the playing of the game of reversi between two human players.

13 Namespace

This chapter describes the namespace feature in C++. The Namespace directive allows the orderly management of names in the environment and helps prevent the overpopulation of the global namespace. The overpopulation or pollution of the global namespace is all too easy in a large C++ program.

13.1   Introduction to namespace

In a C++ program the names used in the program can be partitioned into several different namespaces. The standard library classes are usually in the namespace std. For example when using the class string the declaration is written as:

```
std::string name = "Corinna";
```

indicating that the name string is contained in the namespace std. The scope resolution operator is used to indicate that string is in the namespace std. Using namespaces thus helps prevent the pollution of the global namespace.

For example, a red oriented view of the world can be encapsulated in the namespace Red as follows:

```
#include <iostream>
#include <string>
```

```
namespace Red            //The red world
{
  std::string colour() { return "red"; }
  std::string fruit()  { return "strawberries"; }
}
```

whilst a blue view of the word can be encapsulated in the namespace Blue as follows:

```
namespace Blue           //The blue world
{
  std::string colour() { return "blue"; }
  std::string fruit()  { return "blueberries"; }
}
```

A name space is introduced into a program by means of the `using` keyword as follows:

```
int main()
{
  using namespace Red;
  std::cout << "My favourite colour is " << colour()
          << " and fruit is " << fruit() << "\n";
  return 0;
}
```

which when run would produce:

```
My favourite colour is red and fruit is strawberries
```

However, if the above code for `main` had been written as:

```
int main()
{
  using namespace Blue;
  std::cout << "My favourite colour is " << colour()
          << " and fruit is " << fruit() << "\n";
  return 0;
}
```

Then the result when executed would be:

```
My favourite colour is blue and fruit is blueberries
```

13.1.1   Scope of `using` directive

The scope of the `using` keyword is the scope of the unit in which it is used. In the previous examples, the keyword `using` is used inside a function so its scope is the function. Had it been used outside of any unit then its scope would be file scope. File scope is from the point at which the item is introduced to the end of the file, or the end of the file that included the file.

13.2   Selectively using names in different namespace

The scope resolution operator is used to introduce individual names from specific namespaces into a code sequence. For example, the following code uses functions from both the `red` and `blue` namespaces.

```
int main()
{
  using Blue::colour;
  using Red::fruit;
  std::cout << "My favourite colour is " << colour()
           << " and fruit is " << fruit() << "\n";
  return 0;
}
```

Note: The two forms of **using**

```
using Blue::colour;   // An item in the namespace
using namespace Blue; // All items in the namespace
```

Which when compiled and run produces the following output:

```
My favourite colour is blue and fruit is strawberries
```

Alternatively an item from a namespace can be explicitly accessed as follows:

```
int main()
{
  std::cout << "My favourite colour is " << Blue::colour()
           << " and fruit is " << Red::fruit() << "\n";
  return 0;
}
```

This is the approach taken when accessing items in the namespace std in the example programs shown in this book.

13.3 Nested namespaces

A namespace may itself contain other namespaces, as in the following example of a namespace for Pastel that contains the namespaces Yellow and Pink.

```
namespace Pastel         //The world of Pastel colours
{
  namespace Yellow
  {
    std::string colour() { return "light yellow"; }
    std::string fruit()  { return "banana"; }
  }
  namespace Pink
  {
    std::string colour() { return "light pink"; }
    std::string fruit()  { return "papaya"; }
  }
}
```

Which is used below, to select names from the two namespaces `Yellow` and Red.

```
int main()
{
  using Pastel::Yellow::colour;
  using Red::fruit;
  std::cout << "My favourite colour is " << colour()
          << " and fruit is " << fruit() << "\n";
  return 0;
}
```

Note: To include all names from the `Yellow` namespace the using directive:
      `using Pastal::Yellow;`
      would be used.

Which when run, produces the following output:

```
My favourite colour is light yellow and fruit is strawberries
```

13.4   Namespace alias

A name space may be aliased to another name, for example, an alias `Favourite` is created for the namespace `Pastal::Yellow` with the following declaration.

```
namespace Favourite=Pastal::Yellow;
```

Which would allow the following code:

```
int main()
{
  using namespace Favourite;
  std::cout << "My favourite colour is " << colour()
          << " and fruit is " << fruit() << "\n";
  return 0;
}
```

to be written. Which when compiled and run produces:

```
My favourite colour is light yellow and fruit is banana
```

13.5 Adding to a namespace

At all times other names may be added to a namespace using the `namespace` directive. For example, to add to the `Blue` namespace the following is used:

```
namespace Blue          //Add to the blue world
{
  std::string drink() { return "blue lagoon"; }
}
```

The namespace `Blue` is used in the normal way. For example, the following program:

```
int main()
{
  using namespace Blue;
  std::cout << "My favourite colour is " << colour() << "\n";
  std::cout << "My favourite fruit  is " << fruit()  << "\n";
  std::cout << "My favourite drink  is " << drink()  << "\n";
  return 0;
}
```

when compiled and run produces the following output:

```
My favourite colour is blue
My favourite fruit  is blueberries
My favourite drink  is blue lagoon
```

13.6 Self-assessment

- What is contained in the namespace `std`?

- How can the use of the namespace directive improve the maintainability of a program?

- How can a programmer use names selectively from several different namespaces?

13.7 Exercises

- Re-write the noughts and crosses program using the namespace `Games` for the class `Board`.

- Re-write the C4 Game program using the namespace `Games` for the classes in the program.

14 Exceptions

This chapter looks at the way errors and exceptions are handled by the C++ run-time system.

14.1 Exceptions

An exception is an event generated in a program in exceptional circumstances. For example, the failure to allocate storage for a data structure. The raised exception can be caught and the abnormal event handled in a sanitary fashion by the code which initiated this process. An exception is in effect a clean way for program code to abandon processing and return control to the calling code. The calling code has the responsibility of handling this exception in a clean way. If it does not capture the exception the exception is propagated up until either it is handled by user supplied code or the outer system exception handler. If the system exception handler captures the exception, the program is abandoned with an appropriate error message.

An exception is raised by the `throw` construct. For example, while processing user supplied data, the program code may abandon the process as insufficient storage is available to store an audit trail. The writer of this processing code raises an exception with the following statement:

```
throw "Too many items";
```

Note: In this particular case the code processing the data has throw a C++ string.

The caller of this code has the responsibility of capturing the exception. This is achieved by a `try` block as follows:

```
{
  try {
    //Some code
    throw "Too many items";
  }
  catch ( char exception_mes[] )
  {
    cout << "Fail: " << exception_mes << "\n";
  }
}
```

Note: The item thrown may be any instance of an inbuilt data type or user defined class.

The compiler generates a temporary copy of the thrown item, this temporary is then passed to the appropriate catch handler. A copy constructor may be required to make a safe copy of the object.

Any items constructed in the `try` *block will be destructed before the exception is handled. Only fully constructed items will be destructed. Thus raising an exception in a constructor is not advisable.*

In the above example, a C++ string is thrown. In C++ a string is represented by an array of characters. An array object is represented by the address of its first character. Thus if a local array had been the object thrown, the actual value thrown would have been a pointer to the first element of this local array. The storage for this local array which is allocated on the run-time stack will be released when the function is exited. If the code to catch the exception is not in the function, then the storage for the array will have been released before the `catch` code is executed. This will result in the exception handler processing undefined data values for the contents of the thrown array.

However, if a string constant is thrown this will be safe, as a string is held as a `static` data item in global storage. Hence the lifetime of a static data item is the lifetime of the program.

14.1.1   The exception classes

The following standard classes are provided, so that instances of the class may be thrown for specific types of error's. These classes are defined in the header file `<stdexcept>`.

Logical errors thrown: `logic_error`, `domain_error`, `invalid_argument`, `length_error` and `out_of_range`.

Run-time errors thrown: `runtime_error`, `range_error` and `overflow_error`.

Note: A class constant for these classes takes a string parameter which is to be associated with the exception. The method `what` *returns a* `C_str` *representing the text of this message.*

The classes are defined in the namespace `std`.

For example, to throw a run-time error the following code is used:

```
int main()
{
  try {

    if ( data_values > MAX_DATA_VALUES )
      throw std::runtime_error("Too many items");
  }
  catch ( std::runtime_error& err )
  {
    cout << "Fail: " << err.what() << "\n";
  }
  return 0;
}
```

which would produce the following output if the exception occurred:

```
Fail: Too many items
```

14.2   Capturing any exception

To capture any exception the statement `catch( ... )` is used. For example, the following code will capture a range error thrown by code called from within the `try` block plus any other exception which might occur.

```cpp
{
  try {
    //Some code

  }
  catch ( std::range_error& err )
  {
    std::cout << "Fail: " << err.what() << "\n";
  }
  catch ( ... )
  {
    std::cout << "Fail: An unexpected exception has occurred" << "\n";
  }
}
```

Note: The `catch( ... )` *statement must be the last of any* `catch` *statements.*

14.2.1   Capturing any exception derived from class `exception`

A catch block for the base class `exception` will match any exception derived from this class.

```cpp
try {
  //Some code

}
catch ( std::range_error& err )
{
  std::cout << "Fail: Range error: " << err.what() << "\n";
}
catch ( std::exception& err )
{
  std::cout << "Fail: Unexpected exception: " << err.what() << "\n";
}
catch ( ... )
{
  std::cout << "Fail: An unexpected exception has occurred" << "\n";
}
```

Note: The `catch ( ... )` *handler is still used to capture exceptions that do not use the standard exception classes.*

The advantage of capturing an unexpected exception in this way is that it may be interrogated for more information.

14.3   Specifying exceptions which may be propagated

When an exception is thrown and a handler is not available in the current function the exception will be propagated out to a potential handler in the code that called the function. However, in the definition of a function a list of exceptions that are to be propagated to the outside environment may be explicitly specified. For example, in the following function `twice`:

```
int twice(int) throw( std::overflow_error& );

//Only if 2's complement arithmetic is used is this code valid
//....

int twice( int n ) throw( std::overflow_error& )
{
  const max_int = ~( 1 << (sizeof(int)*8-1) );
  if ( n > ( max_int/2+1 ) )
   throw std::overflow_error("Number too big");
  return n + n;
}
```

Note: `const max_int = ~( 1 << (sizeof(int)*8-1) );`
will set `max_int` *to the largest positive representable number for an int in a 2's complement machine.*
If no throw specification is included with a function then all exceptions will be propagated to the outside environment,

the exception `overflow_error` may be propagated to the calling code of the function `twice`. However the function `trusting_twice` which is not allowed to propagate an exception is defined as:

```
int trusting_twice(int) throw();

int trusting_twice( int n ) throw()
{
  return twice( n );
}
```

Note: The `throw()` *in the specification of the function* `trusting_twice` *defines that no exceptions may be propagated out of the function.*

14.4   Putting it all together

The above function `trusting_twice` when compiled with suitable declarations and the following code:

```
int main()
{
  try {
    std::cout << "Twice 123   is " << trusting_twice(123)   << "\n";
    std::cout << "Twice 20000 is " << trusting_twice(20000) << "";
  }
  catch ( std::overflow_error& err )
  {
    std::cout << "Fail: " << err.what() << "\n";
  }
  return 0;
}
```

would produce output of the form:

```
Twice 123   is 246
Abnormal program termination
```

Note: The exception of an `overflow_error` will not be propagated out from the function `trusting_twice`. Instead the standard function `unexpected` is called to deliver a fatal error message onto the user's terminal.

14.5   Self-assessment

●   When should an exception be used, when should an exception not be used.

●   How may a programmer capture a thrown exception.

●   What problems can occur if the thrown object contains a pointer.

●   How is the exception generated by the expression `throw 2+3;` caught.

●   What happens when an exception is not caught by the program code.

●   Describe how a programmer can write a function which:
●   Will not propagate an exception.
●   Will generate a fatal error if the function attempts to propagate an exception.

14.6   Exercises

● *Store*

A random access store for data items whose specification is shown below:

Method	Responsibility
put	Adds a [key,data] pair to the store.
get	Using the supplied key retrieves the data item associated with the key from the data store.
contains	Returns true if the key is present in the data store.

```
#ifndef CLASS_STORE_SPEC
#define CLASS_STORE_SPEC

template <class Index_type, class Item_type, const int MAX=5>
class Store {
public:
  Store();
  void put( const Index_type key, const Item_type data);
  Item_type& get( const Index_type key );
  const Item_type& get( const Index_type key );
  bool contains( const Index_type key);
private:

};

#endif
```

In using an instance of this class the following exceptions may be generated.

Eventuality	Exception thrown
Item not stored	range_error("Not there")
Data store full	domain_error("Full")

15 Operator overloading

This chapter shows how operators in C++ may be overloaded with a new meaning. This is usually used in the context of a class, enabling the user to extend the language to manipulate instances of this class in a way specific to their needs.

15.1 Defining operators in C++

In defining a class to represent money, it would be convenient to be able to write:

```
Money i_have, gift;
i_have = i_have + gift;
```

rather than having to perform the add using a member function like:

```
i_have.add( gift );
```

There may in addition be cases when the user needs to redefine an existing operator so that the new definition overloads the existing meaning or meanings.

15.2 The class Money

For example, in a program which deals with money a new class Money could be defined which holds an amount of money in credits and pence. The operator + could then be overloaded to work between instances of class Money.

The responsibilities of the class Money are:

Method	Responsibility
print	Print the value.
+	Add together two money objects returning a new object.
++	Increment the 'pence' component by 1.

The C++ specification of this class is:

```
#ifndef CLASS_MONEY_SPEC
#define CLASS_MONEY_SPEC
#include <iostream>;
```

```
class Money {
public:
  Money( const long = 0, const int = 0 );  //Constructor
  Money operator + ( const Money );        //add operator
  Money operator ++();                      //prefix increment
  Money operator ++(int);                   //@postfix increment
  void print(std::ostream&);                //print
private:
  long the_credits;                         //In Units
  int  the_hundredths;                      //In Hundredths
};
#endif
```

Note: That there are two distinct definitions for ++; as a prefix operator and another as a postfix operator.

`Money operator ++();`	Definition of prefix ++.
`Money operator ++(int);`	Definition of postfix ++. Note the dummy parameter that is used to distinguish between the two cases.

Returning to the class `Money`, its constructor is defined as :

```
#ifndef CLASS_MONEY_IMP
#define CLASS_MONEY_IMP
#include "Money.h"

Money::Money( const long credits, const int pence )
{
  the_credits = credits; the_hundredths = pence;
}
```

The constructor has parameters defined with default values of 0 so that an instance of class `Money` may, if desired, be initialized to a predefined value rather than 0.

The member function `print` will display the value stored in an appropriate form for a monetary quantity to the selected output stream.

```
void Money::print(std::ostream& str)
{
  str << "#" << the_credits << "."
      << (the_hundredths < 10 ? "0" : "" )
      << the_hundredths;
}
```

The definition of an operator, in this case +, is very like the definition of a member function, except that instead of the name of the member function `operator + ` is specified.

```
Money Money::operator + ( const Money p1 )
{
  Money res;
  res.the_hundredths = p1.the_hundredths + the_hundredths;
  res.the_credits    = res.the_hundredths / 100;
  res.the_hundredths = res.the_hundredths % 100;
  res.the_credits    = res.the_credits + p1.the_credits + the_credits;
  return res;
}
```

Note: Even though + is a binary operator, only the second argument is specified because the compiler treats an expression involving instances of Money such as:

```
instance_of_money + another_instance_of_money
```

as

```
instance_of_money.operator+( another_instance_of_money );
```

It is of course permissible to use the second form of the expression, though this is rarely used in practice.

The code for the increment operators is as follows:

```
Money Money::operator ++()      //Prefix ++
{
  the_hundredths = the_hundredths + 1;
  the_credits    = the_credits + (the_hundredths / 100);
  the_hundredths = the_hundredths % 100;
  return *this;
}
```

```
Money Money::operator ++(int)   //Postfix ++
{
  Money res      = *this;
  the_hundredths = the_hundredths + 1;
  the_credits    = the_credits + (the_hundredths / 100);
  the_hundredths = the_hundredths % 100;
  return res;
}

#endif
```

15.2.1   `*this` the object to which a message is sent

In producing the code bodies for the overloaded operator ++, the actual instance of the class which the operator ++ operates on, must be returned as the result.

In a method `*this` is the instance of the class to which the message was sent. Why it is known as `*this` will be explained later in Chapter 17, where a full explanation of the monadic operator `*` is contained.

15.3   Declaration of instances of a class with an initial value(s)

In the above case of a class dealing with money, it might be convenient to be able to declare a new instance of the class `Money` which has a specified initial value #23.45.

This can be done as follows:

```
Money bill(23,45);
```

To make life even easier for the user, parameters which are omitted can be given a default value. So, to declare `revised_bill` with an initial value of #24.00 the following declaration can be used:

```
Money revised_bill(24);
```

or even

```
Money revised_bill = 24;
```

Note: This form of initialization can be prevented by declaring the constructor as `explicit`. *The keyword* `explicit` *is used to prevent implicit conversions of an item to an instance of* `Money`. *As in this case 24 is converted to an instance of class* `Money`.

If `bill` had been declared as:

```
Money bill;
```

then both parameters to the constructor `Money` would take their default values.

Note: When giving a parameter a default value, all other parameters to the right of it must also have a default value.

15.3.1   Putting it all together

The following fragment of code uses the class Money to calculate the amount of a bill:

```
#include <iostream>
#include "Money.h"

int main()
{
  Money ham_pizza(4,75), extra_cheese = Money(0,50);
  Money tuna_pizza = ham_pizza + Money(1);

  std::cout << "A ham pizza costs "; ham_pizza.print(std::cout);
  std::cout << "\n";
  std::cout << "A ham pizza with extra cheese costs ";
  (ham_pizza+extra_cheese).print(std::cout); cout << "\n";
  std::cout << "A tuna pizza costs "; tuna_pizza.print(std::cout);
  std::cout << "\n";
  return 0;
}
```

Note: The message print *is sent to the object created by the result of* ham_pizza+extra_cheese.

When compiled and run it will produce the following output:

```
A ham pizza costs #4.75
A ham pizza with extra cheese costs #5.25
A tuna pizza costs #5.75
```

15.4   Class constants

A class constant is an instance of a class which is used as a constant in a program. For example, the following fragment of code uses a class constant Money(1,0) to represent 1 unit of money.

```
Money tuna_pizza = ham_pizza + Money(1,0);
```

The expression Money(1,0) calls the constructor in the class Money to generate a temporary constant instance of the class Money. The lifetime of this class constant is implementation dependent.

Note: The compiler can use the constructor of the class Money to generate an implicit class constant. For example, in the expression:
    Money tuna_pizza = ham_pizza + 1;
    the integer 1 will be converted to the class constant Money(1,0).

15.4.1   Restrictions

In Section 15.2 the operator + was defined implicitly with a (Left Hand Side) LHS of type Money.

In most cases this will not be a problem. However, there will be cases when it is required to have a LHS that is not the same type as the class. This can be achieved using friend functions and will be described in the next section.

```
bill = bill + 1;   //Will compile
bill = 1 + bill;   //Will not compile as the LHS of +
                   //  is not of type Money
```

Note: The first case will work, as a constructor in Money is provided to turn an integer into an instance of the class Money.
bill = bill + 1;   =>   bill = bill.operator+(1).
However, the second case will fail to compile as the compiler treats this as:
bill = 1 + bill;   =>   bill = 1.operator+(bill).

15.4.2   Friend functions

The class for Money could have been defined as follows, using friend functions:

```
#ifndef CLASS_MONEY_SPEC
#define CLASS_MONEY_SPEC
#include <iostream>

class Money {
public:
  Money(const long = 0, const int = 0);
  void print(std::ostream&);                    //print
  friend Money operator + (const Money, const Money);
  friend Money operator ++(Money&);             //prefix increment
  friend Money operator ++(Money&, int);        //@postfix increment
private:
  long the_credits;                             //In Units
  int  the_hundredths;                          //In Hundredths
};

#endif
```

A friend function has the following main properties:

●   It is not a member of the class but is allowed to access members of the class as if it were a member. The implication of this is that is can access private and protected members in an instance of the class.

●   Both the LHS and the RHS of dyadic operator function are specified and both sides are subject to assignment compatible conversions.

● Assignment compatible conversions take effect if the conversion of the actual parameter to the type required is defined in the program. For example, there is a constructor to perform this action.

Note: As the friend functions are not members of the class Money, *they are not subject to the visibility access restrictions imposed in the class. In keeping with this 'unrestricted visibility' they are shown as* public *members.*

As can be seen when using a friend function the LHS of the operator is also specified in the parameter list to the overloaded operators + and ++.

```cpp
#ifndef CLASS_MONEY_IMP
#define CLASS_MONEY_IMP

Money::Money( const long credits, const int pence )
{
  the_credits = credits; the_hundredths = pence;
}

void Money::print(std::ostream& str)
{
  str << "#" << the_credits << "."
      << (the_hundredths < 10 ? "0" : "" )
      << the_hundredths;
}

Money operator + ( const Money p1, const Money p2 )
{
  Money res;
  res.the_hundredths = p1.the_hundredths + p2.the_hundredths;
  res.the_credits    = res.the_hundredths / 100;
  res.the_hundredths = res.the_hundredths % 100;
  res.the_credits    = res.the_credits + p1.the_credits + p2.the_credits;
  return res;
}

Money operator ++ ( Money& p1 ) //prefix ++
{
  p1.the_hundredths = p1.the_hundredths + 1;
  p1.the_credits    = p1.the_credits + (p1.the_hundredths / 100);
  p1.the_hundredths = p1.the_hundredths % 100;
  return p1;
}

Money operator ++ ( Money& p1, int) //Postfix
{
  Money res = p1;
  p1.the_hundredths = p1.the_hundredths + 1;
  p1.the_credits    = p1.the_credits + (p1.the_hundredths / 100);
  p1.the_hundredths = p1.the_hundredths % 100;
  return res;
}

#endif
```

Note: The operators + and ++ are not members of the class money, so when they are declared, the scope resolution operator is not required.

15.5 Use of friend functions

A friend function is a way of allowing a function to have all the privileges of membership of a class, without having to belong to that class. Thus, a friend function could in fact be a member of another class.

However, this escaping from strict type checking and data hiding can easily lead to programming errors.

Friend functions vs. member functions

Characteristics	Friend function	Member function
Access to all components of the class.	Yes	Yes
Specify all arguments to an operator function.	Yes	Specify only the RHS of a dyadic operator.
Arguments to the operator function subject to assignment compatible conversions.	Yes (either the LHS or the RHS)	Only the RHS of a dyadic operator.
A member of the class.	No	Yes

15.5.1 Friend classes

A whole class may be made a friend of another class by specifying its name as a friend class. For example, to make all members of a class visible to the class Account, the following line would be included in the class specification.

```
friend class Account;
```

15.5.2 Assignment compatible conversions

Using the revised class Money would now allow the following code to be written:

```
bill = 1 + Money(0,30) + 2;
```

Because + was defined as a friend function, its arguments are subject to assignment compatible conversions. In 1 + Money(0,30) the 1 is converted to type Money by using the constructor Money(const long=0,const int=0). The overloaded operator + can then be used to deliver the result of the addition.

Note: The above expression would involve the generation of several temporary class constants for Money.

15.5.3   Overloading of <<

A `friend` function can be defined in the class `Money` to overload the << operator so that output on an instance of Money may be performed in the C++ idiom.

The specification of the class now becomes:

```
#ifndef CLASS_MONEY_SPEC
#define CLASS_MONEY_SPEC
#include <iostream>

class Money {
public:
  Money( const long = 0, const int = 0 );
  friend Money operator + ( const Money, const Money );
  friend Money operator ++ ( Money& );        //prefix increment
  friend Money operator ++ ( Money&, int );//postfix increment
  friend std::ostream& operator << ( std::ostream& s, const Money m );
private:
  long the_credits;                           //In Units
  int  the_hundredths;                        //In hundredths
};
#endif
```

The overloaded operator << is defined as follows.

```
std::ostream& operator << ( std::ostream& s , const Money m )
{
  s << "#" << m.the_credits << "."
    << (m.the_hundredths < 10 ? "0" : "" )
    << m.the_hundredths;
  return s;
}
```

Note: << is overloaded so that the C++ style of output can be carried over to printing the contents of an item of type `Money`.

The function returns a reference to an object of type `ostream`, so that the overloaded operator can be used in expressions such as:

```
cout << "The value of the item is " <<  Money(9,99) << "\n";
```

Remember, the stream object passed as a parameter cannot be copied.

15.5.4   Putting it all together

Using the latest version of the class Money it is now possible to write:

```
//Final definition of the class Money
int main()
{
  Money ham_pizza(4,75), extra_cheese = Money(0,50);
  Money tuna_pizza = ham_pizza + 1;

  std::cout << "A ham pizza costs " << ham_pizza << "\n";
  std::cout << "A ham pizza with extra cheese costs " <<
             (ham_pizza+extra_cheese) << "\n";
  std::cout << "A tuna pizza costs " << tuna_pizza << "\n";
  return 0;
}
```

When run, this produces the following output:

```
A ham pizza costs #4.75
A ham pizza with extra cheese costs #5.25
A tuna pizza costs #5.75
```

15.5.5   Functional notation for overloaded operators

Overloaded operators can be expressed, using a functional notation. For example, the overloaded operators + and ++ in the class Money are defined by the following specification:

```
Money operator + ( const Money );      //add operator
Money operator ++();                    //prefix increment
Money operator ++(int);                 //@postfix increment
```

Using functional notation, the programmer could write:

```
Money prefix,postfix,sum,cheese,onion;

prefix.operator++();                    //++prefix
postfix.operator++(1);                  //postfix++
sum = cheese.operator+(onion);          //sum = cheese + onion
```

Note: Normally this syntax would not be used. However, there are circumstances when it becomes necessary to use an overloaded operator hidden by a current definition. In these cases, the functional notation, combined with the scope modification operator, allows the hidden function to be accessed.

Alternatively, if the same operations in the class had the following specification:

```
friend Money operator + ( const Money, const Money );
friend Money operator ++ ( Money& );       //prefix increment
friend Money operator ++ ( Money&, int );//postfix increment
```

functional notation could be used to write

```
Money prefix,postfix,sum,cheese,onion;

operator++(prefix);                //++prefix
operator++(postfix,1);             //postfix++
sum = operator+(cheese,onion);     //sum = cheese + onion
```

Note: The extra parameter, in this case 1 to distinguish the postfix and prefix cases of the overloaded operator ++.

15.6   Restrictions on overloading operators

Only existing operators in the language can be used for the definition of a new operator. As the definer of the operator cannot specify an operator precedence, the operators retain their original precedence.

All operators (See Appendix J) can be overloaded except for:

> .   .*   ::   ? :

When an operator is overloaded, at least one of the operands must be an instance of either:

- A class type or reference to a class type.
- An Enumeration type, or reference to enumeration type.

This prevents, the overloading of the inbuilt definition for + between two `int` operands.

15.7   Conversion operators

In earlier examples, an instance of a class has been copied from one storage location to another using the assignment operator. This has involved simply copying the storage represented by the instance of the class to a new memory location.

Note: It will be shown later in Chapter 23 how to overload the assignment operator, so that effects other than simply copying the contents of the instance of the class can be specified.

Using the class `Money` the following code can be written:

```
Money mine,yours;

mine  = Money( 10,50 )
yours = mine;
```

If classes for `Pounds` and Swiss `Francs` existed it would be convenient to be able to write:

```
Pounds to_spend(10,50);      //Have in Brighton
Francs holiday_money;        //Will have in Swiss Francs

holiday_money = to_spend;

std::cout << "Holiday money = " << holiday_money << "\n";
```

The value delivered by `to_spend` depends on the value expected. In the above case the value expected from `to_spend` is the amount in Swiss Francs. Likewise it would be convenient to use a cast to covert between currencies. For example, to convert from Swiss `Francs` to `Dollars` the programmer could write:

```
std::cout << "Holiday money = " << (Francs) to_spend << "\n";
```

To achieve this, a conversion operator is defined in the class `Pounds`, which contains code which will convert between the different types of objects. In the above example of a currency transaction, the operator would simply use the prevailing exchange rate between the two currencies.

15.7.1   Specification and implementation of a conversion operator

A conversion operator in the class `Pounds` which converts an object of type `Pounds` to an object of type `Francs` is specified as follows:

```
class Pounds
{
public:
  operator Francs() const;      //Conversion operator Francs

};
```

and implemented as

```
Pounds::operator Francs() const
{
  long francs; int centime;
  // Conversion to Francs and centime's from Pounds and pence
  return Francs( francs, centime );
}
```

Note: This assumes that there is a constructor in the class Francs to construct an instance of Francs from an amount in Francs and centimes.

15.8   The class Money as a base class

In building a program to work in Dollars, Swiss Francs and Pounds the inheritance structure as illustrated in Figure 15.1 will be used.

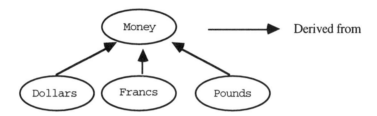

Figure 15.1 Class hierarchy for Dollars, Swiss Francs and Pounds.

The original class Money, however cannot be used for the following reasons:

- Friend functions are not inherited. This means that if + is used between objects of type Pounds, the operands will have to be converted to type Money before the friend function in the class Money can be used. In addition the result will have to be converted back to type Pounds. Whilst this is possible, many needless conversions will be generated.

- The return type in an inherited function is not changed to the type of the inheriting class.
  For example, the function in the class Money with the following signature
    ```
    Money operator+( Money )
    ```
  would be inherited in Pounds as
    ```
    Money operator+( Pounds ).
    ```

For these reasons a new class Money will be developed. The C++ specification for this new class Money is as follows:

```
#ifndef CLASS_MONEY_SPEC
#define CLASS_MONEY_SPEC

class Money {
public:
  explicit Money( const long = 0L, const int = 0 );
  static void add( Money& , Money, Money );
  friend std::ostream& operator << (std::ostream&, const Money);
  long units() const;              //return the units
  int hundredths() const;          //return the hundredths
private:
  long the_credits;                //In Units
  int  the_hundredths;             //In Pence
};
```

Note: Only the method to implement add is shown to save space.
       Rather than implementing the add function as an operator it is implemented as a static void function taking three parameters. To implement, the expression:

```
cost = #10.50 + #5.60;
```

this would be coded as

```
Money cost; Money::add( cost, Money(10, 50), Money(5,60) );
```

The reason for the choice of this implementation technique is discussed later in Section 15.8.3.

15.8.1 Constructor prefix `explicit`

The prefix `explicit` in the specification of the constructor prevents assignment compatible conversions taking place when constructing an instance of the class `Money`. However, calling the constructor directly will not be affected. For example, the assignment of `10L` to an instance of `Money` will now fail.

```
Money to_spend  = 10L;     // Error!
                           // Cannot covert long to Money
Money to_spend( 1, 'a' );  // Ok by compiler (But dubious)
```

Note: That the dubious use of the call of Money's constructor in `to_spend(1,'a')` will still compile.

15.8.2 Implementation of the new class for `Money`

The following methods are implemented as inline functions for efficiency reasons. Hence they are defined in the same file as the specification of the class.

```
inline Money::Money( const long credits, const int pence )
{
  the_credits = credits; the_hundredths = pence;
}

inline long Money::units() const
{
  return the_credits;
}

inline int Money::hundredths() const
{
  return the_hundredths;
}

#endif
```

The rest of the implementation of the class Money which may be separately compiled is implemented as:

```
#ifndef CLASS_MONEY_IMP
#define CLASS_MONEY_IMP

void Money::add( Money& res, Money lhs, Money rhs)
{
  res.the_hundredths = lhs.the_hundredths + rhs.the_hundredths;
  res.the_credits    = res.the_hundredths / 100;
  res.the_hundredths = res.the_hundredths % 100;
  res.the_credits    = res.the_credits +
                       lhs.the_credits + rhs.the_credits;
}

ostream& operator << ( std::ostream& s, const Money m )
{
  s << "#" << m.units()
    << "." << (m.hundredths() < 10 ? "0" : "" )
    << m.hundredths();
  return s;
}

#endif
```

The C++ specification of the derived class Pounds is:

```
#ifndef CLASS_POUNDS_SPEC
#define CLASS_POUNDS_SPEC

class Pounds : public Money {
public:
  static void prelude( const double, const double );
  explicit Pounds( const long = 0L, const int = 0 );
  operator Dollars() const;        //Conversion operator Dollars
  operator Francs() const;         //Conversion operator Francs
  friend std::ostream& operator << ( std::ostream& s, Pounds m );
```

```
private:
  static double the_dollar_rate;    //Dollar rate
  static double the_franc_rate;     //Franc rate
};

#endif
```

By using inheritance, all the member methods from Money will be incorporated into the new class Pounds. The only methods that need to be supplied are the conversion operators to Swiss Francs and Dollars, a few constructors, and the overloaded output operator <<.

Note: The syntax for the specification of a conversion operator is very similar to the syntax for the specification of an overloaded operator.

The code for the constructors in the class Pounds, the prelude function and the overloaded operator << are as follows:

```
#ifndef CLASS_POUNDS_IMP
#define CLASS_POUNDS_IMP

#include <math>

double Pounds::the_dollar_rate = 1.0;
double Pounds::the_franc_rate  = 1.0;

Pounds::Pounds( const long pounds, const int pence ) :
     Money( pounds, pence )
{
}

void Pounds::prelude( const double dollar_rate, const double franc_rate
)
{
  the_dollar_rate = dollar_rate;
  the_franc_rate  = franc_rate;
}

std::ostream& operator << ( std::ostream& s, Pounds m )
{
  s << "£" << m.units() << "."
    << (m.hundredths() < 10 ? "0" : "" )
    << m.hundredths();
  return s;
}
```

The conversion operators below convert the value held in the class Pounds to Dollars and Swiss Francs respectively.

```
Francs::operator Dollars() const
{
  long cents = (long) floor( the_dollar_rate * hundredths() +
                             the_dollar_rate * units() * 100.0 + 0.5);
  long dollars = cents / 100;
  cents        = cents % 100;
  return Dollars( dollars, cents );
}

Francs::operator Pounds() const
{
  long pence  = (long) floor( the_pound_rate * hundredths() +
                              the_pound_rate * units() * 100.0 + 0.5 );
  long pounds = pence / 100;
  pence       = pence % 100;
  return Pounds( pounds, pence );
}

#endif
```

This code will be called whenever an instance of class `Pounds` is required to deliver an object of type `Dollars` or Swiss Francs.

Note: The use of the library function floor (prototype in <maths>). This delivers the largest double which is smaller than its double argument.
This assumes perhaps naively that the double value can be converted into a long. *It might have been better to have used* typedef *to define a new type which could represent the Swiss Francs, centimes, etc.*

The code for the classes `Francs` and `Dollars` are developed in a similar way.

15.8.3 Providing the operator + interface to the **add** method

The interface for the addition of `Pounds`, `Dollars` or Swiss `Francs` as implemented is not very elegant. The user of the class `Pounds` for example, would need to write:

```
int main()
{
  Pounds camera(60,0);
  Pounds bag(10,0);
  std::cout << "Cost of camera + bag is "
  Pounds res; Pounds::add( res, camera, bag );
  std::cout << res << "\n";
  return 0;
}
```

By providing the template function:

```
template <class Type>
inline Type operator + ( Type lhs, Type rhs )
{
  Type res;
  Type::add( res, lhs, rhs );
  return res;
}
```

A user of the class Pounds can now write:

```
int main()
{
  Pounds camera(60,0);
  Pounds bag(10,0);
  std::cout << "Cost of camera + bag is " << camera + bag << "\n;
  return 0;
}
```

In addition to this template function the following templated functions are provided to allow an instance of Pounds to be added to an Integer value.

```
template <class Type>
inline Type operator + ( Type lhs, int rhs )
{
  Type res;
  Type::add( res, lhs, Type(rhs) );
  return res;
}
template <class Type>
inline Type operator + ( int lhs, Type rhs )
{
  Type res;
  Type::add( res, Type(lhs), rhs );
  return res;
}
```

Note: This will result in a rather unusual error message if a user wrote:

```
object = object + 1;
```

where object is an instance of a class Object which does not provide either:
* *an overload + operator*
* *a function with the signature add(Object, Object, Object)*
and a constructor to turn an integer into an instance of Object.

15.8.4 Putting it all together

The following program illustrates the use of conversion operators implemented in the classes `Dollars`, `Pounds` and `France`. Firstly, the various currency conversion rates are set up.

```
void process();

int main()
{
  const double Dollar_Pound_rate = 0.6105;    //Dollars -> Pound
  const double Dollar_Franc_rate = 1.4613;    //Dollars -> Swiss Francs

  Dollars::prelude( Dollar_Pound_rate, Dollar_Franc_rate );

  //The money market would have precise rates which would
  //allow a small profit on conversions

  const double Pound_Dollar_rate= 1/Dollar_Pound_rate;
  const double Pound_Franc_rate = Pound_Dollar_rate* Dollar_Franc_rate;

  Pounds::prelude( Pound_Dollar_rate, Pound_Franc_rate );

  const double Franc_Dollar_rate= 1/Pound_Franc_rate*Pound_Dollar_rate;
  const double Franc_Pound_rate = 1/Pound_Franc_rate;

  Francs::prelude( Franc_Dollar_rate, Franc_Pound_rate );

  process();
  return 0;
}
```

Then the following conversions are performed to show how much US $100.00 is worth in Swiss Francs and UK Pounds.

```
void process()
{
  Dollars to_pay(100,0);
  cout << "Amount to pay  = " << to_pay << "\n";
  cout << "Amount to pay  = " << (Pounds) to_pay << "\n";
  cout << "Amount to pay  = " << (Francs) to_pay << "\n";
}
```

When compiled with the classes `Pounds`, `Dollars` and `Swiss Francs` would produce the following results:

```
Amount to pay  = $100.00
Amount to pay  = £61.05
Amount to pay  = SF146.13
```

The normal + operator may be used as illustrated in the revised program to calculate the price of different pizzas.

```
int main()
{
  Dollars ham_pizza(4,75);
  Dollars extra_cheese = Dollars(0,50);
  Dollars tuna_pizza = ham_pizza + 1;

  std::cout << "A ham pizza costs " << ham_pizza << "\n";
  std::cout << "A ham pizza with extra cheese costs " <<
              (ham_pizza+extra_cheese) << "\n";
  std::cout << "A tuna pizza costs " << tuna_pizza << "\n";
  return 0;
}
```

When compiled with the class `Dollars` and the template functions for the operator + would produce the following results:

```
A ham pizza costs $4.75
A ham pizza with extra cheese costs $5.25
A tuna pizza costs $5.75
```

15.9   Initializing arrays of objects

When a constructor in a class has parameters (e.g. class `Dollars`), an array of objects of this class may be initialized as follows:

```
Dollars  prices[4] = { 1, Dollars(2,50), 3 };
```

Note: *If the initializers are not all provided, then the default constructor (in this case `Dollars()` would be used).*
A constructor will be used to turn the `int`s 1 and 3 into an object of type `Dollars`.

15.9.1   Inherited operators

The table below summarizes the properties of member operators.

Operator	Inherited	Created by default
() [] ->	Yes	No
=	No	Yes (member by member copy)
The rest (see note)	Yes	No
Conversion	Yes	No

Note: *The operators `new` and `delete` are described in Chapter 17 and the overloading of the operator = in Chapter 23.*

15.10 Self-assessment

●   What operators can be overloaded with a new meaning in C++?

●   Can the operator + be redefined to have a new meaning when both operands are of type `int`?

●   Can a user invent new operators? For example, could a user define the monadic operator +++ to add two to an integer?

●   Why might excessive use of overloading the standard operators lead to a program that is difficult to follow?

15.11 Exercises

Construct the following classes

●   *Imperial_Weight*
A class that stores a weight in the old English imperial units of pounds and ounces. In this system there are 16 ounces in each pound. Thus the following fragment of code:

```
Imperial_Weight apples  = Imperial_Weight(2, 4);
Imperial_Weight oranges = Imperial_Weight(3, 14);
std::cout << "Combined weight is: " << apples + oranges << "\n";
```

would produce the following output:

```
Combined weight is: 6 Pounds 2 ounces
```

●   *Number*
The class number that holds an integer number to a precision of 200 digits. This allows the following code to be written:

```
Number  large = Number("1_000_000_000_000_000_000_000_000_000");

large = large + 1;
```

The constructor for the class can take either a `long`, `int` or `string` parameter. If a string is used to initialize the number then the underscore character can be used to break up the digits to make the number more readable.

One approach to solving this problem is to hold the number in decimal form in an array. The overloaded operator + then implements the arithmetic operation by adding together individually each digit in its two operands to form the result.

16 Polymorphism

In the processes described so far, when a message is sent to an object, the method executed has been determinable at compile-time. This is referred to as static binding. If however, the type of object is unknown at compile-time then the binding between the method and the message is deferred until run-time. Dynamic binding leads to polymorphism, which is when a message sent to an object causes the execution of a method that is dependent on the type of the object.

16.1 Rooms in a building

A partial classification of the different types of accommodation found in an office building is shown in Figure 16.1.

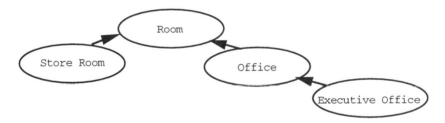

Figure 16.1 Partial classification of types of accommodation in a building.

The type of accommodation in each part of the building can be modelled using the C++ inheritance mechanism. First, a class Room to describe a general room is created. This class is then used as the base class for a series of derived classes that represent more specialized types of room. For example, an executive office is a more luxurious office, perhaps with wall-to-wall carpets and an outside view.

Each class derived from the class Room, including Room, has a function describe which returns a description of the accommodation.

A program is able to send the message describe to an instance of any type of accommodation and have the appropriate code executed. This is accomplished with function name overriding.

Figure 16.2 illustrates the call of a function describe on an instance of a class derived from Room.

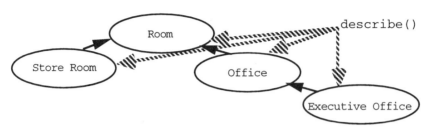

Figure 16.2 Call of `describe` on any instance of an object derived from Room.

16.1.1   Dynamic binding

So far the binding between a message and a method in an object has been resolved at compile-time. Figure 16.3 illustrates the sending of a message to an object.

```
Object

┌─────────────────────────┐            Message
│  std::string describe() │
│  {                      │            describe()
│     return the_use;     │  ◄─────────────────────
│  }                      │
├─────────────────────────┤
│  the_use                │
└─────────────────────────┘
```

Figure 16.3 Sending the message `describe` to an object.

The binding between the message and the method may however, be deferred to run-time, if the type of the object is unknown at compile time. This can occur when the object is a member of a collection which contains objects of many different types or the object is the formal parameter to a function whose actual parameter has been passed by reference. The exact details of these two special cases will be explained later.

The sending of a message to an object is implemented by a call to the member function (representing the method) in the objects class. Dynamic binding to a member function is requested by prefixing the specification of the function with the keyword `virtual`.

16.2   The classes for `Office` and `Room`

The responsibilities of a Room are as follows:

Method	Responsibility
`describe`	Deliver a string containing a description of the room.
`room_number`	Deliver the room's number.
`use`	Deliver the room use
`Room`	Set up information about the state of a particular room.

The C++ specification for this class is shown below:

```
#ifndef CLASS_ROOM_SPEC
#define CLASS_ROOM_SPEC

#include <string>                      //C++ string class

class Room {
public:
  Room(const int=0, const std::string = "");
  virtual ~Room();
  virtual std::string describe() const;     //Describe the room
  int room_number() const;                  //The room number
  std::string use() const;                  //The room use
private:
  int          the_room_number;             //Room number
  std::string the_use;                      //Use of room
};
#endif
```

The member function describe and the destructor ~Room are prefixed with the keyword virtual. The keyword virtual instructs the compiler to use dynamic binding when either of these methods is called. The full consequences of this will become apparent when a new class is derived from the class Room.

Note: When a method in a class is described as virtual *the destructor in the class should also be described as* virtual. *The reason for this is fully explained in Section 16.4.2.*

The implementation of the class Room is:

```
#ifndef CLASS_ROOM_IMP
#define CLASS_ROOM_IMP

Room::Room(const int number, const std::string use )
{
  the_room_number = number;
  the_use         = use;
}

Room::~Room()
{
}

int Room::room_number() const
{
  return the_room_number;
}

std::string Room::use() const
{
  return the_use;
}
```

```
std::string Room::describe() const
{
  return the_use;
}

#endif
```

The responsibilities of an `Office` are those of the `Room` plus:

Method	Responsibility
describe	Returns a string describing an office.
Office	Set up information about the state of a particular office.

The specification for a class `Office` extends the specification for a class `Room` as follows:

```
#ifndef CLASS_OFFICE_SPEC
#define CLASS_OFFICE_SPEC

#include <string>                   //C++ string class
#include <Room.h>
class Office :public Room {
public:
  Office(const int=0, const std::string="", const int=0);
  std::string describe() const;
  int occupiers() const;
private:
  int the_occupiers;              //Number of occupiers
};
#endif
```

In the implementation of the class `Office` the constructor for an `Office` calls explicitly the constructor for a `Room`. This is so the physical room number and description can be passed to the constructor in `Room`.

```
#ifndef CLASS_OFFICE_IMP
#define CLASS_OFFICE_IMP

#include <iostream>          //Normal I/O
#include <strstream>

Office::Office(const int number, const std::string use,
               const int occupiers) : Room(number,use)
{
  the_occupiers = occupiers;
}
```

The function `describe` is overridden with a new meaning which returns details about an office.

```
std::string Office::describe() const
{
  const int MAX_BUF = 100;              //Max size of text area
  char buf[MAX_BUF];                    //Holds written text
  std::ostrstream s(buf, MAX_BUF);      //s is a string stream
  s << use();
  s << " occupied by " << the_occupiers;
  s << " people ";
  s << '\0';
  return std::string( buf );
}
```

The function `occupiers` returns the number of people in the office.

```
int Office::occupiers() const
{
  return the_occupiers;
}
#endif
```

Note: The use of the string stream class `ostrstream` *which is used in the creation of the description of an office.*

16.2.1   Putting it all together

The above classes can be combined into a program which prints details about various rooms or offices in a building. The program is as follows:

```
void about( Room &accommodation )
{
  std::cout << "Room " << accommodation.room_number() << " : ";
  std::cout << accommodation.describe();
  std::cout <<  "\n";
}

int main()
{
  Room            w420(420,"Reception");
  Office          w414(414,"QA",4);

  about( w420 );
  about( w414 );
  return 0;
}
```

The function `about` can take either an instance of the class `Room` or an `Office` as its single parameter. This is achieved by describing the formal parameter as `Room&`. A formal parameter of type `Room&` will match an instance of `Room` or an instance of any type which is derived directly or indirectly from a `Room`. This concession to the strict type checking of C++ will help facilitate the deferring of the binding between a message and a method until run-time. Remember a reference to an object will be implemented as the objects address in memory.

The call to the member function `describe()` in the function `about` is not resolvable at compile-time, as the object passed and represented by the formal parameter `place` may be either an instance of a `Room` or an instance of an `Office`. At run-time when the type of `place` is known by the executing program, this call can be resolved. Thus, either `describe` in the class `Room` or `describe` in the class `Office` will be called.

Note: One way to implement the dynamic binding is for the object to contain information about which function `describe` is to be called. This information can then be interrogated at run-time to allow the appropriate version of the function `describe` to be executed. By careful optimization, the overhead of dynamic binding can be limited to a few machine cycles.

When run, this program will produce the following output:

```
Room 420 : Reception
Room 414 : QA occupied by 4 people
```

16.3   Heterogeneous collections of objects

The real benefits of polymorphism accrue when a heterogeneous collection of related items is created. For example, a program which maintains details about accommodation in a building could use an array to hold objects which represent the different types of accommodation. Unfortunately, this technique cannot be implemented directly in C++, as the size of individual members of the collection may vary. The solution in C++ is to use an array of pointers to the different kinds of object which represent the accommodation. In C++, a pointer is usually implemented as the physical address in memory of the referenced object. An array of pointers to objects of type `Room` and `Office` is illustrated in Figure 16.4.

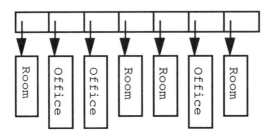

Figure 16.4 Heterogeneous collection of `Room`s and `Office`s.

16.3.1   An array as a heterogeneous collection

A heterogeneous collection of different types of accommodation can be modelled in an array. The array will contain for each type of accommodation a pointer to either an instance of a Room or an instance of an Office. For example, the following array declaration defines an array the_rooms which can hold pointers to an instance of a Room or an instance of any class which is derived from a Room.

```
Room *the_rooms[MAX];                    //Heterogeneous collection
```

Note: In C++ an object of type Room can be assigned a pointer to an instance of a Room or a pointer to any object which is an instance of a class derived from a Room.*

The heterogeneous collection is then built by assigning to individual elements of the array pointers to the various objects that represent the types of accommodation in the building. For example, to enter details about room 420 into the heterogeneous array, the following code is used.

```
the_rooms[0] = new Room(420,"Reception")
```

The operator new allocates storage for a class constant of type Room. However, this storage must be explicitly returned by using the operator delete. If this is not done, then the storage will stay in existence till the program terminates.

16.4   A building information program

A class Building, which is used as a container to store and retrieve details about the accommodation in a building, has the following responsibilities:

Method	Responsibility
add	Add a description of a room.
about	Return a description of a specific room.

The C++ specification for the class Building is:

```
#ifndef CLASS_BUILDING_SPEC
#define CLASS_BUILDING_SPEC

#include <string>
```

```
class Building {
public:
  Building();
  ~Building();
  std::string about(const int) const;      //Describe the room
  void add(Room*);                         //Add a room
private:
  static const int MAX=20;
  Room *the_rooms[MAX];                    //Heterogeneous collection
  int    the_next_free;                    //Next free Room
};

#endif
```

The constructor for the class, simply sets the_next_free, the next free entry in the array the_rooms to be 0.

```
#ifndef CLASS_BUILDING_IMP
#define CLASS_BUILDING_IMP
#include "Building.h"

Building::Building()
{
  the_next_free=0;
}
```

As the collection is represented by storage claimed by the operator new the storage must be explicitly returned by the operator delete. The destructor for the class Building performs this function.

```
Building::~Building()
{
  for ( int i=0; i<the_next_free; i++ )  //Return storage
  {
    delete the_rooms[i];
  }
}
```

The function add adds new data to the next available position in the array.

```
void Building::add(Room* a_room )
{
  if ( the_next_free < MAX )
  {
    the_rooms[ the_next_free++ ] = a_room;    //Save
    return;
  }
  throw std::range_error("No room");
}
```

Note: The exception range_error is raised if there is no more free space in the array.

The function about uses a linear search to find the selected room number. If the room number does not exist, the returned string contains the text "Sorry room not known".

```
std::string Building::about(const int room ) const
{
  if ( the_next_free > 0 )
  {
    for ( int i=0; i<the_next_free; i++ )
    {
      if ( the_rooms[i]->room_number() == room )
        return the_rooms[i]->describe();
    }
  }
  return "Sorry room not known";
}

#endif
```

16.4.1 Putting it all together

The classes Room, Office and Building can be used to build a program to allow visitors to a building to find out details about individual rooms. A simple test program for this would be:

```
// Include specs for Building Room Office

void populate(Building& block)
{
  block.add( new Room(420,"Reception") );
  block.add( new Office(414,"QA",4) );
}

int main()
{
  try
  {
    Building watts;
    int       room;
    populate( watts );                     // Populate building
    while ( std::cout << "Room number: ",
            std::cin >> room,
            !std::cin.eof() )
    {
      std::cout << "Room " << room << " : "
              << watts.about( room ) << "\n";
    }
  }
  catch ( std::range_error& err )
  {
    std::cout << "\n" << "Fail: " << err.what() << "\n";
  }
  return 0;
}
```

An example interaction using the program would be as follows:

```
Room number: 414
Room 414 : QA occupied by 4 people
Room number: 420
Room 420 : Reception
Room number: 500
Room 500 : Sorry room not known
```

16.4.2   Destructors and polymorphism

When the storage for the instance of a class item is released, the destructor for it and all its base classes is called. For example, if the storage for an instance of the class Office is released, then the destructor in Room will be called.

When an instance of a class is created dynamically with new, and the pointer to the object is assigned to an item of type pointer to the base class, then the base class destructor must be declared virtual, otherwise only the destructor in the base class will be called when the instance of the class is destroyed. The concepts behind pointers and dynamic storage relevant to the creation of instances of a class, are covered in the next chapter.

The simplest strategy is always to declare a virtual destructor in any base class that has virtual member functions.

16.5   Advantages and disadvantages of polymorphism

Advantages

Additions and modifications to a program are simplified. For example, in the bank account program in Section 8.10 the introduction of a new type of account would simply require the creation of a new derived class. The code which deals with the general processing of the transactions on that account, need not change.

In essence, this should mean that changes to the program are encapsulated in any new class which is implemented. This does, however, pre-suppose that the program has been written with enhancement and extensibility in mind.

Disadvantages

There is a code overhead each time dynamic binding is used. The reason for this overhead is that the location (address) of the member function to be called must be resolved at run-time, rather than compile time.

The use of virtual functions may well involve the use of pointers, which are discussed more fully in the following chapter on pointers.

16.6 Program maintenance and polymorphism

To modify the above program so that details about executive offices in the building are also displayed would involve the following changes:

● The creation of a new derived class `Executive_office`.

● Adding extra code to populate the building with instances of an `Executive_office`.

No other components of the program would need to be changed. In carrying out these modifications, the following points are evident:

● Changes are localized to specific parts of the program.

● The modifier of the program does not have to understand all the details of the program to carry out maintenance.

● Maintenance will be easier.

Thus, if a program using polymorphism is carefully designed, there can be considerable cost saving when the program is maintained/updated.

16.6 Virtual items in a class

The table below summarizes the components in a class that can be virtual.

Item in class	Can be virtual
The constructors	✗
The destructor	✓
operators (see note)	✓
conversion operators	✓
member functions	✓
friend functions	✗

Note: *The operators new and delete which cannot be virtual are described in Chapter 17.*
If any member function in a class is virtual then it is advisable to make the destructor virtual as well.

16.7   Self-assessment

- What is the difference between static and dynamic binding?

- What is a heterogeneous collection of objects? How are heterogeneous collections of objects created and used in C++?

- How does the use of polymorphism help in simplifying program maintenance?

- Can you convert a derived class to a base class? Can you convert a base class to a derived class? Are these conversions safe? Explain your answer.

16.8   Exercises

Construct the following:

- The class `Executive_office` which will extend a normal office by including biographical details about the occupants. For example, 'Ms C Lord, Programming manager'.

- A new information program for a building which will include details about rooms, offices and executive offices. You should try and re-use as much code as possible.

- A program to record transactions made on different types of bank account. For example, the program should be able to deal with at least the following types of account:

    - A deposit account on which interest is paid.

    - An account on which no interest is paid and the user is not allowed to be overdrawn.

17 Pointers and dynamic storage

This chapter describes the low level features of C++, which allow direct allocation and manipulation of memory. This process is inherently dangerous and can easily lead to programs which fail in unexpected and unusual ways. Debugging programs which contain errors due to the wrong use of pointers can be difficult and time consuming.

However, the code produce by the correct use of pointers will usually be smaller and faster executing than code developed without the use of pointers.

17.1   Introduction

C++ retains many of the low level features of C; one such feature is the ability to manipulate memory directly using the lvalue and rvalue of a variable.

These features of C++ are carried out at a low level. If at all possible, these operations should only be used to implement classes which are used in the building of a solution to a problem. An undisciplined use of pointers can lead to code which is error-prone and very difficult to maintain.

In C++ there are two monadic operators which are used to manipulate memory addresses directly. These are:

Operator	Delivers the	Terminology
`&item`	Physical byte address in memory of `item`	lvalue
`*item`	Contents of the location whose byte address is held in `item`	rvalue

Note: When, for example, an int parameter is passed by reference, the argument is described by `int&`. This requests the compiler to pass the address of the item, rather than its contents. The C++ compiler generates the correct code in the function, to access the contents of the location.

Consider the following snapshot of memory, from byte address 1000 to byte address 1028 illustrated below:

Snapshot of store			Using & and *	
Byte address	Contents	C++ name	index	Would deliver 1004
1000	1028	of store location		
1004	2		&index	Would deliver 1016
1008	3			
1012	4	cost	*index	Would deliver 2
1016	1004	index		[contents of location 1004]
1020	1000	tricky		
1024	0		**tricky	Would deliver 42
1028	42			[double indirect]

In the expression statement 'message[20]=character;', message[20] delivers a lvalue and character delivers a rvalue. This is illustrated in Figure 17.1.

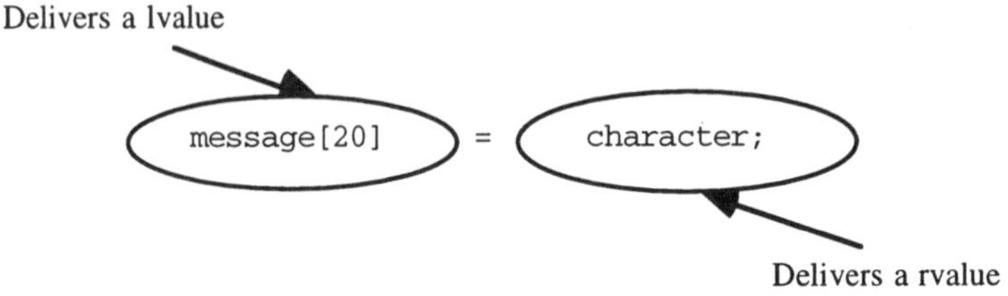

Figure 17.1 Rvalues and lvalues in C++.

In C++ the subscripting operator can be implemented by using address arithmetic. Consider the following code fragment that declares a vector and then assigns the address of the first element to a pointer variable.

```
const int SIZE = 10;

char ch_vec[SIZE];        char *p_ch = ch_vec;
int  int_vec[SIZE];       int  *p_int= int_vec;
```

Note: In C++ the name of the vector delivers the address of the first element. Thus ch_vec and &ch_vec[0] both deliver the address of the first element of ch_vec.

Element 4 of the vector of characters and integers may be output using either:

Using array access	Using address arithmetic
`cout << ch_vec[4];` `cout << int_vec[4];`	`cout << *(p_ch+4);` `cout << *(p_int+4);`

Note: In C++ when an integer value is added to an address it is scaled by the byte size of the addressed item. If an int was represented in 4 bytes then 16 would be added to the byte address in p_int.

17.2 Use of pointers in C++

Consider the following C++ declaration, which declares an array of 100 characters initialized with the characters 'B', 'r', 'i', etc.

```
char name[100] = "Brighton East Sussex";
```

The declaration:

```
char *p_ch;
```

would declare a variable p_ch which holds the address of a character variable. The following fragment of code:

```
char name[100] = "Brighton East Sussex";
char *p_ch;

  p_ch = &name[3];
```

stores the address of the third element of the array name into p_ch, this can be visualized as illustrated in Figure 17.2.

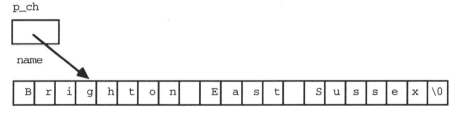

Figure 17.2 A pointer to name[3].

17.3 From arrays to pointers

In C++ a C string is simply a sequence of characters in store, followed by the special character '\0' to mark the end. This special character '\0' has the numeric value of 0 which is also the truth value for false. C++ has no inbuilt language facilities to manipulate C strings, though there are library functions which provide these facilities.

The class string implements a more advanced form of string handling, this however is not part of the language, but a standard class library. Appendix C lists some of the library functions for handling C++ strings and Appendix D lists some of the member functions of the class string.

A function to copy a C++ string from one area of store to another is implemented as follows:

Firstly, using arrays, this is expressed as:

```
void strcpy_V1( char to[], const char from[] )
{
 int i=0;                       //Start of array
 while ( from[i] != '\0' )      //While not EOS
 {
  to[i] = from[i];              //copy char from src to dst
  i++;                          //Next character
 }
 to[i] = '\0';                  //Add EOS to destination
}
```

Note: The fact that the string is terminated by '\0', which is used to end the copy of the characters.

Changing the code to use pointers instead of arrays would give the following new implementation:

```
void strcpy_V2( char* to, const char* from )
{
 while ( *from != '\0' )        //While from src != EOS
 {
  *to = *from;                  //copy char from src to dst
  to++; from++;                 //Increment pointers
 }
 *to = '\0';                    //Add EOS to destination
}
```

Note: A parameter, which contains a pointer to a character is described as char *.
from++ increments from *to point to the next item, which in this case is by one byte.*

This source code can be reduced in size by using the idiom *from++ to deliver the character pointed to by from, and then to increment the address in from to point to the next storage location.

```
void strcpy_V3( char* to, const char* from )
{
 while ( *from != '\0' )        //While from src != EOS
 {
  *to++ = *from++;              //copy and increment pointer
 }
 *to = '\0';                    //Add EOS to destination
}
```

Further reductions in size can be achieved by observing that `*from != '\0'` is identical to `*from` in the condition. Remember that C++ takes 0 as `false` and any other value as `true`.

```
void strcpy_V4( char* to, const char* from )
{
 while ( *from )                  //While from src != EOS
 {
   *to++ = *from++;               //Copy and increment pointer
 }
 *to = '\0';                      //Add EOS to destination
}
```

Finally, the body of the while loop can be substituted into the condition, to produce the following shorter code:

```
void strcpy( char* to, const char* from)
{
 while ( *to++ = *from++ );       //Copy stop when copied EOS
}
```

Note: The end string terminator is copied before the test for end is made.

If the parameters are placed in a register, optimum code will usually be produced on a register file architecture machine.

```
void strcpy( register char* to, const register char* from )
{
 while ( *to++ = *from++ );       //Copy stop when copied EOS
}
```

Note: The C standard library function strcpy *in the header file* <string.h> *returns as a result of the function the address of the EOS character copied to the destination.*

At first sight this is not very obvious, but it is one of the idioms of C++. Normally all this would be hidden from the users, as they would employ a string class to manipulate strings. The code in this class, however, would most likely be written using the above techniques.

This illustrates well the C++ philosophy of allowing the programmer access, if required, to very low-level machine constructs. However, it is expected that these features will only be used when absolutely necessary, and will be hidden by the class mechanism.

Note: Any local variable or parameter which can be contained in a machine word can be nominated by the programmer to be contained in a CPU register. This nomination is done by preceding the declaration by register. *The compiler may of course ignore this suggestion.*
The library function strcpy *also delivers the address of the area in which the string has been copied.*

17.4. Pointers vs. arrays

The following programs implement a function to count the number of characters in a string. In the first program the C++ string is described as an array of characters, and in the second it is described as a pointer to characters.

Firstly, using an array:

```cpp
#include <iostream>

namespace strlen_array
{
  int strlen( const char str[] )
  {
    int position = 0;
    while ( str[ position ] != '\0' )
    {
      position++;
    }
    return( position );
  }
}

int main()
{
  static char str[] = "University of Brighton";

  std::cout << "The length of " << str << " is "
            << strlen_array::strlen(str)  << " characters" << "\n";
  return 0;
}
```

Note: The use of the namespace `strlen_array` *to hold the definition of* `strlen` *this is so there will not be a clash of name with the system* `strlen`.

which will print:

```
The length of University of Brighton is 22 characters
```

Secondly, using a pointer to count the characters in the string:

```cpp
#include <iostream>

namespace strlen_ptr
{
  int strlen( const register char* str )
  {
    int count = 0;
    while ( *str++ ) count++;
    return( count );
  }
}
```

```
int main()
{
  static char str[] = "University of Brighton";

  std::cout << "The length of " << str << " is "
          << strlen_ptr::strlen(str)  << " characters" << "\n";
  return 0;
}
```

which will print:

```
The length of University of Brighton is 22 characters
```

Although this is not an obvious way of implementing this function, it will, however, produce very efficient code.

In many cases the choice of using either pointers or arrays is left to the implementor, but there will be occasions when only pointers will provide a solution.

Note: One of the design aims of C++ as well as C was to produce efficient code on a register file architecture machine.

That when an array is passed to a function the formal parameter can be described by either of the following declarations:

```
Type *formal_parameter
Type formal_parameter[]
```

17.4.1 Parameter access rights for pointers and arrays

In passing an array or a pointer to a function, the user can control the write access made to the item(s) described by the formal parameter. Read access, however, cannot be controlled and is therefore always allowed.

This can be summarized with the following six function skeletons.

```
void process( char * vec )
{
  //vec is a pointer to a char
  vec++;              //OK
  vec[1] = 'Z';       //OK
  *(vec+1) = 'Z';     //OK
}
```

```
void process( const char * vec )
{
  //vec is a pointer to a const char
  vec++;              //OK
  vec[1] = 'Z';       //Compile fail
  *(vec+1) = 'Z';     //Compile fail
}
```

```
void process( const char * const vec )
{
  //vec is const pointer to a const char
  vec++;              //Compile fail
  vec[1] = 'Z';       //Compile fail
  *(vec+1) = 'Z';     //Compile fail
}
```

```
void process( char * const vec )
{
  //vec is a const pointer to a char
  vec++;              //Compile fail
  vec[1] = 'Z';       //OK
  *(vec+1) = 'Z';     //OK
}
```

```
void print_vec4( const char vec [] )        void print_vec5( char vec [] )
{                                           {
  //vec is a const array                      //vec is an array
  vec++;            //Compile fail            vec++;            // OK
  vec[1] = 'Z';     //Compile fail            vec[1] = 'Z';     // OK
  *(vec+1) = 'Z';   //Compile fail            *(vec+1) = 'Z';   // OK
                                            }
```

Note: There is no equivalent to const char* vec *when it is described as an array. The assignment statements* vec[1] = 'Z'; *and* *(vec+1) = 'Z'; *are identical in effect.*

Read Access to the parameter vec *can be made using a subscript '*vec[i]*' or by using the indirection operation '**(vec+i)*' in all cases.*

17.5. Dynamic storage allocation

In C++, storage can be claimed dynamically from the system. In the example below, storage for 10 characters is claimed and a pointer to this store is assigned to p_ch.

```
char *p_ch;
p_ch = new char[10];              //Allocate storage
```

This storage can be released back to the system with:

```
delete [] p_ch;                   //Release storage
```

Note: The use of the [] brackets to signify that an array of items are being disposed of. In this particular case the [] brackets are not necessary, but when the array contains instances of a class the destructor for each element would not be called if the [] were omitted.

17.5.1. Alternative syntax

If only a single item is to be allocated then the [] may be omitted. For example, the following code sequences are identical:

Using []s	Without []s
```char *p_ch; p_ch = new char[1]; delete [] p_ch;```	```char *p_ch; p_ch = new char; delete p_ch;```

Note: The exception bad_alloc *is raised if no storage can be allocated. Legacy compilers will however return a NULL pointer.*

17.5.2 Access to dynamic storage

Dynamic storage is usually used to allocate storage for a class that contains no functions. This structure can also be described using the `struct` syntax. The struct construct originated in the language C.

Using the class definition syntax	Using the struct definition syntax

<pre>const int MAX_NAME = 40;
 	
class Person {
public:
  int birthdate;
  char sex;
  char name[MAX_NAME];
};</pre>
	<pre>const int MAX_NAME = 40;
	
	struct Person {
	  int birthdate;
	  char sex;
	  char name[MAX_NAME];
	};</pre>

Note: The use of an array of characters to represent the person's name rather than an instance of the class string. When using an array of characters to represent a string standard library functions are used to copy characters to and from the array. Section 17.4. compares the use of character arrays and instances of the class `string` *to hold strings.*

The above definition of storage describes a person. Which can be used as follows:

```
Person father;

father.birthdate = 1918;
father.sex = 'M';
strcpy( father.name, "James Smith" );
```

Note: The use of `strcpy` *to copy the name of the person into the name field.*

Rather than allocate storage for mother directly, a pointer to the structure can be described as follows:

```
Person *p_mother;
```

In the machine, the storage would look like:

p_mother [   ]

Note: That `p_mother` *is simply a variable which can hold a pointer to some storage of type* `Person`. *The contents of* `p_mother` *is currently undefined.*

At some later stage the storage for an instance of `Person` is allocated as follows:

```
p_mother = new Person[1];
```

An illustration of the storage for this data structure is shown in Figure 17.3.

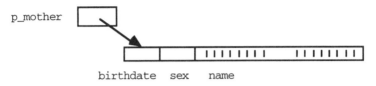

Figure 17.3 Layout of storage for `p_mother = new Person[1];`.

Note: The allocation for 1 element of storage of type `Person`.

To access the individual elements of `mother` is as follows:

```
p_mother->birthdate = 1918;
p_mother->sex = 'F';
strcpy( p_mother->name, "Margaret Smith" );
```

Note: How `->` *is used to access members of the class. The selection operator* `->` *is used instead of* `.` *when an instance of the class is represented by a pointer to the object.*
p_mother->birthdate = 1918; could have been expressed as
(*p_mother).birthdate = 1918;

17.6   Use of dynamic storage

The `Stack` class shown earlier in Section 8.9, could be rewritten using dynamic storage allocation as follows. In rewriting this class, the user interface to the class has not changed. Thus, a user of this class would not need to modify their existing program.

However, this class cannot be used, if instances of the class are to be copied. Chapter 23 describes why this will not produce the expected result, and how to implement a class using dynamic storage that can be copied. In essence copying an instance of this class will result in both objects pointing to the same data. The destructor for each of these objects will eventually attempt to deallocate the shared storage.

17.6.1   Specification of the **Class Stack**

```
#ifndef CLASS_STACK_SPEC
#define CLASS_STACK_SPEC

#include <ctype.h>
```

```
template <class Type>
class Stack {
public:
  Stack();
  ~Stack();
  bool empty() const;              //Stack empty
  size_t size() const;             //Size of collection
  const Type& top() const;         //Return top item on stack
  Type& top();                     //Return top item on stack
  void push(const Type);           //Push item on to stack
  void pop();                      //Pop top item from stack
private:
  class Element;                   //Tentative declaration
  typedef Element *P_Element;      //
  class Element {                  //Full declaration
  public:
    Type       the_value;          //Stored item
    P_Element the_p_next;          //Pointer to next element
  };
  P_Element the_p_tos;             //Pointer to first item
  int the_no_elements;             //Number of elements in stack
};

#endif
```

Note: The tentative declaration of P_Element.

17.6.2   Implementation of the **Class Stack**

The empty list is represented by the the_p_tos containing the nil pointer NULL. The nil pointer is used to indicate that currently the variable the_p_tos does not point to any storage. This can be imagined as illustrated in Figure 17.4:

Figure 17.4 Illustration of a null pointer.

The constructor for Stack sets this initial value and sets the number of elements held in the stack to be zero.

```
#ifndef CLASS_STACK_IMP
#define CLASS_STACK_IMP
#include "stack.h"

template <class Type>
Stack<Type>::Stack()
{
  the_p_tos = NULL;                //Empty stack
  the_no_elements = 0;             //No elements
}
```

The destructor releases any storage still active back to the system.

```
template <class Type>
Stack<Type>::~Stack()
{
  while ( !empty() ) pop();              //Free storage
}
```

Note: The member function pop will release the storage for the stored item.

The member function `size` returns the number of elements held in the stack.

```
template <class Type>
bool Stack<Type>::empty() const
{
  return the_p_tos == NULL;             //Is empty
}
```

The member function `empty` returns `true` when the stack is empty.

```
template <class Type>
size_t Stack<Type>::size() const
{
  return the_no_elements;               //Elements in stack
}
```

The storage allocated when the single integer value 3 is stored in an instance of an `<int>` Stack is shown in Figure 17.5.

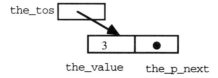

Figure 17.5 A stack containing 1 element.

If `the_tos` contains a pointer to an instance of the data structure `Element`. Then to access the member `the_value` of the data structure `Element` the following code is used:

```
the_tos->the_value = 3;
```

The function `push` creates a new element and chains this into a linked list of elements which hold the items pushed onto the stack.

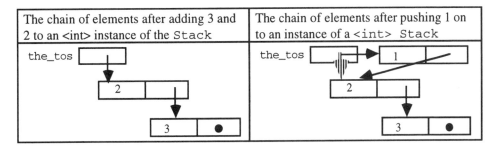

The chain of elements after adding 3 and 2 to an <int> instance of the Stack	The chain of elements after pushing 1 on to an instance of a <int> Stack

In the implementation of push if there is no storage available then an exception is thrown which is caught and the new exception range_error is thrown to indicate the failure to add a new element.

```
template <class Type>
void Stack<Type>::push(const Type item)
{
  P_Element p_new_item = NULL;
  try
  {
    p_new_item = new Element[1];                    //Allocate
  }
  catch ( bad_alloc& exp )
  {
    throw std::range_error("Stack: out of mem");    //Failed
  }
  p_new_item->the_value = item;                      //Store data
  p_new_item->the_p_next = the_p_tos;                //Chain in
  the_p_tos = p_new_item;                            //
  the_no_elements++;                                 //One more
}
```

Note: Section 26.5 on legacy compilers details the old action taken when storage is not available.

In catching the exception bad_alloc there may be insufficient dynamic memory to raise the new exception range_error.

The member function pop releases the storage for the top item in the stack back to the system.

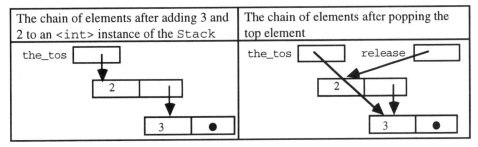

The chain of elements after adding 3 and 2 to an <int> instance of the Stack	The chain of elements after popping the top element

```
template <class Type>
void Stack<Type>::pop()
{
  if ( the_p_tos ==  NULL ) {              //Stack empty
    throw std::range_error("Stack: underflow");
  }
  P_Element release = the_p_tos;           //Remove top item
  the_p_tos = the_p_tos->the_p_next;
  delete [] release;
  the_no_elements--;                       //One less
}
```

The member function `top` returns the contents of the top item on the stack. There are two versions of this method to cater for const and non const collections of objects.

```
template <class Type>
Type& Stack<Type>::top()
{
  if ( the_p_tos == NULL )
    throw std::range_error("Stack: underflow");
  return the_p_tos->the_value;             //Element at top
}

template <class Type>
const Type& Stack<Type>::top() const
{
  if ( the_p_tos == NULL )
    throw std::range_error("Stack: underflow");
  return the_p_tos->the_value;             //Element at top
}

#endif
```

17.6.3   Putting it all together

```
int main()
{
  Stack <int> numbers;
  char ch;

  try
  {
    while ( std::cin >> ch, !std::cin.eof() )
    {
      switch ( ch )
      {
        case '+' :                    //push item onto stack
        {
          int num; std::cin >> num;
          numbers.push(num);
          break;
        }
```

```
      case '-' :                //pop item from stack
      {
        int num = numbers.top();
        std::cout << "Num = " << num << "\n";
        numbers.pop();
        break;
      }
    }
  }
}
catch ( std::range_error& err )
{
  std::cerr << "\n" << "Fail: " << err.what() << "\n";
}
return 0;
}
```

When run with the data

```
+1 +2 +3 +4 - - - - -
```

this will produce the following results:

```
Num = 4
Num = 3
Num = 2
Num = 1

Fail: Stack: underflow
```

This is the same interface as used previously for a stack. This time, however, the implementation code of the stack uses dynamically allocated storage.

17.7 struct vs. class

The struct construct originated in the language C and could only contain data members. In C++ a struct acts like a class except that by default its members are public. Thus in C++ a struct can contain member functions.

For example, the class:

```
class Element;
typedef Element *P_Element;
class Element {
public:
  Type      the_value;        //Stored item
  P_Element the_p_next;       //Pointer to next element
};
```

could have been declared as the following structure:

```
struct Element;
typedef Element *P_Element;
struct Element {
  Type       the_value;        //Stored item
  P_Element the_p_next;        //Pointer to next element
};
```

A `struct` is a class containing members which are by default all public.

17.8   Dynamic vs. static storage allocation

The following table summarizes the pros and cons of using dynamic and static storage allocation:

Metric	Dynamic (linked) storage allocation	Fixed (sequential) storage allocation
Space used (exact size not known in advance)	Optimum	Wasted space for elements not used.
Space used (exact size known in advance)	Extra space required for links.	Optimum
Complexity of code	Code to manipulate the storage may be complex.	Simple
Random access to data items in the structure.	May be very slow.	Fast
Sequential access to data items in the structure.	Fast	Fast

Note: Fixed storage allocation is when the size of the area to be allocated is fixed at compile time. A C++ array is an example of a structure where the size is fixed at compile time.

17.9   Overloading the operators `new` and `delete`

The operators `new` and `delete` may be overloaded in a class. This allows implementors of the class to provide, among other things, their own storage management routines.

The following class `Float` stores a floating point number and overloads `new` and `delete` to provide diagnostic information when an instance of the class is created dynamically.

```
#ifndef CLASS_FLOAT_SPEC
#define CLASS_FLOAT_SPEC
```

```
class Float
{
public:
  Float( float = 0.0 );                       //constructor
  void* operator new(size_t);                 //Single object
  void* operator new[](size_t);               // Array of objects
  void  operator delete(void *, size_t);      //Single object
  void  operator delete[](void *, size_t);    // Array of objects
  operator float();                           //conversion operator
private:
  float the_storage;                          //storage
};

#endif
```

Note: The overloaded operator `new` *returns a pointer to an untyped area of store*
(void*).

The implementation of the class `Float` is:

```
#ifndef CLASS_FLOAT_IMP
#define CLASS_FLOAT_IMP

Float::Float(float f)
{
  the_storage = f;
}
```

There are two overloading for the operator `new`, the first for single objects and the second when an array of class objects is allocated.

```
void* Float::operator new( size_t s )
{
  std::cout << " [ new       Bytes = " << s << " ]" << "\n";
  return (void *) ::new char[s];              //The global new
}
void* Float::operator new[]( size_t s )
{
  std::cout << " [ new[]     Bytes = " << s << " ]" << "\n";
  return (void *) ::new char[s];              //The global new
}
```

There are two overloading for the operator `delete` the first for single objects and the second when an array of class objects is de-allocated.

```
void Float::operator delete( void *p, size_t s )
{
  std::cout << " [ delete    Bytes = " << s << " ]" << "\n";
  ::delete p;                                 //The global delete
}
```

```
void Float::operator delete[]( void *p, size_t s )
{
  std::cout << " [ delete[] Bytes = " << s << " ]" << "\n";
  ::delete [] p;                         //The global delete
}

#endif
```

Note: *The overloaded operators* new *and* delete *are implicitly declared static. This means that they are not allowed to access data members of the class.*

The parameter to delete, which provides the size of the individual storage unit in bytes to be deleted.

size_t *is defined in the header file* stddef.h *as an integer value.*

void * *indicates a pointer to any type of storage.*

The class Float can be used to provide diagnostic information about the use of floating point numbers:

```
int main()
{
  std::cout << "Float *s1 = new Float(3.14);" << "\n";
  Float *s1 = new Float(3.14);              //New in class Float
  std::cout << "Float *s2 = new Float[10];" << "\n";
  Float *s2 = new Float[10];                //New in class Float

  std::cout << "Contents of s1 = " << *s1 << "\n";

  std::cout << "delete s1;" << "\n";
  delete s1;                                //Delete in class Float
  std::cout << "delete [] s2;" << "\n";
  delete [] s2;                             //Delete in class Float
  return 0;
}
```

which when compiled and run would produces the following output:

```
Float *s1 = new Float(3.14);
 [ new      Bytes  = 4 ]
Float *s2 = new Float[10];
 [ new[]    Bytes  = 40 ]
Contents of s1 = 3.14
delete s1;
 [ delete   Bytes = 4 ]
delete [] s2;
 [ delete[] Bytes = 4 ]
```

17.9.1 Overloading the global operators **new** and `delete`

The global operators new and delete may also be overloaded. However, great care must be exercised as many library functions use new and delete. In particular, the C++ I/O systems allocates buffers using dynamically allocated storage.

17.9.2 Additional parameters to the operator new

The operators new may be passed additional parameters. When used in this form the signature of new is:

Signature of new	Example call for a class Type
void* operator new(size_t, parameters)	new (*parameters*) Type;
void* operator new[](size_t, parameters)	new (*parameters*) Type[5];

One use of this form of the new operator is the creation of an object over existing storage. For example, the following overloading of the operator new returns the second actual parameter as the storage allocated for the object.

```
void* operator new( size_t, void* storage )
{
  return storage;
}

void* operator new[]( size_t, void* storage )
{
  return storage;
}
```

After this overloaded new operator is executed the constructor for the object is implicitly called. Using the above overloading of the operator new the following code allocates an instance of the class Office (described in Section 16.2) over existing storage.

```
int main()
{
  char *p_object   = new char[ sizeof(Office) ]; //Raw storage
  Office *p_office = reinterpret_cast<Office*>(p_object);
  new( p_office ) Office(420, "QA", 3);           //Calls constructor
  std::cout << p_office->describe() << "\n";
  p_office->~Office();                            //Destructor call
  delete [] p_object;                             //Return storage
  return 0;
}
```

Note: *The explicit call of the destructor for the instance of* Office *allocated using this form of the new operator. This is required as the compiler will not automatically call the destructor for the instance of Room, as the compiler thinks the storage holds characters.*

The use of `reinterpret_cast` *to cast from a pointer from type char* to type* Office**.*

The above code is used when raw storage is required to be turned into storage for a class object. Section 20.2.6 illustrates an example of this use.

17.10 Standard operators `new` and `delete`

The table below summarizes the standard declarations of `new` and `delete` defined in the header file `<new>`. When `new` or `delete` are defined as class member functions they are considered as static members, which can be inherited, but cannot be virtual.

Operator	Declaration	Notes
new	`void* operator new(size_t size) throw(bad_alloc);`	[1]
	`void* operator new[](size_t size) throw(bad_alloc);`	[1]
	`void* operator new(size_t size, const nothrow&) throw();`	[2]
	`void* operator new[](size_t size, const nothrow&) throw();`	[2]
	`void* operator new  (size_t size, void* p) throw();`	[2]
	`void* operator new[](size_t size, void* p) throw();`	[2]
delete	`void operator delete  (void* p, void*) throw();`	[3]
	`void operator delete(void* p) throw();`	
	`void operator delete[](void* p) throw();`	
	`void operator delete[](void* p, void*) throw();`	

Note:
[1]   If storage cannot be allocated the exception `bad_alloc` is thrown.
[2]   If storage cannot be allocated a null pointer (NULL) is returned.
[3]   `delete` may not be overloaded to have two or more definitions `size_t` is defined in the header file `ctype.h`.

17.10.1 Failure to allocate storage

When storage is exhausted the system attempts to call a handler for this eventuality. This handler function will usually release storage back to the heap so that `new` may satisfy the current request. The handler is made known to the system by calling the function `set_new_handler` whose prototype is defined in the header file `<new>` as:

```
typedef void (*new_handler)();
new_handler set_new_handler(new_handler fun);
```

The default value for the handler is NULL, that indicates no function is to be called. When the systems new operator is invoked the following process illustrated below in pseudo code is performed:

```
while( true )
{
  allocate_memory();
  if ( memory_is_allocated ) return pointer_to_memory;
  if ( new_handler == NULL )
  {
    if ( no_throw ) return NULL; else throw bad_alloc( "" );
  }
  new_handler();
}
```

Note: The different actions depending on whether the operator new throws an exception or returns a null pointer.

17.11 Operators . * and ->*

It is sometimes useful to reference a class member through its address. For this to work correctly a special process has to be used.

This process is illustrated in the example below, in which the class Record is used to create instances of objects that contain a message passed at creation time. The two member functions print this message followed by their parameter either in decimal or hexadecimal.

```
#ifndef CLASS_RECORD_SPEC
#define CLASS_RECORD_SPEC

class Record
{
public:
  Record( const char [] );           //Record name
  void display_dec( const int) const; //Display parameter in dec
  void display_hex( const int) const; //Display parameter in hex
private:
  static const int SIZE=40;
  char the_str[ SIZE ];              //The message
};

#endif
```

```
#ifndef CLASS_RECORD_IMP
#define CLASS_RECORD_IMP

Record::Record( const char text[] )
{
  strcpy( the_str, text );           //Save the message
}

void Record::display_dec( const int i ) const
{
  std::cout << the_str << " in decimal " << dec << i << "\n";
}
```

```
void Record::display_hex( const int i ) const
{
  std::cout << the_str << " in hex     " << hex << i << "\n";
}

#endif
```

A member pointer p_fun to a member function of class Record which takes an int parameter and returns void can be declared as:

```
void (Record::*p_fun)( const int ) const;
```

p_fun can be assigned either the address of display_dec or display_hex as they both have the desired specification.

An instance of Record with the message "Display point 1 " is created with the declaration:

```
Record mes1("Display point 1 ");
```

The address of the member function display_dec can be assigned to the member pointer p_fun as follows:

```
p_fun = &Record::display_dec;
```

Note: The compiler will type check this assignment at compile time.

Calling the function represented by p_fun in the object mes1 requires the use of the operator '.*'. This is required so that the correct association between the function and the instance of the class can be made.

17.11.1 Putting it all together

The following program uses both .* and ->* to access functions display_dec and display_hex.

```
int main()
{
  Record mes1("Display point 1 ");
  Record *p_mes2 = new Record("Display point 2 ");

  void (Record::*p_fun)( const int ) const;

  p_fun = &Record::display_dec;
  (mes1.*p_fun)(100);                        //in mes1
  (p_mes2->*p_fun)(100);                     //in mes2
```

```
    p_fun = &Record::display_hex;
    (mes1.*p_fun)(100);                          //in mes1
    (p_mes2->*p_fun)(100);                       //in mes2

    delete p_mes2;
    return 0;
}
```

Note: That -> is the equivalent of . * when using a pointer to the object rather than the object directly.*

When run this will give the following results:

```
Display point 1  in decimal 100
Display point 2  in decimal 100
Display point 1  in hex      64
Display point 2  in hex      64
```

17.12 Pointers and polymorphism

The normal way of using polymorphism is through the pointer mechanism. The code below can be written using the classes Abstract_Account, Account_IB, and Account_IT described in Section 18.2.

```
    const int MAX_CUSTOMERS = 3;
    Abstract_Account *customers[MAX_CUSTOMERS];

    customers[0] = new Account    ( 100.00 );
    customers[1] = new Account_IB( 10000.00 );
    customers[2] = new Account_IT( 25000.00 );
```

Note: A pointer to any derived object from a particular base class can be assigned to a location of type pointer to base class.
This can lead to errors if used unwisely.

This sets the elements of customers to three different types of account.

In writing a program to process transactions on bank accounts, the following fragment of code may be used to calculate any interest accrued on the account at the end of each day.

```
    for (int i=0; i<MAX_CUSTOMERS; i++ )
    {
       customers[i]->end_of_day(365);
    }
```

The interest accrued on each account is credited to the account at the end of the first day of the new accounting period.

```
for (int i=0; i<MAX_CUSTOMERS; i++ )
{
    customers[i]->end_of_day(1);
}
```

The bank can print a statement for each of its customers, using the following code:

```
for (int i=0; i<MAX_CUSTOMERS; i++ )
{
    cout << "Customer " << i << " :" << "\n" <<
            customers[i]->statement() << "\n";
}
```

If the bank was to introduce a new type of account, the code responsible for processing transactions on the accounts would not change. The code changes required to introduce a new account would be encapsulated in the class for the new account.

Note: For polymorphic access to take place, the binding between the object and the function call must be made at run-time. For this to happen the function must be virtual and called either by using a pointer or a reference to the object.

17.13 Opaque types

By using dynamic storage, the state information about an object can be removed from the specification part of a class. The classes constructor has the responsibility of allocating the storage for the object and the destructor for returning the storage. For example, the class Account's specification is:

```
#ifndef CLASS_ACCOUNT_SPEC
#define CLASS_ACCOUNT_SPEC

class Account {
public:
    Account(const float = 0.00, const float= 0.00);
    ~Account();
    float account_balance() const;         //Return the balance
    float withdraw( const float );          //Withdraw from account
    void deposit( const float );            //Deposit into account
    void set_min_balance( const float );//Set min balance
private:
    struct Account_data;                    //Tentative declaration
    Account_data* the_storage;              //Pointer to storage for object
};
#endif
```

The implementation of the classes constructor and destructor are:

```
#ifndef CLASS_ACCOUNT_IMP
#define CLASS_ACCOUNT_IMP

struct Account::Account_data {        //Physical storage for object
  float the_balance;
  float the_min_balance;
};

Account::Account( const float money, const float overdraft )
{
  the_storage = new Account_data[1];
  the_storage->the_balance     = money;
  the_storage->the_min_balance = overdraft;
}

Account::~Account()
{
  delete [] the_storage;
}
```

The implementation code for the member functions now access the member data of an object indirectly.

```
float Account::account_balance() const
{
  return the_storage->the_balance;
}

float Account::withdraw( const float money )
{
  if ( the_storage->the_balance-money >= the_storage->the_min_balance )
  {
    the_storage->the_balance = the_storage->the_balance - money;
    return money;
  } else {
    return 0;
  }
}

void Account::deposit( const float money )
{
  the_storage->the_balance = the_storage->the_balance + money;
}

void Account::set_min_balance( const float money )
{
  the_storage->the_min_balance = money;
}

#endif
```

Warning

An instance of this class Account may not be copied as it contains pointers. The consequences of copying such an object will produce undefined and probably fatal consequences. The reasons for the copying restriction together with a solution are described in Chapter 23 on Deep and shallow copying.

17.13.1 Hidden vs. visible storage in a class

The main benefit of this approach is that a client of the class does not need to recompile their code when the storage structure of the class is changed. The client code only needs to be relinked with the new implementation code. This would usually occur when a new improved class library is provided by a software supplier. Naturally, this assumes that the interface with the library stays the same.

The pros and cons of the two approaches are:

Criteria	Using an opaque type (Hidden storage)	Normal type
Compilation efficiency	Fewer resources required, as only a recompile of the class and then a re-link need to be performed.	Greater as all units that use the class need to be recompiled.
Run-time efficiency	Worse as there is the overhead of dynamic storage allocation.	No extra run-time overhead.
Client access to data components of an object.	None	None
Code complexity	Increased complexity in the implementation as storage must be explicitly managed. See Chapter 17.	-

Note: The extra cost of re-compiling and re-linking all units of a program may be marginal when compared with just re-linking.

17.14 Class component *this

In a class the reserved word this is used to indicate a pointer to the current instance of the class. To access the actual instance of the class *this is used. In an early example, in Section 15.2, the class Money had the operator ++ defined to add 1 to the monetary amount. The overloaded operator ++ delivers the current instance of the class as its result using *this.

17.14.1 Implementation of messages and methods

A hidden first parameter is inserted by the compiler into all non static member functions. The hidden parameter this is a pointer to the object on which the method is called. For example, the sending of the message deposit to the object mike shown below:

```
Account mike;

mike.deposit(250.00);
```

is implemented by the compiler as:

```
deposit( &mike, 250.00);
```

The method `deposit` that is invoked by the message is written by a programmer as:

```
void Account::deposit( float money )
{
  the_balance = the_balance + money;
}
```

and implemented by the compiler as:

```
void deposit( Account *this, float money )
{
  this->the_balance = this->the_balance + money;
}
```

Note: Naturally there are compile time checks for the validity of the specified operations.

By explicitly using `this` the implementor can access the object to which the message has been sent.

17.15 Self-assessment

- What is the difference between dynamic storage allocation and storage allocated by the normal declaration of variables?

- What are the advantages of using dynamic storage in a program?

- Is the operator `->` redundant? Explain your answer?

- What is the result printed for the following code fragment?

```
char first[1], second[1];
*first = 'A'; *second = 'A';
cout << ( *first == *second ? "Equal" : "Not equal" );
cout << (  first ==  second ? "Equal" : "Not equal" );
```

- What do the following mean:
    - `int *p_int;`
    - `int **p_p_int;`
    - `int *process(int)`

● Is the [] operator absolutely necessary in C++? Explain your answer.

● Using dynamic storage is often considered to be difficult. Do you agree? Can you suggest any ways of making access to dynamic storage easier?

● Why can the use of pointers be dangerous?

● If an object contains a pointer to some storage, why should it not usually be copied.

● What is the purpose of the operators .* and ->*?

17.16 Exercises

Construct the following classes:

● String Class

Write your own string manipulation class using dynamic storage. This should contain methods/functions to allow the user of your class to write:

```
String s1,s2;

s1.set("Hello world"); s2.set(" from Brighton");  s1.join_with( s2 );

cout << s1 << "\n";
```

Note: You will need to be careful that you de-allocate any storage you have created.

Warning

There is an implied assignment when an object is passed by value to a function or returned as the result of a function. This implied assignment is handled by a copy constructor that is described in Chapter 23. If an instance of the class String is passed by value to a function or returned as a result of a function then without having the copy constructor defined only the pointer and not the data structure will be copied.

● Number Class

Develop a class to deal with arbitrary precision integer arithmetic. Such a class might, for example, enable a user to write the following:

```
Number n1,n2;

n1.set("1234567789012345676890"); n2.set(12); n1.add( n2 );

cout << n1 << "\n";
```

18 Polymorphism revisited

This chapter explores some of the advanced uses of polymorphism. In particular the use of abstract classes and run-time type identity are set in context.

18.1 Abstract class

When defining a class with virtual member functions only the specification need be defined. This allows a designer to define the protocol that a class should obey without having to fill in the details. This type of class is termed an abstract class, as illustrated by the protocol for a bank account class with the following responsibilities:

Method	Responsibility
account_balance	Return the balance of the account.
deposit	Deposit money into the account.
end_of_day	Perform end of day processing, such as adding interest gained for that day.
set_min_balance	Set the overdraft limit 0.00 no overdraft.
statement	Return a string representing a summary of the state of the account.
withdraw	Withdraw money from the account, but only if there is sufficient funds or an overdraft is allowed.

is specified in C++ as:

```
#ifndef CLASS_ABSTRACT_ACCOUNT_SPEC
#define CLASS_ABSTRACT_ACCOUNT_SPEC
#include <string>

class Abstract_Account {
public:
  virtual double account_balance() const     = 0; //Balance
  virtual double withdraw( const double ) = 0;     //Withdraw
  virtual void deposit( const double ) = 0;        //Deposit
  virtual void set_min_balance(const double) = 0; //Overdraft
  virtual void end_of_day( const int ) = 0;        //End of day
  virtual std::string statement() const      = 0;  //Summary
  virtual ~Abstract_Account() {};
};

#endif
```

Note: In the specification of an abstract class (or any class which contains the base definition of a virtual function), the destructor should be specified as virtual. This

is important, as otherwise the wrong destructor may be called when a derived object's storage is released.
The body of the virtual function is specified as '= 0' to indicate its abstract nature.

An abstract class may only be used in the following ways:

- As the base class of a new derived class.
- As the description of a parameter passed by reference.
- As the description of a pointer.

Then, the following declaration is invalid:

```
Abstract_Account mine;          // would produce a compile time error
```

whilst the following declarations are valid:

```
void process(Abstract_Account&); // Is OK
Abstract_Account *mine;          // Is OK
```

18.1.1 A normal account

A normal account which does not offer any interest, is derived from the class `Abstract_Account`. The specification for this class is as follows:

```
#ifndef CLASS_ACCOUNT_SPEC
#define CLASS_ACCOUNT_SPEC
#include "Abstract_account.h"

class Account : public Abstract_Account {
public:
  Account( const double = 0.0 );
  ~Account();
  double account_balance() const;        //Balance
  double withdraw( const double );       //Withdraw
  void deposit( const double );          //Deposit
  void set_min_balance(const double);    //Overdraft
  void end_of_day( const int );          //End of day
  std::string statement() const;         //Summary
private:
  double  the_balance;                   //The account balance
  double  the_min_balance;               //Overdraft
};

#endif
```

Note: The function end_of_day will be defined to take no action.

The implementation of this class is as follows:

```
#ifndef CLASS_ACCOUNT_IMP
#define CLASS_ACCOUNT_IMP
#include <iostream>
#include <strstream>
#include <iopmanip>

Account::Account(const double initial)
{
  the_balance    = initial;            //Opening balance
  the_min_balance = 0.00;              //No overdraft allowed
}
```

The implementation of `account_balance`, `withdraw`, `deposit` and `set_min_balance` are implemented as follows:

```
double Account::account_balance() const
{
  return the_balance;
}

double Account::withdraw( const double money )
{
  if ( the_balance-money >= the_min_balance )
  {
    the_balance = the_balance - money;
    return money;
  } else {
    return 0.00;
  }
}

void Account::deposit( const double money )
{
  the_balance = the_balance + money;
}

void Account::set_min_balance( const double money )
{
  the_min_balance = money;
}
```

The function `end_of_day` performs no action in the class `Account` so it is defined with an empty body.

```
void Account::end_of_day( const int day)
{
  //Null action
}
```

Note: In the base class of Abstract_Account *a pure virtual function is defined for the method* end_of_day. *Therefore, if an instance of the class* Account *is to be created, there must be a concrete definition for the method* end_of_day.

The function `statement` returns a string representing summary information about the account.

```
std::string Account::statement() const
{
  const int MAX_BUF = 256;                    //Max size of text area
  char buf[MAX_BUF];                          //Holds written text
  ostrstream text(buf, MAX_BUF);             //text is a std::string stream
  text << setiosflags( ios::fixed );         //Fixed point x.y
  text << setiosflags( ios::showpoint );     //Show all dec places
  text << setprecision(2);                    //2 places of decimals
  text << "Balance of account is £" << account_balance();
  text << "\n" << '\0';
  return std::string(buf);
}
```

The destructor writes a warning to the error stream if an account is closed that contains money.

```
Account::~Account()
{
  if ( account_balance() != 0.00 )
  {
    cerr << "Warning account contains £" << account_balance();
    cerr << "\n";
  }
}
#endif
```

Note: Each pure virtual function has been overridden in `Account`. *This prevents a pure virtual function from being accidentally called. The compiler will prevent a user creating an instance of a class which contains a pure virtual function.*

18.2   A derived interest-bearing account

An interest bearing account has the following responsibilities in addition to those of a normal bank account:

Method	Responsibility
`prelude`	Set the global interest rate for this class of accounts.
`interest_today`	Calculate the day's interest due on the outstanding balance.
`credit_interest_day`	Return true if this is the end of the accounting period.

plus a specialization of the existing methods:

Method	Responsibility
`statement`	Print summary details about this type of account.
`set_min_balance`	Prevent an overdraft being set.

The C++ specification for this class `Account_IB` is:

```
#ifndef CLASS_INTEREST_ACCOUNT_SPEC
#define CLASS_INTEREST_ACCOUNT_SPEC

class  Account_IB : public Account {
public:
  Account_IB(const double = 0.0 );          //Account
  ~Account_IB();                            //Destructor
  static void prelude( const double );
  std::string statement() const;            //Summary of account
  void end_of_day( const int );             //End of day
  void set_min_balance(const double);       //Overdraft
protected:
  virtual double interest_today();          //Calc interest
  virtual bool credit_interest_day(const int);//End accounting per.
private:
  static double the_rate;                   //Interest rate
  double the_accumulated_interest;          //Interest gained
};

#endif
```

Note: The reason why the member functions `interest_today` and `credit_interest_day` are declared virtual is described later in Section 18.3.3.

The implementation for this class is as follows:

```
#ifndef CLASS_INTEREST_ACCOUNT_IMP
#define CLASS_INTEREST_ACCOUNT_IMP

const double DAILY_RATE = 0.00026116;       //10% Annual rate

double Account_IB::the_rate;                //Declare the storage

Account_IB::Account_IB(const double amount) : Account(amount)
{
  the_accumulated_interest = 0.00;
}

void Account_IB::prelude(const double rate)
{
  the_rate = rate;
}
```

Note: A static member is used to record the interest rate payable on this account.

The destructor causes the end of day processing for the special day 0 to be called. This special day invokes any closing actions required for the account.

```
Account_IB::~Account_IB()
{
  end_of_day(0);                              //Force add interest
}
```

The function `end_of_day` is called daily to calculate and store interest accrued on the account. On the day specified as the interest credit day, the accrued interest is credited to the account.

```
void Account_IB::end_of_day( const int day )
{
  if ( day != 0 )
    the_accumulated_interest += interest_today(); //Real day
  if ( credit_interest_day(day) )                 //End
  {
    deposit( the_accumulated_interest );          //Into account
    the_accumulated_interest = 0.0;
  }
}
```

Note: The special action for day 0. This day is used to invoke closing actions for an account.

A polymorphic call will be constructed for the member functions `interest_today` and `credit_interest_day`. Remember, in the implementation of the body of the function, the line:

```
the_accumulated_interest += interest_today();
```

will be implemented as:

```
the_accumulated_interest += this->interest_today();
```

The function `interest_today` returns the amount of interest gained on the day's outstanding balance.

```
double Account_IB::interest_today()
{
  return account_balance() * the_rate;
}
```

At the end of the accounting period interest will be credited to the account, the function `credit_interest_day` returns true when this day is reached,

```
bool Account_IB::credit_interest_day( const int day )
{
  return day == 1 || day == 0;               //Hard wired
}
```

The member function `set_min_balance` overrides the method in the base class and hence prevents a direct call of this method.

```
void Account_IB::set_min_balance( const double )
{
  return;                                    //No action
}
```

The member function `statement` uses the scope resolution operator `::` to call `statement` in the class `Account`.

```
std::string Account_IB::statement() const
{
  return std::string("Interest bearing Account:") + "\n" +
         Account::statement();
}

#endif
```

Note: The 1st string needs to be converted to an instance of the class `string` *so that the concatenation of the 1st and 2nd strings will be performed.*

18.3   A derived higher interest account

An interest bearing account with tiered rates of interest has the following responsibility in addition to those of an interest bearing bank account:

Method	Responsibility
prelude	Set the global interest rates.

as well as a specialization of the existing methods:

Method	Responsibility
interest_today	Calculate the interest due on the outstanding balance.
statement	Returns a string representing a summary of the account.

The C++ specification for this class `Account_IB` is:

```
#ifndef CLASS_SPECIAL_INTEREST_ACCOUNT_SPEC
#define CLASS_SPECIAL_INTEREST_ACCOUNT_SPEC

class  Account_IT : public Account_IB {
public:
  Account_IT(const double = 0.0 );
  static void prelude(const double, const double, const double );
  std::string statement() const;          //Summary of account
protected:
  double interest_today();                //Calculate interest today
private:
  static double the_interest_rate1;       //Interest Rate 1
  static double the_interest_rate2;       //Interest Rate 2
  static double the_interest_rate3;       //Interest Rate 3
};

#endif
```

The implementation part of this class is as follows:

```
#ifndef CLASS_SPECIAL_INTEREST_ACCOUNT_IMP
#define CLASS_SPECIAL_INTEREST_ACCOUNT_IMP

const double DAILY_RATE_R1 = 0.00026116;  //10% Annual rate
const double DAILY_RATE_R2 = 0.00028596;  //11% Annual rate
const double DAILY_RATE_R3 = 0.00031054;  //12% Annual rate

double Account_IT::the_interest_rate1;    //Interest Rate 1
double Account_IT::the_interest_rate2;    //Interest Rate 2
double Account_IT::the_interest_rate3;    //Interest Rate 3
```

The constructor calls the constructor in `Account_IB`.

```
Account_IT::Account_IT(const double amount)  : Account_IB(amount)
{
}
```

The static member function `prelude` sets the tiered interest rates which the objects in the class use.

```
void Account_IT::prelude(
  const double r1=DAILY_RATE_R1, const double r2=DAILY_RATE_R2,
  const double r3=DAILY_RATE_R3 )
{
  the_interest_rate1 = r1;
  the_interest_rate2 = r2;
  the_interest_rate3 = r3;
}
```

The implementation of the specialization of the member functions `interest_today` and `statement` is as follows:

```
double Account_IT::interest_today()
{
  double money =  account_balance();
  if ( money < 10000.00 )
    return money*the_interest_rate1;        //Interest band 1
  else if ( money < 25000.00 )
    return money*the_interest_rate2;        //Interest band 2
  else
    return money*the_interest_rate3;        //Interest band 3
}

std::string Account_IT::statement() const
{
  return std::string("Special Interest bearing Account:") + "\n" +
         Account::statement();
}

#endif
```

18.3.1   Putting it all together

Using the above classes the following function illustrates the use of the three types of account. In the illustrated code the inclusion of the header files and the setting up of the previously illustrated interest rates is omitted.

```
// Inclusion of appropriate header files
// Setting up the interest rates for the accounts

void process()
{
  const int MAX_CUSTOMERS = 7;
  Abstract_Account *customers[MAX_CUSTOMERS];
  int i;

  customers[0] = new Account    ( 10000.00 );
  customers[1] = new Account_IB( 10000.00-0.01 );
  customers[2] = new Account_IB( 10000.00 );
  customers[3] = new Account_IT( 10000.00-0.01 );
  customers[4] = new Account_IT( 10000.00 );
  customers[5] = new Account_IT( 25000.00-0.01 );
  customers[6] = new Account_IT( 25000.00 );

  //At the end of each day the bank would calculate the interest
  // if any to be credited to each account

  for (i=0; i<MAX_CUSTOMERS; i++ )
  {
    customers[i]->end_of_day(365);
  }
```

```
//At the end of each accounting period interest
// To be credited to each account

for (i=0; i<MAX_CUSTOMERS; i++ )
{
    customers[i]->end_of_day(1);
}
for (i=0; i<MAX_CUSTOMERS; i++ )
{
    std::cout << "Customer " << i << " :" << "\n" <<
                 customers[i]->statement() << "\n";
}

for (i=0; i<MAX_CUSTOMERS; i++ )
{
    delete customers[i];
}
}
```

When run, this will produce the following output:

```
Customer 0 :
Balance of account is £10000.00

Customer 1 :
Interest bearing Account:
Balance of account is £10005.21

Customer 2 :
Interest bearing Account:
Balance of account is £10005.22

Customer 3 :
Special Interest bearing Account:
Balance of account is £10005.21

Customer 4 :
Special Interest bearing Account:
Balance of account is £10005.72

Customer 5 :
Special Interest bearing Account:
Balance of account is £25014.29

Customer 6 :
Special Interest bearing Account:
Balance of account is £25015.53
```

The following warning message are produced as when the accounts are closed they still contain money.

```
Warning account contains £10000
Warning account contains £10005.2
Warning account contains £10005.2
Warning account contains £10005.2
Warning account contains £10005.7
Warning account contains £25014.3
Warning account contains £25015.5
```

18.3.2   Member functions called

The following table shows the member functions provided by each class. If a member function is called on an instance of a class and it is not defined in that class, then the definition will be taken from the most recent base class in the class hierarchy Abstract_Account » Account » Account_IB » Account_IT.

This is why the class Account must have code for each virtual function; if this is not provided in this class, the compiler will generate a compile-time error message stating that an implementation has not been provided for a pure virtual function.

Abstract_Account	Account	Account_IB	Account_IT
account_balance Δ	account_balance	➜	➜
		interest_today Δ	interest_today
		credit_interest_day Δ	➜
deposit Δ	deposit	➜	➜
end_of_day Δ	end_of_day	end_of_day	➜
		prelude	prelude
set_min_balance Δ	set_min_balance	set_min_balance	➜
statement Δ	statement	statement	statement
withdraw Δ	withdraw	➜	➜
	Constructor	Constructor	Constructor
~Destructor Δ		~Destructor	

Note: ➜ *is used to denote an inherited method.*
Δ is used to denote the definition of a virtual function.
The Abstract class does not have a constructor but it does have a virtual destructor. This ensures that an object created from any inherited class will have the correct destructor called. If a constructor or destructor is not provided in a class, a default implementation is provided by the compiler.

18.3.3   Re-dispatching

In the implementation of the method interest_today in the class Account_IB shown below:

```
void Account_IB::end_of_day( const int day )
{
  if ( day != 0 )
    the_accumulated_interest += interest_today(); //Real day
  if ( credit_interest_day(day) )                 //End
  {
    deposit( the_accumulated_interest );          //Into account
    the_accumulated_interest = 0.0;
  }
}
```

the actual method called when the messages interest_today and credit_interest_day are dispatched, depends on the type of object to which the message end_of_day was sent.

For example, with the following declarations:

```
Abstract_Account *object_ib = new Account_IB( 25000.00 );
Abstract_Account *object_it = new Account_IT( 25000.00 );
```

results in the following methods being called when the message end_of_day is sent to the respective objects.

object_ib->end_of_day();	object_it->end_of_day();
Account_IB::end_of_day()	Account_IB::end_of_day()
Account_IB::interest_today()	*Account_IT::interest_today()*
Account_IB::credit_interest_day()	Account_IB::credit_interest_day()
Account ::deposit(...)	Account ::deposit(...)

As can be seen, the actual method interest_today called depends on the type of the object the message end_of_day is sent to. The writer of the class Account_IB does not know which method interest_today will be called, as it is declared virtual and may be overloaded by a new method in an inheriting class.

Warning

Whilst it is a very powerful facility, it is dangerous to rely on this implementation of end_of_day if it has not been documented as working this way. A new implementation of the class Account_IB may implement the method end_of_day in a way which does not involve a polymorphic call of interest_today.

18.4   Run-time `typeid`

As objects in a heterogeneous collection are described as a pointer to the base class, a user of the collection has lost the original type information about the object. Fortunately, C++ provides type identity for all objects. The keyword `typeid` is used to return the type of an object. For example, the following code prints a statement summary for all interest bearing accounts held in the heterogeneous collection customers:

```
int main()
{
  const int NO = 4;
  Account   *customers[NO];

  customers[0] =  new Account    (100.00);
  customers[1] =  new Account_IB(200.00);
  customers[2] =  new Account    (300.00);
  customers[3] =  new Account_IB(400.00);

  std::cout << "List of interest bearing accounts:" << "\n";

  for( int i=0; i<NO; i++ )
  {
    if ( typeid(*customers[i]) == typeid(Account_IB) )
    {
      std::cout << "Customers account # " << i << "  " <<
                   customers[i]->statement();
    }
  }

  for ( int r=0; r<NO; r++ )
  {
    delete customers[r];
  }
  return 0;
}
```

Note: The use of `typeid(Account_IB)` *to return the internal representation for the type* `Account_IB`.

When compiled and run the following output will be produced:

```
List of interest bearing accounts:
Customers account # 1  Interest bearing Account:
Balance of account is £200.00

Customers account # 3  Interest bearing Account:
Balance of account is £400.00
```

18.4.1   The class `type_info`

Run-time `typeid` provides a programmer with the ability to interrogate an object at run-time and determine its type. As seen above, this facility is useful when determining the real type of an object in a heterogeneous collection. `typeid` returns a reference to an object of type `type_info`. The class `type_info`'s public specification is:

```
class type_info {
public:
  virtual ~type_info();
  bool operator==(cosnt type_info& rhs) cosnt;
  bool operator!=(cosnt type_info& rhs) cosnt;
  bool before(cosnt type_info& rhs) cosnt;
  cosnt char* name() cosnt;
};
```

The header file `<typeinfo>` contains the definition for the class `type_info`.

18.5   Downcasting

Downcasting is the conversion of an instance of a base class to an instance of a derived class. This conversion is normally impossible as extra information needs to be added to the base type object to allow it to be turned into an instance of a derived type. However, in a program, it is possible to describe a pointer to an instance of a derived type as a pointer to an instance of the base type. This will usually occur when a heterogeneous collection is created. The data members of a heterogeneous collection, though consisting of many different types, are each defined as a pointer to the base type of the collection.

The conversion from a base type to a derived type must, of course be possible. For example, the following code fragment copies the interest bearing accounts in the heterogeneous array `customers` into the array `better_accs`.

```
Account_IB better_accs[NO];
int     number_better_accs = 0;

for( i=0; i<NO; i++ )
{
  Account_IB *p_acc = dynamic_cast<Account_IB*>( customers[i] );
  if ( p_acc != NULL )
  {
    better_accs[number_better_accs++] = *p_acc;
  }
}
```

Note: The operator dynamic_cast returns NULL if the cast cannot be performed.

The operator `dynamic_cast` ensure that the cast is valid by performing run-time type checking. The format of the `dynamic_cast` operator is shown in Figure 18.1.

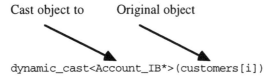

Figure 18.1 Components of the operator `dynamic_cast`.

This and other casts are further explained in Section 19.6.

18.6   Self-assessment

- Why can an abstract class not be used to declare storage?

- Why would an implementor provide an abstract specification of a class?

- How can you find the class that an object is an instance of.

- Why is Run-Time Type Identity needed?

- Why would a programmer need to use downcasting?

18.7 Exercises

- *Bank*

  Build a framework for a bank that allows normal transactions to take place on different types of account. The objective of the framework is to allow new types of account to be added at a later stage, without the code for the framework having to change.

- *C4 with a human and computer player*

  Re-implement the game of C4 shown in Chapter 12 using pointers and polymorphism. For example, the method get_move in the class Player could be made virtual so that the array contestants contains a 'human' player as well as a computer player. The declaration for contestants would now become:

  ```
  Board   c_4;

  Player* contestant[] = {
     new Player( Counter(Counter::BLACK) ),
     new Computer_Player( Counter(Counter::WHITE), c_4 ),
   };
  ```

  The method get_move would be made virtual in the base class Basic_player. The constructor for Computer_Player in addition to storing the counter used, also stores a pointer to the board. Thus, the method get_move can interrogate the board. The code for processing a move in the method play would now become:

  ```
      move = contestant[no]->get_move(terminal);
      while ( !c_4.move_ok_for_column(move) )
      {
        move = contestant[no]->get_move(terminal, true);
      }
      c_4.drop_in_column(move, contestant[no]->counter_is());
  ```

19 Declarations and casts

This chapter will describe how storage is declared for derived types in C++. When declaring storage it is important to explicitly allocate storage for the parts of the data structure which have not be implicitly allocated. In addition the explicit casting mechanism is explored.

19.1 Storage declarations of derived types

C++ allows the direct declaration of many complex structures made from a single type. However, in many of these declarations for derived types, only part of the storage is allocated implicitly, the rest must be explicitly allocated and chained together to form the total storage specified for the structure.

For example:

```
int *table;
```

declares a storage location `table` which can hold a pointer to an int. The contents of the location `table` are undefined and an explicit assignment must be made to `table`, providing it with a pointer to a storage cell which can contain an int.

In these declarations the priority of operators is important. In particular, note the operator priority of [] () and *.

19.1.1 Priority of [] () and *

This is illustrated in Figure 19.1.

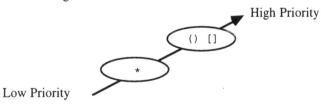

Figure 19.1 Priority of [] () and *.

Summary

Operator	Associates	Notes	Priority
[]	Left to right	Array declaration	High equal to ()
()	Left to right	Function declaration	High equal to []
*	Right to left	Indirection	Low

Thus, in the C++ declaration:

```
int *table[3];
```

which describes an array of three pointers to items of type integer, only the storage for the array is allocated. The storage to hold the three integers must be allocated separately.

This declaration is read as follows:

int *<u>table[3]</u>;	*An array of 3*
int <u>*table[3]</u>;	*An array of 3 pointers*
int <u>*table[3]</u>;	*An array of 3 pointers to items of type int*

Note: It is a good idea to allocate any extra storage required for a structure immediately after the declaration.

The declaration:

```
int (*table)[3]
```

describes a pointer to an array of three items of type integer. This time, only the location to hold the pointer to the structure is allocated.

For this example, the way to read it is as follows, using the above rules for operator precedence:

int (<u>*table</u>)[3];	*A pointer to*
int <u>(*table)[3]</u>;	*A pointer to an array of 3 items*
int <u>(*table)[3]</u>;	*A pointer to an array of 3 items of type int*

*Note: That [] has higher priority than *.*

19.2 Structures allocated

A declaration in C++ has two distinct attributes:

- Creation of the storage for all or part of the data structure.
- Describes to the compiler how to access elements of the data structure.

In the examples below for each declaration the storage described is shown diagrammatically. In the diagram the solid area represents storage implicitly allocated and the dotted area indicates storage which has to be explicitly allocated later.

Declaration	Data structure
`int value;`	
`int *value;` "A pointer to an int"	
`int value[3];` "An array of 3 ints"	
`int *value[3];` "An array of 3 pointers to an int"	
`int (*value)[3];` "A pointer to an array of 3 ints"	
`char *(*argv)[];` "A pointer to an open array of pointers to a character"	

19.3   Function prototypes

As seen previously, all functions must be declared with a function prototype statement before they can be used. However, in these examples the item returned has been a relatively simple item.

Consider the function prototype:

```
char *return_str();
```

Which is a function `return_str` with no parameters which returns a pointer to an item of type char.

The way to read this is as follows:

`char *return_str();`   *A function with no parameters*

`char *return str();`   *A function with no parameters which returns a pointer to an item of type char*

Note: As the name given to the function is `return_str`, *it is very likely that the pointer will in fact point to the first character of an array of characters which will make up a C++ string.*

Another more complex example would be:

```
char * ( *fun( int ) ) ();
```

A function with no parameters returning a pointer to a function taking an int parameter which returns a pointer to a C++ string.

The way to read this is as follows:

`char * ( *fun( int ) ) ();`	*A pointer to a function taking an int parameter*
`char * ( *fun( int ) ) ();`	*A function with no parameters returning a pointer to a function taking an int parameter*
`char * ( *fun( int ) ) ();`	*A function with no parameters returning a pointer to a function taking an int parameter which returns a pointer to a C++ string*

This however, can more easily be expressed using `typedef`:

```
typedef char*    C_string;       //C++ string
typedef C_string F_C_string(int); //Function returning C_string

F_C_string*      fun();          //Function returning
                                 // pointer to F_C_string
```

19.3.1   Formal parameter declarations

Like declarations of storage, parameters to a function also need to be declared.

19.4   Union

A `union` specifies that several data items are to share the same physical storage. This will allow for very efficient use of memory when the items are not stored and used concurrently. The dangers inherent in using this mechanism are, principally, the destruction of a data item previously stored in the union when a new data item is inserted, and the extraction of a data item that has been stored as another type. For example, a union that holds an `int`, `char`, and `float` may be used to store an integer value and then this integer value may be extracted as if it were a floating point number.

Note: There can occasionally be valid reasons for extracting a data item as a different type.

In the following program a `union` is used to define a type `Store` which can hold a char, int or a float.

```
int main()
{
  union Store
  {
    char  as_a_char;          //All occupy the
    int   as_an_int;          // same storage
    float as_a_float;         // space
  };

  Store item;
  item.as_a_char = 'A';       //Use item to hold a  character
  item.as_an_int = 42;        //Use item to hold an integer
  item.as_a_float= 3.14;      //Use item to hold a  float

  cout << "int = " << item.as_an_int << "\n";
  return 0;
}
```

When run the program will give the following result:

```
int = -2621
```

which may not have been what was expected.

19.5   Bit-field

A `struct` can have the bit-field qualifier to indicate the exact number of bits occupied by an integer type. How this is achieved is up to the implementors of the compiler.

The following program declares a `struct` named `Flags` held in a machine word that represents various status flags.

```
int main()
{
  struct Flags
  {
    unsigned int status : 3;      //status is 3 bits wide
    unsigned int size   : 6;      //size  is 6 bits wide
    unsigned int ok     : 1;      //ok    is 1 bit  wide
  };

  Flags operation;                //Operation to be performed
  operation.status= 3;            //Set bits for operation
  operation.size = 5;
  operation.ok   = 1;

  std::cout << "status : " << (int) operation.status << "\n";
  std::cout << "size   : " << (int) operation.size << "\n";
  std::cout << "ok     : " << (int) operation.ok << "\n";

  std::cout << "word   : " << oct <<
              *(reinterpret_cast<int*>(&operation)) << "\n";
  return 0;
}
```

Note: The cast reinterpret_cast *is used to convert a pointer to* Flags *into a pointer to an int.*

When run the above program produces the following results:

```
status : 3
size   : 5
ok     : 1
word   : 1053
```

Note: unsigned int *is used to guarantee that sign extension will not take place.*

19.6   Casts

C++ provide several explicit ways of converting an object from one type to another type. These explicit casting mechanisms are:

- const_cast<T>(arg)
- dynamic_cast<T>(arg)
- reinterpret_cast<T>(arg)
- static_cast<T>(arg)

where arg is the expression which is to be cast to type T.

- const_cast<T>(arg)

  A const cast is used to add or remove the const or volatile modifier from an object.

  For example, in the following code the const modifier is added and then removed:

  ```
  const char *const_name = "mike";

  char *name = const_cast<char*>( const_name );

  const char *const_name2 = const_cast< const char* >( name );
  ```

- dynamic_cast<T>(arg)

  A dynamic cast is used to convert between pointer or reference to an object to a pointer or reference to another object. One important use of this cast is to convert between base and derived classes. Importantly the feasibility of the cast is checked at run-time. If a pointer cast fails then 0 is returned, whilst if a reference cast fails then the exception bad_cast is thrown.

  For example, the following code recovers an instance of a derived class from a heterogeneous collection.

```
Base *collection[2];
collection[0] = new Derived[1];
collection[1] = new Derived[1];

Derived *d =  dynamic_cast<Derived*>(collection[0]);
if ( d == 0 )
{
   // Failed
}
```

- reinterpret_cast<T>(arg)

  Used in general to cast one kind of pointer to another. This includes converting int's to pointers and vice-versa. In the conversion T must be a pointer, reference, arithmetic type, pointer to function or pointer to member.

  For example, the following code illustrates the conversion of a literal constant to a char pointer and then to an int pointer.

```
char *p_ch  = reinterpret_cast<char*>( 0x0000FA00 );
int  *p_int = reinterpret_cast<int*>( p_ch );
```

- static_cast<T>(arg)

  Used to cast an expression to a type the compiler can perform by an existing conversion mechanism.

  For example, the following code converts a char to an int and a derived class to a base class:

```
char c = 'M';
int as_int = static_cast<int>(c);

Derived d;
Base    b = static_cast<Base>( d );
```

19.7   Self-assessment

- What is the difference between the two declarations:
  ```
  int value[3];
  int *value[3];
  ```

- How would you declare the object data that represents an array of 3 pointers which point to pointers which in turn points to a character object?

- Why is a union a dangerous structure to use?

- When would you use a dynamic_cast?

20 Container classes

This chapter describes how the operator [] can be overloaded to provide a safe implementation of a vector in C++. This is modelled in part on the interface of the STL templated class `vector`. The STL library is described in Chapters 24 and 25.

20.1 Introduction

In the discussion about arrays in C++, one of the main points under discussion was that at run-time the array bounds are not checked. This naturally can lead to some serious run-time errors, which can cause an unexpected crash. Worse still, there will be occasions when the error is not observed and wrong results are produced.

In C++, array access using subscripting is just a shorthand way of using pointers and addresses. For example, with the following declaration:

```
int vec[10]
```

The subscripting expression:

```
int res = vec[5];
```

could have been written as:

```
int res = *( &vec[0] + 5 );
```

When adding or subtracting a value from a pointer, C++, like its ancestor language C, multiples the value by the size of the storage pointed at. For example:

Expression	Interpreted by the compiler as:
`*( &vec[0] + 5 )`	`*( &vec[0] + 5 * sizeof(int))`

This technique is used by the compiler to also evaluate normal subscripting of an array. The actual code generated is very simple, as many of the items in the expression are known at compile time.

20.1.1 A solution

The risk of undetected run-time errors can be avoided, as C++ fortunately allows the [] operator to be re-defined. A class to implement this safe vector is shown below. In implementing this class, features are provided which allow an instance of this class to be used in the creation of a safe two-dimensional array.

20.2   A safe vector

The responsibilities of a safe vector are:

Method/Constructor	Responsibility
( )	Access an element with no bounds checking
[ ]	Access an element with bound checking
back	Return the last element in the vector
front	Return the first element in the vector
pop_back	Re-size the vector by removing an element from the end
push_back	Re-size the vector by adding an element to the end
set_def_size	Set the default size for vector creation
size	Return the length of the vector
Vector	Construct the safe vector

Note: The operator [] is the low-level subscripting operator and () is the function call operator.

20.2.1   Restriction in use of an instance of the class Vector

An instance of Vector has the restriction that it may not be copied. However, this restriction is not enforced by the compiler. The reasons for the disallowing of copying are explained fully in Chapter 23, together with a mechanism to enforce the restriction and an illustration of the process required to allow objects that contain a pointer to be copied.

20.2.2   C++ specification

The specification for this class is:

```
template <class Type>
class Vector {
public:
  typedef Type Value_type;            //Make Visible
  explicit Vector( size_t = 0 );      //Constructor
  ~Vector();                          //Destructor
  Type& operator()( size_t );         //Access no checking
  const Type& operator()( size_t ) const;  //Access no checking const
  Type& operator[]( size_t );         //Access checking
  const Type& operator[]( size_t ) const;  //Access checking const
  size_t size() const;                //Length
  void push_back(const Type&);        //Add element at end
  void pop_back();                    //Remove element at end
  inline const Type& front() const;   //Front element
  inline Type& front();               //Front element
  inline const Type& back() const;    //Back element
  inline Type& back();                //Back element
  static void set_def_size( size_t ); 
```

```
protected:
  void fail( const char[],  size_t  ) const;
  Type* new_vec(  size_t  );
private:
  static const int INC_SIZE=10;          //Size of expansion
  Type*  the_p_item;                     //Pointer to array store
  size_t the_vec_size;                   //Elements in array
  size_t the_vec_actual_size;            //Real size of array
  static int the_def_size;               //Default size
};
```

Note: The two versions for the overloaded operator [] and (), to cater for const and
       non const instances of a class.
       The two version of the methods front and back, to cater for const and non
       const instances of a class.

       An integer vector can be declared using:

```
Vector <int> numbers;
Vector <int> many_numbers(25);
```

This is similar to the way vectors are normally declared in C++. However, the
size of the array need not be a compile time constant.
The header file <ctype.h> contains the definition for size_t, a type used to
specify a size.

An instance of the class Vector represents a vector of 10 elements as illustrated in
Figure 20.1.

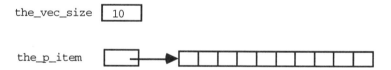

Figure 20.1 Storage for an instance of a Vector.

The class through the use of its constructor and destructor ensures that the storage is
allocated and de-allocated correctly.
Remember, an instance of this class may not be assigned.

20.2.3   Implementation

The static member function set_def_size sets the default vector creation size. This
default setting for the vector size will be used, when for example, a vector of objects of
type Vector is created. It is not possible to explicitly set a parameter for an objects
constructor when a variable number of objects are created.

```
#include <string>
#include <strstream>
#include <stdexcept>

template <class Type>
size_t Vector <Type>::the_def_size = 0;

template <class Type>
void Vector <Type>::set_def_size( size_t s )
{
  the_def_size = s;
}
```

The constructor uses the protected member function `new_vec` to allocate the storage for the vector.

```
template <class Type>
Vector <Type>::Vector( size_t s )
{
  if ( s > 0 )                                  //Size
    the_vec_size = s;
  else
    the_vec_size = the_def_size;
  the_vec_actual_size = the_vec_size;           //Space allocated
  the_p_item = NULL;                            //May fail
  the_p_item = new_vec(the_vec_size);
}
```

Note: If the default value for the constructor is used then the actual elements allocated is defined by `the_def_size`.

The destructor releases the claimed storage.

```
template <class Type>
Vector <Type>::~Vector()
{
  if ( the_p_item != NULL )                     //Not allocated
    delete [] the_p_item;
}
```

Access to an individual element uses the overloaded operator []:

```
template <class Type>
Type& Vector <Type>::operator[]( size_t i )
{
  if ( i < 0 || i >= the_vec_size ) {           //Subscript check
    fail( "subscript is", i );                  //Failure
    return the_p_item[0];                       //Compiler check
  }
  return the_p_item[i];                         //OK
}
```

The point of interest here is that the address of the object selected is returned, rather than the object itself.

```
Type& Vector <Type>::operator[]( size_t i )
```

This allows the use of subscripting on the LHS of an expression. Remember, the lvalue must be returned for an item on the LHS of an assignment operator. The compiler, however, will convert this to an rvalue if the operator is used on the RHS of an assignment operator.

Note: Normally, if the overloaded operator [], has been declared inline, *and is used on the RHS of an expression, then the compiler will optimize away the conversion rvalue -> lvalue -> rvalue for the returned result.*

The const version of the method that is used on a const instance of the class is defined as:

```
template <class Type>
const Type& Vector <Type>::operator[]( size_t i ) const
{
  if ( i < 0 || i >= the_vec_size ) {        //Subscript check
    fail( "subscript is", i );               //Failure
    return the_p_item[0];                    //Compiler check
  }
  return the_p_item[i];                      //OK
}
```

Note: This is required as a reference to a const object is returned.

However, should a user require efficient access to the structure they can use:

```
template <class Type>
Type& Vector <Type>::operator()( size_t i )
{
  return the_p_item[i];                      //Fast
}
```

which, if declared inline, would normally generate the same code as one would expect to see when using inbuilt C++ arrays. The const version of the method is implemented as:

```
template <class Type>
const Type& Vector <Type>::operator()( size_t i ) const
{
  return the_p_item[i];                      //Fast
}
```

The member function `size` returns the number of active cells in the vector. This may be different from the storage allocated.

```
template <class Type>
size_t Vector <Type>::size() const
{
  return the_vec_size;                    //Elements stored
}
```

The member function, `push_back` re-sizes the vector by adding an extra element at the end. This is implemented by creating a new array and copying the old contents plus the additional element to the newly allocated storage. To make the process more efficient, `INC_SIZE` elements are added, thus subsequent invocations of `push_back` can simply copy the new element into the free storage.

```
template <class Type>
void Vector <Type>::push_back(const Type& val)
{
  if ( the_vec_size+1 > the_vec_actual_size )      //No room
  {
    Type* old_vec  = the_p_item;                   //Original

    the_vec_actual_size = the_vec_size + INC_SIZE; //New size
    the_p_item = new_vec(the_vec_actual_size);
    for ( size_t i=0; i<the_vec_size; i++ )
    {
      the_p_item[i] = old_vec[i];
    }
    if ( old_vec != NULL ) delete [] old_vec;      //Dispose
  }
  the_p_item[ the_vec_size ] = val;                //Store
  the_vec_size++;                                  //Adjust size
}
```

The member function, `pop_back` re-sizes the vector by removing the last element from the vector. There is no attempt to reduce the actual storage occupied by the array.

```
template <class Type>
void Vector <Type>::pop_back()
{
  if ( the_vec_size > 0 )
  {
    the_vec_size--;                         //Adjust size
  } else {
    fail("pop_back", 0);
  }
}
```

The first and last elements of the vector can be accessed directly using the methods front and back respectively. A reference to the item selected is returned to avoid any unnecessary copying of items from the collection. There are two versions of each method so that a const and non const instance of a Vector can be processed.

```
template <class Type>
const Type& Vector <Type>::front() const
{
  return operator [] (0) ;                    //Retrieve
}
template <class Type>
Type& Vector <Type>::front()
{
  return operator [] (0) ;                    //Retrieve
}
template <class Type>
const Type& Vector <Type>::back() const
{
  return operator [] (the_vec_size-1) ;       //Retrieve
}
template <class Type>
Type& Vector <Type>::back()
{
  return operator [] (the_vec_size-1) ;       //Retrieve
}
```

Note: The use of the explicit call to the member operator function [ ]. The operator
function [ ] call:
```
        return operator [] (0);
```
could also have been written as
```
        return (*this)[0];.
```

The member function new_vec is responsible for allocating memory for holding the contents of the vector.

```
template <class Type>
Type* Vector<Type>::new_vec( size_t n )
{
  Type* p_store;
  p_store = new Type[n];                      //Allocate
  //  Warning
  //  This may fail due to lack of memory
  //  If it does then the exception
  //    bad_alloc will be thrown
  return p_store;                             //Storage
}
```

The member function `fail` generates an exception.

```
template <class Type>
void Vector <Type>::fail( const char mes[], size_t  i ) const
{
  char storage[120];                              //Message
  std::ostrstream text(storage,120);              //As stream
  text << "Vector [Bounds 0.." << ((int)the_vec_size-1)
       << " - " << mes << " " << i << "]" << '\0';
  throw std::range_error( std::string(storage) );  //Exception
}
```

20.2.4   Putting it all together

A small test program to populate a vector and attempt an invalid access is:

```
#include <iostream>
#include <string>
#include <stdexcept>

#include "Vector.h"

int main()
{
  try
  {
    const int MAX = 9;
    Vector <int> v(MAX);
    int i;

    for ( i=0; i<MAX; i++ ) { v[i] = i; }              //Populate

    for ( i=0; i<MAX; i++ ) std::cout << v[i] << " ";  //Checking
    std::cout << "\n";

    for ( i=0; i<MAX; i++ ) std::cout << v(i) << " ";  //No Checking
    std::cout << "\n";

    std::cout << "\n" << "\n";
    std::cout << "Now access element 100 which does not exist" << "\n";
    std::cout << v[100];
  }
  catch ( std::range_error& err )
  {
    std::cout << "\n" << "Fail: " << err.what() << "\n";
  }
  return 0;
}
```

When run this produces the following output:

```
0 1 2 3 4 5 6 7 8
0 1 2 3 4 5 6 7 8

Now access element 100 which does not exist

Fail: Vector [Bounds 0..8 - subscript is 100]
```

20.2.5 Passing an instance of a `Vector` by reference

Though an instance of a `Vector` cannot be copied (see Section 20.2.6) it can be passed by reference to a function, as the example below illustrates.

```cpp
int sum( Vector <int>& numbers )
{
  int sum = 0;
  for (int i=0; i<numbers.size(); i++) sum += numbers[i];
  return sum;
}

int main()
{
  Vector <int> room(4);
  room[0] = 3;              //People
  room[1] = 2;              //People
  room[2] = 1;              //People
  room[3] = 1;              //People
  std::cout << "Number of people in the rooms is : "
            << sum( room ) << "\n";
  return 0;
}
```

When run this would produce:

```
Number of people in the rooms is : 7
```

20.2.6 Limitations of the implementation

The implementation of the class `Vector` has the following limitations:

● Assignment of an instance of the `Vector` container class will not produce the correct results. Sections 23.1 and 23.4 explains in detail the consequences of such an action together with a solution.

● When class items which have a constructor or destructor are stored, some unnecessary constructions and destruction's will be performed when the array is extended.

A solution to the second limitation is to allocated memory as raw storage and only explicitly call the constructor for the stored object when it is added to the collection. This improvement to the process requires the modification of the methods: ~Vector, push_back, pop_back and new_vec.

As the storage is allocated as raw storage, destructors for the items stored must be explicitly called in the class Vector's destructor. This is implemented as follows:

```
template <class Type>
Vector <Type>::~Vector()
{
  for ( int i=0; i<the_vec_size; i++ )
  {
    (&the_p_item[i])->~Type();              //Force destructor call
  }
  if ( the_p_item != NULL )                 //Not allocated
    delete [] (char*) the_p_item;           // Treat as bytes
}
```

The implementation of the method push_back uses the special form of the new operator shown below:

```
void* operator new(size_t, void* p)          //Initialize
{
  return p;
}
```

to explicitly call the constructor for the item to be stored via the above overloaded version of new.

```
template <class Type>
void Vector <Type>::push_back(const Type& val)
{
  if ( the_vec_size+1 > the_vec_actual_size )       //No room
  {
    Type* old_vec  = the_p_item;                    //Original

    the_p_item = new_vec(the_vec_actual_size+INC_SIZE);
    for ( int i=0; i<the_vec_size; i++ )
      new ( &the_p_item[i] ) Type(old_vec[i]);      //Construct

    the_vec_actual_size += INC_SIZE;                //New size
    for ( int i=0; i<the_vec_size; i++)             //Destructor
      (&old_vec[i])->~Type();                       // For elements
    if ( old_vec != NULL )
      delete [] (char*)old_vec;                     //Raw storage
  }
  new ( &the_p_item[the_vec_size] ) Type(val);      //Construct
  the_vec_size++;                                   //Adjust size
}
```

Note: *The original members of the collection are copied to the newly allocated storage using the overloaded operator new. This mechanism is required so that the proper construction process is performed.*

The method `pop_back` now explicitly calls the destructor on the removed item.

```
template <class Type>
void Vector <Type>::pop_back()
{
  if ( the_vec_size > 0 )
  {
    (&the_p_item[the_vec_size-1])->~Type();  //Force destructor call
    the_vec_size--;                          //Adjust size
  } else { fail("pop_back", 0); }            // Invalid
}
```

The allocation of memory for raw bytes of storage is as follows:

```
template <class Type>
Type* Vector<Type>::new_vec( size_t n )
{
  Type* p_store;
  //   Warning
  //   This may fail due to lack of memory
  //   If it does then the exception
  //      bad_alloc will be thrown
  p_store = (Type*)new char[n*sizeof(Type)];       //Allocate

  return p_store;                                  //Storage
}
```

20.3 Implementing a stack with the class `Vector`

The Class `Stack` described in Section 8.9 can be re-implemented using a container class to provide the storage of the data items. Any container class can be used provided it implements the following methods: `size`, `push_back`, `pop_back` and `back`. As the container class `Vector` implements these methods it may be used. The C++ specification for the class `Stack` using a container class for the storage of data is:

```
#ifndef CLASS_STACK_SPEC
#define CLASS_STACK_SPEC
template <class Type, class Container >
class Stack {
public:
  typedef Container::Value_type Value_type; //In Container
  Stack();
  inline bool empty() const;                //Stack empty
  inline size_t size() const;               //Size of collection
  inline Value_type& top();                 //Return top item
  inline const Value_type& top() const;     //Return top item
  inline void push( const Value_type );     //Push item onto stack
  inline void pop();                        //Pop top item from stack
private:
  Container the_elements;                    //Storage
};
```

Note: The typedef to make `Value_type` *in the container visible. The type of objects stored in the container are of* `Value_type`*.*

The implementation of the class `Stack` is:

```
template <class Type, class Container>
Stack<Type, Container>::Stack()
{
}

template <class Type, class Container>
bool Stack<Type, Container>::empty() const
{
  return the_elements.size() <= 0;      //Is empty
}


template <class Type, class Container>
size_t Stack<Type, Container>::size() const
{
  return the_elements.size();           //Elements in stack
}

template <class Type, class Container>
Value_type& Stack<Type, Container>::top()
{
  return the_elements.back();           //Top item
}

template <class Type, class Container>
const Value_type& Stack<Type, Container>::top() const
{
  return the_elements.back();           //Top item
}


template <class Type, class Container>
void Stack<Type, Container>::push( const Value_type item )
{
  the_elements.push_back( item );       //Push onto stack
}

template <class Type, class Container>
void Stack<Type, Container>::pop()
{
  the_elements.pop_back();              //Remove
}

#endif
```

20.3.1 Putting it all together

A stack of `int`'s using a `Vector` as the storage container is declared as:

```
Stack < int, Vector<int> > numbers;
```

*Note: That there must be a space between the `>`'s in `Stack < Vector<int> >`
otherwise the compiler will confuse the construct with the use of the `>>` operator.*

Whilst a stack of `char`'s using a `Vector` as the storage container is declared as:

```
Stack < char, Vector<char> > letters;
```

Any other container for storage could be used provided it implements the methods:
`size`, `push_back`, `pop_back` and `back`. For example, if there is a container class
`List` whose implementation uses a linked list and provides the above interface. Then a
stack of integers using a linked list for its storage technique is declared as:

```
Stack < int, List<int> > numbers;
```

20.3.2 Default parameters to a templated class

As with functions, default parameters can also be given to the arguments to a templated
class. For example, the class `Stack` could have been defined as:

```
template <class Type, class Container = Vector<Type> >
class Stack {
public:

}
```

Then an instantiation of this class to use an instance of the class `vector` to store the
elements would be declared as:

```
Stack < char > letters;
```

20.4 Hashtable

As the operator [] can be redefined, this allows new structures to be associated with
traditional arrays. In some applications, an array is required with indexes or keys that
can take the form of an arbitrary string. For example, in an application for a car
manufacturer which records how many cars of different colours are constructed each
day, it would be convenient to be able to write:

```
std::cout << "Number of Green cars = " << cars[ "green" ] << "\n";
```

This can be implemented by using hashing to convert the key into an index. The hashed key is then used to access a hash table of pointers to a chain of cells, which contain the pair (`"green"`, `20`). The first component is the key, in this case green, the second component is the value associated with the key.

Hashing is simply the conversion of the key into a number in the range 0 to the maximum number of elements of the hash table minus one. This hashed key is then used to access the hash table. As the hash value may not be unique, the key and data value are stored as a pair in a chain of items which hash to the same value; this is to ensure that the correct key is selected when access is made to an element for which several keys hash.

For example, after executing the following code:

```
cars[ "green" ] = 2;   cars[ "blue" ] = 3;
```

the structure used to store the number of cars of each colour would be as illustrated in Figure 20.2, if both the key strings (`green`, `blue`) converted to a hash value of 4.

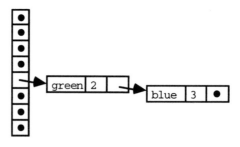

Figure 20.2 Hash table for two items with the same hash value.

The specification for this class `Hashtable` is:

Method/Constructor	Responsibility
Hashtable	Allocate storage for the object.
[]	Access the data associated with a key.

The C++ specification for class `Hashtable` where the user can specify the type of the key and data is:

```
#ifndef CLASS_STRING_VEC_SPEC
#define CLASS_STRING_VEC_SPEC
```

```
template <class Key, class Data>
class Hashtable {
public:
  explicit Hashtable(const unsigned int,
                     unsigned long (*f)(const Key&) );
  ~Hashtable();                               //Release storage
  Data& operator[]( const Key );              //Subscript
  const Data& operator[]( const Key ) const;  //Subscript const
protected:
  void fail( const char mes[], const int ) const;
private:
  struct Cell;                                //Tentative declaration
  typedef Cell *P_Cell;
  struct Cell {
    Key     key_value;                        //Key value
    Data    value;                            //Data value
    P_Cell p_next;                            //Next item in list
  };
  P_Cell  *the_p_cell_vec;                    //Pointer to a P_Cell
  int      the_no_elements;                   //Number of elements
  unsigned long (*the_hash_fun)(const Key&);  //Pointer to hash function
};

#endif
```

The structure manipulated by the class Hashtable is illustrated in Figure 20.3.

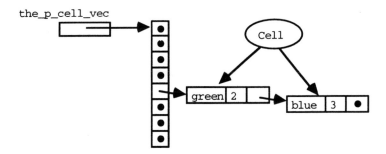

Figure 20.3 Storage used by the class Hashtable.

Note: The declaration of Cell describes the storage for the individually stored items.

The construct for the class Hashtable has the following parameters:

- The size of the hashtable to use
- The address of a function f whose signature is:
  unsigned long f(const Key&)
  which converts the key into an integer number.

and is implemented as follows:

```
#ifndef CLASS_STRING_VEC_IMP
#define CLASS_STRING_VEC_IMP
```

```
#include <string>
#include <strstream>
#include <stdexcept>

template <class Key, class Data>
Hashtable<Key,Data>::Hashtable(const unsigned int size,
                               unsigned long (*f)(const Key&) )
{
  the_no_elements = size;

  if ( the_no_elements < 1 )
    fail("Invalid bounds - ", the_no_elements );   //Invalid hash size

  //   Warning
  //   This may fail due to lack of memory
  //   If it does then the exception
  //      bad_alloc will be thrown

  the_p_cell_vec = new P_Cell[the_no_elements];    //Hash table


  for( int i=0; i<the_no_elements; i++ )           //Set pointers in
    the_p_cell_vec[i]=NULL;                         // hash table to null

  the_hash_fun = f;                                //Address of hash fun
}
```

Note: The size of the hashtable should be a prime number which is near the size of the number of unique keys used.

The destructor carefully releases all storage that has been created.

```
template <class Key, class Data>
Hashtable<Key,Data>::~Hashtable()
{
  for(int i=0; i<the_no_elements; i++)         //All lists
  {
    P_Cell p_cell = the_p_cell_vec[i];
    while ( p_cell != NULL )                    //List
    {
      P_Cell p_current = p_cell;                //
      p_cell = p_cell->p_next;                  //Next cell in chain
      delete [] p_current;                      //Current cell
    }
  }

  delete [] the_p_cell_vec;                     // Release hashtable
}
```

The fail function is defined as follows:

```
template <class Key, class Data>
void Hashtable<Key,Data>::fail(const char mes[], const int i ) const
{
  char storage[120];
  std::ostrstream text(storage,120);
  text << "Hashtable ["
       << mes << " " << i << "]" << '\0';
  throw std::range_error( storage );
}
```

Note: This is only called when storage can not be allocated.

The overloaded operator [] is used to index the associative array. The version shown below is for mutable objects. When a key is used that does not exist in the hash table a new entry is created for the key.

```
template <class Key, class Data>
Data& Hashtable<Key,Data>::operator[]( const Key key_value )
{
  unsigned int h = (*the_hash_fun)(key_value)%the_no_elements;
  P_Cell *p = &the_p_cell_vec[h];              //Pointer to P_Cell

  while ( *p != NULL ) {                        //
    if ( (*p)->key_value == key_value ) {
      return (*p)->value;                       //Found cell
    }
    p = &((*p)->p_next);                         //Next in list
  }

  //Non existing key create cell and chain in

  //  Warning
  //  This may fail due to lack of memory
  //  If it does then the exception
  //    bad_alloc will be thrown

  *p = new Cell[1];                              //Build cell

  (*p)->key_value = key_value;                   //Store key
  (*p)->p_next    = NULL;                        //
  return (*p)->value;                            //Data value (Undefined)
}
```

Note: If a key element is accessed and is not already stored, an entry is created for it with an undefined value. This may lead to an error later on if this undefined value is used. This is done so that a hashtable of any type may be created. A better mechanism would have been to use the identity element or nil value of the type, but this presupposes that all types can provide an identity or nil value.

The const version of this method is:

```
template <class Key, class Data>
const Data& Hashtable<Key,Data>::operator[]( const Key key_value )
const
{
  unsigned int h = (*the_hash_fun)(key_value)%the_no_elements;
  P_Cell *p = &the_p_cell_vec[h];              //Pointer to P_Cell

  while ( *p != NULL ) {                       //
    if ( (*p)->key_value == key_value ) {
      return (*p)->value;                      //Found cell
    }
    p = &((*p)->p_next);                       //Next in list
  }

  //Can not create an element in a const object

  fail("Element undefined (Reading const hashtable)", 0);
  return (*p)->value; //Never gets here - prevents warning
}

#endif
```

Note: The failure raised, if access to a non existent member of a const object is attempted.

20.4.1   Putting it all together

A user can now write:

```
int main()
{
  Hashtable<std::string, int> cars( 11, hash );

  cars[ "green" ] = 20;   cars[ "blue" ] = 30;

  cars[ "green" ]++;
  cars[ "blue" ] = cars[ "blue" ] + 3;

  std::cout << "Number of Green cars = " << cars[ "green" ] << "\n";
  std::cout << "Number of Blue  cars = " << cars[ "blue" ] << "\n";
  return 0;
}
```

Where the hashing function `hash` is defined as:

```
unsigned long hash( const std::string& str )  //Hash string to number
{
  unsigned long h = 0;
  for ( int i=0; i < str.length(); i++ )
  {
    h = h + (unsigned long) str[i];              //Sum letters in string
  }
  return h;
}
```

Note: The scaling of the hash value to be within the range of the hashtable is performed during the subscripting process.

Which when compiled with suitable header files and run will produce:

```
Number of Green cars = 21
Number of Blue  cars = 33
```

20.4.2 Sparse arrays

The class `Hashtable` can also be used to implement sparse arrays. For example, a fragment of a program which uses a sparse integer array is shown below:

```
unsigned long hash_index( const unsigned long& value )
{
  return value;
}

int main()
{
  Hashtable< unsigned long, int >  sparse_array( 17, hash_index );

  sparse_array[ 12345 ]     = 56;
  sparse_array[ 123456789 ] = 42;

  std::cout << sparse_array[ 123456789 ] << "\n";
  return 0;
}
```

20.5   Self-assessment

- Why has the constructor for Vector been declared as explicit?

- Why does the class Vector return a reference to the object selected?

- Why can a programmer not successfully assign a copy of an instance of the Vector class?

- If an instance of the class Hashtable where declared to only consist of a hashtable of 1 element would it still be able to store many data items?

20.6   Exercises

- *Re-sizeable Array*
  Modify the class Array so that a user can re-size the array. In re-sizing the array the original contents of cells which are common to the original array and the re-sized array should be preserved. This preservation may be implemented by copying.

  Remember, an instance of an Array may not be copied.

- *Cube*
  Implement and test a class to provide a safe array that has three dimensions.

- *Binary_tree*
  Implement and test a class to implement the storing and retrieving of a key, data pair using a binary tree as the underlying storage mechanism.

21 Pre-processing directives

This chapter describes the macro language provided as a pre-processor for C++ . In essence, a macro provides the means of replacing a sequence of program symbols by another set of symbols. Macros are a very powerful facility when correctly used. However, when incorrectly used they can make a program unreadable, and un-modifiable.

21.1 Introduction

A macro is the textual substitution of one set of program tokens by another set of tokens. This macro processing is performed before the source text is presented to the compiler proper. A macro definition is introduced by a # in column 1 of the text file.

In many cases in C++ the use of inline functions and const declarations eliminates the need for macros.

21.2 Source inclusion of files

One of the useful features of a macro processor is the source inclusion of the contents of a file into the program text.

```
#include "filename"     /* Taken from current working directory */

#include <filename>     /* Taken from system directories */
```

21.3 Text substitution

These should in most cases be done by `const` declarations and by the use of `inline` functions.

The following will define the symbol MAX to be replaced by 120:

```
#define  MAX 120
```

Note: *The scope of the macro is to the end of the compilation unit in which it has been defined.*
A semi-colon should not be placed at the end of a macro definition as this could cause problems.

For example, the C++ code sequence:

```
#define MAX 120;    // The # must be in column 1
int table[MAX];
```

would be seen by the compiler as:

```
int table[120;];
```

which would cause a compile time error, that would not be obvious to spot.

The definition of a macro may be removed with:

```
#undef MAX
```

From now on, no replacement of the symbol MAX with 120 will be performed.

The following will define a macro, that uses a condition expression to deliver the larger of x and y:

```
#define larger(x,y)   ( (x)>(y) ? (x) : (y) )
```

Note: Be careful, with the use of brackets when defining a macro.

For example, if `larger` had been defined as:

```
#define larger(x,y)   x>y ? x:   y
```

then the replacement text for:

```
max = larger( count+1, last )*2;
```

would have been as follows:

```
max = count+1 > last   ? count+1 : last*2;
```

Note: Only the result returned by larger when the result is false is multiplied by 2.

More useful is an assert macro which can be defined as:

```
#inclfude <stdlib>
#define assert(ex)                                                 \
{                                                                  \
  if (!(ex))                                                       \
  {                                                                \
    std::cerr << "assert failed File " << __FILE__ << " line "; \
    std::cerr << __LINE__ << "\n";                                 \
    std::exit( -1 );                                               \
  }                                                                \
}
```

which can then be placed in a program under development to assert various conditions during the execution of the program. For example, the method `withdraw` in the class `Account` seen in Section 5.3.1 could have been implemented as:

```
float Account::withdraw( const float money )
{
  assert( money >= 0.00 );                        //Pre-condition
  float get = 0.00;
  if ( the_balance-money >= the_min_balance )
  {
    the_balance = the_balance - money;
    get = money;
  }
  assert( get >= 0.00 );                          //Post-condition
  return get;
}
```

When the program works correctly the macro can be changed to:

```
#define assert(ex)
```

When the program is recompiled, this will considerably reduce the program size. Of course, this does mean that the checks in the program will no longer be made.

Note: If a macro extends over more than one line \ is used to indicate the continuation.
__FILE__ is a system macro which is replaced by the name of the current file.
__LINE__ is a system macro which is replaced by the current line number.
The macro `assert` is defined in the header file `<assert>`

21.4 Conditional compilation

Great care should be exercised in the use of conditional compilation. While to a builder of an application it offers the powerful feature of allowing several different versions of the program to be contained in the same source files, it can easily lead to confusion over which code has actually been used to compile a particular version.

For example:

```
#include <iostream>
#include "local.h"

int main()
{
#ifdef  DEBUG
  std::cerr << "Entering function main" << "\n";
#endif
  std::cout << "Hello world" << "\n";
  return 0;
}
```

Then, if the file `local.h` contained:

```
#define  DEBUG  1
```

the C++ compiler would compile the text as follows:

```cpp
#include <iostream>
#include "local.h"
int main()
{
  std::cerr << "Entering function main" << "\n";

  std::cout << "Hello world" << "\n";
  return 0;
}
```

Alternatively, if the file `local.h` did not contain the definition of the symbol DEBUG:

```cpp
//#define  DEBUG  1
```

the C++ compiler would compile the text as follows:

```cpp
#include <iostream>
#include "local.h"
int main()
{

  std::cout << "Hello world" << "\n";
  return 0;
}
```

The important point about conditional compilation is that the substitution is done before the text is presented to the C++ compiler proper.

Other conditions may be employed for example:

```cpp
//#define  MAX     10

#ifndef MAX
  std::cout << "MAX not defined";
#endif
```

This would compile code to print the message:

```
MAX not defined
```

The conditional expression may have an `else` part as in:

```
#define  Intel 7

#ifdef Mips
  std::cout << "Mips CPU" << "\n";
#elif  Intel
  std::cout << "Intel CPU" << "\n";
#else
  std::cout << "Not a Mips or Intel CPU" << "\n";
#endif
```

which would compile code to print:

```
Intel CPU
```

The condition may also be a compile time condition made up of defined symbols as in:

```
#define Intel 8

#if   Intel == 7
  std::cout << "P7 CPU" << "\n";
#elif Intel == 8
  std::cout << "P8 CPU" << "\n";
#else
  std::cout << "Intel CPU" << "\n";
#endif
```

which would compile code to print:

```
P8 CPU
```

The monadic operator `defined` may be used with #if to test if several symbols are defined.

```
#if defined Intel && defined Linux
  std::cout << "Intel CPU running Linux" << "\n";
#endif
```

21.5   The `error` directive

The `#error` directive is used to cause a fatal error in compilation. For example, in a program the implementors may enforce the requirement that the value of the defined symbol MAX is in the range 0 .. 100 by means of the following code sequence.

```
#if MAX < 0 || MAX > 100
#error MAX must be in range 0 .. 100
#endif
```

If as part of the compilation process the defined symbol MAX is set outside of the prescribed range then the compilation will be aborted with a message of the form:

```
Fatal example.cpp 9: Error directive: MAX must be in range 0 .. 100 in
function main()
```

21.6   The `pragma` directive

The implementation dependant directive #pragma is used to set compile specific options. For example, to select space optimization for the code of a program the pragma directive might be:

```
#pragma space_optimization
```

Note: This is a made up pragma directive, the exact pragmas supported will be found with the documentation for the specific compiler used.

The compiler will ignore pragma directives that it does not recognize.

21.7   The `line` directive

Used to tell the compiler what the original line number and file name was before pre-processing. This is usually generated automatically by the C++ pre-processor which performs the inclusion of source files specified by the #include directive. In this way the compiler can give the source line number and file name of the original files rather than the line and file name of the file generated by the pre-processor.

```
# line 27
# line  1    "Account.h"
```

21.8   Predefined names

The following macro names have the following predefined values:

Name	Explanation
__cplusplus	defined if the compiler is a C++ compiler.
__DATE__	The current date (Mmm dd yyyy).
__FILE__	The current file name.
__LINE__	The current line number.
__TIME__	The current time (hh:mm:ss).

Note: __cplusplus can be used if a header file is to be shared between C++ programs and C programs.

21.9.   Creating a string

Macro replacement does not take place inside of a string, to create a string dynamically the # operator is used. The # operator when used inside a macro causes the next token to be enclosed in string quotes. For example, a macro `AS_STRING` which generates a string from its argument is defined as follows:

```
#define AS_STRING( name ) # name

std::cout << AS_STRING( Mike ) << "\n";
```

This would generate the output line:

```
std::cout << "Mike" << "\n";
```

21.10. Pasting tokens together

The ## operator is used inside a macro to paste tokens together, so that further macro substitutions may be performed. For example, with the following macro definitions:

```
#define ENGLISH_1    "one"
#define ENGLISH_2    "two"

#define FRENCH_1     "un"
#define FRENCH_2     "deux"

#define REAL_PASTE( x, y ) x ## y
```

The result of processing the line:

```
std::cout << REAL_PASTE( ENGLISH, _1 ) << "\n";
```

is the line:

```
std::cout << "one" << "\n";
```

By using a second level of macro replacement, macro replacement on the arguments can also be included. For example:

```
#define PASTE( x, y ) REAL_PASTE(x,y)

#define LANGUAGE FRENCH
#define NUMBER_2 PASTE( LANGUAGE, _2 )
```

would cause:

```
std::cout << NUMBER_2 << "\n";
```

to be replaced by the line:

```
std::cout << "deux" << "\n";
```

21.11 Overuse of macros

The use of macros, however, can be taken to extremes, as in the following program, in which the very nature of the language has been changed to make C++ look like a Pascal or Ada style programming language.

```
#define IF     if(
#define THEN   ){
#define ELSE   } else {
#define ELIF   } else if (
#define FI     ;}
#define BEGIN  {
#define END    }
#define WHILE  while(
#define DO     ){
#define OD     ;}
```

```
#include <iostream>
int main()
BEGIN
  int countdown;
  countdown = 4;
  WHILE countdown > 0 DO
    cout << countdown << "\n";
    IF countdown == 3 THEN
      std::cout << "Ignition" << "\n";
    FI
    countdown = countdown - 1;
  OD
  std::cout << "Blast off" << "\n";
  return 0;
END;
```

When run this program would produce the results:

```
4
3
Ignition
2
1
Blast Off
```

21.12 Inclusion of header files

A header file in C++ is usually constructed as follows:

```
#ifndef   CLASS_NAME_SPEC
#define   CLASS_NAME_SPEC

//Specification of the class
//Which will only be source included once

#endif
```

This allows a header file to be included many times in a program, but only has the compiler process the contents of the file once.

Note: This can occur, for example, in the following situation, where a program uses the following class specifications for a Car and a Person which both contain the inclusion of a class specification for holding a name.

Specification for class Person	Specification for class Car

```#include "name.h"```
 	
```class Person {```
``` //class specification```
```}```
	```#include "name.h"```
	
	```class Car {```
	``` //class specification```
	```}```

21.13 Parameter specification: variable number of parameters

In C++ it is possible to declare and use a function which has a variable number of parameters. For example, a function sum_params can be written which forms the sum of its parameters. The parameter list is terminated by a parameter with a value of 0. This can be implemented as follows:

```
#include <stdarg.h>

int sum_params( const int, ... );           //Prototype

int sum_params( const int first, ... )
{
  va_list p_arg;                            //Pointer to arguments
  va_start( p_arg, first );                 //Set pointer to first
  int sum = 0, value = first;
  while ( value != 0 )
  {
    sum += value;
    value = va_arg( p_arg, int );           //next value in list
  }
```

```
        va_end(p_arg);                              //Clean up
        return sum;
}
```

Note: The use of . . . to indicate that the function has a variable number of parameters.
The use of the zero value to terminate the parameter list.
Using the above macros requires that at least one parameter has to be specified.
The use of this technique means that the compiler is unable to check the type and number of parameters supplied.

The macros contained in `stdarg.h` are used because they allow access to the parameters in a machine independent way. Their function is as follows:

`va_list`	Declares a pointer `p_arg` to the argument list.
`va_start`	Initializes `p_arg` with a pointer to the argument after argument `first`.
`va_arg`	Returns the argument pointed at by `p_arg`, in this case of type `int`, then advances `p_arg` to the next argument.
`va_end`	Cleans up afterwards.

The function `sum_params` could then be used in the following program:

```
int main()
{
    std::cout << "The sum of 1, 2, 3, 4, 5 is ";
    std::cout << sum_params( 1, 2, 3, 4, 5, 0 ) << "\n";
    return 0;
}
```

which would produce the results:

```
The sum of 1, 2, 3, 4, 5 is 15
```

Note: The possibility for error in this process cannot be overstated.

21.14 Self-assessment

- In C++ the use of the macro facility is almost redundant, why is this?
- Why is it better to use a templated function rather than a macro?
- When is it appropriate to use a macro?

21.15 Exercises

- `assert_to_file`
  construct the macro:
  `assert_to_file( condition, string, file_name )`
  that writes `string` and any other appropriate debugging information to the file `file_name` when the asserted condition is false. The file is to be opened and closed for each invocation of the macro.

22 C++ input and output

This chapter describes the C++ input and output system. In particular it shows how to construct manipulators for changing the format of information read and written to a stream.

22.1 Overview of the C++ I/O system

The C++ I/O system is implemented by a collection of classes, an overview of the inheritance structure of these classes is shown in Figure 22.1.

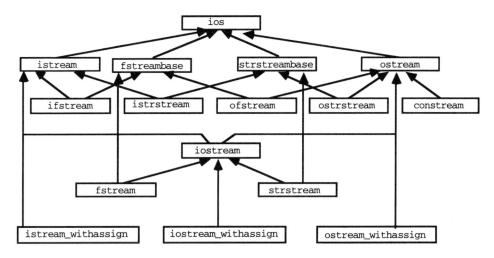

Figure 22.1 Inheritance diagram of C++ I/O classes.

22.1.1 The class `ios`

The class `ios` is the base for all the input and output classes. In particular it defines the following values:

Value	Description
in	File is input
out	File is output

Value	Description
app	Append to file.
beg	Seek relative to start of file.
binary	Binary data.
cur	Seek relative to current position in file.
end	Seek relative to end of file.
trunc	Truncate file on create.

22.1.2. The class `ostream`

The class `ostream` which is derived from the class `ios` provide formatted output to the standard output device. In the header file `<iostream>` there is the following declaration for the objects `cout`:

```
extern ostream cout;
```

The class `ostream` implements the following major methods:

Method	Description
<<	The overloaded extraction operator for all the standard types.

22.1.3. The class `istream`

The class `istream` which is derived from the class `ios` provide formatted output to the standard output device. In the header file `<iostream>` there is the following declaration for the objects `cout`:

```
extern istream cin;
```

The class `istream` implements the following major methods:

Method	Description
>>	The overloaded insertion operator for all the standard types.

22.1.4. The classes `ifstream` and `ofstream`

The classes `ifstream` and `ofstream` allow I/O to be performed to and from a disk file.

The class `ifstream` (Input file stream) implements the following additional methods to `istream`:

Method	Description
open(name, mode)	Opens a file, where name is a c++ string and mode has a default value of `ios:in`.
close()	Close the stream.
is_open()	Returns true if the stream is open.

The class `ofstream` (Output file stream) implements the following additional methods to `ostream`:

Method	Description
open(name, mode)	Opens a file, where name is a c++ string and mode has a default value of ios:out || ios::trunc.
close()	Close the stream.
is_open()	Returns true if the stream is open.

22.1.5   The classes `istrstream` and `ostrstream`

The classes `istrstream` and `ostrstream` allow I/O to be performed to and from memory locations in the program. These streams are useful for formatting text that is to be used internally in the program. The class ostrstream has all the methods of `ostream` plus the addition method of:

Method	Description
str()	Returns a C++ string (char*) to the text entered into the stream.

22.1.6   Standard streams

The following standard streams are defined in the header file `<iostream>`

For char	For wchar_t	Description
extern istream cin;	extern wistream win;	Standard input.
extern ostream cout;	extern wostream wout;	Standard output.
extern ostream cerr;	extern wostream werr;	Error output (Unbuffered).
extern ostream clog;	extern wostream wlog;	Log output.

22.2   Inserters, extractors and IO manipulators

The stream IO system can be customized, to allow IO to be performed directly on objects declared in a program. For example, using the class `Account` defined in Section 5.3.1 whose specification is:

```cpp
class Account {
public:
  Account();
  float account_balance() const;      //Return the balance
  float withdraw( const float );      //Withdraw from account
  void deposit( const float );        //Deposit into account
  void set_min_balance( const float ); //Set minimum balance
private:
  float the_balance;                  //The outstanding balance
  float the_min_balance;              //The minimum balance
};
```

The next sections, illustrate how to implement the following features:

- An extractor
  Extracts and prints the contents of an object
- An inserter
  Inserts from a C++ stream a value into an object
- IO Manipulators
  Change the way the IO system works. This is usually a change to the format of the way information is displayed.

22.2.1 An extractor

An extractor allows the contents of an object to be written directly using the stream IO system defined in `<iostream>`. This is implemented for an instance of the class `Account` by overloading the extractor operator << as follows:

```
std::ostream& operator << ( std::ostream &s, Account acc )
{
  s << std::setiosflags( std::ios::fixed );      //x.y format
  s << std::setprecision(2);                     //2 dec places
  s << std::setiosflags( std::ios::showpoint ); //Show all places
  s << "£" << acc.account_balance();             //Print details
  return s;
}
```

Note: This function takes as its 1st parameter a reference to an `ostream` *object and delivers as its result a reference to this object.*
A reference to an instance of `ostream` *is required as the object may not be copied as it contains state information about the management of the output to the stream.*

Using this overloading of the extractor operator << allows the following code to be written:

```
int main()
{
  Account mike;
  mike.deposit( 100.00 );
  std::cout << "Mike's account contains " << mike << "\n";
  return 0;
}
```

Which when compiled with suitable header files and executed will produce the following output:

```
Mike's account contains £100.00
```

22.2.2   An inserter

An inserter allows the contents of an object to be read directly using the IO system defined in <iostream>. This is implemented for the class Account by overloading the insertion operator >> as follows:

```
std::istream& operator >> ( std::istream &s, Account& acc )
{
  float money;
  s >> money;                        //Read
  acc.deposit( money );              //Update object
  return s;
}
```

Using this overloading of the insertion operator >> allows the following code to be written:

```
int main()
{
  Account mike;
  std::cin >> mike;
  std::cout << "Mike's account contains " << mike << "\n";
  return 0;
}
```

Which when compiled with suitable header files and executed will produce the following output, when the input is 50.0.

```
Mike's account contains £50.00
```

22.2.3   IO manipulators

IO manipulators allow the state of the stream to be changed. A manipulator money_format to format an instance of a float in a way suitable for the writing of monetary amounts is used as follows:

```
int main()
{
  Account mike;
  float   gift = 100.00;
  std::cout << "Deposit " << money_format << gift << "\n";
  mike.deposit( gift );
  std::cout << "Mike's account contains " << mike << "\n";
  return 0;
}
```

Which when compiled with suitable header files and executed will produce the following output:

```
Deposit 100.00
Mike's account contains £100.00
```

The IO manipulator `money_format` is created in a two stage process as follows:

22.2.1.1   Manipulator creation Stage 1

Create a function to implement the manipulator as follows:

```
std::ostream& money_format( std::ostream &s )
{
  s << std::setiosflags( std::ios::fixed );       //x.y format
  s << std::setprecision(2);                      //2 dec places
  s << std::setiosflags( std::ios::showpoint );   //Show all places
  return s;
}
```

Note: This function takes as its single parameter a reference to an `ostream` object and delivers as its result a reference to this object.

22.2.1.2   Manipulator creation Stage 2

Overload the operator `<<` between an ostream object and a pointer to the function `money_format` as follows:

```
std::ostream& operator << ( std::ostream& s,
                            ostream& (*fun)(std::ostream&) )
{
  return (*fun)(s);                     // Call manipulator
}
```

Note: `ostream& (*fun)(ostream&)` is a pointer to a function which takes a single parameter of type `ostream` and delivers an object of type `ostream`. The overloaded function, implements the call of the manipulator.

22.2.1.3   The process

When the manipulator `money_format` in the following expression is executed:

```
std::cout << "Deposit " << money_format << gift << "\n";
```

the following functions are called:

●   The function:
```
    std::ostream& operator << (std::ostream& s,
                               std::ostream& (*fun)(ostream&) )
```
is executed which calls the manipulator `money_format`.

● The manipulator function
```
std::ostream& money_format( std::ostream &s )
```
then implements the manipulators functionality.

22.2.4. IO manipulators with a single parameter

A manipulator `money_format_width(8)` to format `float`'s in a monetary format in a field width of 8 characters is used as follows:

```
#include <iomanip>

int main()
{
  Account mike;
  float   gift = 100.00;
  std::cout << "Deposit " << money_format_width(8) << gift << "\n";
  mike.deposit( gift );
  std::cout << "Mike's account contains " << mike << "\n";
  return 0;
}
```

Note: This process requires the inclusion of the header file <iomanip>

Which when compiled with suitable header files and executed will produce the following output:

```
Deposit   100.00
Mike's account contains £100.00
```

Unfortunately the process illustrated in Section 22.2.3 above for manipulators with no parameters cannot be extended directly to deal with manipulators which take a single parameter.

The IO manipulator `money_format_width` is created in a two stage process as follows:

22.2.4.1   Creation of a manipulator with single parameter stage 1

Create a function to implement the manipulator's functionality as follows:

```
std::ostream &money_format_width( std::ostream &s, int field_width )
{
  s << std::setiosflags( std::ios::fixed );      //x.y format
  s << std::setprecision(2);                     //2 dec places
  s << std::setiosflags( std::ios::showpoint ); //Show all places
  s << std::setw( field_width );                 //Nextin field_width
  return s;
}
```

Note: The second parameter is the IO manipulator's 1st parameter.

22.3.4.2   Creation of a manipulator with single parameter stage 2

Define the following templated function, which returns an instance of the templated class omanip.

```
omanip <int>
money_format_width( int field_width )
{
    return omanip<int> (money_format_width, field_width);
}
```

Note: The type used in the template is the type of the manipulator's parameter.

22.3.4.3   The process

The class omanip defined in the header file <iomanip> (specific implementations may differ in detail) is defined as follows:

```
template<class T>
class omanip
{
public:

    omanip(ostream& (*f)(std::ostream&, T), T z ) : fun(f), arg(z)
    {
    }
    friend std:ostream& operator<<(std:ostream &s, omanip<T> f)
    {
        return(*f.fun)(s, f.arg);
    }

private:

    std:ostream& (*fun)(std:ostream&, T);
    T arg;
};
```

When an instance of the class omanip is created, the address of the manipulator and its single parameter are stored in the created object. The friend function: ostream& operator<<(ostream &s, omanip<T> f) of the class omanip calls the manipulator.

When the manipulator `money_format_width(8)` in the following expression is executed:

```
std:cout << "Deposit " << money_format_width(8) << gift << "\n";
```

the following functions are called:

- The function:
  `omanip <int> money_format_width( int field_width )`
  is executed which returns an instance of the class `omanip`.

- The constructor for `omanip` stores the manipulator's address and parameter.

- The friend function of `omanip`:
  `std:ostream& operator<<(std:ostream &s, omanip<T> f)`
  is called which calls the function `money_format_width(8)`.

- The manipulator function:
  ```
  std:ostream &money_format_width( std:ostream &s,
                                   int field_width )
  ```
  then implements the functionality of the manipulator.

22.3   A computerized bank system (using binary data)

The computerised bank system seen in Section 8.10 can be re-implemented to store the data about individual customer's bank accounts in a randomly accessed disk file, rather than an internal array. Using this implementation technique the data is made persistent. To implement this a class `Bank` is defined which has the following responsibilities:

Method	Responsibility
account_balance	Return the balance for a particular customer's account.
deposit	Deposit money into a specified customer's account.
extend	Add new accounts to the persistent collection
set_min_balance	Set the overdraft limit for a customer.
statement_summary	Print a summary statement of the account.
last_account_no	Return the last account number.
withdraw	Withdraw if possible money from a customer's account.

The C++ specification for the class Bank is:

```
#ifndef CLASS_BANK_SPEC
#define CLASS_BANK_SPEC
#include <iostream>
#include <fstream>
```

```
class Bank {
public:
  Bank( char [] );
  ~Bank();
  void extend( long );                       //Extend accounts
  float account_balance(const int) const;    //Balance
  float withdraw( const int, const float );  //Withdraw
  void deposit( const int, const float );    //Deposit
  void set_min_balance(const int, const float);//Set minimum balance
  void statement_summary( std:ostream&, const int ) const;
  int last_account_no() const;               //Last account no.
protected:
  void read( Account& data, long pos );      //Read Account
  void write( Account& data, long pos );     //Write Account
private:
  long     the_max_customers;                //Max Customers
  mutable std::fstream the_customers;        //File descriptor
  bool     the_fs_ok;                        //All ok
};

#endif
```

Note: The member variable `the_customers` *of type* `fstream` *is marked as
mutable, so that* `const` *member functions may modify this value. The reason is
that the stream is modified even if only a read operation is performed. This
preserves the notion of constness for a user of the class using operation such as*
`account_balance.`

22.3.1   Implementation

In the implementation of the class Bank a binary file is used to hold saved images of
instances of customers' accounts. The construct for the class bank opens this file and by
determining the size of the file calculates the number of accounts held.

```
#ifndef CLASS_BANK_IMP
#define CLASS_BANK_IMP

Bank::Bank( char vol_name[] )
{
  the_customers.open( vol_name,
                      std:ios::binary | std:ios::in | std:ios::out );
  the_fs_ok = the_customers.fail() == 0;
  if ( !the_fs_ok )
  {
    throw std::runtime_error("Can not open bank accounts file");
  }
  the_customers.seekp( 0L, std:ios::end );
  the_max_customers = (the_customers.tellg()) / (sizeof( Account ));
}
```

The destructor closes the open file.

```
Bank::~Bank()
{
  if ( the_fs_ok ) the_customers.close();
}
```

Note: The file is opened for both reading and writing.
If the file does not exist it will be created with a zero length.

The method `extend`, adds new customers' accounts to the end of the file.

```
void Bank::extend( long size )
{
  Account new_account;
  for ( long pos=0; pos<size; pos++ )
  {
    the_customers.seekp( (the_max_customers+pos)*sizeof(Account) );
    the_customers.write( (char*)&new_account, sizeof(Account) );
  }
  the_max_customers = the_max_customers + size;
}
```

These accounts will have account numbers up to and including the account number returned by the member function `last_account_no`.

```
int Bank::last_account_no() const
{
  return the_max_customers-1;
}
```

In the implementation of the member function `account_balance` the function `read` reads the state of a previously saved `Account` object and restores it into the object `customer`. Once this has been done the message `account_balance` is sent to the restored customer's object in memory.

```
float Bank::account_balance(const int client) const
{
  Account customer;              //Instance of Account
  read( customer, client );      //Overwrite with saved state
  return customer.account_balance();
}
```

The implementation of `withdraw` follows a similar strategy, except that as the state of the object is changed this must be saved back to disk. The method `write` performs this function by writing the state of the object `customer` to disk.

```
float Bank::withdraw( const int client, const float money )
{
  Account customer;                    //Instance of Account
  read( customer, client );            //Overwrite with saved state
  float get = customer.withdraw( money );
  write( customer, client );           //Save state to disk
  return get;
}
```

The functions deposit, set_min_balance and statement_summary are implemented in a similar way as follows:

```
void Bank::deposit(const int client, const float money)
{
  Account customer;                    //Instance of Account
  read( customer, client );            //Overwrite with saved state
  customer.deposit( money );
  write( customer, client );           //Save state to disk
}

void Bank::set_min_balance(const int client, const float money)
{
  Account customer;                    //Instance of Account
  read( customer, client );            //Overwrite with saved state
  customer.set_min_balance( money );
  write( customer, client );           //Save state to disk
}

void Bank::statement_summary( std:ostream& s, const int client ) const
{
  Account customer;                    //Instance of Account
  read( customer, client );            //Overwrite with saved state
  s << "Bank statement summary -";
  s << " account number " << client << "\n";
  s << "£" << customer.account_balance();
  s << " on deposit" << "\n";
}
```

The functions read and write perform the actual I/O to and from the disk file. The only minor problem is that the interface to read and write require a pointer to an array of characters. This is easily solved by casting a pointer to an Account object to a pointer to an array of characters.

```
void Bank::read( Account& data, long pos )
{
  char *buf = (char*) &data;                         //As chars
  if ( !the_fs_ok )
    throw std::runtime_error("File not open");       //Internal error
  the_customers.seekg( pos * sizeof(Account) );      //Seek to pos
  the_customers.read( buf, sizeof(Account) );        //Read
  if (the_customers.gcount() != sizeof(Account) )
    throw std::runtime_error("Failed to read record"); //Read failed
}
```

```
void Bank::write( Account& data, long pos )
{
  char *buf = (char*) &data;                     //As chars
  if ( !the_fs_ok )
    throw std::runtime_error("File not open");    //Internal error
  the_customers.seekp( pos * sizeof(Account) );   //Seek to pos
  the_customers.write( buf, sizeof(Account) );    //Write
  if (the_customers.gcount() != sizeof(Account) )
    throw std::runtime_error("Failed to write record");//Write failed
}

#endif
```

Warning the process of reading and writing an image of an object will only work when:

● The object contains no pointers.

● The architecture of the machines on which the reading and writing take place are compatible. For example, the representation of a `float` is identical.

22.3.2 Putting it all together

Using the above classes and suitable include directives the following separately executing programs can be written. The first program sets up the bank with 6 accounts numbered 0—5 and deposits £50.00 into account number 5.

```
int main()
{
  Bank  piggy( "piggy.bnk" );              //A very small bank
  piggy.extend( 6L );
  int customer = piggy.last_account_no(); //Last customer
  piggy.deposit(customer, 50.00);
  return 0;
}
```

The second program withdraws £20 from the last account.

```
int main()
{
  Bank  piggy( "piggy.bnk" );              //A very small bank
  float obtained;
  int customer = piggy.last_account_no();

  piggy.statement_summary(std::cout, customer);

  std::cout << "\n" << "Transaction withdraw £20.00" << "\n";
  obtained = piggy.withdraw(customer, 20.00);
  std::cout << "piggy Bank gives £" << obtained << "\n";
  piggy.statement_summary(std::cout, customer);
  return 0;
}
```

The output from this second program is:

```
Bank statement summary - account number 5
£50 on deposit

Transaction withdraw £20.00
piggy Bank gives £20
Bank statement summary - account number 5
£30 on deposit
```

The third program interrogates the last account:

```
int main()
{
  Bank  piggy( "piggy.bnk" );              //A very small bank
  int customer = piggy.last_account_no();  //Last customer
  piggy.statement_summary(std::cout, customer);  // Statement
  return 0;
}
```

the output from this program is:

```
Bank statement summary - account number 5
£30 on deposit
```

22.4   Self-assessment

● What is an inserter and extractor?

● How can the following be printed?

Object	Format
float temperature	In a field width of 8 characters with 3 decimal places.
int number	In a field width of 8 characters.
int pattern	As a binary bit pattern.

22.5   Exercises

● Re-write the Bank class described in this chapter such that the method withdraw can be implemented in the following way :

```
float Bank::withdraw( const int client, const float money )
{
  Account customer;
  the_customers >> seek( client ) >> customer;
  float get =  customer.withdraw( money );
  the_customers << seek( client ) << customer;
  return get;
}
```

23 Deep and shallow copying

This chapter looks at a technique of counting references to storage that is shared between several objects. Using shared memory in this way involves deep and shallow copies of an object's storage. By using a shallow copy of an object's storage more efficient use of memory and sometimes execution time can be made. The implementation of this process involves the overloading of the assignment operator, and the copy constructor.

23.1 Descriptors

A pointer to a data structure is often referred to as a descriptor. When copying such a data structure, it is usual to copy the descriptor, rather than the data structure itself. However, this copy results in two objects sharing the same storage. This is safe as long as the underlying storage is not modified. If the storage is modified a copy of the underlying data structure must first be made.

The use of a descriptor in representing an objects storage can lead to efficient implementations, but has the side effect of requiring more complex code. Fortunately, the resulting complexity is easily hidden from a user of the object by the encapsulation provided by the class mechanism.

Note: The following example illustrates the use of a descriptor. However, for such a trivial data case, the descriptor mechanism would not normally be employed.

A number of people could be a described by a number descriptor as illustrated in Figure 23.1.

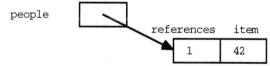

Figure 23.1 Representation of a number descriptor.

The descriptor `people` is a pointer to the described item which contains two values:

- A count of the number of references to this item.
- The physical storage for the number.

By using a descriptor with a reference count several objects may share the same data structure. For example, in the following code:

```
Number  people, computing;

computing = 42;
people = computing;
```

The storage for the number 42 is shared between the two objects `people` and `computing`.

After the execution of the above code, the storage inside the computer for `people` and `computing` is as shown in Figure 23.2.

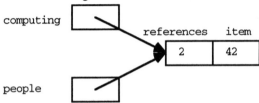

Figure 23.2 Two objects sharing the same storage.

This can result in a considerable saving in storage and execution time if the object stored is large. However, care must be taken in writing the code for the class `Number` as now more than one variable may reference the same data area.

The main items to consider when writing the code for the class `Number` are:

● There are now two types of copy for a data item:

  ● A deep copy, in which the storage for the item is physically duplicated.

  ● A shallow copy, in which only the reference count is incremented to indicate two or more objects share the same copy of the physical storage.

● The assignment operator must be overloaded.

  When a variable is overwritten its previous contents must be released back to the system in a sanitary way.

● A copy constructor must be provided.

  This is so that implied assignments, such as passing a value to a function, can be processed sensibly. A copy constructor is called in the following situations:

  ● A parameter is passed by value. The copy constructor is used to initialize the actual value of the parameter.

  ● A functions returns an expression. The copy constructor is used to convert the expression into a temporary instance of the returned object.

● The destructor for `Number` can only release the storage when the reference count is 1.

This process is illustrated below for a linked list of colours:

● Assignment

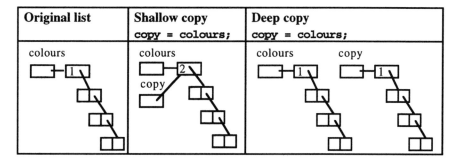

● Equality

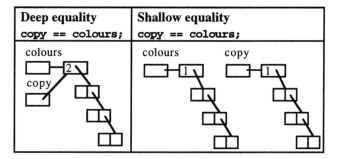

23.2 A class to perform deep and shallow copying

The template class RC implements a reference counting mechanism that implements deep and shallow copying for any existing C++ type or class. For example the following declaration:

```
typedef RC <double> Real;
Real number1,number2;
```

defines Real to be a reference counted descriptor for a double object. By defining a conversion function in the parameterized type RC to deliver an object of the type of its actual parameter (in this case double), number1 and number2 can be used in arithmetic expressions in the normal way.

This mechanism can be used when many instances of a type contain the same value. For example, a grid of spot heights for a surface can be described using a reference counted long double as follows:

```
typedef RC<long double> Real;

void main()
{
  const int SIZE=10;
  Real heights[SIZE][SIZE];

  for (int i=0; i<SIZE; i++)
    for( int j=0; j<SIZE; j++ )
      heights[i][j] = Real(0.0);

  return 0;
}
```

When all the values are zero, as in the above example there will only be one physical instance of the `long double` value 0.0 with `SIZE*SIZE` pointers to it.

The C++ specification for the class RC is as follows:

```
#ifndef CLASS_REFERENCE_COUNT_SPEC
#define CLASS_REFERENCE_COUNT_SPEC

template <class Type>
class RC {
public:
  RC();
  RC( const Type );
  RC( const RC<Type>& );                  //Copy constructor
  ~RC();                                  //Destructor

  RC& operator    = ( const RC<Type>& ); //Shallow
  RC& operator <<= ( const RC<Type>& ); //Deep
  operator Type&() const;                 //Conversion operator
  void describe() const;                  //Describe the item
protected:
  Type& stored() const;                   //Contents
  int  refs() const;                      //Number of references
  void change( Type );                    //Change to
  void split();                           //Split [Two unique objects]
  void release_storage();                 //Return storage for item
  void fail( const char[] ) const;        //Give up
private:
  struct Desc_RC {
    Type item;                            //The stored data object
    int references;                       //References to object
  };
  Desc_RC *the_p_desc;     //Pointer to descriptor for number
};

#endif
```

The parameterless constructor for RC creates a descriptor to an undefined instance of the type used-as the parameterized type for this class. If this is a class item then it must have a parameterless constructor which will be called to initialize the value.

```
#ifndef CLASS_REFERENCE_COUNT_IMP
#define CLASS_REFERENCE_COUNT_IMP

#include <string>
#include <strstream>
#include <stdexcept>

template <class Type>
RC<Type>::RC()
{
  //  Warning
  //  This may fail due to lack of memory
  //  If it does then the exception
  //     bad_alloc will be thrown

  the_p_desc = new Desc_RC[1];

  the_p_desc->references = 1;
}
```

The next constructor has as its parameter an instance of the parameterized type, which is used to initialize the descriptor.

```
template <class Type>
RC<Type>::RC( const Type value )
{

  //  Warning
  //  This may fail due to lack of memory
  //  If it does then the exception
  //     bad_alloc will be thrown

  the_p_desc = new Desc_RC[1];

  the_p_desc->item       = value;
  the_p_desc->references = 1;
}
```

The destructor calls `release_storage` which will only release the storage if the reference count is 1.

```
template <class Type>
RC<Type>::~RC()
{
  release_storage();
}
```

The copy constructor is called when there is an implicit assignment, for example when an actual parameter is passed by value. As the target has not been initialized no storage for the target needs to be released. Once the pointer has been assigned, the reference count is incremented by 1 to reflect the extra reference to this object.

```
template <class Type>
RC<Type>::RC( const RC<Type>& copy )
{
    the_p_desc = copy.the_p_desc;      //Copy pointer to descriptor
    (the_p_desc->references)++;        //Increment references
}
```

The overloaded operator = (used for a shallow copy) increments the reference count of the source object, releases any storage for the target and then assigns the pointer to the from descriptor to the target descriptor pointer.

```
template <class Type>
RC<Type>& RC<Type>::operator =
                         ( const RC<Type>& from )
{
    if ( the_p_desc != from.the_p_desc )    //Not a = a
    {
        (from.the_p_desc->references)++;    //RC copied
        release_storage();                  //Overwritten RC
        the_p_desc = from.the_p_desc;       //Perform the copy
    }
    return *this;
}
```

Note: The order of these operations is important as a user may have written:
```
        object = object; //Target and source are the same item
```

The overloaded operator <<= (used for a deep copy) creates a new instance of storage for the actual object and assigns to this the source object. The targets reference count is decremented and the pointer to it is overwritten by a pointer to the descriptor for the new object.

```
template <class Type>
RC<Type>& RC<Type>::operator <<=
                (const RC<Type>& from) //Deep copy
{
    Desc_RC *p_desc;

    //   Warning
    //   This may fail due to lack of memory
    //   If it does then the exception
    //      bad_alloc will be thrown

    p_desc = new Desc_RC[1];

    p_desc->item       = from.the_p_desc->item;    //MUST BE DEEP
    p_desc->references = 1;
    release_storage();               //Now release storage for target
    the_p_desc = p_desc;             //Set up target
    return *this;
}
```

The next three member functions are used for accessing components in the descriptor. This approach is taken so that derived classes of this class can access its private data members.

```
template <class Type>
Type& RC<Type>::stored() const
{
  return the_p_desc->item;              // Stored item
}

template <class Type>
int  RC<Type>::refs() const
{
  return the_p_desc->references;        //Number of references
}

template <class Type>
void RC<Type>::change( Type new_value )
{
  the_p_desc->item = new_value;         //Change item
}
```

The protected member function `split` is used to split a reference counted item into two distinct objects. The current object that has a single reference to it, and the remaining object that may have 1 or more references to it.

This is used when implementing a mutator method, on an object that has more than one reference to it.

```
template <class Type>
void RC<Type>::split()
{
  if ( refs() >= 2 )
  {
    Desc_RC *p_desc;

    //  Warning
    //  This may fail due to lack of memory
    //  If it does then the exception
    //     bad_alloc will be thrown

    p_desc = new Desc_RC[1];

    p_desc->item       = the_p_desc->item;    //Deep copy
    p_desc->references = 1;

    the_p_desc->references--;                 //1 less ref
    the_p_desc = p_desc;                      //this 1 ref
  }
}
```

The member function `release_storage` decrements the reference count for the object and if it is 0 will then physically release any storage for the object.

```
template <class Type>
void RC<Type>::release_storage()
{
  if ( --(the_p_desc->references) == 0 ) {
     delete [] the_p_desc;                      //its descriptor
  }
}
```

The member function `fail`, generates a `runtime_error` exception.

```
template <class Type>
void RC<Type>::fail( const char message[] ) const
{
  char storage[120];                           //Message
  ostrstream text(storage,120);                //As stream
  text << "RC: " << message << '\0';
  throw std::runtime_error( std::string(storage) ); //Exception
}
```

The conversion operator return a reference to an instance of the stored object. A reference is returned so that the stored object may be modified.

```
template <class Type>
RC<Type>::operator Type&() const
{
  return the_p_desc->item;      // Stored item
}

#endif
```

23.3   Example of usage

The following program uses a reference counted integer to store the number of apples and pears. As can be seen the details that the `Int` is referenced counted is 'hidden' from the writer of the code.

```
typedef RC<int> Int;

int main()
{
  Int total_fruit = 0, apples = 20, pears = 30;
  std::cout << "total_fruit = apples + pears" << "\n";
  total_fruit = apples + pears;
  std::cout << "total_fruit = " << (int) total_fruit;
  std::cout << " apples = "     << (int) apples;
  std::cout << " pears = "      << (int) pears << "\n";
  return 0;
}
```

The above program when compiled and run would produce the output:

```
total_fruit = 50 apples = 20 pears = 30
```

However, in evaluating: `total_fruit = apples + pears;`

the following operations take place:

```
apples + pears;
```
- conversion operator in class `RC` applied to `apples` and `pears` to `deliver an int`.
  - `apples` delivers 20 as an `int`
  - `pears` delivers 30 as an `int`
- `operator +` (Standard C++ int operator)
  Delivers 50

```
total_fruit = 50 ( result of 20 + 30 )
```
- Constructor `RC<int>(50)`
  Delivers a temporary
- `operator = temporary`
  - Call `release_storage` on `total_fruit`
  - Perform the assignment of the pointer to the object
  - return `*this`

```
temporary ( result of apples + pears ) goes out of scope
```
- `~RC <int>()`
  But will not release the storage for 50 as the reference count is not zero.

Note: A simple arithmetic operation will execute a 'considerable' amount of code. The code path for the above could be reduced by creating specialization's of assignment. For example the function:
         `RC& operator = ( const Type& );.`

23.4.   Preventing assignment of an object

By defining the overloaded operator = and the copy constructor to be private or protected members of a class prevents a user of the class copying an object from the class. The compile issues an error message to say that the operation is not visible to the user of the class. For example, the class `Account` in Section 5.3.1 could have been defined as:

```
#ifndef CLASS_ACCOUNT_SPEC
#define CLASS_ACCOUNT_SPEC
```

```
class Account {
public:
  Account( const float=0.00 , const float=0.00 );
  ~Account();
  float account_balance() const;        //return the balance
  float withdraw( const float );        //withdraw from account
  void deposit( const float );          //deposit into account
  void set_min_balance( const float ); //Set minimum balance
protected:
  Account( Account& );                  //Copy constructor
  Account& operator = ( Account );      //Assignment
private:
  struct Account_data;                  //Tentative declaration
  Account_data* the_storage;            //Pointer to storage for object
};

#endif
```

Note: The implementation of assignment and the copy constructor will be a null action.

Using this new definition for the class Account the dubious code below which duplicates money in bank account is prevented from compiling.

```
int main()
{
  Account mike, corinna;
  mike.deposit( 100.00 );
  corinna = mike;            //Compile time error message
  return 0;
}
```

23.5   Self-assessment

- What is the difference between a deep and a shallow copy of an object?

- What is the difference between a deep and a shallow comparison of an object?

- When might using a shallow copy of an object cause problems?

- When might using a deep comparison of an object cause problems?

23.6   Exercises

- *class Person_RC*
  Implement the class Person_RC that implements a reference counted Person class that is described in Section 8.13. A user of this new class should be unaware of the underlying deep and shallow copies that take place.

- *class Vector*
  Re-implement the class Vector seen in Section 20.2 so that now instances of the class may be correctly copied.

24 Pointers and generic algorithms

This chapter looks at the use of pointers used in the implementation of algorithms found in the Standard Template Library. The STL (Standard Template Library) defines a standard way of manipulating and processing data and is available with all ANSI C++ compilers.

24.1 Generic algorithms

The following generic algorithms are based on those found in the STL (Standard Template Library). This library of useful functions is based around a pointer-centred view of access to storage. The reasoning behind this is to allow the algorithms to work with instances of inbuilt types as well as instances of classes.

In addition the STL implements a range of containers to ease the management of stored items. This feature of the STL is described in detail in Chapter 25. The STL was originally designed at Hewlett-Packard and is freely available over the internet. The HP distribution contains the following copyright message:

```
/*
 *
 * Copyright (c) 1994
 * Hewlett-Packard Company
 *
 * Permission to use, copy, modify, distribute and sell this software


 * and its documentation for any purpose is hereby granted without fee,
 * provided that the above copyright notice appear in all copies and
 * that both that copyright notice and this permission notice appear
 * in supporting documentation.  Hewlett-Packard Company makes no
 * representations about the suitability of this software for any
 * purpose. It is provided "as is" without express or implied warranty.
 *
 */
```

In the ANSI standard for C++ these generic algorithms are implemented in the namespace std. Rather than using the directive using namespace std; that would result in the pollution of the global namespace, each generic algorithm is made visible by using the scope resolution operator :: to individually select it from the namespace std. The header file <algorithm> contains these generic algorithms.

24.2   Generic algorithm `copy`

A generic algorithm to copy data from one location to another is implemented by the templated function `copy` shown below:

```
template <class I_It, class O_It>
O_It copy( I_It first, I_It last, O_It too )
{
  while ( first != last ) *too++ = *first++;
  return too;
}
```

Note: This would be implemented in the namespace `std` as part of the standard library.

In implementing the algorithm the parameters to the templated function `copy` are:

Parameter	Explanation
`first`	An input pointer to the first element of the collection to be copied.
`last`	An input pointer to the element after the last element of the collection to be copied.
`too`	An output pointer to the area where the data is to be moved to.

Note: The pointer iterators used to denote the area to be copied, point to the first element and the element after the area to be copied.

24.2.1   Putting it all together

Using the above generic algorithm `copy` the following fragment of code copies the elements of the integer array `numbers` to the integer array `copy_of`.

```
# include <algorithm>

int main()
{
  int numbers[] = { 10,9,8,7,6,5,4,3,2,1 };
  const int BEGIN = 0;                          //Index
  const int SIZE  = sizeof(numbers)/sizeof(int); //No Elements
  const int END   = SIZE;                       //Index

  int copy_of[SIZE];

  std::copy( &numbers[BEGIN], &numbers[END], &copy_of[0] );

  return 0;
}
```

Note: &numbers[BEGIN] returns a pointer to the start of the collection to be copied. &numbers[END] returns a pointer to the element after the end of the elements in the collection to be copied.
The algorithms are contained in the header file `<algorithm>`.

24.3   Generic algorithm for_each

The templated function `for_each` applies a function to each element of a collection. The parameters to the templated function `for_each` are:

Parameter	Explanation
`first`	An input pointer to the start of the collection.
`last`	An input pointer to the element after the last element of the collection.
`f`	A function whose signature is `void f(Type&)` which is applied to each of the elements in the range `first .. last-1`.

The templated function `for_each` is implemented as:

```
template <class IO_It, class Unary_function>
Unary_function for_each( IO_It first, IO_It last, Unary_function f )
{
  while ( first != last )            //For each element
  {
    f(*first++);                     // apply function f to it
  }
  return f;
}
```

24.3.1   Putting it all together

Using the above algorithm `for_each` the following fragment of code prints the contents of each of the elements of the integer array `numbers`:

```
# include <algorithm>
void print_int( int& val )
{
  std::cout << val << " ";
}

int main()
{
  int numbers[] = { 10,9,8,7,6,5,4,3,2,1 };
  const int BEGIN = 0;                          //Index
  const int SIZE  = sizeof(numbers)/sizeof(int); //No Elements
  const int END   = SIZE;                        //Index

  std::for_each( &numbers[BEGIN], &numbers[END], print_int );
  std::cout << "\n";
  return 0;
}
```

which when compiled with suitable header files will produce the following output:

```
10 9 8 7 6 5 4 3 2 1
```

24.3.2   Function objects (Implementing a generic `print`)

The limitation to the solution seen above is that there needs to be a specific instance of the function `print` for each data type that is to be printed. In the example above, the function `print_int` can only print integer values.

A function object is an instance of a class which overloads the function call operator `()`. This allows the function object to be used just like a normal function. For example, if `print` is a function object then `print()` will call the method `.operator()` that implements the functionality of the function. The class that the function object belongs to can be a generic class and hence a specific instance of a function object can be instantiated to process a specific type of data.

Shown below is a function object `print<Type>()` which implements the printing of arguments of type `Type`.

```
template <class Arg1, class Result>
class unary_function
{
public:
  typedef Arg1   first_arg_type;
  typedef Result result_type;
};

template <class Type>
class print : unary_function<Type, void>
{
public:
  void operator()(const Type& x) const
  {
    std::cout << x << " ";
  }
};
```

Note: The class `unary_function` *is used so that there is a common base class for all function objects. In particular this names the types used in the function object.*

The function object `print<int>()` is used below to print the contents of the integer array `numbers` as follows :

```
int main()
{
  int numbers[] = { 10,9,8,7,6,5,4,3,2,1 };
  const int BEGIN = 0;                        //Index
  const int SIZE  = sizeof(numbers)/sizeof(int); //No Elements
  const int END   = SIZE;                     //Index

  std::for_each( &numbers[BEGIN], &numbers[END], print<int>() );
  std::cout << "\n";
  return 0;
}
```

Note: The class constant `print<int>()` *is an instance of the generic class* `print<int>`.

24.3.3 How a function object works

In the generic algorithm `for_each` the third parameter is used as a function which is applied to each element of the collection.

In the call of:

```
for_each( &numbers[START], &numbers[END], print<int>() );
```

the third actual parameter `print<int>()` is an instance of the generic class `print`, which is applied to each element of the collection. The specific line in the algorithm `for_each` (see Section 24.3) that is responsible for the call of the function is the line:

```
f(*first++);
```

which is compiled as:

```
instance_of_print( *first++ );
```

and is implemented as:

```
instance_of_print.operator() ( *first++ );
```

Note: This is because the class `print` *has overloaded the function call operator* `()`.

24.4   Sorting

Some of the simplest sorting algorithms are based on the idea of a bubble sort. In an ascending order bubble sort, consecutive pairs of items are compared, and arranged if necessary into their correct ascending order. The effect of this process is to move the larger items to the end of the list. However, in a single pass through the list only the largest item not already in the correct position will be guaranteed to be moved to the correct position. The process of passing through the list exchanging consecutive items is repeated until all the items in the list are in the correct order. For example, the following list of numbers is to be sorted into ascending order:

| 20 | 10 | 17 | 18 | 15 | 11 |

The first pass of the bubble sort compares consecutive pairs of numbers and orders each pair into ascending order. This is illustrated in Figure 24.1 below.

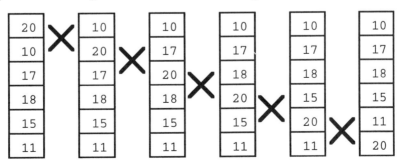

Figure 24.1 The first pass of the bubble sort.

Each pass through the list of numbers moves the larger numbers towards the end of the list and the smaller numbers towards the start of the list. However, only one additional larger number in the list is guaranteed to be in the correct position. The result of successive passes through the list of numbers is illustrated in the table below.

List of numbers						Commentary
20	10	17	18	15	11	The original list.
10	17	18	15	11	20	After the 1st pass through the list.
10	17	15	11	18	20	After the 2nd pass through the list.
10	15	11	17	18	20	After the 3rd pass through the list.
10	11	15	17	18	20	After the 4th pass through the list.

The process is repeated until there have been no swaps during a single pass through the list. Thus, after the 4th pass an additional pass through the list will be made in which no changes will occur. This indicates that the list is sorted into ascending order.

24.4.1   Efficiency

This variation on the bubble sort is not a very efficient algorithm, as in the worse case it will take n passes through the list to rearrange the data into ascending order, where n is the size of the list. Each pass through the list will result in n-p comparisons, where p is the number of the pass.

The big O notation is used to give an approximation of the order of an algorithm. For this modified bubble sort the order (number of comparisons) will be approximately $O(n^2)$. For a small amount of data this is not important, but if n is large, then the number of comparisons will be very large, and hence the time taken to sort the data will be lengthy.

24.5   Generic algorithm `sort`

The following code uses a modified form of the bubble sort to order data into ascending order. After each pass through the data the last item will be in the correct order. Subsequent passes can thus ignore the last item from the previous pass. The STL implementation of the `sort` generic algorithm uses the far superior quick sort algorithm.

```
template <class IO_It>
void sort( IO_It first, IO_It last_plus_one )
{
  bool swaps = true;                 //Not sorted
  IO_It last = last_plus_one-1;      //Real last value
```

```
while ( swaps )
{
  swaps = false;                      //Assume sorted
  for(IO_It p=first; p!=last; p++)    //Scan array
  {
    IO_It q = p+1;                    //q points at next item
    if ( *p > *q )                    //Pair (p,q) in wrong order
    {
      swaps = true;                   // So not sorted
      swap( *p, *q );                 // Put (p,q) in correct order
    }
  }
  last--;                             //last item is correct
}
}
```

The function swap is implemented as the templated function:

```
template <class Type>
void swap( Type& first, Type& second )
{
  Type tmp = first;                   //Temporary copy
  first = second;                     //Change first
  second = tmp;                       //Change second
}
```

24.5.1 Putting it all together

Using the above algorithm sort the following fragment of code sorts an array of numbers into the correct order:

```
const int BEGIN = 0;                           //Index
const int SIZE  = sizeof(numbers)/sizeof(int); //No Elements
const int END   = SIZE;                        //Index
sort( &numbers[START], &numbers[END] );
```

Note: The collection of items to be sorted is described by a pointer to the first item and a pointer to after the last item.
The STL sort algorithm is std::sort.

24.5.2 Generic algorithm sort with order

The overloaded templated function sort has a third parameter which is used to determine the sort order.

Parameter	Explanation
first	An input pointer to the start of the collection.
last	An input pointer to the element after the last element of the collection.
cmp	Returns true if two items are in the correct order.

The overloaded templated function `sort` is implemented as:

```
template <class IO_It, class Compare_function>
void sort( IO_It first, IO_It last_plus_one, Compare_function cmp )
{
  bool swaps = true;                   //Not sorted
  IO_It last = last_plus_one-1;        //Real last value
  while ( swaps )
  {
    swaps = false;                     //Assume sorted
    for(IO_It p=first; p!=last; p++)   //Scan array
    {
      IO_It q = p+1;                   //q points at next item
      if ( !cmp(*p, *q) )              //Pair (p,q) in wrong order
      {
        swaps = true;                  // So not sorted
        swap( *p, *q );                // Put (p,q) in correct order
      }
    }
    last--;                            //last item is correct
  }
}
```

Note: *The implementation of the templated function* swap *is shown with the previous version of the generic algorithm* sort.

24.5.3   Putting it all together

A class `Person` has the following methods:

Method	Responsibility
Person	Construct an instance of a person storing their name and height.
name	Return a person's name as a string.
height	Return a person's height in Cm's.

The specification of the class `Person` is:

```
#ifndef CLASS_ACCOUNT_SPEC
#define CLASS_ACCOUNT_SPEC
#include <string>
```

```
class Person
{
public:
  Person( std::string="", int=0 );
  std::string name() const;       //Name of person
  int     height() const;         //Height of person in Cm's
private:
  std::string the_name;           //Name
  int         the_height;         //Height in Cm's
};

#endif
```

The implementation of the class is:

```
#ifndef CLASS_ACCOUNT_IMP
#define CLASS_ACCOUNT_IMP

Person::Person ( std::string name, int height )
{
  the_name = name; the_height = height;   //Store details
}

std::string Person::name() const
{
  return the_name;                        //Return persons name
}

int Person::height() const
{
  return the_height;                      //Return person height
}

#endif
```

A program to sort a collection of people is show below. The program uses two functions: `cmp_name` that returns true if the first person's name collates lower in the alphabet than the second person's and the second function `cmp_height` returns true if the first person is shorter than the second.

```
bool cmp_name( Person first, Person second )
{
  return first.name() < second.name();
}

bool cmp_height( Person first, Person second )
{
  return first.height() < second.height();
}
```

The following overloading of the extractor operator allows the printing of an instance of the class `Person`.

```
ostream& operator << ( ostream& s, const Person& individual )
{
  s << "[" << individual.name() << "," << individual.height() << "]";
  return s;
}
```

A program to sort people into height and name order is shown below:

```
int main()
{
  Person friends[] = { Person("Paul", 165), Person("Carol", 147),
                       Person("Mike", 183), Person("Corinna", 171)  };

  const int NUM_FRIENDS  = sizeof(friends)/sizeof(Person);
  const int BEGIN = 0;
  const int END   = NUM_FRIENDS;
  const int LAST  = NUM_FRIENDS-1;


  std::sort( &friends[BEGIN], &friends[END], cmp_height );
  std::cout << "Tallest person is          :" << friends[LAST] << "\n";

  std::sort( &friends[BEGIN], &friends[END], cmp_name );
  std::cout << "Highest collating name is :" << friends[LAST] << "\n";

  return 0;
}
```

Note: This fragment of code uses the real STL sort *function.*

which when compiled with suitable header files will produce the following output:

```
Tallest person is          :[Mike,183]
Highest collating name is :[Paul,165]
```

24.6   Generic algorithm `find`

The templated function `find` returns a pointer to the element matching the supplied object. If no object is found then the pointer `last` is returned.

Parameter	Explanation
`first`	An input pointer to the start of the collection.
`last`	An input pointer to the element after the last element of the collection.
`value`	The value to be searched for.

The templated function find is implemented as:

```
template <class I_It, class Type>
I_It find(I_It first, I_It const last, const Type& value)
{
  while ( (first != last) && (*first != value) ) ++first;
  return first;
}
```

24.6.1   Putting it all together

Using the above algorithm find the following fragment of code determines if Blue is a colour in the rainbow:

```
int main()
{
  std::string colours[] = { "Violet", "Blue", "Green",
                            "Yellow", "Orange", "Red" };
  const int BEGIN = 0;                                //Index
  const int SIZE  = sizeof(colours)/sizeof(std::string); //No Elements
  const int END   = SIZE;                             //Index

  std::string* pos;
  pos = std::find( &colours[BEGIN], &colours[END], "Blue");
  if ( pos != &colours[END] )
  {
    std::cout << *pos << " is a colour in the rainbow" << "\n";
  }
  pos = std::find( &colours[BEGIN], &colours[END], "Pink");
  if ( pos != &colours[END] )
  {
    std::cout << *pos << " is a colour in the rainbow" << "\n";
  }
  return 0;
}
```

which when compiled with suitable header files will produce the following output:

```
Blue is a colour in the rainbow
```

24.7   Generic algorithm find with criteria

The overloaded templated function find returns a pointer to the element matching the supplied object. If no object is found then the pointer last is returned.

Parameter	Explanation
`first`	An input pointer to the start of the collection.
`last`	An input pointer to the element after the last element of the collection.
`pred`	A condition to determine the found object.

The overloaded templated function `find` is implemented as:

```
template <class I_It, class Predicate>
I_It find_if(I_It first, I_It const last, Predicate pred)
{
  while (first != last && !pred(*first)) ++first;
  return first;
}
```

24.7.1   Putting it all together

Using the above algorithm `find` the following fragment of code determines if there is a colour of the rainbow with three characters. Firstly a class to create a function object that is used to test if a string has # characters is defined as follows:

```
class length_is
{
public:
  explicit length_is( int len ) : the_length( len )
  {
  }
  bool operator()(const std::string& str) const
  {
    return str.length() == the_length;
  }
private:
  const int the_length;                          //Length to check for
};
```

Note: The constructor for the function object `length_is` *records the length of string to look for.*
The function object `length_is` *is not part of the standard library.*

This is then used in the following program to find a colour of the rainbow with three characters.

```
int main()
{
  std::string colours[] = { "Violet", "Blue", "Green",
                            "Yellow", "Orange", "Red" };
  const int BEGIN = 0;                                  //Index
  const int SIZE  = sizeof(colours)/sizeof(std::string); //No Elements
  const int END   = SIZE;                               //Index
```

```
    std::string* pos;
    pos = std::find_if( &colours[BEGIN], &colours[END], length_is(3) );
    if ( pos != &colours[END] )
    {
      std::cout << "A colour of the rainbow with 3 characters is "
               << *pos << "\n";
    }
    return 0;
}
```

which when compiled with suitable header files will produce the following output:

```
A colour of the rainbow with 3 characters is Red
```

24.7.2 How it works

In the generic algorithm `find` the third parameter is a function object which is applied to each element of the collection. The function object returns `true` when the appropriate element of the collection is found. In the call of:

```
    find_if( &colours[BEGIN], &colours[END], length_is(3) );
```

the third actual parameter `length_is(3)` is an instance of the class `length_is`. The constructor for the class initializes the instance variable `the_length` with the value 3. In the body of the generic algorithm `find` the formal parameter `pred` takes the value of an instance of the class `length_is` in the line:

```
    while (first < last && !pred(*first)) ++first;
```

the expression `!pred(*first))` is interpreted as:

```
    !instance_of_length_is(*first);
```

which is implemented as:

```
    !instance_of_length_is.operator () (*first);.
```

In the class `length_is` the function call operator `()` is overloaded with code that determines if the parameter is equal to the value that the object was constructed with. If no match is found for the search then the iterator `last` is returned.

24.8 Generic algorithm `transform`

The generic algorithm `transform` applies a function to each member of a source collection. The results of applying the function to each member of the source collection are stored into a results collection. The algorithm is in two forms: a unary version that is used to transform a single collection into a result collection and a binary version in which a binary function is applied to corresponding elements from two input collections to create the result collection. The generic algorithm transform is defined as follows:

Parameter	Explanation
`first1`	An input iterator to the start of the 1st source collection.
`last1`	An input iterator to the element after the last element of the 1st source collection.
`first2` Δ	An input iterator to the start of the 2nd source collection.
`result`	An output iterator to the start of the result collection.

`f`	A function that transforms the collection
	Binary transform:
	     results = f(collection_1st, collection_2nd)
	Unary transform:
	     results = f(collection_1st)

Note: Δ *Only for the binary transform generic algorithm.*

The two versions of transform are shown below:

```
template <class I_It, class O_It, class Unary_function>
O_It transform (I_It first, I_It last, O_It result,
                Unary_function f)
{
    while (first != last) *result++ = f(*first++);
    return result;
}
```

```
template <class I_It1, class I_It2, class O_It, class binary_function>
O_It transform ( I_It1 first1, I_It1 last1,
                 I_It2 first2, O_It  result,
                 binary_function f)
{
    while (first1 != last1) *result++ = f(*first1++, *first2++);
    return result;
}
```

24.8.1   Example of the use of `transform`

The following example program uses the function `print_array` to print elements from an array of integers. This is implemented by using the generic algorithm `copy` with a second parameter of an `ostream_iterator`. When elements are copied to an instance of an `ostream_iterator` they are written to the specified output stream. This is more fully explained in Section 25.3.5.

```
void print_array(std::string title, int *from, int *too )
{
  std::cout << title;
  std::copy( from, too,
             std::ostream_iterator<int>( std::cout, " " ) );
  std::cout << "\n";
}
```

In the main function of the program the following generic function objects are used in the transformation:

Function object	Implements
`std::plus<int>()`	+
`std::negate<int>()`	Unary –

Note: Section 24.9 lists other useful function objects.

```
int main()
{
  const int BEGIN = 0;
  const int END   = 10;
  const int SIZE  = END;
  int source1[SIZE], source2[SIZE], target[SIZE];

  for ( int i=0; i<SIZE; i++ )
  {
    source1[i]  = 10+i;
    source2[i]  = 20+i;
  }

  print_array( "source1 = ", &source1[BEGIN], &source1[END] );
  print_array( "source2 = ", &source2[BEGIN], &source2[END] );

  std::cout << "Evaluate: target = source1 + source2 " << "\n";

  std::transform( &source1[BEGIN], &source1[END],
                  &source2[BEGIN], &target[BEGIN], std::plus<int>() );

  print_array( "target  = ", &target[BEGIN],  &target[END] );

  std::cout << "Evaluate: target = -source1" << "\n";

  std::transform( &source1[BEGIN], &source1[END],
                  &target[BEGIN],  std::negate<int>() );

  print_array( "target  = ", &target[BEGIN], &target[END] );

  return 0;
}
```

24.8.2 Putting it all together

Which when compiled and run with suitable declarations produces the following output:

```
source1 = 10 11 12 13 14 15 16 17 18 19
source2 = 20 21 22 23 24 25 26 27 28 29
Evaluate: target = source1 + source2
target  = 30 32 34 36 38 40 42 44 46 48
Evaluate: target = -source1
target  = -10 -11 -12 -13 -14 -15 -16 -17 -18 -19
```

24.9   Useful function objects

The following generic function objects are provided in the header file `<algorithm>`. In the table below only the name of the function object is shown. For example, a function object to multiply two `int` numbers together is `times<int>()`, whilst a function object to concatenate two strings together is `plus<std::string>()`.

Name	operation	Name	operation
plus	x + y	minus	x - y
multiplies	x * y	divides	x / y
modulus	x % y	negate	- x

equal_to	x == y	not_equal_to	x != y
greater	x > y	less	x < y
greater_equal	x >=y	less_equal	x <= y

logical_and	x && y	logical_or	x || y
logical_not	! x		

24.10   Generic algorithm `generate`

The templated function `generate` stores the result of the generator function in successive elements of the indexed collection.

Parameter	Explanation
first	An input pointer to the start of the input collection.
last	An input pointer to the element after the last element of the input collection.
f	A generator function which delivers a potentially different result each time it is called.

The templated function `generate` is implemented as:

```
template <class O_It, class Generator>
void generate(O_It first, O_It last, Generator  f )
{
    while (first != last) *first++ = f();
}
```

24.10.1 A generator function

A generator is a function which returns potentially different values each time it is called. For example, the templated generator `fibonacci` that returns successive values of the fibonacci sequence is defined as follows:

```
template <class Type>
class fibonacci : unary_function<Type, void>
{
public:
  fibonacci()
  {
    the_first = 0; the_second = 1;        //Initial values of window
  }
  Type operator()()
  {
    Type next = the_first + the_second;   //Next in sequence
    the_first = the_second;               //Move window down
    the_second = next;
    return the_first;                     //Return next in sequence
  }
private:
  Type the_first;                         //First  in window
  Type the_second;                        //Second in window
};
```

*Note: The constructor sets the initial values of the window used in calculating the next
term of the sequence.*
The method operator *( ) delivers successive terms in the fibonacci sequence.*

24.10.2 Putting it all together

Using the above algorithm generate and the generator function fibonacci the
following fragment of code populates the array numbers with terms from the fibonacci
sequence:

```
int main()
{
  int numbers[15];                                    //std::vector

  const int BEGIN = 0;                                //Index first
  const int SIZE  = sizeof(numbers)/sizeof(int);      //No Elements
  const int END   = SIZE;                             //Index last

  std::generate( &numbers[BEGIN], &numbers[END], fibonacci<int>() );

  std::cout << "Fibonacci sequence is : ";
  std::for_each( &numbers[BEGIN], &numbers[END], print<int>() );
  std::cout << "\n";

  return 0;
}
```

Note: The function object print<***int***> *( ) is defined in Section 24.3.2.*

which when compiled with suitable declarations and run will produce the following
output:

```
Fibonacci sequence is : 1 1 2 3 5 8 13 21 34 55 89 144 233 377 610
```

24.11 Function adapters

A function adapter is used to build a new function out of an existing function object. By using a function adapter new function objects can be created out of existing function objects.

24.11.1 The function adapter `not1`

The function adapter `not1` is used to produce a new function that delivers the not of an existing function object.

The function object `even` is defined as follows:

```
template <class Type>
class even : public unary_function<Type, bool>
{
public:
  bool operator()(const Type& val) const
  {
    return val%2==0;
  }
};
```

and delivers true when supplied with an even integer parameter. For example, the following fragment of code will deliver true.

```
even<int>() ( 4 )
```

Note: An instance of the function object even is created by:

```
even<int>()
```

The function in the function object is called by applying the function call brackets to this object.

The function adapter `not1` delivers a new function object that will deliver the not of the result of the function object passed as a parameter to it. For example, to create a new function object to deliver true when an odd parameter is passed to it can be created out of the existing function object `even` as follows:

```
std::not1( even<int>() )
```

Note: not1(even<int>()) creates a function adapter to deliver the not of the function object even<int>().

This new function object is used in the following fragment of code to test if an integer value is odd:

```
int main()
{
  int i = 2;
  std::cout << "The number " << i << " is "
            << (not1( even<int>() )( i ) ? "odd" : "not odd") << "\n";
  return 0;
}
```

Note: The function call brackets ( ) are used to invoke the function.

24.11.2 How it works

The constructor for the function adapter `not1` stores the function object `even<int>()`. When the function call brackets are applied to the function adapter, method `operator` `()` is invoked which calls the stored function object `even<int>()` and delivers the not of its result. This process is illustrated in Figure 24.2.

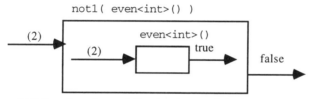

Figure 24.2 Function adapter delivering the not of the function object even.

The function adapter `not1` is defined as the two templated classes as follows:

```
template <class Predicate>
class unary_negate :
  public unary_function<typename Predicate::first_arg_type, bool>
{
public:
  explicit unary_negate (const Predicate& x) : pred(x) {}
  bool operator() (const first_arg_type& x) const { return !pred(x); }
private:
  Predicate pred;
};

template <class Predicate>
unary_negate<Predicate> not1(const Predicate& pred)
{
  return unary_negate<Predicate>(pred);
}
```

Note: The use of the reserved word `typename` to indicate that `Predicate::first_arg_type` is a type.

An adapter function works in a similar way to a normal function object, except this time the item stored is a function object.

24.11.3 Putting it all together

Using the above adapter `not1` and the function object `even` the following code will find the first even and odd numbers in the fibonacci sequence:

```cpp
int main()
{
    int numbers[15];                                  //std::vector
    const int BEGIN = 0;                              //Index first
    const int SIZE  = sizeof(numbers)/sizeof(int);    //No Elements
    const int END   = SIZE;                           //Index last

    generate( &numbers[BEGIN], &numbers[END], fibonacci<int>() );
    int *p;
    p = find_if( &numbers[BEGIN], &numbers[END], even<int>() );
    std::cout << "first     even number is " << *p << "\n";

    p = find_if( &numbers[BEGIN], &numbers[END], not1( even<int>() ) );
    std::cout << "first not even number is " << *p << "\n";
    return 0;
}
```

which when compiled and run will produce the output:

```
first     even number is 2
first not even number is 1
```

24.11.4 The function adapters `bind2nd` and `bind1st`

The function adapter `bind2nd` takes two parameters:

1st Parameter	A function with the following signature: T fun(T2 first, T2 second).
2nd Parameter	A value of type T2.

and delivers a function which has the new signature `T  fun_new(T2  x)` and implements `T fun(T1 x, T2 value)`.

For example, a function which tests if its single integer parameter is greater than 100 is constructed as follows: `bind2nd( greater <int>(), 100 )`.

The constructor for the function adapter `bind2nd` stores the function object `greater<int>()`, and the integer value `100`. Then when the function call brackets with an actual parameter of say `999` are applied to the function adapter, the method `operator (999)` is invoked which calls the function object `greater<int>()` with actual parameters of `999` and `100`. This process is illustrated in Figure 24.3.

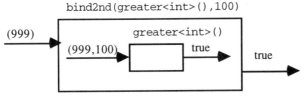

Figure 24.3 A function adapter delivering true if its parameter is greater than 100.

The function adapter `bind1st` takes two parameters:

1st Parameter	A function with the following signature:
	T fun(T2 first, T2 second
2nd Parameter	A value of type T2.

and delivers a function which has the new signature `T fun_new(T2 x)` and implements `T fun(T2 value, T2 x)`.

For example, a function which tests if its single integer parameter is greater than 100 is constructed as follows:

```
bind1st( less <int>(), 100 ).
```

The constructor for the function adapter `bind1st` stores the function object `greater<int>()`, and the integer value `100`. Then when the function call brackets with an actual parameter of 999 is applied to the function adapter the method `operator (999)` is invoked which calls the function object `greater<int>()` with actual parameters of `100` and `999`. This process is illustrated in Figure 24.4.

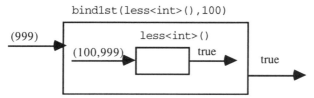

Figure 24.4 A function adapter delivering true if its parameter is greater than 100.

24.11.5 Using the function adapters `bind1st` and `bind2nd`

The following fragment of code finds the first number in the fibonacci series greater than 100:

```
int main()
{
  int numbers[15];                               //std::vector
  const int BEGIN = 0;                           //Index first
  const int SIZE  = sizeof(numbers)/sizeof(int); //No Elements
  const int END   = SIZE;                        //Index last

  std::generate( &numbers[BEGIN], &numbers[END], fibonacci<int>() );
  int *p = NULL;

  //x > 100

  p = std::find_if( &numbers[BEGIN], &numbers[END],
               std::bind2nd( std::greater<int>(), 100 ) );
  std::cout << "first number in sequence greater than 100 is "
       << *p << "\n";
  return 0;
}
```

Note: There is no check that a number greater than 100 does not exist.

When compiled with suitable declarations and run, the following output will be produced:

```
first number in sequence greater than 100 is 144
```

The code to find the first number greater than 100 could have been written using bind1st as:

```
p = std::find_if( &numbers[BEGIN], &numbers[END],
                  std::bind1st( std::less<int>(), 100 ) );
```

24.12 The STL library

The Standard Template Library provides many generic algorithms. Appendix E lists selected algorithms, function objects and function adapters in the STL.

24.13 Self-assessment

- Using the generic sort algorithm, why would a user of this templated function get compile-time error messages when sorting instances of the class Account?

- What are the advantages and disadvantages of using generic algorithms?

- What is a function object and how is it used?

- What is a function adapter and how is it used?

24.14 Exercises

Construct the following generic algorithms based on pointer semantics:

- void count(I_It first, I_It last, const T& val, Size& count)

  which increments count for each element that matches val.

- void count_if(I_It first, I_It last, Predicate f, Size& count)

  which increments count for each element that matches the Predicate defined by the function f, the signature of which is:
  ```
  bool f( I_It element ).
  ```

  In the generic algorithms the type I_It is an input iterator, a pointer to an element of the collection.

Construct the following function adapter:

- *as_string*
  That converts a function object that delivers an int, into a function object that delivers a string representation of the int result.

25 STL containers

This chapter describes the use of containers defined in the Standard Template Library. The use of these standard containers, simplifies the construction of programs, though in some cases there is a penalty in resources used due to the generality of the container.

25.1   Introduction to STL containers

The STL library provides several different types of container, the exact choice of which container to use will depend on many factors including: efficiency of access, ability to insert and remove elements, and storage used.

Container	Description of characteristics
vector	Efficient random access and insertion of new elements at the end of the container.
list	Efficient insertion and removal of elements anywhere in the container.
deque	Efficient insertion and removal at the front and back of the container.
set	Elements held in order, efficient test for inclusion, insertion and removal from the container.
multiset	A set with duplicate values.
map	Efficient access to values using a key. Efficient insertion and removal of key data pairs from the container.
multimap	A map with duplicate keys.
stack	Insertion and removal from the front only.
queue	Removal of items at the front and insertion at the back only.
Priority queue	Efficient access to and removal of the (largest/smallest) value from the container.

25.2   The `vector` container

The `vector` container class provides for efficient access to elements using either an iterator or a subscript. The container is extended by adding additional elements to the end of the container. To make this process efficient the container's storage is expanded by a user definable increment size. Any unused space will be used on subsequent insertions. The implementation of the class `Vector` described in Section 20.2 implements a small set of the features of the `vector` container.

The major methods implemented by the vector container are:

Method	Responsibility
vector<T>	Where T is the type of the collection. Constructor variations: () Empty container. (size) Indicates number of elements. (size,value) Number of elements initial contents value.
at(i)	Returns the i'th element. The exception out_of_range is thrown if the element does not exist.
back()	Returns the last element of the vector.
begin()	Returns an instance of a random access iterator pointing to the first element of the vector.
empty()	Returns true if the vector is empty.
end()	Returns an instance of a random access iterator pointing to 1 element beyond the end of the vector.
erase(RAI) erase(RAI,RAI)	Removes the element from the vector pointed at by the iterator or the range specified by the iterators. All iterators and references after the erasure are invalidated.
front()	Returns the front element of the vector.
insert(RAI,T)	insert(p, item) inserts item before the element pointed at by iterator p. All iterators and references after the insertion are invalidated.
max_size()	Returns the maximum size used. (This may be more than the storage required for the currently stored elements.)
operator =	Implement a copy of the vector.
operator []	Returns a reference to the selected element, allowing the normal subscripting operator to be used.
pop_back()	Removes the element at the back end of the vector.
push_back(T)	Adds a new element to the back end of the vector.
rbegin()	Returns a reverse iterator to the beginning of the vector.
rend()	Returns a reverse iterator to the end of the vector.
reserve(size_type)	Sets the size of the area to be reserved when additional space is added to the vector.
size()	Returns the number of elements in the vector.

Note: The vector container is defined in the header file <vector>.
       RAI is a Random Access Iterator.

The main embedded classes in a vector are:

Class	Used for declaring
`vector<T>::iterator`	A random access iterator used for read and write access to an instance of vector<T>.
`vector<T>::const_iterator`	A const random access iterator used for read access to an instance of vector<T>. *Note: If the container is const then a* `const_iterator` *must be used.*
`vector<T>::reverse_iterator`	A random access reverse iterator.
`vector<T>:: const_reverse_iterator`	A constant random access reverse iterator.

The main embedded types in a vector container are:

Class	Describes
`vector<T>::value_type`	The type of item stored in the vector.
`vector<T>::reference`	A reference to the item stored in the container.
`vector<T>::const_reference`	A constant reference to the item stored in the container.
`vector<T>::size_type`	A type used to represent a size and array index.

25.2.1   An insertion sort using the `vector` container

In an insertion sort, items are inserted into a sorted collection of items in the correct position. Normally this algorithm is not used for sorting data as insertion operations are expensive. For example, to sort the numbers: 20, 10, 17, and 18 using an insertion sort

Item to be inserted	Before insertion	After insertion
20		20
10	20	10 20
17	10 20	10 17 20
18	10 17 20	10 17 18 20

An implement of this algorithm for sorting data using an instance of a `vector` container is shown below. The method `insert` is used to insert a data item in the correct position in the array. Data for the sort algorithm is taken from an instance of a string stream `cin`.

```
#include <iostream>
#include <vector>
#include <algorithm>
```

```
typedef std::vector <int> Numbers;

int main()
{
  char data[] = "20 10 17 18 15 11";
  std::istrstream cin( data , strlen(data) );        //String stream

  Numbers sorted(0);                                 //Vector of 0 elements
  int     num;

  while ( cin >> num, !cin.eof() )
  {
    Numbers::size_type i=0;                          //Initial position
    while( i<sorted.size() )                         //In sorted array
    {
      if ( sorted[i] > num ) break;                  //Position to insert
      i++;
    }
    sorted.insert( &sorted[i],  num );               //Insert in order
  }

  std::cout << "Numbers sorted are: ";

  for ( unsigned int i=0; i<sorted.size(); i++ ) //Print array
  {
    std::cout << sorted[i] << " ";                   // using array access
  }
  std::cout << "\n";

  return 0;
}
```

Note: The use of the method `insert` to insert a new element into the container. This is not efficient, as the elements in the higher collating cells must be moved to make room for the newly inserted element.
That class `vector` is in the namespace `std`.
That `Numbers::size_type` is a type representing the value returned by size().

Which when run will produce the following results:

```
Numbers sorted are: 10 11 15 17 18 20
```

25.3   Containers and iterators

The elegance of the container classes is that they are used in a way analogous to how the inbuilt C++ container of an array is used. However, in addition the container classes provide many extra facilities that help simplify program construction. Classes defined in the container class allow the declaration of iterators that are used to access elements in a container using pointer semantics. To facilitate the use of iterators the container classes contain several iterator classes that overload the following standard operators:

*	De-reference iterator delivering value pointed at.
+	Advance the pointer by n units in the forward direction.
++	Advance the pointer by 1 unit in the forward direction.
–	Advance the pointer by n units in the reverse direction.
– –	Advance the iterator by 1 unit in the reverse direction.

25.3.1 Iterators in the container classes

The iterators in the container classes are categorised into a hierarchy of usage. Iterators at a particular point in the hierarchy support all the operations allowed on iterators lower down the hierarchy. The iterator hierarchy is shown below:

Iterator	Properties	
Random Access	Random access.	Highest
Bi-directional	May be moved in a forward or reverse direction.	
Forward	May only be moved in a forward direction.	
Input/Output	Used to extract insert data to a stream.	Lowest

25.3.2 An insertion sort using pointer semantics

The code to implement an insertion sort using pointer semantics is developed in a similar way to the code shown in Section 25.2.1. In the following code the function object `print` is used to facilitate the printing of the sorted array:

```
template <class Type>
class print : std::unary_function<Type, void>      //Common base
{
public:
  void operator()(const Type& x) const
  {
    std::cout << x << " ";                         //Insertion operator
  }
};
```

The actual code that performs the insertion sort is:

```
#include <iostream>
#include <vector>
#include <algorithm>

typedef std::vector <int> Numbers;

int main()
{
  char data[] = "20 10 17 18 15 11";
  std::istrstream cin( data , strlen(data) );    //String stream

  Numbers sorted(0);                             //Vector of 0 elements
  int     num;
```

```
while ( cin >> num, !cin.eof() )
{
  Numbers::iterator cur = sorted.begin();    //Start
  Numbers::iterator end = sorted.end();      //End
  while ( cur != end )                       //For sorted
  {
    if ( *cur > num ) break;                 //Position to insert
    cur++;                                   //Next
  }
  sorted.insert( cur, num );                 //Insert in order
}

std::cout << "Numbers sorted are: ";

std::for_each( sorted.begin(), sorted.end(), print<int>() );
std::cout << "\n";
return 0;
}
```

Note: The use of the type Numbers::iterator *to declare the iterators.*

When compiled with suitable declaration and run, it will produce the following results:

```
Numbers sorted are: 10 11 15 17 18 20
```

25.3.3   Using const iterators

When working with const containers, const iterators must be used to iterate through the values of the container. If a normal iterator is used compile-time error messages will be generated as the operations performed by a normal iterator are not compatible with a const container. For example, a function print_strings that prints all the strings in a container is implemented as follows:

```
typedef std::vector<std::string> Strings;

void print_strings( const Strings& col )
{
  Strings::const_iterator cur = col.begin();
  Strings::const_iterator end = col.end();
  while ( cur != end )                       //For each
  {
    std::cout << *cur++ << " ";
  }
  std::cout << "\n";
}
```

25.3.4 Copying between containers

The copy algorithm may be used to transfer data between different types of containers. When the amount of data to be transferred is unknown, the back inserter adapter is used to generate an iterator that calls the container's push_back method to insert a new data value.

For example, to copy an array of strings into a vector container, the following code is used.

```
// Declaration of the function print_strings ( See Section 25.3.3 )
int main()
{
  Strings rainbow(0);
  std::string colours[] = { "Violet", "Blue", "Green",
                            "Yellow", "Orange", "Red" };
  const int BEGIN = 0;                                  //Index
  const int SIZE  = sizeof(colours)/sizeof(std::string); //No Elements
  const int END   = SIZE;                               //Index
  std::copy( &colours[BEGIN], &colours[END],
             std::back_inserter( rainbow ) );
  print_strings( rainbow );
  return 0;
}
```

Note: *The adapter* `back_inserter(rainbow)` *returns an iterator that uses the container's* `push_back` *method to extend the container.*

Which when compiled with suitable declarations and run will produce the following results:

```
Violet Blue Green Yellow Orange Red
```

25.3.5 The ostream_iterator adapter

The ostream_iterator is used to insert a data item into an output stream. For example, the function print_strings in Section 25.3.3 could have been implemented as:

```
typedef std::vector<std::string> Strings;
void print_strings( ostream& ostr, const Strings& container )
{
  std::copy( container.begin(), container.end(),
             std::ostream_iterator<std::string>( ostr, " " ) );
  std::cout << "\n";
}
```

Note: *The adapter* `ostream_iterator` *is parameterized with the type of object stored in the container.*
       The two parameters to the constructor are:
           An instance of an `ostream`.
           The separator written between instances of the output objects.

25.3.6 The `istream_iterator` adapter

The `istream_iterator` is used to extract a data item from an input stream. For example, the following demonstration program, reads integer values from a string stream into the container `temperatures`. In this program the following two instances of an `istream_iterator` are used:

Instance of the `istream_iterator`	Explanation
`ints( cin )`	An iterator to the stream `cin` which extracts the integer number from the stream.
`eof`	An iterator that represents the end of file. The name is unimportant, what is important is the object is constructed with no parameters.

The `istream_iterator` is parameterized with two types:

- The type of the values to be extracted from the stream.
- A type used to represent the difference between two pointers.

```
int main()
{
  typedef std::vector<int> Numbers;
  char data[] = "20 10 17 18 15 11";
  istrstream cin( data , strlen(data) );   //String stream

  Numbers temperatures(0);                 //Collection of temperatures

  std::istream_iterator<int,ptrdiff_t> ints(cin), eof;
  std::copy( ints,
             eof,
             std::back_inserter( temperatures ) );

  std::copy( temperatures.begin(), temperatures.end(),
             std::ostream_iterator<int>( std::cout, " " ) );
  return 0;
}
```

Which when compiled with suitable declarations and run will produce:

```
20 10 17 18 15 11
```

25.3.7 Reverse iterators

The methods `rbegin` and `rend` return reverse iterators, these are in essence the inverse of a normal iterator. The method `rbegin` returns an iterator pointing at the end of the container and `rend` returns an iterator pointing at one element before the first element of the container. The operator `++` on a reverse iterator advances the iterator to the previous element and the operator `--` advances the iterator to the next element. For example, the following code writes out the contents of a `vector` in forward and reverse order.

```
# include <iostream>
# include <string>
# include <vector>

int main()
{
  typedef std::vector<std::string> Strings;
  Strings c(0);
  c.push_back("Violet");
  c.push_back("Blue");
  c.push_back("Green");
  c.push_back("Yellow");
  c.push_back("Orange");
  c.push_back("Red");

  std::for_each( c.begin(), c.end(), print<std::string>() );
  std::cout << "\n";

  std::for_each( c.rbegin(), c.rend(), print<std::string>() );
  std::cout << "\n";

  return 0;
}
```

Which when compiled and run will produce the following results:

```
Violet Blue Green Yellow Orange Red
Red Orange Yellow Green Blue Violet
```

25.4   Adding range checking to the `vector` container

Range checking can be added to the `vector` container, by using inheritance to derive a new class `Vector`. In the new class `Vector` the `[]` operator is overloaded to provide subscript checking on access.

```
#ifndef CLASS_VECTOR_SPEC
#define CLASS_VECTOR_SPEC

template <class Type>
class Vector : public std::vector<Type>
{
public:
  Vector(const size_type);
  const_reference operator [](const size_type) const;
  reference operator [](const size_type);
protected:
  void fail( char [], const size_type ) const;
};

#endif
```

Note: The use of the inherited types:

`reference`	*For a reference to the stored object.*
`const_reference`	*For a constant reference to the stored object.*
`size_type`	*For a type used to describe the array subscript.*

The implementation of this class is as follows:

```
#ifndef CLASS_VECTOR_IMP
#define CLASS_VECTOR_IMP
#include <stdexcept>
template <class Type>
Vector<Type>::Vector(const size_type i)  : std::vector<Type>( i )
{
}
```

Note: Only a single constructor is overloaded, if others were required then these too must be overloaded in the class `Vector`.

The `[]` operator is overloaded twice firstly for a const object and secondly for a mutable object as follows:

```
template <class Type>
const_reference Vector<Type>::operator[] ( const size_type i ) const
{
  if ( i < 0 || i >= size() )
    fail( "access", i);
  return std::vector<Type>::operator[]( i );

}

template <class Type>
reference Vector<Type>::operator[] ( const size_type i )
{
  if ( i < 0 || i >= size() )
    fail( "access", i);
  return std::vector<Type>::operator[]( i );
}
```

The method `fail` throws an exception to indicate the failure:

```
template <class Type>
void Vector<Type>::fail( char mes[], const size_type i ) const
{
  char storage[120];                          //Message
  ostrstream text(storage,120);               //As stream
  text << "Vector [Bounds 0.." << (size()-1) <<
          " - " << mes << " Subscript: " <<
          i << "]" << '\0';
  throw std::range_error( std::string(storage) );    //Exception
}

#endif
```

25.4.1 Putting it all together

The following code shows the use of the class Vector that implements subscript checking.

```
// Include of the new Vector class
int main()
{
  Vector<std::string> colours(0);
  colours.push_back( "Red" );
  colours.push_back( "Blue" );
  colours.push_back( "Green" );
  colours.push_back( "Orange" );
  colours.push_back( "Yellow" );
  colours.push_back( "Violet" );
  try
  {
    std::cout << "Colours of rainbow : ";
    for ( Vector<std::string>::size_type i=0; i<colours.size(); i++ )
    {
      std::cout << colours[i] << " ";
    }
    std::cout << "\n";

    std::cout << "Colours of rainbow : ";
    for ( Vector<std::string>::size_type i=0; i<colours.size()+1; i++ )
    {
      std::cout << colours[i] << " ";
    }
    std::cout << "\n";
  }
  catch ( std::exception& err )
  {
    cerr << "\n" << "Failure: " << err.what() << "\n";
  }
  return 0;
}
```

Which when compiled and run will produce the following output:

```
Colours of rainbow : Red Blue Green Orange Yellow Violet
Colours of rainbow : Red Blue Green Orange Yellow Violet
Failure: Vector [Bounds 0..5 - access Subscript: 6]
```

25.5   The list container

The list container class provides for efficient sequential access to elements using an iterator. The container may be extended efficiently by adding additional elements to any part of the list.

The major methods implemented by the `list` container are:

Method	Responsibility:
`list<T>`	Where `T` is the type of the collection. Constructor variations: `()` Empty container. `(size)` Indicates number of elements. `(size,value)` Number of elements initial contents `value`.
`back()`	Returns last element of the list.
`begin()`	Returns a bi-directional iterator pointing to the start of list.
`empty()`	Returns true if the list is empty.
`end()`	Returns bi-directional iterator pointing to 1 element beyond the end of the list.
`erase(BDI)`	Removes the element from the list pointed at by the iterator. Δ
`front()`	Returns the front element of the list.
`insert(BDI,T)`	Inserts an element into the list before the iterator. Δ
`max_size()`	Returns the maximum possible size of the list.
`operator =`	Implement a copying of the list.
`pop_back()`	Removes the element at the back end of the list.
`pop_front()`	Removes the element at the front end of the list.
`push_back(T)`	Adds a new element to the back end of the list.
`push_front(T)`	Adds a new element to the front end of the list.
`rbegin()`	Returns a reverse iterator to the beginning of the list.
`rend()`	Returns a reverse iterator to the start of the list.
`size()`	Returns the number of elements in the list.

Note: The list container is defined in the header file `<list>`.
BDI is a bi-directional iterator.
Δ   All iterators and references after the erasure or insertion are invalidated.

This is very similar to a `vector` container except that:

- The subscripting operator [ ] may not be used.
- The additional methods of `push_front` and `pop_front` are available to add and remove data to and from the front of the list.

The main embedded classes in the class `list` are:

Class	Used for declaring
`list<T>::iterator`	A bi-directional iterator used for read and write access to an instance of `list<T>`.
`list<T>::const_iterator`	A const bi-directional iterator used for read access to an instance of `list<T>`. *Note: If the container is const then a `const_iterator` must be used.*
`list<T>::reverse_iterator`	A bi-directional reverse iterator.
`list<T>::` `const_reverse_iterator`	A constant bi-directional reverse iterator.

The main embedded type in a list container are:

Class	Describes
list<T>::value_type	The type of item stored in the container.
list<T>::reference	A reference to the item stored in the container.
list<T>::const_reference	A constant reference to the item stored in the container.
list<T>::size_type	A type use to represent a size.

25.5.1 An insertion sort using pointer semantics

For example, a program to illustrate the insertion sort algorithm using a list container and then print the results is shown below:

```
#include <iostream>
#include <list>
#include <algorithm>

typedef std::list <int> Numbers;

int main()
{
  char data[] = "20 10 17 18 15 11";
  istrstream cin( data , strlen(data) );      //String stream

  Numbers sorted(0);                          //Vector of 0 elements
  int    num;

  while ( cin >> num, !cin.eof() )
  {
    Numbers::iterator cur = sorted.begin();   //Start
    Numbers::iterator end = sorted.end();     //End
    while ( cur != end )                      //For sorted
    {
      if ( *cur > num ) break;                //Position to insert
      cur++;                                  //Next
    }
    sorted.insert( cur, num );                //Insert in order
  }

  std::cout << "Numbers sorted are: ";

  std::for_each( sorted.begin(), sorted.end(), print<int>() );
  std::cout << "\n";
  return 0;
}
```

Note: This is the same code as used previously for an insertion sort using a vector container, except that the 'type' Numbers is now an instance of a list container.

When run, the above code will produce the following results:

```
Numbers sorted are: 10 11 15 17 18 20
```

25.5.2   Copying between containers

As the list container supports insertion of data at the front of a list, the `front_inserter` adapter may be used to insert data. For example, the following code copies the colours of the rainbow to the front of the list `rainbow`.

```cpp
typedef std::list<std::string> Strings;

int main()
{
  Strings rainbow(0);

  std::string colours[] = { "Violet", "Blue", "Green",
                            "Yellow", "Orange", "Red" };
  const int BEGIN = 0;                                  //Index
  const int SIZE  = sizeof(colours)/sizeof(std::string); //No Elements
  const int END   = SIZE;                               //Index

  std::copy( &colours[BEGIN], &colours[END],
             std::front_inserter( rainbow ) );

  std::copy( rainbow.start(), rainbow.end(),
             std::ostream_iterator<std::string>( std::cout, " " ) );
  std::cout << "\n";
  return 0;
}
```

When compiled and run it will produce the following results:

```
Red Orange Yellow Green Blue Violet
```

25.6   The `deque` container

The deque container class is a cross between the `vector` and the `list` container. The container provides for random access to elements and efficient insertion at the back or front of the deque.

The major methods implemented by the `deque` container are:

Method	Responsibility

deque<T>	Where
	    T is the type of the collection.
	Constructor variations:
	  () Empty container.
	  (size) Indicates number of elements.
	  (size,value) Number of elements initial contents value.

Method	Responsibility
`at(i)`	Returns the i'th element. The exception `out_of_range` is thrown if the element does not exist.
`back()`	Returns last element of the deque.
`begin()`	Returns a random access iterator pointing to start of deque.
`empty()`	Returns true if the deque is empty.
`end()`	Returns a random access iterator pointing to 1 element beyond the end of the deque.
`erase(RAI)`	Removes the element from the deque pointed at by the iterator. Δ
`front()`	Returns the front element of the deque.
`insert(RAI,T)`	Inserts an element into the deque before the iterator. Δ
`max_size()`	Returns the maximum possible size of the deque
`operator =`	Implement copying of the deque.
`operator []`	Return a reference to the selected element, allowing the normal subscripting operator to be used.
`pop_back()`	Removes the element at the back end of the deque.
`pop_front()`	Removes the element at the front end of the deque.
`push_back(T)`	Adds a new element to the back end of the deque.
`push_front(T)`	Adds a new element to the front end of the deque.
`rbegin()`	Returns a reverse iterator to the beginning of the deque.
`rend()`	Returns a reverse iterator to the start of the deque.
`size()`	Returns the number of elements in the deque.

Note: The deque container is defined in the header file `<deque>`.
RAI is a random access iterator.
Δ   All iterators and references after the erasure or insertion are invalidated.

The main embedded classes in a deque are:

Class	Used for declaring
`deque<T>::iterator`	A bi-directional iterator used for read and write access to an instance of deque<T>.
`deque<T>::const_iterator`	A const bi-directional iterator used for read access to an instance of deque<T>. *Note: If the container is const then a `const_iterator` must be used.*
`deque<T>::reverse_iterator`	A bi-directional reverse iterator.
`deque<T>::const_reverse_iterator`	A constant bi-directional reverse iterator.

The main embedded type in a deque container are:

Class	Describes
`deque<T>::value_type`	The type of item stored in the container
`deque<T>::reference`	A reference to the item stored in the container.
`deque<T>::const_reference`	A constant reference to the item stored in the container.
`deque<T>::size_type`	A type use to represent a size.

The following example program uses a deque to sort numbers using an insertion sort. The numbers in the deque are printed using the normal subscripting operator.

```cpp
#include <string>
#include <deque>
#include <algorithm>
#include <iostream>
#include <strstream>

int main()
{
  typedef std::deque <int> Numbers;
  char data[] = "20 10 17 18 15 11";
  istrstream cin( data , strlen(data) );      //String stream

  Numbers sorted(0);                          //Vector of 0 elements
  int     num;

  while ( cin >> num, !cin.eof() )
  {
    Numbers::iterator cur = sorted.begin();   //Start
    Numbers::iterator end = sorted.end();     //End
    while ( cur != end )                      //For sorted
    {
      if ( *cur > num ) break;                //Position to insert
      cur++;                                  //Next
    }
    sorted.insert( cur, num );                //Insert in order
  }

  std::cout << "Numbers sorted are: ";

  for ( Numbers::size_type i = 0; i < sorted.size(); i++ )
  {
    std::cout << sorted[i] << " ";
  }
  std::cout << "\n";
  return 0;
}
```

Which when compiled and run will produce the following output:

```
Numbers sorted are: 10 11 15 17 18 20
```

25.7   The `stack` container

The `stack` container class stores and retrieves data items using a first in last out access mechanism.

The major methods implemented by the stack container are:

Method	Responsibility:

stack<T,Con>
stack<T>
	Where
	    T is the type of the collection.
	    Con is a container used to store the data items.
	Constructor variations:
	  () Empty container

empty()	Returns true if the stack is empty.
operator =	Implement a copying of the Stack.
pop()	Removes the top item from the stack.
push(T)	Adds a new element to stack.
size()	Returns the number of elements in the stack.
top()	Returns the top item on the stack, but does not remove it.

The main embedded type in a stack container is:

Class	Describes
stack<T,Con>::value_type	The type of item stored in the container.

25.8   The queue container

The queue container class stores and retrieves data items using a first in first out access mechanism

The major methods implemented by the stack container are:

Method	Responsibility:

queue<T,Con>	Where
	    T is the type of the collection
	    Con is a container used to store the data items
	Constructor variations:
	  () Empty container

back()	Returns the element at the end of the queue.
empty()	Returns true if the queue is empty.
front()	Returns the element at the front of the queue, but does not remove it.
pop()	Removes the element at the front of the queue.
push(T)	Push a new element onto the end of the queue.
size()	Returns the number of elements in the queue.

The main embedded type in a stack container is:

Class	Describes
queue<T,Con>::value_type	The type of item stored in the container.

25.9   The priority `queue` container

The `priority_queue` container class allows the fast retrieval of the smallest or largest item in the collection.

The major methods implemented by the `priority_queue` container are:

Method	Responsibility
priority_queue <T,Con,Cmp>	Where T is the type of the collection. Con is a container used to store the data items. Cmp is a function object to order items in the priority queue. Constructor variations: () Empty container
empty()	Returns true if the priority queue is empty.
top()	Returns the element at the front of the priority queue, but does not remove it.
pop()	Removes the element at the front of the priority queue.
push(T)	Push a new element onto the end of the priority queue.
size()	Returns the number of elements in the priority queue.

The main embedded type in a priority queue container is:

Class	Describes
priority_queue<T,Con,Cmp>:: value_type	The type of item stored in the container.

25.9.1   A sort program using a priority queue

The following demonstration program reads numbers into a priority queue collection and then removes the smallest number from the collection so that it can be added to the end of a list, hence ordering the numbers.

The parameters to the instantiation of a priority queue are:

- The type of the items stored.
- The container used to store the data items.
- The function object used to order data items in the priority queue. The order determines the lowest collating item that will be removed using the method `top`.

```
#include <iostream>
#include <string>
#include <queue>            // Priority queue and queue
#include <vector>           // Container used by priority queue
#include <list>
#include <algorithm>
#include <strstream>
```

```
template <class Type>
class print : std::unary_function<Type, void>       //Common base
{
public:
  void operator()(const Type& x) const
  {
    std::cout << x << " ";                          //Extraction operator
  }
};
```

```
int main()
{
  typedef std::priority_queue < int, std::vector<int>,
                                std::greater<int> > Pq;
  typedef std::list <int> Numbers;
  Pq numbers;                                 //Priority queue of numbers
  Numbers sorted;                             //List of 0 elements
  char data[] = "20 10 17 18 15 11";
  istrstream cin( data , strlen(data) );      //String stream

  int     num;

  while ( cin >> num, !cin.eof() )            //Put numbers in P queue
  {
    numbers.push( num );
  }

  while ( numbers.size() > 0 )
  {
    sorted.push_back( numbers.top() );        //Add smallest (list)
    numbers.pop();                            //Remove smallest (pq)
  }

  std::cout << "Numbers sorted are: ";

  std::for_each( sorted.begin(), sorted.end(), print<int>() );
  std::cout << "\n";
  return 0;
}
```

Which when compiled and run produces the following output:

```
Numbers sorted are: 10 11 15 17 18 20
```

The order of the sort can be reversed by changing the declaration of the priority queue to:

```
typedef std::priority_queue < int, std::vector<int>,
                              std::less<int> > Pq;
```

25.10   The `map` and `multimap` containers

The `map` and multimap container classes implement the storage and retrieval of information using the key data metaphor. The pair (key, data) is stored and is retrieved by using the key.

The major methods implemented by the `map` and `multimap` containers are:

Method	Responsibility

`map<T1,T2,FO>`	Where
	    `T1` is the type of the key.
	    `T2` is the type of the item associated with the key.
	    `FO` is a function object used to order items in the collection.
	Constructor variations:
	    () Empty map

`begin()`	Returns a random access iterator pointing to the start of the map.
`empty()`	Returns true if the map is empty.
`end()`	Returns a bi-directional iterator pointing to 1 element beyond the end of map.
`erase(T1)`	Removes the key from the map.
`find(T1)`	Returns a bi-directional iterator to the (key, data) pair.
`insert(VT)`	Inserts an element into the map.
`max_size()`	Returns the maximum possible size of the map.
`operator =`	Implements a copy of the map.
`operator []`	Returns a reference to the selected key, allowing the normal subscripting operator to be used.
`rbegin()`	Returns a bi-directional iterator used to transverse the map in a reverse direction.
`rend()`	Returns a bi-directional iterator used to transverse the map in a reverse direction.
`size()`	Returns the number of elements in the map.

Note: The vector map is defined in the header file `<map>`.
   VT is the class `map<T1,T2,FO>::value_type` an instance of this class is used to store the (key, data) pair. For example:
   `map<T1,T2,FO>::value_type ( instance_of_T1, instance_of_T2)`

Class	Used for declaring
`map<T1,T2,FO>::iterator`	A bi-directional iterator used for read and write access to an instance of `map<T1,T2,FO>`.
`map<T1,T2,FO>::const_iterator`	A const bi-directional iterator used for read access to an instance of `map<T1,T2,FO>`. Note if the container is const then a `const_iterator` must be used.

The main embedded types in a map container are:

Type	Describes
map<T1,T2,FO>::value_type	The type of the values stored in the map. pair<**const** key, Data>. Individual members of the pair are selected using the names first and second.
map<T1,T2,FO>::key_type	The type of the key in the map.

25.10.1 Use of the **map** container

A car dealership wishes to record the number of different coloured cars they have in stock. A map Stock is created with an index field of type string and data field of type int using the following typedef statement:

```
typedef map< std::string, int, std::less<string> > Stock;
```

Note: The parameters to the map are:
- *The index used to access the stored data.*
- *The data stored with the index.*
- *A definition of < between instances of the index. This will determine the collating sequence of keys held in the map.*

In the above example the definition of < between strings is provided by the function object less<std::string>*. Section 24.9 lists other useful function objects.*

Data may be entered into the map container using normal subscripting operations as follows:

```
# include <iostream>
# include <string>
# include <algorithm>
# include <map>

typedef map< std::string, int, std::less<string> > Stock;

int main()
{
  Stock cars;

  cars[ "red" ]    = 2;                 //Initial stock
  cars[ "blue" ]   = 5;
  cars[ "silver" ] = 4;
  cars[ "green" ]  = 4;

  cars[ "red" ] = cars[ "red" ] + 2;    //2 new red cars

  std::for_each( cars.begin(), cars.end(), print_car );
  std::cout << "\n";

  return 0;
}
```

The function `print_car` that is applied to each element in the `Stock` collection is implemented as follows:

```cpp
void print_car( Stock::value_type& entry)
{
  std::cout << "There are " << std::setw( 3 ) << entry.second
            << " " << entry.first << " cars" << "\n";
}
```

Note: Each entry in the collection is stored as a pair (key, data). An instance of the pair is created using the function object `Stock::value_type`. *Individual members of the pair are selected using the names* `first` *and* `second`.

When compiled and run the above code produces the following results:

```
There are    5 blue cars
There are    4 green cars
There are    4 red cars
There are    4 silver cars
```

The code may be written using explicit references to the (key, data) pairs as follows:

```cpp
# include <iostream>
# include <string>
# include <algorithm>
# include <map>
int main()
{
  Stock cars;

  cars.insert( Stock::value_type( "red", 2 ) );        //Initial Stock
  cars.insert( Stock::value_type( "blue", 5 ) );
  cars.insert( Stock::value_type( "silver", 4 ) );
  cars.insert( Stock::value_type( "green", 4 ) );

  cars.erase( "red" );                                 //Update
  cars.insert( Stock::value_type( "red", 4 ) );

  Stock::iterator p = cars.begin();

  while ( p != cars.end() )
  {
    std::cout << "There are " << std::setw( 3 ) << (*p).second
              << " " << (*p).first << " cars" << "\n";
    p++;
  }
  return 0;
}
```

Which when run will produce the following results:

```
There are    5 blue cars
There are    4 green cars
There are    4 red cars
There are    4 silver cars
```

25.10.2 Checking if an item is in a map

The following function uses the method `find` to check if a particular car colour is stored in an instance of the map `Stock` used previously in Section 25.10.1. If the colour is contained in the map then the number of cars of that particular colour that are held in stock are printed, otherwise the message "We do not stock" is printed.

```cpp
void how_many( Stock& cars, std::string colour )
{
  if ( cars.find( colour ) != cars.end() )
  {
    std::cout << "There are " << std::setw( 3 ) << cars[colour]
              << " " << colour << " cars" << "\n";
  } else {
    std::cout << "There are  no "
              << colour << " cars in stock" << "\n";
  }
}
```

The demonstration program below populates the map with cars and then uses the function `how_many` to interrogate the map. In addition the method `erase` is used to remove items from the map.

```cpp
# include <iostream>
# include <string>
# include <algorithm>
# include <map>

typedef std::map< std::string,int, std::less<std::string> > Stock;

// The functions how_many, print_car

int main()
{
  cars[ "red" ]    = 2;    cars[ "blue" ]  = 5;
  cars[ "silver" ] = 4;    cars[ "green" ] = 4;

  std::cout << "List of cars" << "\n";
  std::for_each( cars.begin(), cars.end(), print_car );

  std::cout << "\n" << "Interrogate and manipulate stock" << "\n";
  how_many( cars, "red" );        //Print how many red cars
  how_many( cars, "pink" );       //            pink cars

  cars.erase( "red" );            //Remove red cars from map
  how_many( cars, "red" );        //Print how many red cars
```

```
    std::cout << "\n" << "List of cars" << "\n";
    std::for_each( cars.begin(), cars.end(), print_car );
    return 0;
}
```

Which when compiled and run will produce the following output.

```
List of cars
There are    5 blue cars
There are    4 green cars
There are    2 red cars
There are    4 silver cars

Interrogate and manipulate stock
There are    2 red cars
There are   no pink cars in stock
There are   no red cars in stock

List of cars
There are    5 blue cars
There are    4 green cars
There are    4 silver cars
```

25.10.3 Use of a multimap

A multimap is like a map except that it can hold multiple copies of the same key. For example, the following example program populates a map with the colours of cars in which the key green occurs twice.

The method f ind is then used to locate the green key and then a loop is executed that prints all keys that are green. After which the colour green is removed from the map, the effect of which is to remove both occurrences of key.

```
typedef std::multimap< std::string,int,std::less<std::string> > Stock;

int main()
{
  Stock cars;

  cars.insert( Stock::value_type( "red", 2 ) );      //Initial Stock
  cars.insert( Stock::value_type( "blue", 5 ) );     //
  cars.insert( Stock::value_type( "green", 4 ) );
  cars.insert( Stock::value_type( "green", 8 ) );    //Duplicate key
  cars.insert( Stock::value_type( "silver", 4 ) );

  std::cout << "List all keys in multimap" << "\n";

  Stock::iterator p = cars.begin();
  while ( p != cars.end() )
  {
    std::cout << "There are " << std::setw( 3 ) << (*p).second
              << " " << (*p).first << " cars" << "\n";
    p++;
  }
```

```
std::cout << "\n" << "Print multiple keys for green cars" << "\n";

std::string key = "green";
p = cars.find( key );
while ( p != cars.end() && (*p).first == key )
{
  std::cout << "There are " << std::setw( 3 ) << (*p).second
          << " " << (*p).first << " cars" << "\n";
  p++;
}

cars.erase( "green" );

std::cout << "\n" << "Erase green key " << "\n"
        << "List all keys in multimap" << "\n";

p = cars.begin();
while ( p != cars.end() )
{
  std::cout << "There are " << std::setw( 3 ) << (*p).second
          << " " << (*p).first << " cars" << "\n";
  p++;
}

return 0;
}
```

Which when compiled and run produces the following output:

```
List all keys in multimap
There are   5 blue cars
There are   4 green cars
There are   8 green cars
There are   2 red cars
There are   4 silver cars
Print multiple keys for green cars
There are   4 green cars
There are   8 green cars
Erase green key
List all keys in multimap
There are   5 blue cars
There are   2 red cars
There are   4 silver cars
```

25.11 The `set` and `multiset` containers

The `set` and `multiset` container classes implement the storage and retrieval of single data items. Items in a set are ordered using the function object specified when the set is created.

The major methods implemented by the `set` and `multiset` containers are:

Method	Responsibility

set<T,FO>	Where
	    T is the type of the collection.
	    FO is a function object used to order items in the collection.
	Constructor variations:
	    () Empty set

begin()	Returns a bi-directional iterator pointing to the start of the set.
empty()	Returns true if set empty.
end()	Returns a bi-directional iterator pointing to 1 element beyond the end of the set.
erase(T)	Removes the element(s) from the set.
find(T)	Returns a bi-directional iterator to the element.
insert(T)	Inserts an element into the set.
max_size()	Returns the maximum possible size of the set.
operator =	Implements a copy of the set.
rbegin()	Returns a bi-directional iterator used to transverse the set in a reverse direction.
rend()	Returns a bi-directional iterator used to transverse the set in a reverse direction.
size()	Returns the number of elements in the set.

Note: The set is defined in the header file `<set>`

Class	Used for declaring
set<T,FO>::iterator	A bi-directional iterator used for read and write access to an instance of set<T,FO>.
set<T,FO>::const_iterator	A const bi-directional iterator used for read access to an instance of set<T1,FO>. *Note: if the container is const then a* `const_iterator` *must be used.*

The main embedded types in a set container are:

Type	Describes
set<T,FO>::value_type	The type of the values stored in the set.

25.11.1 Use of the `set` container

For example, a set to hold strings is defined as follows:

```
typedef std::set< std::string, std::less<std::string> > Strings;
```

Note: The parameters to the `set` *are:*
- *The type of item stored in the set.*
- *A definition of < between instances of the set.*

In the above example the definition of < between strings is provided by the function object `less<std::string>`.

The following example program, populates a set with different colours, and then removes the colour that is not a colour of the rainbow.

```
typedef std::set< std::string, std::less<std::string> > Strings;
int main()
{
  Strings colours;
  colours.insert("Violet");      colours.insert("Blue");
  colours.insert("Green");       colours.insert("Yellow");
  colours.insert("Orange");      colours.insert("Red");
  colours.insert("Olive");

  std::copy( colours.begin(), colours.end(),
          std::ostream_iterator<std::string>( std::cout, " " ) );
  std::cout << "\n";

  colours.erase( std::string("Olive") );
  std::copy( colours.begin(), colours.end(),
          std::ostream_iterator<std::string>( std::cout, " " ) );
  std::cout << "\n";
  return 0;
}
```

Which when compiled and run will produce the following results:

```
Blue Green Olive Orange Red Violet Yellow
Blue Green Orange Red Violet Yellow
```

25.11.2 Use of the multiset container

A multiset is like a set except that it can hold multiple copies of the same item. For example, the following example program populates a set with the colours of the rainbow in which the colour red occurs twice. Then the colour red is removed from the set, the effect of which is to remove both occurrences of this colour.

```
typedef std::multiset< std::string, std::less<std::string> > Strings;
int main()
{
  Strings colours;
  colours.insert("Violet");      colours.insert("Blue");
  colours.insert("Green");       colours.insert("Yellow");
  colours.insert("Orange");      colours.insert("Red");
  colours.insert("Red");

  std::copy( colours.begin(), colours.end(),
          std::ostream_iterator<std::string>( std::cout, " " ) );
  std::cout << "\n";

  colours.erase( std::string("Red") );   //Erases all Red elements
  std::copy( colours.begin(), colours.end(),
          std::ostream_iterator<std::string>( std::cout, " " ) );
  std::cout << "\n";
  return 0;
}
```

Which when compiled and run produces the following output:

```
Blue Green Orange Red Red Violet Yellow
Blue Green Orange Violet Yellow
```

25.12 Self-assessment

- What are the advantages of using the container classes in a program?

- Under what circumstances would it be better to use a list container instead of a vector container? When might the reverse be true?

- If an instance of an object is stored in a container, what operations must it support and why?

- Why should the user be wary of storing pointers in a container?

25.13 Exercises

Construct the following:

- *Account*
  A class representing a bank account, in which transactions are stored as part of the audit trail mechanism. The account class implements in addition to the normal methods associated with an account the additional methods of:

Method	Responsibility
`clear_audit_trail`	Clears the audit trail.
`return_audit_trail`	Returns a collection of audit trail entries.

- *Bank*
  A class representing a bank in which individual accounts are stored in an appropriate container. The bank class should support the addition of new accounts and the processing of normal bank transactions.

- *Spell checker*
  Construct a simple spell checker using appropriate containers. A simple strategy for a spell checker is to use a container to hold a dictionary of correctly spelt words. A word is considered correctly spelt if it is in the dictionary. If a word is not in the dictionary the user is asked if the word is spelt correctly if yes, then the word is added to a user dictionary.

26 Using legacy C++ compilers

This chapter describes how to overcome some of the limitations of pre ANSI C++ compilers. This is achieved by converting ANSI constructs where possible into existing language components implemented by the legacy compiler. This conversion process is usually though not exclusively implemented using the macro processor. In some cases however, hand editing of the ANSI C++ source code will be required.

26.1   Overview

The aim of this chapter is to highlight some of the differences between compilers that support the ANSI standard and legacy compilers. However, as C++ has evolved over many years I have not attempted to cover differences from the early days of C++.

26.2   Include directive

In the ANSI standard the C++ header files do not have an extension. For example, to include the header file iostream the following is written:

```
#include <iostream>
```

In earlier versions of C++ the header files had an explicit .h extension. For legacy compilers that do not support this form of include directive, the inclusion of the header file iostream is written as:

```
#include <iostream.h>
```

26.3   The **bool** type not implemented

Define the following macro's at the top of the program:

```
#define bool int
#define true 1
#define false 0
```

Unfortunately the more elegant:

```
enum bool { false, true };
```

will not work in all cases.

26.4   Scope of the `for-init-statement` in a `for` loop

In a `for` statement if there is a `for-init-statement`, then the scope of the declared object is to the end of the `for` statement. In previous versions of the language the scope of this variable was to the end of the enclosing block.

For compilers that have the old scope rule enclose the whole of the `for` statement in enclosing {}'s. For example:

```
{
  for ( int i=0; i<10; i++ )   // for-init-statement -> int i=0
  {
    // Body of first for loop
  }
}

{
  for ( int i=0; i<10; i++ )   // for-init-statement -> int i=0
  {
    // Body of second for loop
  }
}
```

will effectively restrict the scope of the declaration `int  i=0` to the body of the `for` loop.

26.5   Dynamic memory allocation with `new`

A call to new using the form:

```
char *p_chs = new char[10];
```

will raise the exception `bad_alloc` when no more storage is available to be allocated. However, the original effect when storage could not be allocated was to return a `NULL` pointer. The old effect can be obtained by re-writing the call to `new` as:

```
char *p_chs = new char (nothrow) [10];
```

26.6   The exception mechanism not implemented

This is difficult to fake completely. An intermediate solution that will work in cases where the standard exceptions have been used is:

```
# define throw
# define try
# define catch( parameter ) exception err; if ( false )
```

Note: There can only be one catch in each block.
The exception classes needs to be defined.

This will at least allow the code to compile and will run correctly provided no exception is generated.

26.7   The exception classes not implemented

Include definitions for the exception classes as follows:

```
class exception
{
public:
  exception( const string& arg="" )
  {
    the_message = arg;
  }
  virtual ~exception(){};
  virtual const char* what()
  {
    return the_message.c_str();
  }
private:
  string the_message;
};
```

Then for each exception used provide a derived class from the class exception for it. For example, for the exception logic_error, provide the following class definition:

```
class logic_error: public exception
{
public:
  logic_error( const string& arg ) : exception( arg ) {};
};
```

26.8   The namespace directive not implemented

The effect of different namespaces is difficult to fake using existing constructs. The only solution will be to comment out the directives and prefix each name in the namespace with its namespace name and amend the code to reflect the new names. This could take some time. In the examples shown in the book the following macro will remove the namespace `std` prefix from standard library class use.

```
#define std
```

26.9   The template mechanism not implemented

During the early development of C++ the template construct was simulated by using the macro facility. This simulation of templates is implemented by defining a macro for the generic class. The macro has as its parameter the type for which the class is to be instantiated. This macro is then used to declare specific instantiations of the class.

For example, a templated class that defines a generator for a sequence of numbers is implemented by using macros as follows:

```
#define generate_seq(Type)                                      \
class generate_seq_##Type                                       \
{                                                               \
public:                                                         \
  generate_seq_##Type( Type initial_val, Type inc )             \
    : the_next(initial_val) , the_increment(inc)                \
  {                                                             \
  };                                                            \
  Type operator()()                                             \
  {                                                             \
    Type res = the_next;                                        \
    the_next = the_next + the_increment;                        \
    return res;                                                 \
  }                                                             \
private:                                                        \
  Type the_next;                                                \
  Type the_increment;                                           \
};                                                              \
```

Note: The use of ## to allow part of a symbol to be substituted. This needs to be used so that Type *may be substituted by the specific type to form a new symbol for* generate_seq_##Type.

The macro `declare`, defined as:

```
#define    declare( Object, Type ) Object(Type)
```

is used to instantiate the specific class `generate_seq_int` as follows:

```
declare( generate_seq, int )
```

The macro `implement`, defined as:

```
#define  implement( Object, Type ) Object##_##Type
```

is used to implement an instance `init_seq` of the class `generate_seq_int` as follows:

```
implement(generate_seq,int)      int_seq(1,1);
```

Note: Macros, for `implement` *and* `declare` *are defined in the header file* `<generic>`.

26.9.1   Putting it all together

These could then be used in a program as follows:

```
#include <iostream>

declare( generate_seq,  int )
declare( generate_seq,  float )

int main()
{
   implement(generate_seq,int)      int_seq(1,1);
   implement(generate_seq,float)    float_seq(10.2, 0.1);

   std::cout << "Next int is    : " << int_seq()    << "\n";
   std::cout << "Next int is    : " << int_seq()    << "\n";
   std::cout << "Next float is  : " << float_seq()  << "\n";
   std::cout << "Next float is  : " << float_seq()  << "\n";
   return 0;
}
```

which when run would produce the results:

```
Next int is    : 1
Next int is    : 2
Next float is  : 10.2
Next float is  : 10.3
```

26.10   The `mutable` qualifier not implemented

Define the following macro at the top of the program:

```
#define mutable
```

Then surround the class that uses `mutable` with a macro to define `const` as the null string. This causes inspector member functions to be regarded as mutable member functions as the `const` attribute has been removed from a functions specification.

```
#define const

class Uses_mutable { };

#undef const
```

This does assume that there is not a const and a non const version of an overloaded operator in the class.

26.11 The `explicit` qualifier not implemented

Define the following macro at the top of the program:

```
#define explicit
```

This will remove the qualifier from the program.

26.12 No initialized const members in a class

Use an enumeration to define the value. For example, if in the private part of a class MAX is declared as follows:

```
private:
  static const int MAX = 100;
```

change this to:

```
private:
  enum { MAX = 100 };
```

26.13 Self-assessment

● To what extent can the provision of ANSI C++ features for legacy compilers be automated by using suitable macros?

26.14 Exercises

● Write a pre-processor in C++ to implement features of ANSI C++ not implemented in your version of C++.

● Implement a new extension to the language C++.

27 Attributes

This chapter describes the attributes of C++ items, and how they are implemented during execution.

27.1 Introduction

The attributes of an item in C++ are far from simple, and no general description of their properties can hope to cover all cases. With these qualifications in mind, a variable can be said to have the following attributes:

- Duration.
- Linkage.
- Scope.
- Storage class.
- Type.
- Visibility.

These are established by many factors, some of which are explicit, and others implicit.

27.2 Lifetime

Lifetime specifies the active duration of an item. It can be either:

- For the lifetime of the program   (static).
- For the lifetime of the executing function   (auto).
- As decided by the programmer   (dynamic).

For example, the following program features the lifetimes static, auto, and dynamic:

```
#include <iostream>
int blue_cars = 3;
int main()
{
  int   red_cars    = 4;
  int* green_cars = new int[1]; *green_cars = 5;
  std::cout << "Cars: Red  =  " <<  red_cars << "\n";
  std::cout << "Cars: Blue = " <<  blue_cars << "\n";
  std::cout << "Cars: Green=  " <<  *green_cars << "\n";
  delete green_cars;
  return 0;
}
```

Note: The lifetimes static *and* auto *are implicitly defined.*

Static   The storage for `blue_cars` has static duration, which means that the storage will stay in existence for the lifetime of the program. Variables declared outside a function will always have static duration.

Auto   The storage for `red_cars` has auto duration, which means that the storage will stay in existence for the lifetime of the function. The storage for this variable is allocated in the run-time stack.

Dynamic   The programmer explicitly allocates storage for `green_cars` with the operator `new` and de-allocates it with `delete`.

The above program could have been written with explicit `auto` and `static` declarations as follows:

```
#include <iostream>

static int blue_cars = 3;

int main()
{
  auto int  red_cars   = 4;
  int* green_cars = new int[1]; *green_cars = 5;
  std::cout << "Cars: Red  = " <<  red_cars << "\n";
  std::cout << "Cars: Blue = " <<  blue_cars << "\n";
  std::cout << "Cars: Green= " <<  *green_cars << "\n";
  delete green_cars;
  return 0;
}
```

Note: *A local variable to a function may be preceded by static:*
        `static int red_cars;`
        in which case the variable would be allocated in global data storage and would stay in existence for the lifetime of the program. This can be used to enable functions to remember values.
        It is good programming practice to let local variables to a function have auto duration.

27.2.1 Summary

Item declared	Default duration (No declaration required)	May also be (Declaration required)
In function	auto	static
Outside function	static	—

27.3 Linkage

When building a program out of several separately compiled modules, there may be cases where items are declared in one module but used in another. Linkage is the attribute which allows this association to be performed. All items can be said to have the following attributes.

- No linkage.
- Internal linkage   `static int not_visible_outside.`
- External linkage   `extern int visible_outside.`

Note: By default functions have external linkage and variables have internal linkage.

The following program illustrates linkage. Two programs `ex1.cpp` and `ex2.cpp` are separately compiled using the common header file `ex.h`.

```
//Header file ex.h

#ifndef  HEADER_FILE_EX
#define  HEADER_FILE_EX

extern int shared;          //Shared has external linkage
void process();             //Function prototype for process

#endif
```

The program file `ex1.cpp`	The program file `ex2.cpp`
``#include "ex.h"

int shared; // storage alloc.
int main()
{
  shared = 42;
  process();
  return 0;
}``` | ```#include "ex.h"
#include <iostream>
void process(void)
{
  std::cout << "Shared = ";
  std::cout << shared << "\n";
  return;
}``` |

The two object code files are linked together and the resultant program when run would print the result:

```
Shared = 42
```

Note: The function `process` has by default external linkage.
The common header file instructs the compiler that shared is to have external linkage. In file `ex1.cpp` the compiler will generate an 'I am here' reference in the object code. Whilst in the file `ex2.cpp` it will generate a 'link to' reference in the object code file.

27.4   Scope

In a C++ program scope determines the area in which an item is active. This may, in some cases, be different from the area in which the item can be referenced. Consider the following program:

```
std::string var_is_a = "Global declaration";

int main()
{
  std::string var_is_a = "Local declaration";
  {
    std::string var_is_a = "Local inner declaration";
    std::cout << "var_is_a is : " << var_is_a << "\n";    //Local inner
    std::cout << "var_is_a is : " << ::var_is_a << "\n"; //Global
  }
  std::cout << "var_is_a is : " << var_is_a << "\n";      //Local
  return 0;
}
```

In the function `main` the first declaration of `var_is_the` will be in scope for all of the duration of the function `main`, but will be hidden for the duration of the block in which the second declaration is made. The scope resolution operator `::` is used to access the global `var_is_a`.

There are four kinds of scope:

- Class.
- File.
- Function.
- Local.

Class   Items declared in a class are local to that class. Access can be made to the members of the class using the `::` or `.` or `->` operators provided they are not hidden by a private or protected access right.

File   An item that is declared outside of a class, function or block is visible from the point of declaration to the end of the compilation unit.

Function   All labels declared in a function can be accessed from any point in the function. A label is the destination of a `goto` statement.

```
void nasty(const int data)
{
  //label exit is in scope through out the function
  if ( data < 10 ) goto exit;

exit:
  return;
}
```

Local   An item declared in a function is local to the block (enclosing {}s) from the point of declaration to the end of the block.

27.5   Visibility

Visibility defines the area in which the item may be accessed. This may, as seen above in the case of var_is_a, be less than the scope of an item.

Each type name declared in C++ shares the same name space. If there are two different types with the same name then there must be a way of uniquely identifying which type is being referred to.

27.6   Storage class

This determines where and how an item is stored in the machine during its lifetime. The storage classes available are:

- auto   auto   local_variable
- extern   extern   static_variable
- register register   local_variable
- static   static   life_time_of_program
- mutable   mutable   writable class data member

auto   This can only be used with items local to a function and indicates that the item is to be stored in the run-time stack.

```
void process() {
  auto int temp;
}
```

extern   This indicates that external linkage is to be made to this item. Obviously the placement of such an item must be known at compile time and hence must be implicitly static.

register   This is a hint to the compiler to hold the item in a CPU register if possible. Only items of an appropriate size and defined as auto are eligible for this treatment. The compiler may ignore the hint to place the item in a register.

In C++ it is possible to take the address of an item which has the storage class register. The most likely effect of this is for the compiler to ignore the hint to place the item in a register.

```
void process()
{
  register int used_frequently; //Held in CPU register

}
```

static   This indicates that the item has internal linkage and its lifetime will be that of
         the program.

```
int new_product_code()
{
   static int number = 0;   //Delivers a unique product
   return ++number;         //code each time it is called.
}
```

mutable Applied to a data member of a class to nullify a const specifier to a method.
        For example, a const method (inspector) may modify a mutable data member
        of the class.

```
class Bank
{
public:
   float account_balance( const int ) const;

private:
   mutable fstream the_customers;

}
```

The inspector method `account_balance` will change the stream pointer
`the_customers` when it reads an individual customer details from disk.
However, this method `account_balance` is const (to a client of the class)
as it does not change the file, and would be confusing to the client if shown
as a mutating method. The use of mutable should be used with care.

27.7   Modifiers

A declaration may be modified by the following:

const
         Indicates that the item is read only.

```
const int MAX = 10;   //MAX number of items
```

*Note: An instance of a class can be declared as `const`, in which case the functions
operating on the const object must also be declared as const.*

`volatile`

> Warn the compiler that the item may be changed by a source other than the program. For example, using memory mapped I/O, a device register would appear as a normal store location. A program that accessed this location must be sure that the compiler will not shadow its value in a CPU register or otherwise optimize the code.

```cpp
struct Acia {
  char      status;        //Status information
  char      dummy1;        //1 byte pad
  char      data;          //Data register
};

volatile Acia * base_vdu = reinterpret_cast<Acia*>(0x0C0080);

const int ACIA_RM  =  0x01;
const int ACIA_TM  =  0x02;

//
//     Wait for device to become free
//              Read a character from the terminal
//

char getchar()
{
  while( (base_vdu->status & ACIA_RM) == 0 );
  return base_vdu->data;
}
```

Note: An instance of a class can be declared as volatile. In which case the messages sent to this object must invoke a volatile method.

27.8.   Type

There are several categories of types which can be declared. These are:

- Aggregate.
- Function.
- Fundamental.
- Void.

27.8.1. Aggregate

The aggregate types are derived from the fundamental types. These aggregate types are:

- Array   `int vec[4];.`
- Class   `Class Account {  };.`
- Pointer   `char *p_ch;.`
- Reference   `char& passed.`
- Structure   `struct Person {  };.`
- Union   `union Overlay {  };.`

27.8.2   Function

The function type defines a code sequence which may be executed in the program.

27.8.3   Fundamental

An instance of these types will usually be contained in a single machine-based component, and are collectively known as the arithmetic types:

- Integral types :   enumeration's, `char` and `int` all sizes.
- Floating point: `float, double, long double`.

27.8.4   Void

This, as its name suggests, indicates the absence of any value. It is mainly used to:

- Indicate that a function has no return value.
- Indicate that a function has no parameters.
- Describe a pointer to any type of storage.

For example:

```
void hello();         //Function prototype

void *not_sure;       //A pointer to storage of any type

void hello() { std::cout << "Hello" << "\n"; }
```

27.9   Run-time execution of a program

The execution of a C++ program such as:

```
#include <iostream>

typedef char* C_string;

C_string str_letters( int );

int length = 10;

int main()
{
  C_string letters = str_letters( length );
  std::cout << "The first " << length;
  std::cout << " letters are " << letters << "\n";
  delete [] letters;
  return 0;
}

C_string str_letters( int len )
{
  C_string text = new char[ len+1 ];
  for( int i=0; i<len; i++ ) text[i] = char( i+int('a') );
  text[len] = '\0';
  return text;
}
```

when run, would produce the following result:

```
The first 10 letters are abcdefghij
```

To support the execution of the C++ program, items will be allocated in different areas of memory. Though there may be minor differences in implementation, the areas involved will be as shown in Figure 27.1.

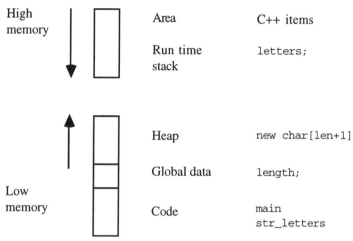

Figure 27.1 Layout of store.

27.9.1   Run-time stack

A run-time stack will contain the individual stack frames, which support the execution of called functions in the C++ program. Each time a function is called, a new stack frame will be created.

For example, when the function `str_letters` is called, its stack frame would be as illustrated in Figure 27.2.

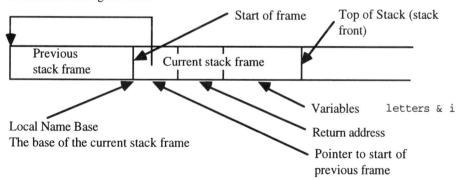

Figure 27.2 Run-time stack of a C++ program.

In the Figure 27.2:

- The LNB (Local Name Base) is used as a pointer, from which items in the current stack frame can be accessed. The stack frame contains the current local variables.

- The TOS (Top Of Stack) marks the upper limit of the frame.

The items in the stack frame for `str_letters` are:

A pointer to the previous stack frame:
> This will become the active LNB when an exit is made from the current function.

The return address:
> This denotes the code address from which execution will resume, when an exit is made from the current function.

Variables `letters` and `i`:
> The auto variables declared in a function are allocated in the stack frame. Hence, when the function is exited, this space can be released back to the system.

Temporary work space:
> In evaluating the code for the function, temporary values may be stored by expanding the stack frame at the stack front.

27.9.2   The heap

Any storage allocated by `new` has existence until it is explicitly released with `delete`. This storage comes from the heap, which is managed by a garbage collector that will try to re-allocate returned storage. If no storage can be re-allocated, then new storage is allocated by expanding the heap towards the run-time stack.

Optimism dictates that the run-time stack and the heap will never meet.

Note: This is usually enforced by the memory management unit. However, on some implementations this will not be checked for, and disaster will ensue if the two regions meet and overrun each other.

27.9.3   Global data

The global data area is where all the statically allocated data items are usually held. Normally this is data items declared outside of a function.

27.9.4   Code

The code area contains the physical machine code of the program.

28 C++: a summary

The following chapter contains a summary of the main language features of C++.

Declarations in C++

```
char    c;   unsigned char c;
wchar_t wc;
bool    b;
int     i;   unsigned int i;    signed int i;
             short int i;       unsigned short int i;
                                signed short int i;
             long int i;        unsigned long int i;
                                signed long int i;
float f;     double f;          long double f;

Account mike;
```

Enumeration declaration

```
enum Colour { RED, GREEN, BLUE };

Colour : car = RED;
```

Array declaration

```
char text[120];                 //Array of 120 characters
char mes[] = "Hello world";     //Array
char table[3][3];               //Two dimensional array
```

Dynamic memory allocation

```
int main()
{
  float *p_f = new float[1];        //Allocate storage
  *p_f = 12.3; std::cout << *p_f;   //Use
  delete [] p_f;                    //De-allocate;
}
```

Lifetime

```
char global;          //Global lifetime global visibility

int main()
{
  char l;             //Local to function
  static char c;      //Global lifetime local visibility

  char *d = new[10];  //Dynamic allocation

  delete [] d;        //De-allocation
}
```

Class declaration and implementation

```
class Account {
public:
  Account();
  float account_balance() const;     //Return the balance
  float withdraw( const float );     //Withdraw from account
  void deposit( const float );       //Deposit into account
protected:
  void set_min_balance( const float ); //Set minimum balance
private:
  float the_balance;                 //The outstanding balance
  float the_min_balance;             //The minimum balance
};
```

```
Account::Account() { the_amount = the_min_balance = 0.00; }

float Account::account_balance() const { return the_balance; }
```

```
void Account::deposit( const float money )
{
  the_balance = the_balance + money;
}
```

```
float Account::withdraw( const float money )
{
  if ( the_balance-money >= the_min_balance )
  {
    the_balance = the_balance - money;
    return money;
  } else {
    return 0.00;
  }
}
```

```
void Account::set_min_balance( const float money )
{
  the_min_balance = money;
}
```

Inheritance

```
class  Interest_Account : public Account
{
  public:        //Functions specialising an Account
  protected:     //Functions specialising an Account
  private:       //Instance variables specialising an Account
};
```

Operator and assignment overloading

```
class List {
public:
  List();                    //Constructor
  ~List();                   //Destructor
  List( List& )              //Copy constructor
  List operator = ( List );  //Assignment operator
  List operator + ( List );  //Addition operator
  operator int();            //Conversion operator
private:
};
```

Run-time type identity

```
int main()
{
  Account mike;
  std::cout << "Type of mas = " <<
          typeid( mike ).name() << "\n";
  return 0;
}
```

Casts

```
int main()
{
  float i = (float) 2;
  float j = float(2);     //Functional notation

  Account *p = new Restricted_account[1];
  Restricted_account *r =
    dynamic_cast<Restricted_account*>(*p);   //Downcast
  return 0;
}
```

Functions

```
int twice( int );                    //Function prototype

int main()                           //Entry point
{
  int actual_param = 2;
  std::cout << "Twice actual is " << twice( actual_param );
  return 0;
}

int twice( int formal_param )        //Function body
{
  return formal_param + formal_param;
}
```

Statement expressions

```
a = 2+3;                //Assignment expression
bank_statement();       //Function call
mas.deposit(10);        //send message deposit #10 to mas
```

Compound statement

```
{
  char character;
  character = 'M'; std::cout << character;
}
```

Selection statements

```
if ( temperature < 15 ) std::cout << "Cold";

if ( temperature < 15 )
  std::cout << "Cold";
else
  std::cout << "Warm";

switch ( number )
{
  case 2+3  :  std::cout << "Is 5";
               break;
  case 7    :  std::cout << "Is 7";
               break;
  default   :  std::cout << "Not 5 or 7";
}

std::cout << ( temperature < 15 ? "Cold" : "Warm" );
```

Looping statements

```
while ( raining ) work();

do
  play();
while ( sunny );

for( i = 1; i < MAX ; i++ ) std::cout << i << "\n";
```

Arithmetic operators

```
res = a + b;  //plus
res = a - b;  //minus
res = a * b;  //multiplication
res = a / b;  //division (Integer if a and b both integer)
res = a % b;  //Modulus  (remainder)
```

Conditional expressions

```
if( a == b )   //Equal to
if( a > b )    //Greater than
if( a < b )    //less than
if( a != b )   //Not equal
if( a >= b )   //Greater or
               //equal
if( a <= b )   //Less or
               //equal
```

```
if( wet && monday )   //and
if( dry || tuesday )  //or
```

```
if ( cost > 15 && number <= 100  )
{
    std::cout << "Cost greater than 15 and the number of" <<
            " items is less than 100";
}
```

Note: *The conditional expression will only be evaluated as far as necessary to produce the result*
of the condition. Thus in the if *statement:*

> if (fun_one() || fun_two()) perform();

fun_two() *will not be called if* fun_one() *delivered true.*

Logical operators

```
res = a << 2;   //Shift a left  2 binary places
res = a >> 2;   //Shift a right 2 binary places

res = a & b;    //Logical and of a b
res = a | b;    //Logical or  of a b
res = a ^ b;    //logical xor of a b
res = !a;       //logical not of a
res = ~a;       //1's complement of a
```

Short cuts

```
a++;            //equivalent to a = a + 1;
a--;            //equivalent to a = a - 1;
res += a * b;   //equivalent to res = res + (a * b)
                //also for -=, *=, /=, %= etc.
```

Changing the flow of control in a loop

```
while ( raining )
{
  work();
  if ( tied ) break;              // Exit from loop if tied now!
  work();
}

while ( raining )
{
  work()
  if ( may_have_stoped ) continue;   // jump to start of loop
  work();
}
```

Exceptions

```
try {

    //Code which may raise an exception
    throw std::runtime_error("It went wrong");

}
catch ( std::runtime_error& err )
{
    std::cout << "Problem " << err.what() << "\n";
}
```

Address operations

```
char string[] = "Hello world";
char  *p_ch;          //p_ch will contain a pointer to a char

p_ch = &string[0];   //Assigns the address
                     //of the first element of string to p_ch
```

The following code will print the characters in the string pointed at by p_ch:

```
while (*p_ch) std::cout << *p_ch++;
```

Function templates

```
template <class Type>
Type max( Type first, Type second )
{
    return first > second ? first : second;
}
```

```
int main()
{
    std::cout << max( 4.64, 3.14 ) << "\n";
    std::cout << max( 'M', 'S' ) << "\n";
    return 0;
}
```

Class templates

```
template <class Type, const int MAX_ELEMENTS=5>
class Stack {
public:
  Stack();
  void push( const Type );        //Push item onto stack
  Type pop();                     //Pop top item from stack
  bool empty();                   //Stack empty
private:
  Type the_elements[MAX_ELEMENTS]; //Items in Stack
  int  the_tos;                   //Top of Stack pointer
};
```

```
template <class Type, const int MAX_ELEMENTS>
Stack<Type,MAX_ELEMENTS>::Stack()
{
  the_tos = -1;                   //Empty
}
```

```
int main()
{
  Stack <int,10> numbers;   //Stack of integers max depth 10
  Stack <float> values;     //Stack of floats max depth 5

}
```

Appendix A: C++ style input/output

Default streams

`std::cout`	Normally the terminal screen.
`std::cin`	Normally the terminal keyboard.
`std::cerr`	It is usual that this stream will always cause output to go to the user's terminal.

Note: `std::cout, std::cin,` *and* `std::cerr` *are of type* `std::ostream.`

Output manipulators

Output manipulators are used as if they are a normal data item to be output. However, instead of data being output, changes are set which determine how the data to be output should be formatted. For example, to set the field width to 5 places in which the number 42 is printed, a user could write:

```
std::cout << std::setw(5) << 42;
```

To use many of these manipulators, a program would need to include the header file iomanip.h. `#include <iomanip>`

Manipulator	Item	Effect
`std::setw(int n)`	next	Sets the field width in which the next item will be printed to n spaces.
`std::hex`	all	Sets the output base for all subsequent integer items to be base 16 (hexadecimal).
`std::oct`	all	Sets the output base for all subsequent integer items to be base 8 (octal).
`std::dec`	all	Sets the output base for all subsequent integer items to be base 10 (decimal).
`std::setfill(int c)`	next	Sets the fill character to make up the characters to pad the next item to field width size to be c.
`std::setprecision(int n)`	all	Sets the number of decimal places to be display for all subsequent floating point numbers.
`std::endl`	next	Inserts new line and flushes stream.
`std::flush`	next	Flushes the stream.
`std::ends`	next	Inserts the end of string terminator.
`std::boolalpha`	all	Inserts a bool type in alphabetic format.
`std::uppercase`	all	Replaces certain lower-case letters with their upper-case equivalent.
`std::unitbuf`	all	Flushes output after each operation.

Note: The second column indicates if the effect is for all subsequent items to be output or just the next item output.

Parameters to the selectors setiosflags and resetiosflags

Input output selector (ios) flags are set or unset with the respective manipulators `setiosflags` and `resetiosflags`. For example, to set all subsequent output to be right aligned in its selected output field width, a user could write:

```
cout << setiosflags( ios::right );
```

The flags listed below are defined in the class `ios`, and act as parameters for the manipulators `setiosflags` and `resetiosflags`.

ios flag	Item	Effect
std::ios::left	all	Items are left aligned in the output field width.
std::ios::right	all	Items are right aligned in the output field width.
std::ios::scientific	all	Floating point items are output in scientific notation. For example 42.2 would be displayed as 4.22E+01.
std::ios::fixed	all	Floating point items are output in decimal notation. For example 42.2 would be displayed as 42.2.
std::ios::showpoint	all	Floating point numbers are displayed with all the specified decimal places even if zero. For example 4.2 with 2 decimal places set would be displayed as 4.20.
std::ios::showpos	all	Show the + sign on output for positive numbers. For example 42 would be displayed as +42.

For example, the following fragment of code:

```
std::cout << "The programming language [";
std::cout << std::setiosflags( ios::left );
std::cout << std::setw(3) << std::setfill('+') << "C" << "]" << "\n";
```

would produce the output:

```
The programming language [C++]
```

Input manipulators

The following manipulators can be used on an input stream:

Manipulators	Item	Effect
std::ws		Reads white space characters in input.
std::oct, std::dec, std::hex	all	Set the input base to: octal, decimal or hexadecimal.
std::boolalpha	all	inserts a bool type in alphabetic format.

Parameters to the selectors `setiosflags` and `resetiosflags`

These are set or unset with the respective manipulators `std::setiosflags` and `std::resetiosflags` which take as a parameter the following flags defined in the class `ios`.

ios flag	Item	Effect
`std::ios::skipws`	all	Input operations will ignore white space characters. `std::resetiosflags( std::ios::skipws )` will cause white space characters to be delivered.

I/O to files

The two classes `ofstream` and `ifstream` are classes derived respectively from `ostream` and `istream`. They add the ability to read and write to files.

For example, the following code will write to the file mas.txt and then read back the data displaying it on a user's terminal.

```
#include <fstream>
#include <iomanip>

int main()
{
  std::ofstream sink;                    //output stream
  std::ifstream source;                  //input stream
  char c;

  sink.open("mas.txt");                  //connect to mas.txt
  if (!sink)                             //Failed to create
  {
    std::cerr << "Failed to create mas.txt" << "\n";
    exit(-1);
  }
  std::sink << "Hello world" << "\n";
  std::sink.close();                     //close stream
```

Once the file is closed it is re-opened as an input source.

```
  source.open("mas.txt");                //connect to mas.txt
  if (!source)                           //Failed to open
  {
    std::cerr << "Failed to open mas.txt" << "\n";
    exit(-2);
  }

  source >> std::resetiosflags( std::ios::skipws );   //Read white space
  while ( source >> c, !source.eof() )        //Copy mas.txt to cout
  {
    cout << c;
  }
  source.close();                        //close stream
}
```

The output from this program would be:

```
Hello world
```

Note: The include file `fstream.h` *which contains the definition of* `ifstream` *and* `ofstream`

String streams

The classes `ostrstream` and `istrstream` are derived respectively from `ostream` and `istream`; they can be used to read and write to and from an area in memory. For example, the following program:

```
#include <strstream>
#include <iomanip>
#include <string>

const int MAX_MES = 100;                      //Size of string

int main()
{
  char mes[MAX_MES];
  char town[] = "Brighton East Sussex";

  std::ostrstream ostr( mes, MAX_MES );       //output str stream

  ostr << "The sum of 2+3 is " << (2+3) << "\n" << '\0';
  std::cout << mes;

  std::istrstream istr( town , strlen(town) );  //input str stream
  istr >> resetiosflags( ios::skipws );

  char c;
  std::cout << "\n" << "[";

  while ( istr >> c , !istr.eof() )            //read characters from
  {
    std::cout << c;                           // String stream
  }
  std::cout << "]" << "\n";
  return 0;
}
```

would produce the following output:

```
The sum of 2+3 is 5

[Brighton East Sussex]
```

Note: The string terminator has to be written to the string stream, if it is to be used as a normal C++ string.
The header file `strstream.h` *contains a #include for* `iostream`*.*

Appendix B: C style input/output

Many C++ compilers will allow the inclusion of C style input and output. In C, like in C++, the I/O routines are not part of the language but are provided by a standard library of functions. In C however, the I/O system is not type safe.

The C I/O philosophy revolves around the concept of a stream pointer which is associated with a file. This stream pointer is then used to read or write information from or to the selected file. Declarations pertaining to this I/O system are held in the header file stdio.h.

A stream pointer is declared with:

```
FILE *sp;
```

and is associated with a file using the library function fopen as follows:

```
sp = fopen( "file.dat" , "r" );
```

The parameters and returned value of fopen are:

Parameter 1:	A string representing the filename.
Parameter 2:	A string representing the way the file is to be accessed:
r	Open for reading.
w	Create for writing.
a	Open for writing at end if exists.
	Create for writing if the file does not exist.
r+	Open an existing file for reading and writing.
w+	Create a new file or reading and writing.
a+	Open for writing at end if exists.
	Create for writing if the file does not exist.
result:	A stream pointer to the file.
	NULL if the file cannot be opened.

Note: When a file is opened for write or append access for the first time it will be created, if it does not already exist.

fopen would normally be called as follows:

```
sp = fopen( "file.dat" , "r" );
if ( sp == NULL )
{
   /* Take an appropriate action: file has not been opened */
}
```

Note: NULL is defined in the header file <stdio>.

Formatted output

Information is written to the file with the library function `fprintf`. This function uses a format string which tells it how to interpolate the contents of its remaining parameters to the stream. This concept is best illustrated by an example:

```
int main()
{
  FILE *sp;
  char ch;
  sp = fopen("tmp.dat", "w" );
  for(int i=100;i<105;i++)
  {
    fprintf(sp,"Character %c has ASCII code %d\n" , i , i );
  }
  fclose(sp);
  return 0;
}
```

which would write into the file tmp.dat:

```
Character d has ASCII code 100
Character e has ASCII code 101
Character f has ASCII code 102
Character g has ASCII code 103
Character h has ASCII code 104
```

Note: That `fprintf` cannot check on the type of arguments supplied; it implicitly trusts the writer of the code to get it right.

The parameters and some of the corresponding returned values of `fprintf` are:

Parameter 1: The stream pointer.

Parameter 2: A string representing how the parameters after this are to be interpolated into the output text. Each parameter to be interpolated is introduced by a % followed by a character or characters indicating the format:

%d   As a decimal number.
%i   As a decimal number.
%u   As an unsigned decimal number.
%c   As a character.
%s   As a string of characters [string terminated with ' \0 '].
%f   As a floating point number [format 1.23].
%e   As a floating point number [format 1.23e45].
%o   As an octal number.
%x   As a hexadecimal number.
%ld   As a long integer.
    %l   As a `long` integer.
    %%   The character %.

The formats may be modified with:

%4d	As a decimal number in a field width of 4 right justified.
%-4d	As a decimal number in a field width of 4 left justified.
%04d	As %4d but with leading zeros.
%8.2f	As a floating number in a field width of 8 right justified by 2 decimal places.

result   Success or failure of the operation.

The following streams are usually pre-defined for the user.

stdout	Normally the terminal screen.
stdin	Normally the terminal keyboard.
stderr	Normally the terminal screen. It is usual that this stream will always cause output to go to the user's terminal.

Single character output

```
fputc( ch, stdout );     //A function call
putc ( ch, stdout );     //May be a macro
```

The parameters and returned value of `fputc` and `putc` are as follows:

Parameter 1	The character to be output.
Parameter 2	The stream to be output on.
result	Success or failure of the operation.

Single character input

```
ch = fgetc( sp );     //A function call
ch = getc ( sp );     //May be a macro
```

The parameters and returned value of `fgetc` and `getc` are as follows:

Parameter 1:	The stream from which the character is to be input.
result:	The character input. If the end of file has been reached on the stream then EOF is returned. EOF is defined in `<stdio>`.

Close the stream

```
fclose( sp );
```

The parameters and returned value of `fclose` are as follows:

Parameter 1:   The stream to be closed.
result: Success or failure of the operation.

Position in file randomly

The example below illustrates a positioning in the file, 12 bytes from the start of the file.

```
fseek( sp , 12L , 0 );
```

The parameters and returned value of `fseek` are as follows:

Parameter 1:   The stream on which a random positioning is to be made.
Parameter 2:   The number of bytes to be moved which must be a long value.
Parameter 3:   0   The file start.
               1   The current position.
               2   The file end.

result: Success or failure of the operation.

Input and output shortcuts

The following functions are special cases of the normal C input/output functions.

Function	Is equivalent to:
`printf( args );`	`fprintf( stdout, args );`
`putchar(ch);`	`putc( ch, stdout );`
`getchar();`	`getc( stdin );`

Appendix C: Useful functions

The routines and macros referred to in this appendix are, part of the normal C standard library.

However, many of the routines operate on very low level structures, such as a C++ string. Care should be exercised in using these routines to make sure that the parameters contain valid data for the function to be performed. In some case the exact effect of the function will be implementation dependent as, for example, the case of the function `system` that will execute a job control language (JCL) command from within a program.

Note: The routines described below perform little error checking on the data supplied to them. In many cases wrong or invalid data will lead to unpredictable results.

Character types and conversions

The following macros are used to determine if a character is an alphabetic character, a digit etc. The character passed must be representable as an unsigned char.

To use these functions the file `ctype.h` which contains the macro definitions will need to be included.

```
#include <ctype>
```

Macro	Description
`int isalnum( int c )`	Returns TRUE if c is a digit or letter character, FALSE otherwise.
`int isalpha( int c )`	Returns TRUE if c is a letter character, FALSE otherwise.
`int iscntrl( int c )`	Returns TRUE if c is a control character, FALSE otherwise.
`int isdigit( int c )`	Returns TRUE if c is a digit character, FALSE otherwise.
`int islower( int c )`	Returns TRUE if c is a lower-case character, FALSE otherwise.
`int isgraph( int c )`	Returns TRUE if c is a printing character, FALSE otherwise.
`int isprint( int c )`	Returns TRUE if c is a printing character including space, FALSE otherwise.
`int ispunct( int c )`	Returns TRUE if c is a punctuation character including space, FALSE otherwise.
`int isspace( int c )`	Returns TRUE if c is a space tab carrage return, new line, vertical tab or formfeed character, FALSE otherwise.
`int isupper( int c )`	Returns TRUE if c is an upper-case character, FALSE otherwise.
`int isxdigit( int c )`	Returns TRUE if c is a hexadecimal digit character, FALSE otherwise.

The following functions convert between the case of a letter. To use these functions the file ctype.h which contains the macro definitions will need to be included.

#include <ctype>

Function	Description
int tolower(int c)	Converts an upper-case character to its lower-case equivalent.
int toupper(int c)	Converts a lower-case character to its upper-case equivalent.

C style string functions

A C style string is represented by a character pointer, which points to an area of store, which contains a vector of characters terminated by the character '\0'.

str

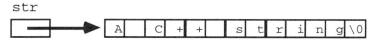

To use these functions the file string.h which contains the function prototype definitions will need to be included.

#include <string>

Function	Description
char *strcat(char *d, const char *s)	Appends a copy of the C style string s onto the end of the C style string d. Returns a pointer to the new string s.
char *strcpy(char *d, const char *s)	Copies the C style string s to d including the terminator '\0'. Returns a pointer to the new string s.
int strcmp(const char *s1, const char *s2)	Performs a comparison of the C style strings s1 & s2 returning an integer which is: < 0 if s1 is less than s2 == 0 if s1 is equal to s2 > 0 if s1 is greater than s2.
size_t strlen(const char *s)	Returns the length of the string s.

Function	Description
char *strncmp(char *d, const char *s, size_t max)	The same as strcmp but only compares up to max characters.
char *strncpy(char *d, const char *s, size_t max)	Copies at most max characters of the C style string s into d terminating with the string terminator '\0' if s is not longer than max.

Note: The header file stddef.h contains the definition of size_t which is defined to be an integer value.

Other string functions

char *strchr(const char * s, int c)	Returns a pointer to the first occurrence in the C style string s of character c scanning from left to right. If character c is not in string s returns null.
size_t strcspn(const char *s1, const char *s2)	Returns the length of the prefix of s1 which consists of characters not in s2.
char *strerror(int n)	Returns a string representing a description of the error number n which has been returned (usually from an I/O function).
int stricmp(const char *s1, const char *s2)	As per strcmp but not case sensitive, e.g. "ABC" and "abc" will be considered equal.
char *strlwr(char *s)	Converts the upper-case letters in s to lower case.
char *strupr(char *s)	Converts the lower-case letters in s to upper case.
char *strncat(char *d, const char *s, size_t max)	Appends at most max characters of d to s and then appends the string terminator ' \0 '.
char *strpbrk(const char *s1, const char *s2)	Returns a pointer into s1 of the first occurrence of a character in the string s2 otherwise returns null.
char *strrchr(const char *s, int c)	As per strchr but scans right to left.
size_t strspn(const char *s1, const char *s2)	Returns the length of the prefix of s1 which consists of characters in s2.
char *strtok(char *s1, const char *s2)	Returns the tokens from s1 that are delimited by characters in s2. Repeated calls to this function will return the next token in s1, a returned value of null indicates no more tokens.

Mathematical functions

To use these functions the file math.h which contains the function prototype definitions will need to be included.

In some cases the result will be undefined if the function is supplied with non-sensible values.

```
#include <math>
```

Function	Description
double sin(double x)	sine of x
double cos(double x)	cosine of x
double tan(double x)	tangent of x

Function	Description
`double asin( double x )`	sine^{-1} of x
`double acos( double x )`	cosine^{-1} of x
`double atan( double x )`	tangent^{-1} of x
`double atan2( double x, double y )`	tangent^{-1} of x/y
`double sinh( double x )`	hyperbolic sine of x
`double cosh( double x )`	hyperbolic cosine of x
`double tanh( double x )`	hyperbolic tangent of x

Function	Description
`double exp( double x )`	e^x
`double log( double x )`	Natural logarithm of x
`double log10( double x )`	Base 10 logarithm of x
`double pow( double x, double y )`	x^y
`double sqrt( double x )`	The square root of x
`double ldexp( double x, int n )`	$x.2^n$
`double fmod( double x, double y )`	Floating point remainder of x/y with the same sign as x.

Function	Description
`double ceil( double x )`	Smallest whole number not less than x.
`double floor( double x )`	Largest whole number not greater than x.
`double fabs( double x )`	Return the absolute value of x. (A negative x is made positive.)

The following functions can be used to find the absolute value of an integer quantity. To use these functions the file `stdlib.h` which contains the function prototype definitions will need to be included.

```
#include <stdlib>
```

Function	Description
`int abs( int n )`	Returns the absolute value of the `int n`.
`long labs( long n )`	Returns the absolute value of the `long n`.

Random number generation

The functions listed below are used in the generation of random numbers. To use these functions the file `stdlib.h` which contains the function prototype definitions will need to be included.

```
#include <stdlib>
```

Function	Description
`int rand( void )`	Returns a pseudo random number in the range 0 to RAND_MAX.
`void srand( unsigned int n )`	Sets the seed for the random number generator. The initial seed is 1.

Character string to number conversions

The following convert between numbers held in a C++ string and the physical representation of that number as an instance of the data type. To use these functions the file stdlib.h which contains the function prototype definitions will need to be included.

```
#include <stdlib>
```

Function	Description
double atof(const char *s)	Converts the number represented by the C++ string s into a double.
int atoi(const char *s)	Converts the number represented by the C++ string s into an int.
long atol(const char *s)	Converts the number represented by the C++ string s into a long.

Exit from a C++ program

The following are used to exit from a C++ program. To use these functions the file stdlib.h which contains the function prototype definitions will need to be included.

```
#include <stdlib>
```

Function	Description
void abort(void)	Aborts the currently running program with an error SIGABRT.
void exit(const int n)	Exits the program with status n. exit(0) is considered the normal completion of a program.
int atexit (void (*fun)(void))	When the program terminates the function fun will be called. The result returned is non zero if the registration of the function cannot be made.

Execution of a command line from within a program

The following is used to execute a command by the host environment from within a running C++ program. To use these functions the file stdlib.h which contains the function prototype definitions will need to be included.

```
#include <stdlib>
```

Function	Description
int system(const char * s)	Executes the JCL command contained in the string s, the value returned is the result from executing the string. This function is very implementation dependent.

Debugging

The macro assert, can be used to test the validity of an assertion in a C++ program. If the symbol NDEBUG is defined `#define NDEBUG` then the macro is ignored and no code is generated.

To use this macro, the file `assert.h` which contains the macro definition will need to be included.

```
#include <assert>
```

Macro	Description

void assert(const int expression)	If the expression is false then an error message of the form:
	`Assertion failed: expression file`
	`filename, line number`
	is written to `stderr`.

Access to variable arguments to a function

If a function is described with a variable number of arguments (...) the following macros allow access in a machine independent manner to these arguments.

For example:

```
int sum_params( const int last_real_arg, ... );
```

To use these macros, the file `stdarg.h` which contains the macro definitions will need to be included. Before the use of any of these macros the variable `p_args` must be declared with:

```
va_list p_args;
```

```
#include <stdarg>
```

Macro	Description
va_start(va_list p_args, last_real_arg)	Sets p_args to the first argument after the argument `last_real_arg` in the argument list. This will address the first of the arguments specified with . . . .
type va_arg(va_list p_args, type)	Returns as type the next argument from the variable argument list.
void va_end(va_list p_args)	After the arguments have been processed this must be called to clean up the process.

Appendix D: The string class

A string is implemented as an instance of the class `string`. The actual implementation of this class involves both templated functions and several base classes.

To use these functions the file `<string>` will need to be included:

```
#include <string>
```

The following is a summarized list of the members of the class `string`. In this summary when a string is returned from a function it is an instance of the class `string` unless otherwise indicated. The following named parameters have the following types:

Parameter	Type	Description
pos	type_t	A position in the string. First position is 0.
str	string	A string.
no	type_t	The number of characters selected.

A selection of the main methods of the class `string` are:

Method	Description
< <= != == >= >	Compare two strings.
+	Returns the concatenation two C++ strings.
[i]	Returns the i'th character of the object name.
capacity()	Returns the capacity of the string this is greater than or equal to its size.
compare(str)	Compars str with the current object.
c_str()	Returns a C++ char* string of the text held.
find(str)	Returns the first occurrence of str in the string.
get_at(pos)	Returns the character at position pos in the string.
insert(pos, str)	Inserts the string str at position pos into the string.
length()	Returns the number of characters in the stored string.
put_at(pos, ch)	Replaces the character at position pos with ch.
remove(pos, no)	Removes no characters starting at position pos in the string.
replace(pos,no,str)	Replaces no characters starting at pos with str.
substr(pos, no)	Returns a new string that starts at position pos and is no characters long.

Note: Failure in a search or extraction is indicated by the returned string `string::npos`.

As the class `string` is a member of the namespace `std` an instance of the class is declared as follows:

```
std::string name;
```

Appendix E: The standard library

In describing the standard library the following type of iterators are used:

Iterator type	Description	Produced by:
IT	Input Iterator: read only, forward moving.	`istream_iterator`
OI	Output Iterator: write only, forward moving.	`ostream_iterator` `inserter, front_inserter,` `back_inserter`
FI	Forward Iterator: read & write, forward moving.	`vector deque, list`
BDI	Bi-directional Iterator: read & write, forward backward moving.	`list, set, multiset, map,` `multimap`
RAI	Random Access Iterator: read & write, random access.	`vector, deque`

The Iterators are hierarchical, thus a forward iterator can be used where an input or output iterator is required and a random access iterator can be used where any other iterator is required.

Initializing algorithms

Algorithm	Description
`void fill( FI first, FI last, const T& val)`	`while ( first != last )` `    *first++ = val;`
`void fill_n( OI p, int size, const T& val)`	`while ( size-- )` `    construct( &*p++, val )`
`OI copy ( IT first, IT last, OI result)`	`while ( first != last )` `    *result++ = *first++;`
`OI copy_backwards ( IT first, IT last, OI result )`	`while ( first != last )` `    *--result++ = --first;`
`void generate( FI first, FI last, Generator g )`	`while ( first != last )` `    *first++ = g();`
`void generate_n( OI p, size, Generator g )`	`while ( size-- )` `    *p = g()`
`void swap_ranges( FI first, FI last, FI first2 )`	`Swap values in range`

Searching algorithms

Algorithm	Description
IT find(FI first, FI last, const T& val)	Returns a pointer to the first occurrence of val.
IT find_if(FI first, FI last, Predicate)	Returns a pointer to the first element which satisfies the `Predicate`.
FI adjacent_find(FI first, FI last [, fun])	Returns a pointer to the first element next to an equal element.
const T& max(const T& f, const T& s [,compare])	Returns the max val of the pair.
const T& max(const T& f, const T& s [,compare])	Returns the min val of the pair.
FI max_element(FI first, FI last [, compare])	Returns a pointer to the max element.
FI min_element(FI first, FI last [, compare])	Returns a pointer to the min element.
pair<IT,IT> mismatch (IT first1, IT last1, IT first2, IT last2 [, fun])	Return a pair of pointers to the first elements which do not match.

Transformation algorithms

Algorithm	Description
void reverse(BDI first, BDI last)	Reverses the order of the elements.
void replace(FI first, FI last, const T& old, const T& new)	Replaces the old element value with the new value.
void replace_if(FI first, FI last, Predicate, const T& new)	Replaces elements with new value where the predicate is true.
void replace_copy(IT first, IT last, OT result, const T& old, const T& new)	Creates new copy
void replace_copy(IT first, IT last, OT result, Predicate, const T& new)	Creates new copy
void rotate(FT first, FT mid, FT last)	Rotates elements around the midpoint.
BDI partition(BDI first, BDI mid, BDI last, Predicate)	Partitions the elements so those satisfying the `Predicate` are moved to the front.
BDI stable_partition(BDI first, BDI mid, BDI last, Predicate)	As above but retaining original order.

Removal algorithms

Algorithm	Description
`FI remove( FI first, FI last, const T& val )`	Moves elements down to overwrite val elements, return pointer to new last.
`FI remove( FI first, FI last, Predicate )`	As above but removed elements match predicate.
`FI remove_copy( IT first, IT last, OI result,` `            const T& val )`	As `remove`, but makes copy.
`FI unique( FI first, FI last [, BinaryPredicate ] )`	Removes duplicate elements, return pointer to new last.

Scalar generating algorithms

Algorithm	Description
`void count( IT first, IT last,` `           const T& val, Size& count)`	Increments count for each element that matches val.
`void count_if( IT first, IT last,` `              Predicate f, Size& count)`	Increments count for each element that matches Predicate.
`ContainerType accumulate( IT first, IT last,` `            ContainerType initial [,BinaryFun ] )`	Returns the result of performing `BinaryFun` (default +) between each element.

Miscellanies algorithm

Algorithm	Description
`Function for_each( IT first, IT last, Function );`	Applies `Function` to each element.

Sorting algorithms

Algorithm	Description
`void sort( RAI first, RAI last [, Compare] )`	sort.
`void stable_sort( RAI first, RAI last [, Compare] )`	sort retain order of equal elements.
`void partial_sort( RAI f, RAI m, RAI l [, Compare] )`	Sort from f .. m.
`void partial_sort_copy( IT f1, IT l1,` `              RAI f, RAI l [, Compare] )`	

Searching algorithms

Algorithm	Description
void nth_element(RAI first, RAI nth, RAI last [, Compare])	Partitions so iterator nth points to nth largest item.
bool binary_search(FI first, FI last, const T& value [,compare])	Returns true if value present (collection must be ordered.)
FI lower_bound(FI first, FI last, const T& value [,compare])	Returns an iterator to the first position that value can be inserted in order.
FI upper_bound(FI first, FI last, const T& value [,compare])	Returns an iterator to the last position that value can be inserted in order.
Pair<FI,FI> equal_range(FI first, FI last, const T& value [,compare])	Returns the result for lower_bound and upper_bound as a pair.

Merging algorithms

Algorithm	Description
OI merge(IT first1, IT last1, IT first2, IT last2, OI result [,compare])	merges range 1 & range 2 into result. If equal range1 first.

Set operations algorithms

Algorithm	Description
OI set_union(IT first1, IT last1, IT first2, IT last2, OI result [,compare])	Set union.
OI set_intersection(IT first1, IT last1, IT first2, IT last2, OI result [,compare])	Set intersection.
OI set_difference(IT first1, IT last1, IT first2, IT last2, OI result [,compare])	Set difference.
OI set_symetric_difference(IT first1, IT last1, IT first2, IT last2, OI result [,compare])	Set symmetric difference.
bool includes(IT first1, IT last1, IT first2, IT last2)	Returns true if set1 is a subset of set2.

Heap operation algorithms

Algorithm	Description
void make_heap(RAI first, RAI last, [,compare])	Make random sequence into heap.
void push_heap(RAI first, RAI last, [,compare])	After adding an element at the end the heap is restored.

Algorithm	Description
`void pop_heap( RAI first, RAI last, [,compare] )`	Swaps first and last elements and restores heap property without last element.
`void sort_heap( RAI first, RAI last, [,compare] )`	Converts into ordered collection. (retains heap property.)

Function objects

Function	operation	Function	operation
`plus`	`x + y`	`minus`	`x - y`
`multiplies`	`x * y`	`divides`	`x / y`
`modulus`	`x % y`	`negate`	`- x`

Function	operation	Function	operation
`equal_to`	`x == y`	`not_equal_to`	`x != y`
`greater`	`x > y`	`less`	`x < y`
`greater_equal`	`x >=y`	`less_equal`	`x <= y`

Function	operation	Function	operation
`logical_and`	`x && y`	`logical_or`	`x || y`
`logical_not`	`! x`		

Example of use:

```
std::cout << "2 + 3 = " << plus<int>()(2,3) << "\n";
```

Function adapters

Function	Description
`not1( unary_function )`	Returns a function which has the same signature as the `unary_function` but now returns the not of the original function.
`not2( binary_function )`	Returns a function which has the same signature as the `binary_function` but now returns the not of the original function.
`bind1st(binary_function, arg1)`	Converts the binary function T f(T2 x, T2 y) into the unary function T f(T2 y) that implements T f(arg1, y)
`bind2nd(binary_function, arg2)`	Converts the binary function T f(T2 x, T2 y) into the unary function T f(T2 x) that implements T f(x, arg2).

Container classes

The standard library provides the following containers:

Container	Description of characteristics	Header file
vector	Efficient random access and insertion of new elements at the end of the vector.	<vector>
list	Efficient insertion and removal of elements anywhere in the list.	<list>
deque	Efficient insertion and removal at the front and back of the structure.	<deque>
set	Elements held in order, efficient test for inclusion, insertion and removal.	<set>
multiset	A set with duplicate values.	<set>
map	Access to values using a key. Efficient insertion and removal.	<map>
multimap	A map with duplicate keys.	<map>
stack	Insertion and removal from the front only.	<stack>
queue	Removal of items at the front and insertion at the back only.	<queue>
Priority queue	Efficient access to and removal of the largest value.	<queue>
bitset	Elements (bits) held in order, efficient test for inclusion, insertion and removal.	<bitset>

Container requirements (all)

Expression	Returns
C::value_type	The type stored in the container.
C::reference	Lvalue (address) of item stored in container.
C::const_reference	Const lvalue of type stored in container.
C::iterator	An iterator type.
C::const_iterator	A const iterator type.
C::difference_type	
C::size_type	A type that can represent the number of items in the container.

Expression	Returns
co.begin()	Iterator for co at start of collection.
co.end()	Iterator for co at start of collection.
ca == cb	Comparison of containers ca & cb.
co.size()	Elements in container co.
co.max_size()	Size of the largest possible container.
co.empty()	If container is empty.
ca < cb	

Reversible container requirements (in addition to container)

These are for a container that can be traversed in the reverse order.
(For example, `vector,list,set,multiset,map,multimap`.)

Expression	Returns
`C::reverse_iterator`	Iterator that can go in the reverse direction.
`C::const_reverse_iterator`	Const iterator that can go in the reverse direction.

Expression	Returns
`co.rbegin()`	Reverse iterator for `co` at end of collection.
`co.rend`	Reverse iterator for `co` at start of collection.

Sequence container requirements (in addition to container)

These are for a container that allows insertion and deletion of items.)
(For example, `vector,list,set,multiset,map,multimap.`)

Expression	Implements
`co.insert(p,item)`	Insert `item` before `p` in container `co`.
`co.insert(p,n,item)`	Insert n items.
`co.erase(p)`	Erase element pointed at by `p`.
`co.erase(p,q)`	Erase elements in the pointer range `p .. q`.

Optional sequence container requirements

These are only provided when the time taken for the operation on a container is constant.
(For example, `vector,list,set,multiset`.)

Expression	Implements
`co.front()`	Returning the first element.
`co.back()`	Returning the last element.
`co.push_front(item)`	Inserting a new item at front.
`co.push_back(item)`	Inserting a new item at back.
`co.pop_front()`	Removing the front element.
`co.pop_back()`	Removing the last element
`co[ i ]`	Returning the element i'th element of the container (`vector` container only.)

Associative sequence container requirements

Expression	Implements
`C::key_type`	Key.
`C::key_compare`	The comparison to put the keys in order.
`C::value_compare`	The comparison used on values.

Appendix F: Priority of operators

Associates	Operators of C++: from high priority to low priority	Notes
Left to Right	`()   []    ->    .    ::`	

Right to Left	`!    ~    ++    --    + -    *`
	`& (type) sizeof new`
	`delete`
		Monadic operators

Left to Right	`.*  ->*`	
Left to Right	`*   /    %`	
Left to Right	`+    -`	
Left to Right	`<<    >>`	
Left to Right	`<    <=    >=    >`	
Left to Right	`==    !=`	
Left to Right	`&`	
Left to Right	`^`	
Left to Right	`|`	
Left to Right	`&&`	
Left to Right	`||`	
Right to Left	`?    :`	conditional expression
Right to Left	`=    *=    /=    etc.`	
Left to Right	`,`	comma operator

Appendix G: String and character escape sequences

The following are the escape sequences for introducing control characters into a string or character constant.

\ "	A double quote "
\ '	A single quote '
\ 0	The end of string marker (\ followed by the digit zero)
\ ?	The question mark ?
\ \	The \ character
\ a	Bell
\ b	Backspace
\ c	Carrage return
\ ddd	The character with octal value ddd
\ f	Form feed
\ n	A newline
\ r	Return
\ t	Tab
\ v	Vertical tab
\ xddd	The character with hexadecimal value ddd

Thus:

```
std::cout << "\"A String\"\n\tWith embedded escape sequences"
```

would print

```
"A String"
  With embedded escape sequences
```

Appendix H: Fundamental types

Type	Abbreviation	Length (bytes)	Min value	Max value
char			0 or -127	255 or 127
signed char		equal to char	-127	+127
unsigned char		equal to char	0	255
w_char				
bool				
int		>= short	-32767	32767
unsigned int		equal to int	0	65535
short int	short	>= char	-32767	32767
unsigned short int	unsigned short	equal short int	0	65535
long int	long	>= int	-2147483647	2147483647
unsigned long int	unsigned long	equal long int	0	4294967295
float			6 dec. places	$10^{\pm37}$ Δ
double		>= float	10 dec. places	$10^{\pm37}$ Δ
long double		>= double	10 dec. places	$10^{\pm37}$ Δ

Type   Is the name of the type.

Abbreviation   Is an allowable abbreviation for the name.

Length   Is the relationship between the types and the bytes of storage occupied.

Min Value   Is the minimal value that must be representable (smaller values are allowed).

Max Value   Is the maximum value that must be representable (larger numbers are allowed).
Δ The minimum range of values.

Note: *The implementor of C++ for a particular machine will decide if* char *is to be* signed *or* unsigned.
signed *may be used as a prefix on the integer types.*

Appendix I: Literals in C++

A literal in C++ has a type, which will effect the way it is processed.

Literal	Example	Type	Commentary
Character	`'A'`	`char`	
Decimal number	`123456`	`int` `long int`	Type dependent on implementation sizes of int etc.
Unsigned number	`1234U`	`unsigned int` `unsigned long int`	Suffix of U or u.
Octal number	`01234`	`int` `long int`	Leading 0 denotes octal number.
Hexadecimal number	`0xFACE`	`int` `long int`	Leading 0x or 0X denotes hexadecimal number.
Large number	`1L`	`long`	Suffix of L or l.
Unsigned large number	`123456UL`	`unsigned long`	Suffix UL or ul or any combination
Real number	`1.23F`	`float`	Suffix of F or f.
Large real number	`1.23`	`double`	
Very Large real number	`1.23L`	`long double`	Suffix of L or l.

Note: An integer number will have the type of the smallest representable unit from (`int`, `unsigned int`, `long int` and `unsigned long int`). Thus, the type of a literal number may differ depending on the size of fundamental types for a particular implementation.

By default a real number (e.g. 1.23) has type double.

A leading 0 to an integer means that the number is octal.

Appendix J: Keywords in C++

asm	auto	bool	break	case
catch	char	class	const	const_cast
continue	default	delete	do	double
dynamic_cast	else	enum	explicit	extern
false	float	for	friend	goto
if	inline	int	long	mutable
namespace	new	operator	private	protected
public	register	reinterpret_cast	return	short
signed	sizeof	static	static_cast	struct
switch	template	this	throw	true
try	typedef	typeid	typename	union
unsigned	using	virtual	void	volatile
wchar_t	while			

Note: asm *is reserved for implementors to include a machine specific facility to pass information to an assembler.*

Operators

^	~	!	!=	%	%=
&	&&	&=	()	*	*=
+	++	+=	,	-	-=
->	->*	.	.*	/	/=
: ?	<	<<	<<=	<=	=
^=	==	>	>=	>>	>>=
delete	new	sizeof	[]	|	||

Alternative representations for operators

Operator	Alternative	Operator	Alternative
&	bitand	&&	and
|	bitor	||	or
^	xor	~	compl
&=	and_eq	|=	or_eq
^=	xor_eq	!	not
!=	not_eq		

Keywords and tokens used by the macro processor

#	##	define	elif	else
endif	error	ifdef	ifndef	include
pragma				
defined				

Appendix K: Passing data to a C++ program

On some computer systems, information can be passed from the outside environment, to an invoked C++ program. This is usually achieved by appending a sequence of string tokens after the name of the binary image of the program. For example, if the binary program was called a.out then to invoke the program and pass it the textual message 'hello world' a user would type:

```
a.out hello world
```

The C++ program would then have its function main called with two parameters, argc and argv. The parameters are defined as:

argc   A count of the number of parameters passed.

argv   An array of pointers to strings which represent the individual tokens of the message.

Note: The value of argc will always be at least 1, because the name of the invoked program is counted as the first string.
If no strings are passed to the program, then argc would equal 1, and argv would be a vector of 1 element containing a pointer to the name of the invoked program.

A program can be written to process these tokens. The program below writes out all tokens except the first, to the stream cout.

```cpp
int main( const int argc, const char * const argv[] )
{
  for ( int i=1; i<argc; i++ )
  {
    std::cout << argv[i] << ( i!=argc ? " " : "" );
  }
  std::cout << "\n";
  return 0;
}
```

This program can then be run as follows on a Unix system:

```
% a.out This should say Hello world
```

and would produce the output:

```
This should say Hello world
```

Note: On a UNIX system, a program similar to this would be known as echo.

Appendix L: Access to C functions in a C++ program

C++ uses type safe linking. This process extends (or mangles) the C++ external function or external variable names to include a description of their type and if appropriate their parameters. The linker is then only able to bind names that have been similarly mangled. Unfortunately this means that it is difficult to link to code which has been written in anything other than C++, as the names will not have been mangled in a compatible fashion.

This name mangling can be stopped by prefixing the function or variable with extern "C". For example, the C function `written_in_c`:

```
float written_in_c( float number )
{
  /*
    * A previously written function
    * which cannot be recompiled with the C++ compiler
    */

}
```

would have its prototype specified in a C++ program as:

```
extern "C" float written_in_c(float);
```

This would stop the name `written_in_c` from being mangled, allowing the linker to be able to bind to the name in the C program.

A C header file may be used in a C++ program as follows:

```
extern "C" {
#include "C_header_file.h"
}
```

This will stop the name mangling on all calls to functions whose function prototype is defined in the header file.

Note: Many C++ compiling systems that can optionally also compile C programs will use conditional compilation to include extern "C" in C header files when included in a C++ program.

Appendix M: Compatibility of code

The programs illustrated in this book were compiler with Borland C++ Builder Version 3 though in the early stages of development many other compilers where used.

Compiler	Problem	Solution
ANSI C++ Compiler	None.	
Borland C++ version 5.02	No initialized const members in a class.	See chapter 26 on legacy compilers.
Borland C++ version 4.5	Scope of the for-init-statement in a for loop. The namespace directive not implemented. The mutable qualifier not implemented. The explicit qualifier not implemented. No initialized const members in a class.	See chapter 26 on legacy compilers.
Borland C++ version 3.0	The bool type not implemented. Scope of the for-init-statement in a for loop. The exception mechanism not implemented. The namespace directive not implemented. The mutable qualifier not implemented. The explicit qualifier not implemented. No initialized const members in a class.	See chapter 26 on legacy compilers.

| GCC egcs- 1.0.2 | The namespace directive not fully implemented. The mutable qualifier not implemented. The explicit qualifier not implemented. | See chapter 26 on legacy compilers. |

References

Margaret A Ellis & Bjarne Stroustrup,
The Annotated C++ Reference Manual. Addison Wesley, 1990.

Bjarne Stroustrup,
The C++ Programming Language, 3nd Edition. Addison Wesley, 1997.

Borland C++ Builder Manuals
(Programmer's guide, User's guide, Library reference, and Tools and utilities guide.)
Borland International., 1998.

X3J16/95-0087 WG21/NO687
Working Paper for Draft Proposed International Standard for Information Systems
Programming Language C++. December 1996.

Index